BUILDING KNOWLEDGE

NICK HAYNES

BUILDING KNOWLEDGE

An Architectural History of the University of Glasgow

Historic Scotland
in association with the University of Glasgow
EDINBURGH & GLASGOW MMXIII

Published by Historic Scotland in association with the University of Glasgow 2013

ISBN 978 1 84917 114 4 PAPERBACK
ISBN 978 1 84917 124 3 HARDBACK

Cover and jacket illustrations: The University of Glasgow, photographed by Keith Hunter
Frontispiece: Design by William Adam for the Old College Library, 1732 [FIG.19]
Opposite introduction: View of the tower and spire of the Gilbert Scott building from the University Library

Designed and typeset in Fleischman by Dalrymple
Printed in England on Condat Matt 150gsm
by Butler Tanner and Dennis

Contents

Forewords

In October 1981 when I first walked up University Avenue as a new student at the University of Glasgow I could not help but be overawed by the scale and magnificence of the architecture. While I knew the buildings from their prominence in the Glasgow skyline it was quite another sensation to experience them close up and to be a part of such an important and historic institution.

The architecture of the University had a profound effect on me and one which I have carried with me throughout life. I can remember being impressed by the Gothic Revival of the Gilbert Scott building, but also finding peace in the simple classicism of the circular McMillan Reading Room. I may not have known the names of the styles of architecture then, but the way they made me feel and the associations I have with them have lasted in my memory and they continue to make me proud to be part of a University with such an outstanding architectural heritage.

The idea of a book first came about when Historic Scotland in conjunction with the University of Glasgow carried out a review of all the listed and unlisted buildings on the Hillhead campus. The review allowed us to take a fresh look at just how important these buildings are and the fascinating information in the University archives shed new light on their history. I am delighted that Historic Scotland and the University of Glasgow have worked together to produce such an informative and beautifully illustrated publication.

The book takes us through the early history of the University right up until the present day when the University is now on the verge of entering another major chapter in its architectural history with the acquisition of the adjacent Western Infirmary site.

Building Knowledge is a remarkable book, and not just for those with a connection with the University. It tells us much about Scotland's rich story of learning and culture through the amazing buildings which continue to inspire thousands of students, residents and visitors alike in Glasgow and beyond.

FIONA HYSLOP
Cabinet Secretary for Culture and External Affairs

The University of Glasgow, in one sense, has never stayed still, never stayed the same. This is one of the key messages that emerges from this excellent book. We have moved from the Cathedral crypt to Old College to the Gilbert Scott building, from the High Street to Gilmorehill. Successive generations have built in stone, then brick, now concrete, steel and glass. It is an eloquent reminder that the University's story has been one of transitions and transformations, in place, space and shape, in materials, styles and uses. These changes mirror the sense in which over our 560 years we have evolved and adapted to reflect the times and meet the changing needs and aspirations of our academics, our students and our community.

But what our architecture and its unfolding story also reveals, are those deep foundations on which each generation has built, and on which we build today. The Old College may have gone, but through the Lion and Unicorn staircase (which was moved and reinstalled at Gilmorehill), its stones lie embedded in today's campus, symbolic of that continuity of purpose, established at our beginnings and which we share today: to be a place that strives after knowledge, and seeks to share its benefits with others. A purpose of which we can be proud.

As this book records, our campus has one of the greatest concentrations of listed buildings in Scotland with distinct buildings of national and international importance. This tells its own story. Our predecessors had the confidence to shape the physical landscape in such bold and impressive ways, because they had the confidence, ambition, and vision that the University could also shape the intellectual landscape. As you will read, they drew on the talent, the commitment, the support of the widest community, public and private, to make their statement in stone, and on a hill, a reality, creating an integral and celebrated part of our landscape, inseparable from the city whose name we bear. And we are the beneficiaries today.

In an age of virtual worlds where the purpose and indeed necessity for physical spaces to learn, to teach, to discover and meet are challenged, I return to the very special feeling I get as I walk through the great south front door and under the University tower. I feel it now as much as I did when I was a student in this University. Now, as then, I sense that I am entering a special place and, with that, comes a reawakening of the thought, which indeed inspired the building in the first place, that as a University, we are indeed engaged in something significant and important beyond our individual endeavours. Our buildings certainly need to be fit for purpose to enable us to deliver our commitment to excellent research and teaching, but, if they similarly inspire us to that end, so much the better.

Looking forward, there are tremendous but exciting architectural challenges. As this book is published, we have just acquired the Western Infirmary site. This will, from 2015 onwards, allow us to extend and reshape our campus, and we have an unparalleled opportunity to build something special. Whatever we build, it must be worthy of our past, be fit for the needs of today and express a statement of confidence in our purpose that resonates and inspires into the future. It also needs to be an enterprise that engages the whole community, as together, we have the opportunity once again, to reshape our landscape for generations to come.

As the University community moved from the High Street to Gilmorehill, the Glasgow Herald of 1 August 1870, stated that the University was moving, not just to a new location, but to a special position to 'place herself at the head of the future ... the foremost in the forefront of all that is fresh in science and speculation'. I can think of no better principle to apply today and one which should inform all that we build as we incorporate the Western Infirmary site and reshape our campus. This great opportunity must, and I believe will, play its part in enabling our University to remain 'at the head of the future' in the pursuit of knowledge, discovery and enterprise.

PROFESSOR ANTON MUSCATELLI
Principal and Vice Chancellor
University of Glasgow

Introduction

The genesis of this book was a collaborative project between Historic Scotland and the University of Glasgow in 2010 to resurvey both the listed and the unlisted buildings of the Gilmorehill and Hillhead campus. The project was intended to support the University's commission to the architects Simpson & Brown to produce a conservation plan for the buildings on the campus. When buildings are assessed for statutory listing, much historical information is gathered in order to gain an understanding of the changes the buildings have undergone over time. It was clear at an early stage that the story behind the University's buildings would be of interest to a wider audience and it was decided to continue the collaboration by publishing the research. The book contains not only the information from the survey but also explores the University's historic roots in the High Street. It concludes with the next stage of development with planning underway for expansion of the main campus into the Western Infirmary site.

For over 560 years the University of Glasgow has acted as a remarkable patron of architecture. Each generation of academics and their architects has sought to maintain and adapt the University's building stock to the constantly changing needs of a world-class teaching and research institution. Often the University has turned to some of the finest architects, engineers, designers and craftsmen working in Scotland to realise its ambitions. An extraordinary record of these creative partnerships survives in the University Archives, the University Library and the Hunterian Museum and Art Gallery in the form of minute books, accounts, correspondence, contracts, plans, drawings, photographs and models. A selection of material from the archives is illustrated here, much of it for the first time. Although the resulting buildings and their methods of construction have differed enormously through the ages, many of the challenges of commissioning new buildings remain the same: finding the finance, finding a site, drawing up the brief, selecting an architect, deciding on a scheme, designing the services, appointing contractors, constructing the building, dealing with delays and snags, and equipping the rooms. The most successful schemes have emerged from strong, purposeful briefs prepared by the client and creative leadership by the designers. A prime example is the Zoology building commissioned by Professor Graham Kerr and designed by Sir John James Burnet in 1921.

From the very beginning in 1451, the University seems to have faced more than its fair share of financial crises, which frequently manifested themselves in decrepit or unfinished buildings. In many cases, the city of Glasgow and grateful alumni of the University as well as businessmen, merchants and industrialists, have come to the rescue. The Crown and town needed to re-endow the University after the disastrous financial effects of the Reformation of 1560. The professors themselves kept the University going following Principal Gillespie's architectural extravagances of the 1650s.

Construction of the Gilbert Scott building on the new site at Gilmorehill from 1865 relied not just on money from the sale of the High Street site and Treasury grants, but on gifts, bequests, and even door-to-door collections. Work ground to a halt in 1870 because the money ran out, and it took four further major benefactions to complete the Bute and Randolph Halls in 1884 and the tower in 1888. The following century, William Whitfield's Library was only half complete when it opened in 1968 because the Treasury's previous largesse had given way under the pressures of a national economic crisis. A decade of Treasury-induced financial uncertainty in the 1980s meant that there were no architectural legacies at all from that period.

As architectural practices working with the University of Glasgow today will acknowledge, it is now a highly professional client with a dedicated buildings team. This was not always the case, as the administration of building projects was often carried out in addition to other academic or administrative duties. Lulls in building activity or changes of staff in the 18th and 19th centuries often led to inexperienced professors managing complex building projects on behalf of a committee of the University's Senate or Court. Sometimes this worked well, but there were occasions where delays or increased costs were attributable to the client's lack of experience. A frequent problem, surprisingly, was omitting to take into account the architect's fee, which was always charged separately as a percentage of the overall project costs.

George Gilbert Scott's appointment to design the principal building at Gilmorehill in October 1864 marked the beginning of a series of successful working relationships between the University and several architectural practices. Although in the 20th century there were many architectural firms involved at Gilmorehill and Hillhead, a few trusted practices dealt not only with new buildings, but also advised on development programmes and looked after the cherished Gilbert Scott building itself. Scott and his son, John Oldrid Scott, initially dominated the University's architectural activity in the latter part of the 19th century. John James Burnet then secured a foothold with a commission for the John McIntyre building (Old Union) in 1886, and went on to design a number of major departmental buildings in the early years of the 20th century. By the 1930s, Professor T. Harold Hughes had taken on the informal mantle of chief architectural advisor. Andrew Graham Henderson of John Keppie & Henderson was particularly influential after the Second World War, to be followed by his business partner Joseph Lea Gleave, who was responsible for the development of the Brutalist campus at Hillhead in the early 1960s. Following Gleave's premature death in 1965, his assistant Ivor Dorward continued the main advisory role. After the building hiatus of the 1980s, much of the architectural direction was taken in-house by the University's own Buildings and Estates department.

In addition to the growth of the University's population and the increasing professionalism of the clients and architects, the history of the University's buildings charts changing residential, teaching and research requirements. Early teaching at the University made do with buildings used for other purposes, such as the crypt of Glasgow Cathedral. The first College buildings in the High Street appear to have incorporated living accommodation. By the early 19th century, teaching was mainly by lecture, which led to the removal of residential accommodation from the Old College to create lecture theatres with raked seating. Research was still conducted in corners of the old High Street buildings. The move to Gilmorehill allowed more research space, but teaching was still mainly undertaken in lecture theatres. Increasingly, specialist scientific research equipment required dedicated buildings, which were distributed around the Gilmorehill site from the 1890s. Halls of residence reintroduced a small amount of accommodation for students, but not on the Gilmorehill campus, which was proving to be too small by the inter-war period. The rise in seminar and tutorial working required different types of accommodation in the departmental blocks of the 1950s and 1960s. Modern computer technology and self-directed learning is again changing the size and organisation of buildings to increase the use of resource centres, touch-down and collaborative working spaces.

Both continuity and renewal emerge as patterns in this long history of patronage. Until the mid-20th century there was a strong awareness of the University's past in the design of its new buildings. Occasionally the two forces of tradition and renewal have clashed, creating great controversy. Most famously, the decision in 1863 to relocate the University from Glasgow's High Street to Gilmorehill caused a furore over both the demolition of the Old College buildings and the appointment of an English architect for the new buildings without a competition. The Gilmorehill architectural controversy was neither the first nor the last: similar regrets surrounded Principal Gillespie's demolition of the ancient College buildings facing the High Street in 1659; and the more recent legacy of Brutalist buildings on the Hillhead campus continues to divide opinion. The contemporary design process is more consultative and inclusive than its 1960s and 1970s predecessors, leading to high-quality buildings that are less confrontational in their context and the environment generally.

As the University approaches its hundred- and-fiftieth anniversary at Gilmorehill, the re-purchase of large parts of the Western Infirmary site provides an exciting potential for continuing its enlightened architectural patronage. NICK HAYNES

AUTHOR'S ACKNOWLEDGEMENTS

For Christine, John and Juliet

The author would particularly like to thank Elly McCrone (HS), Lesley Richmond (GU), Richard Emerson and Ranald MacInnes (HS) for their support, enthusiasm and expertise.

A great many other people have contributed to the research and production of this book, for which the author is extremely grateful: Michelle Andersson (HS); Kyle Armstrong (RCAHMS); Theo van Asperen (Honorary Librarian and Archivist, Glasgow Art Club); Lisa Ballantyne; William Bill (GU); Iain Brodie; Carol Anne Buchanan (GU); Mungo Campbell (GU); Kitty Chilcott; Bob Clark (Campbeltown Museum); Heather Coady; Linda Coxhead; Claire Daniel (GU); Ron Dorran (GU); Rachael Egan (GU); Ian Elder-Cheyne; Robin Evetts; Clive Fenton; Lydia Fisher (RCAHMS); David Fleetwood (HS); Andrew Fleming; Frances Fowler; India Fullarton (GU); David Gaimster (GU); David Sutherland Gleave; Philip Graham (RCAHMS); Simon Green (RCAHMS); Thomas Gübitz; Geoff Hancock (GU); Liz Hancock (GU); Kurt Helfrich (RIBA); Carsten Hermann (HS); Nicky Imrie (GU); Lizzie Jacklin (GU); Fiona Jamieson; David Jones; Michelle Kaye (GU); Euan Leitch; Kirsty Lingstadt (RCAHMS); Andrew Lockwood (Whitfield Lockwood Architects); Donald Macaskill (Glasgow Art Club); Siobhan McDade (GU); Dawn McDowell (HS); Dugald MacInnes; Sam McKinstry (University of the West of Scotland); Gerry McLaren; John Major (GU); Debbie Mays (RIAS); Neil Miller (GU); Sarah Montgomery; Simon Montgomery (HS); Shona Munro; Victoria Murray (HS); David Page (Page\Park Architects); Tom Parnell (Simpson & Brown Architects); Maggie Reilly (GU); Claire Richards; the late Bruce Ritchie; Brian Rodger (GU); Marion Rozowski; Jennifer Russell (GU); John Sanders (Simpson & Brown Architects); Joseph Sharples (GU); Ian Steele; Vanessa Stephen; Steve Sutton (GU); David Taylor; Alma Topen (GU); Gemma Tougher (GU); James Turner (HS); David M Walker; Kristina Watson (RCAHMS); Ruth Whatling; William Whitfield (Whitfield Lockwood Architects); Andrew Wilson; and Emma Yan (GU).

GU	University of Glasgow
HS	Historic Scotland
RCAHMS	Royal Commission on the Ancient & Historical Monuments of Scotland
RIAS	Royal Incorporation of Architects in Scotland
RIBA	Royal Institute of British Architects

Chapter One

The Medieval & Renaissance University 1451–1700

1 Detail from late 17th-century depiction of the University of Glasgow in the High Street by John Slezer
National Library of Scotland, Edinburgh

Glasgow in 1450 was a relatively small settlement or, more accurately, two linked settlements, of about 1,000 people. The first settlement seems to have developed around the site of the cathedral, followed by a mercantile settlement closer to the River Clyde. Both settlements were laid out in the form of a cross. Throughout the early medieval period, the mercantile hub expanded northwards along the High Street towards the ecclesiastical centre until the two became joined. The first cathedral was consecrated in 1136, destroyed by fire in 1189, and rebuilt at least once before construction of the current building began in 1233. Some of the relatively undeveloped lands on the east side of the High Street between the ecclesiastical and mercantile centres were acquired by the Order of Preachers (Dominicans), or 'Black Friars', for construction of a church and priory in 1246.

Sometime between 1175 and 1178 the town became a Bishop's Burgh, granting it trading privileges and enabling it to hold weekly markets. Long, narrow 'burgage' plots were laid out at right angles to the four main streets: High Street; Trongait; Gallowgait; and Walkergait. Housing fronted the streets and the strips of land behind were filled with gardens and outhouses. With the exception of public buildings, many of the early buildings were timber-framed and thatched and probably of one or two storeys. A timber bridge spanned the River Clyde by about 1285. By 1450 the burgh had expanded to become a significant ecclesiastical, political and economic force in Scotland. Glasgow did not have the same easy access to continental ports as the east coast burghs had at this period, so trading was predominantly regional and with Argyll and Ireland. Glasgow was raised to become an archbishopric in 1492, much to the discomfort of St Andrews, Scotland's first archbishopric and university town.

It is in the context of this ambitious ecclesiastical centre that William Turnbull, Bishop of Glasgow, alumnus of St Andrews and former legate to the papal court, persuaded James II to promote the foundation of a new university. A papal bull (letter) of 7 January 1451 by Nicholas V established a 'Studium generale' in Glasgow. The pope was a scholar, bibliophile and key patron of the early Renaissance. Other universities founded during his pontificate were those of Barcelona (1450), Valence (1452) and Trier (1454). The bull was read from Glasgow Mercat Cross on Trinity Sunday, 30 June 1451. Nicholas V's alma mater, the University of Bologna, was to form the teaching model for the new institution in Glasgow.

The early establishment had no buildings of its own and therefore relied to a great extent for accommodation on the Glasgow ecclesiastical bodies that had promoted its foundation. The first meeting of the

2 A late 17th-century depiction of the University of Glasgow in the High Street by John Slezer

National Library of Scotland, Edinburgh

thirty-seven members of the general chapter of the fledgling university was held at an unknown date in 1451 in the chapter house, or meeting room, of the Order of Preachers, commonly called the Black Friars on account of their clothing, in the High Street. The Black Friars were renowned for their intellectual tradition, notably the study of theology and philosophy. The first Chancellor was William Turnbull and his Rector for the day-to-day running of the University was David Cadzow, a precentor and sub-dean of the cathedral. Studies took place either in the Black Friars' chapter house or the cathedral crypt (vaulted area beneath the east end), and the college chapter met in one of the two chapter houses of the cathedral.

Although the Papal Bull authorised teaching of any subject, the syllabus was in practice restricted to a basic 'Arts' course, which included grammar, logic, rhetoric, mathematics, arithmetic and geometry. Divinity, canon law and medicine degrees were awarded in the 15th century, but the teaching of these subjects was more erratic and the Faculty of Arts emerged as the pre-eminent faculty. The fifty or so students were all male and started as young as ten years old. Most were sons of the gentry, burgesses and farmers, training for ministry in the Church. Those of sufficient means were required to live with the regents, while those of lesser means were to pay a set fee and sleep in communal college chambers.[1] When noblemen's sons attended, personal tutors and servants often accompanied them. Individual benefactors endowed bursaries for poorer students. A letter under the great seal of James II of 20 April 1453 granted the officers and students of the University exemption from all taxes. This important privilege was re-confirmed by each of James's successors. The Bishop granted the Rector the right to judge civil and criminal cases involving students or masters of the University. The University guarded this judicial role against infringement by the Church and civil authorities into the 18th century. The Rector also read the statutes publicly once a year to ensure that the regulations were known to all the students.

Within a short period a small tenement on the south

side of Rottenrow, later known as the 'Auld Pedagogy', provided a more discreet setting for 'teaching, lodging and a common table'. In the manner of a monastic institution, the University provided accommodation for study, living and dining together. The origins of the building and its internal arrangement are not known. As the College was unendowed at this stage, it seems likely that the building was a rented pre-existing tenement. The ruins of the 2-storey Auld Pedagogy [FIG.3] survived into the 19th century on the south side of Rottenrow, before being replaced by the Lock (Venereal Disease) Hospital in 1846. The external appearance of the ruinous frontage is known from two lithographs published in Robert Stuart's *Views and Notices of Glasgow in Former Times* of 1848. Archaeological investigation of the site took place in 1986, but little evidence of the medieval structure was found.[2]

There are records of the Faculty of Arts repairing a building on the High Street in 1453 and renting a *pedagogium* in 1456.[3] Further documents record the building of a *pedagogium* between 1458 and 1463, but its location is not clear. In 1460 James, 1st Lord Hamilton, granted a 'tenement lying on the east side of the High Street, between the Convent of the Friars Preachers on the south, and the land of Sir Thomas Arthurlie, Chaplain, on the north, together with four acres of land on the Dovehill, beside the Malyndonore [Molendinar] Burn, under condition that twice in every day, at the close of their noontide and evening meals, the Regents and Students shall rise and pray for the souls of the Lord of Hamilton, the founder of the College, of the Lady Euphame Countess of Douglas and Lady of Bothwell his wife, and of their ancestors, heirs, and successors'.[4] This tenement and land on the High Street to the south of the cathedral was to form the nucleus of the University's properties until the move to Gilmorehill in 1870. The site was further expanded by the gift of an adjacent tenement and croft by Sir Thomas Arthurlie in 1467. The spaciousness of the site probably derived from its position between the two ancient ecclesiastical and mercantile centres, which was developed less intensively until the end of the 18th century.

In spite of the presence of distinguished scholars, the 15th-century and early 16th-century records of the University suggest a relatively impoverished institution, relying on payments by students, small gifts, grants and rentals for its survival. The first record of a communal library is in November 1475 when the Chancellor, Bishop John Laing, presented a manuscript compendium of the works of Aristotle. Printed books were a relatively new invention and still expensive at this time.

The Reformation of 1560 had a disastrous effect on the University, which was intimately bound up in Glasgow's Roman Catholic institutions, hierarchy and patronage. As the ecclesiastical sinecures and benefices that funded the teaching staff dried up, classes virtually ceased for three years. A letter from Mary, Queen of Scots, dated 13 July 1563 describes the lamentable state of the University and its buildings:

Forsamekile as within the citie of Glasgw ane College and Vniuersitie was devisit to be hade quhairin the youthe micht be brocht vp in letres and knawlege the commoune

3 The Auld Pedagogy
After the foundation of the University of Glasgow in 1451, accommodation was rented in Rottenrow near the Cathedral, for living quarters and lecture rooms. The building was occupied by the University for about four years, and became known as the pedagogium or 'Auld Pedagogy'. In 1847 Allan and Ferguson published a lithograph entitled *Views and Notices of Glasgow in Former Times* from which this engraving is derived. The ruined building in the foreground on the left is thought to be the 'Auld Pedagogy'.

welth servit and vertew incressit. Off the quhilk College ane parte of the sculis and chalmeris being biggit the rest thairof alsweill duellingis as provisioune for the pouir bursouris and maisteris to teche ceissit. Sua that the samyn apperit rather to be the decay of ane Vniuersitie nor ony wyse to be reknit ane establisst fundatioun.[5]

(Forasmuch as within the city of Glasgow a College and University was devised to be had wherein the youth might be brought up in letters and knowledge the common wealth served and virtue increased. Of the which College a part of the schools and chambers being built the rest thereof as well as dwellings as provision for the poor bursers and masters to teach ceased. So that the same appeared rather to the decay of a University nor any wise to be reckoned an established foundation.)

The late 16th century saw an increasing interest in education throughout Scotland, which flourished under Mary and her distinguished advisors. Perhaps under the encouragement of the great scholar-poet and later tutor to James VI, George Buchanan, Mary endowed five bursaries for poor students from some of the confiscated revenues of the Black Friars.[6] She also granted the 'kirkroom', manse, 13 acres of land and other property of the Black Friars to the struggling institution. Although not an alumnus of Glasgow, Buchanan took a strong interest in the University, donating twenty Greek books in 1578. Further endowments, including the Blackfriars' Kirk itself, followed from the Town Council of Glasgow in 1572 and a number of other sources until 1577. Another scholar of great repute, Andrew Melville, was recruited as principal regent in 1574 and the teaching began to flourish. In 1577 James VI made a major grant of the some of the revenues of Govan parish for the maintenance of a Provost or Principal, three regents, a steward, four poor students, the Principal's servant, a cook, and janitor. The same charter re-founded the University as a *Nova Erectio* along reformed Protestant lines. Instead of regents teaching the whole arts course, they taught their specialist subjects under a professorial system. In 1581 the Archbishop of Glasgow granted the Tron feu duties (feudal land ownership duties) to the University. James VI granted the teinds (produce tax for maintaining the clergy) of Renfrew and Kilbride parishes in 1618. Although the Reformation of 1560 had removed the clergy of the old Catholic institutions from influence, the University relied on the patronage of the reformed ministers of the west of Scotland, and served primarily as a training college for ministers.

By the later medieval period classes and 'disputations', or formalised debates, were held from Monday to Saturday, and students attended church together twice on Sundays. Students were also required to take meals together at a 'common table'. Teaching was carried out by up to four regents, distinguished graduates of the University, who held office for four to five years. Students were summoned by a bell and each class began with a prayer and calling of a register. General arts courses lasted four years and each regent taught all the subjects in a tutorial system. Until the middle of the 18th century all lectures and most of the tutorials were given in academic Latin. Higher degrees were also awarded.

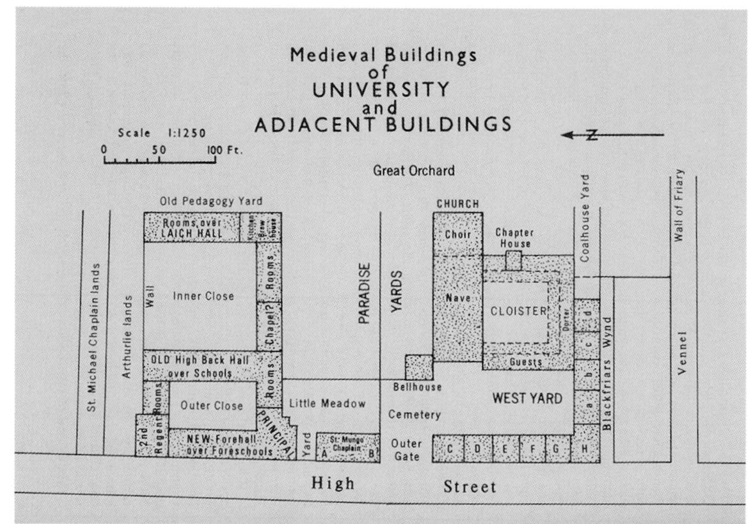

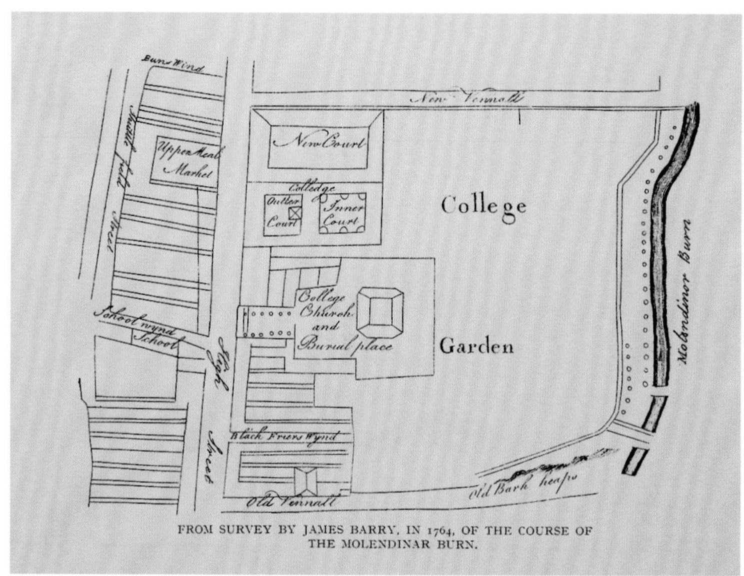

4 Plan of the medieval buildings of the University of Glasgow from *The University of Glasgow 1451–1577* by John Durkan and James Kirk, p.32

5 Plan of the College lands by James Barry, 1764. This plan relates to the College as redeveloped in the 17th century.
GULSC [Mu Add.q17]

LATE 16TH-CENTURY HIGH STREET BUILDINGS

The effect of the re-foundation and new income on the University's buildings is unclear, but it is likely that some repair and enlargement of the High Street structures took place in the late 16th century. In spite of the new revenues, the University's accounts and reports suggest that finances continued to be a matter of concern. The detailed appearance of the medieval buildings is not known, as they were demolished at some time in the first half of the 17th century, but accounts for repairs

6 North range of the Inner Close, rebuilt by John Boyd for Principal Strang in 1631–33 GULSC [B26]

provide evidence of the materials used, such as the thatching of the Principal's house.[7] Sir William Brereton, an English visitor, described those parts of the complex still standing as 'old, strong, plain building' in about 1635.[8] Some sense of the early layout of buildings, yards and gardens in 1577 is provided by the reconstruction plan [FIG.4] drawn up by James Durkan and James Kirk in their book, *The University of Glasgow: 1451–1577*.[9]

For the first century after its foundation the University remained separate from, but closely connected to, the adjoining Blackfriars complex. Like monastic and other contemporary educational establishments, an enclosed, quadrangular plan emerged with an inner and outer close, or courtyard. Accommodation was provided for the Principal, Chaplain, masters and students (who obtained varying standards of room depending on their means). Other components included teaching rooms, a chapel, a kitchen and brewhouse, and three large halls. Brewhouses were standard features of great houses and other large establishments. Student numbers remained low throughout the 15th and 16th centuries, probably never exceeding 100, as was common in most universities of the period.

A *Catalogus librorum communis Bibliothecae Collegii Glasguensis* (library catalogue) was drawn up in 1578, but it is not known at what point a dedicated room was used to house the books. Sir William Brereton described the old library as 'a very little room not twice so large as my old closet'.[10] An account of 1659 records payment of 16 shillings to 'Thomas Joly for two dayes work in takeing doune the roofe of the Bibliothick [Library]', which probably refers to the old buildings fronting the High Street.[11]

REBUILDING OF THE INNER AND OUTER CLOSES, HIGH STREET 1631–1660

Between 1450 and 1600 the population of Glasgow expanded sevenfold to about 7,000.[12] Much of this expansion was in the mercantile centre to the south of the University, and is attributable to increased trade with Ireland, Argyll and the Western Isles, along with some continental trade to France, Flanders and Spain. From

1603, the union of the Scottish and English crowns provided a more stable environment for southern overland trade, particularly in the export of linen and linen yarn and the import of finished cloth. Manufacturing also prospered. The flourishing mercantile and manufacturing classes led in turn to the rise of professional bankers, notaries (lawyers), doctors, apothecaries, clerics, and teachers. The town's population continued to expand to over 14,000 by 1660.

The state of the library appears to have been one of the main factors driving the redevelopment of the University's High Street site from the 1630s. There may also have been a drive to improve the library in response to the rebuilding of the libraries at St Andrews and Edinburgh in 1613 and 1615–18 respectively. As early as 1619, Alexander Boyd, one of the regents, bequeathed a number of books and the sum of 1,000 merks (£666 Scots) for the rebuilding of the college.

James Law, Archbishop of Glasgow and Chancellor of the University, began a more sustained fundraising campaign in July 1630 by the donation of another 1,000 merks. This was closely followed by the promise of 2,000 merks from the Town Council of Glasgow. Charles I pledged £200 sterling in 1633, but it was not until 1654 that the payment was made by Cromwell.

From the early 1630s to the late 1650s a large number of nobles, gentry and clergy throughout Scotland, and expatriate courtiers in London, contributed significant sums towards the 'building of a commoun librarie within the Colledge of Glasgow, furnishing thairof with books and utherways inlarging the fabrick of the said colledge'.[13] Some of the larger donations, such as that by William Alexander, the Earl of Stirling in 1631, were conditional on the use of the donor's name and arms on a room and use of the room by his children in perpetuity.[14] The resulting complex of buildings and gardens on the High Street was described by the great 19th-century antiquarians, David MacGibbon and Thomas Ross, as '... one of the finest, and certainly most extensive specimen of the Scottish civil architecture of the seventeenth century'.[15]

Unlike their predecessor buildings, the construction of the 17th-century University buildings is relatively well documented through accounts, inventories, minutes, descriptions, measured drawings and other records, including an extraordinary late 17th-century bird's-eye view by John Slezer [FIGS 1, 2, 7]. The survival of most of the buildings into the age of photography and Ordnance Survey mapping also provides a good visual record of their appearance, plan-form and dimensions. John Strang, a notable cleric, philosopher and Principal of the University from 1626 to 1651, was a significant force behind the project [FIG. 6]. The designer of the new complex appears to have been the master mason, John Boyd.[16] The employment of a master mason/contractor/architect was entirely in the tradition of building projects before the 18th century. Boyd was Master of Works for the construction of the Glasgow Tolbooth in 1626 (partly demolished in 1814), restored the library in the south-west tower of Glasgow Cathedral in 1628 (demolished 1846–49), worked on Hutcheson's Hospital, Trongate, about 1643 (demolished *c.*1795) and surveyed 'at his Majesties castell of Dumbartone in the yeere of God 1629'.[17]

The royal connection at Dumbarton is of particular interest in that it links Boyd with Sir James Murray, principal master for 'all His Majesty's works and buildings in Scotland', and Master of Works for the Dumbarton project. Murray was a leading member of a circle of architect-masons who brought fashionable classical regularity and Mannerist motifs from French, Italian and Flemish patternbooks, such as strapwork pediments and buckle quoins (decorative corner stones), to the Scottish tradition of building. This hybrid of native style, new classical regularity and patternbook detailing, can still be seen in Boyd's Tolbooth Tower at Glasgow Cross. It was particularly appropriate to an educational establishment that wanted to present itself in a modern, ordered and sophisticated manner. A number of the other tradesmen associated with the Glasgow Tolbooth or Dumbarton Castle, such as Robert Calwall or Caldwell (mason), Robert Boyd (mason), James Rankin (mason), James Johnstone (smith) and Patrick Colquoun (wright), were also employed at the Old College.[18] Boyd was Deacon of the Incorporation of Masons in Glasgow thirteen times between 1609 and 1649.[19]

The new buildings were to occupy the ground plan of the old structures, probably for practical reasons to enable the phasing of work as funds allowed. Demolitions, preparation of the ground and gathering of the building materials from the town quarry, Woodsyd (Woodside) quarry and Craig (probably Craigpark) quarry began in 1631. The following March the masons started work on a range of lodgings on the north side of the Inner Close.[20] The old Inner Close had no buildings on this north side, only an enclosing wall, so the starting point of the protracted building campaign minimised disruption to college life. The University records show accounts for payments to masons, wrights (carpenters), slaters, smiths, 11 wheelbarrow men, who spent 41 days removing the earth and bringing in stone for the foundations, and carters, who delivered the building stone from the quarries. The College met the expense of the gloves for the wrights, masons and slaters, 20,000 sharpenings of the masons' chisels, an hourglass to time the masons' working hours, the pulley for hauling up the roof timbers, and even extra money for a workman 'that had

7 The College buildings and tower are shown in John Slezer's late 17th-century engraving (centre top of the image)
National Library of Scotland, Edinburgh

a sor finger hurt in our work'. Significant stages in the project, for example, the breaking of the ground and the arrival of money from the Town Treasurer, were marked by celebratory ale or wine, supplied by the College.[21]

The new range [FIG.6] comprised three adjoining symmetrical blocks of seven bays, each containing two large rooms per floor, all of very fine and expensive coursed ashlar sandstone. At the centre of each block was a projecting circular stair tower with a tall conical roof, after the manner of a French château. The windows were of two sizes and arranged in bays (in a small-large-small window pattern) on either side of the stair towers. The dormer sizes reflected those of the windows below. The architectural detailing appears to have been relatively conservative: windows and doorways had heavy roll-moulded architraves (surrounds), and the dormer pediments were of simple triangular form. The larger dormerheads had small finials, and at least two of the presumed original six were dated 1632.[22]

The wrights' accounts for 'plenishing the chambers with beds, buirds (boards), formes (benches) *and* studies (partitioned study areas)' before September 1633 reveal that this first range was intended for residential accommodation.[23] Throughout the 17th century, students were required to live within the College. When the buildings were on the point of demolition in 1870, original red floor tiles were recorded in the upper part of the building.[24]

Sir William Brereton described the building project in 1635: 'There is a good, handsome foundation propounded and set out, to add a good, fair and college-like structure to be built quadrangular, one side is already built, and there hath been collections throughout Scotland towards the building of this college, and much more money is collected than is needful to the building hereof.'[25]

John Boyd was contracted by the masters of the College to build the east range of the Inner Close, for which he received final payment and a bonus 'in bounty of his whole attendance and paines in the building of the haille North and East Quarters of the Colledge, beside his weiklie wages' in 1639.[26] This range replaced the old Laigh Hall and kitchen/brewhouse. Boyd's building was demolished in about 1811, but its 1½-storey form (lower than the other sides of the quad) can be seen in John Slezer's engraved bird's-eye view [FIG.1].

The tradesmen's accounts suggest that the old functions were accommodated in the new range: a kitchen, brewhouse and common hall on the ground floor and four large accommodation and/or teaching 'chambers' above.[27] Some degree of ornament is likely to have attached to this block: an oriel window with a tall polygonal roof over a columned doorpiece is visible in Slezer's engraving, and the accounts make particular mention of locks, a knocker, ironwork and lead for the windows, 'pavementing', painting and an iron chimney for the Laigh Hall. Slezer's engraving [FIG.2] indicates that the oriel was fully glazed, while the other windows took the traditional 17th-century form of leaded small-pane windows over shutters. Glass was very expensive in the early 17th century and could only be produced in relatively small sizes. It is likely that the oriel marked the high table location within the Laigh Hall. Although not mentioned in the payments of the 1630s, accounts from the 1650s indicate that the new library was housed in the east range of the Inner Close, probably on the ground floor to the south of the central entrance.[28] A 'large and stately orchard' was also begun at about this time in the Great Yard that stood behind the College.[29] The orchard seems to have been part fruit garden and part pleasure ground for the masters of the College, but definitely out of bounds to the students. By 1640 some £18,200 Scots (£1,516 sterling) had been spent on the new buildings.

The political and religious instability and outbreaks of plague (when the College transferred to Irvine) in the 1640s interrupted fundraising and building progress, but 1641 saw a legacy of 2,000 merks and £1,000 Scots from Thomas Hutcheson and five years later the promise of a major benefaction by Zachary Boyd [FIG.8], Minister of the Barony Kirk, for completion of the Inner Close and construction of the Outer Close [FIG.6]. From 1642 the regenting system of teaching was re-introduced, with many subjects taught by one regent, as happened in the other Scottish universities.

Against the wishes of the College, Oliver Cromwell's Commissioners imposed the energetic and ambitious, but unscholarly, Patrick Gillespie as Principal in 1653. Gillespie appears to have appointed a new mason-architect, John Clark (also spelled 'Clerk' or 'Clarke' in different accounts), at about this period. Little is known of his career prior to the Old College contract, but subsequently Clark became Deacon of the Masons' Incorporation eight times between 1660 and 1674 and he appears to have obtained the lease of the town quarry for fifteen years from 1660.[30] Gillespie is described as having a leading role in the building projects: 'The matters of our Colledge this year [1656] were peaceable; our gallant building goes on vigorously; above twenty-six thousand pounds are already spent upon it; Mr Patrick Gillespie with a very great care, industrie and dexteritie manageing it himself as good as alone.'[31] In 1654 Cromwell re-granted the feudal superiority of the bishopric of Galloway (first granted by Charles I in 1641) along with 200 merks from the customs of Glasgow.[32] By the time of Zachary Boyd's death in 1655, his benefaction was worth about £11,300 Scots and the medieval buildings still remaining within the College site were described as 'ruinous'.[33] A major legacy of £1,000 Scots was received from the estate of Thomas Hutcheson of Lambhill at the same time, and work began on the south and west sides and 'steapell' of the Inner Close. John Snell, alumnus, and benefactor of the Snell Exhibition (an annual scholarship for Glasgow postgraduates to study at Balliol College, Oxford), donated a further 3,000 merks towards the steeple.[34] As not all the donations were in ready cash, the masters of the College ended up lending money against the future realisation of property and rentals.[35] In August 1656 all the masons were given a bonus for completion of the Inner Close and the date was inscribed on one of the dormer pediments of the south range. While the new ranges of the Inner Close mirrored the earlier ranges in general form and regularity, the detailing of the doorways, windows and dormers differed in their flat architraves and strapwork dormer pediments. The gables were crowstepped. The flashier detailing was no doubt intended to contrast with the more sober architecture of the previous regime.

8 Bust of Zachary Boyd at the base of the tower between the Inner and Outer Closes photographed by Thomas Annan
GUAS [Old & New 10]

9 The Forehall arcade and the lion and unicorn staircase, photographed by Thomas Annan
GUAS [Old & New 7]

10 Central range and tower between the Inner and Outer Closes, photographed by Thomas Annan
GUAS [Old & New 11]

The showy pediments were just the start of a far more ambitious scheme. A magnificent 43m-high square-plan steeple was built off-centre in the western range. A pend in the base linked the two quadrangles. String courses defined the upper stages of the tower and the top was finished with a timber arcade, 2-stage ogee lead roof and gilded weather-cock. Initially, it served little practical purpose other than as a prospect tower, as it had neither a clock nor bells and the accommodation was very limited. However, the steeple undoubtedly had symbolic intent, marking the presence and semi-independent jurisdiction of the University as a powerful institution in the city, competing with the steeples of the Tolbooth, Merchant's House (from 1665) and Hutchesons' Hospital, and spires of the Blackfriars' (College Kirk), Tron and cathedral churches.

An account of 1658 records: 'Item, given out for Mr. Zacharie Boyd's statue with the compartment in whyte marbell and the writing tabello (inscription panel) in black, tuinte five poundis sterling'. This statue was commissioned from a London sculptor and set up over the arch at the foot of the steeple in the Inner Close. The bust and inscription were removed to Hunterian Library at Gilmorehill in 1870, and now form part of the sculpture collection of the Hunterian Art Gallery.[36] Later alterations to the steeple included the installation of a clock in 1686 by Walter Corbet, smith of Glasgow, and a large bell in the same year by John Meikle of Edinburgh.[37] A smaller bell of 1703 (now in the tower at Gilmorehill), rung before classes, was also cast by Meikle. The American polymath, Benjamin Franklin, is thought to have advised on the addition of a lightning conductor in 1771 (installed in 1772).[38] Andrew Dickie of Edinburgh made a replacement clock in 1750. The steeple was much admired. As late as 1704, a Liverpool masterbuilder, John Moffatt, was sent to Glasgow to study the Old College steeple as a model for the new Dumfries Tolbooth.[39]

Work continued on the tower and north side of the Outer Close into 1658, followed by the south side. Here the stairs were contained within the buildings or in the semi-engaged stairtowers in the north-west and south-east corners of the close. Strapwork pediments of the type used in the south range of the Inner Close were applied to the Outer Close dormers and an elaborate columned archway was formed to the steeple pend. James Adams, a stone and wood carver, probably created the College arms and flanking urns in 1741.[40] The dormerheads on the outer northern and southern elevations were simple pediments. Robert Baillie, successor to Gillespie, and a particular thorn in his side, chronicled his frustration with the cost, noise, and inconvenience of the long-running building programme:

11 High Street frontage from the south, photographed by Thomas Annan
GUAS [Old & New 3]

12 The Forehall arcade, photographed by Thomas Annan
GULSC [B26]

13 The Forehall, photographed by Thomas Annan
GULSC [B26]

For the Colledge, we have no redresse of our discipline and teaching. Mr. Gillespie's work is building, and pleas [legal pleas]; with the dinn of masons, wrights, carters, smiths, we are vexed every day. Mr. Gillespie, alone for vanitie to make a new quarter in the Colledge, hes cast downe my house to build up ane other of greater show, but farr worse accommodation; in the meane [while] for one full year, I will be, and am exceedingly incommodat, which I bear because I cannot help it. And also because Mr. Gillespie has strange wayes of getting money for it, by his own industry alone; an order he got from the Protector of five hundred pound sterling, (but for an ill-office to the countrie, his delation of so much concealed rent yearly of the Crown); also the vacancy of all churches, wherein the Colledge had entres: this breeds clamour as the unjust spoill of churches and incumbents. Upon these foundations are our palaces builded; but withall our debts grow, and our stipends are not payed; for by his continuall toying our rent is mouldered away. When our magistrates represented this, and much more, in a libell against him, his good friend, Swintoun, obtained to him a fair absolution from all without any cognition of the matter; but to please the Toune, his accusations against them were also as good as waved.[41]

Another early use of the Boyd legacy was a new Principal's house, constructed to the south of the Old College hall on the High Street in 1655, for which Gavan Liteljohn was paid £14 for 'cullouring the new heigh chamber'. This probably refers to a decorative painted scheme on the ceiling or walls. Principal Gillespie's final building project was particularly controversial. Robert Baillie, writing probably in 1659, protested:

We would have been glad he [Gillespie] had rested here; but his nixt motion was, to pull down the whole forework of the Colledge, the high Hall, and Arthurlie, very good houses, all newly dressed at a great charge. I was very grieved at this not only totallie needless but hurtfull motion, and got the most of our number to be in my mind, though he offered to get it builded without any cost to the Colledge, out of the remainder of Mr. Zacharie Boyd's mortification, eight thousand merks in my Lord Loudoun's hands, the vacancies of kirks, and other means he would procure... I reasoned much for a delay, till in the next spring we had gotten some money, and saw how the world would goe; but all in vain: presentlie the Hall was pulled down. All since, I think, repent their rashness, and all beholders cry out on us. This year and the next our Colledge will lye open; want of law makes us void of money, yet now we must goe on by our private borrowings, and any other way he can invent. I am now more ready to further it than any who voted to it, for we cannot now let it lye.[42]

The scale of the medieval loss will never be known, but the replacement structure lining the High Street [FIG.11] was certainly one of the finest architectural creations of 17th-century Scotland. Through its splendidly ornate and monumental design it was intended to express the status and prestige of the College, and probably by extension that of Principal Gillespie and his backer, Oliver Cromwell.

A new contract was drawn up with John Clark in February 1659.[43] On 24 February 1660 the Town Council granted a licence to the University 'to put out their balconie stones att the Colledge yeatt', a reference to the two huge consoled (bracketed) stone balconies that overhung the High Street on either side of the entrance arch. The centrepiece was a symmetrical 2½-storey, 7-bay range containing the Forehall at the first floor and the Divinity Hall in the dormered attic [FIG.13]. The gables were crowstepped, the chimneys were tall with individual offset square-plan flues and all the windows had strapwork pediments. On the outside, fronting the High Street, was the elaborate pedimented archway with banded rustication, flanked by the two balconies at the first floor. Slezer's engraving shows what appears to be a parapet of 'rinceau', or swirling leafy branch, design to the balconies. The archway had two large studded wooden gates, one of which had a smaller wicket gate for pedestrians. The design of the archway was similar to that of Sir James Murray for the main entrance to Parliament House in Edinburgh, completed some twenty years earlier in 1639.[44]

The centrepiece was joined to the 2-bay Principal's house to the south and the 3-bay Professor of Divinity's house to the north. Although the dormer pediments remained consistent throughout the range, the houses had additional floors at different levels. Slezer's engraving shows pediments to all the principal windows of the houses, but photographs from the 1860s show no pediments. Perhaps there was an error in the Slezer engraving, or the pediments were removed from the buildings at a later date. In a reversal of the pattern of new arcaded stone tenements on the High Street, established as a fireproofing measure following the devastating fire of 1652, Gillespie created an arcade facing inwards towards the Outer Close. This fine design reflected the arrangement at Heriot's Hospital in Edinburgh, completed in 1659.

It is possibly no coincidence that a number of aspects of the new Forehall range also corresponded quite closely to details of Moray House in Edinburgh's Canongate, the home to Protector Cromwell on his visits to Scotland in 1648 and 1650. In particular, the corbelled balconies and tall ranks of offset square-plan chimneys of the Forehall had their counterparts in the unusual and sophisticated work of about 1625 at Moray House. Other details of the High Street frontage [FIG.13] also suggest a certain degree of architectural propaganda, or at least provocation, in Principal Gillespie's designs. Initially the college arms, rather than the royal arms, were placed in the panel over the entrance archway. To modern eyes this was hardly a dramatic republican gesture, but following the Restoration of the monarchy on 29 May 1660, replacement of the college arms with those of Charles II was one of the highest priorities for the University. Many of the carved pediments contained emblems representing the constituent parts of the Commonwealth. While the Crown laid claim to the same territories, the emblems may also have had some political symbolism through the selection of the motifs and their distribution.

With the collapse of Richard Cromwell's Second Protectorate, Principal Gillespie fled, leaving the College in severe debt. As Principal Baillie bemoaned: 'I sent ... a list of above twenty-six thousand merks of debt in which Mr. Gillespie has left us, beside which ten thousand pund more will not perfite [perfect] his too magnificent buildings.'[45] The debt was compounded in 1661 by the restoration of the Episcopal system of church governance. Old land taxes and duties, such as those of the bishopric of Galloway, which had previously been granted to the College, were returned to the Church to support the new bishops. Gillespie's rival and critic, Robert Baillie, was appointed Principal. The Town Council had granted a further £1,000 Scots for roofing the half-completed range on 23 October 1660 and the Scottish Parliament granted £600 sterling in 1663.[46]

In view of the financial crisis, the contemporary finishing of the interior of the Forehall was probably relatively restrained. Principal James Fall describes how the disturbances following the 'Glorious Revolution' of November 1688, when Prince William of Orange arrived at Brixham with 15,000 men to claim the thrones of England and Scotland, 'put a stop to all privat designs, and particularly to ours in compleating our begun works and reparations about the College'.[47] However, things were sufficiently settled by June 1690 for some embellishment of the Forehall to begin.

14 The Clerk's Press of 1634, where all the University's important documents were stored. The press is now kept in the Turnbull Room at Gilmorehill.

The Forehall and Principal's house were reached by an external dog-leg staircase, which was ornamented between June and August 1690 by the addition of a stone balustrade with ball finials and sculptures of a unicorn and a lion supplied by the mason, William Riddell, for £192 Scots [FIG.9].[48] A further invoice for £39 Scots itemises 'painting the stone staircase with whyt lead and oyll and guilding the Lyon and Unicorn'.[49] The symbolism of the lion and unicorn is derived from the crowned heraldic supporters of the royal coat of arms, representing Scotland and England respectively. The seated lion, or 'Lion Sejant' in heraldic terms, has a curiously oriental appearance, perhaps after the manner of a Delftware model, and is placed over a carved grotesque. The unicorn is seated on a scrolled frame, or cartouche, containing a skull-like symbol. The lion, unicorn and large stone balls may have been simple decorative finials on the unfinished stair, but their appearance in June 1690 may also have had significance as statements in

15 Parts of the Forehall panelling, including the fireplace of the 1740s were reassembled at Gilmorehill. The photograph by Thomas Annan was taken in the late 1860s, just before the removal to Gilmorehill. The Clerk's Press was kept in the Forehall. GUAS [Old & New 5]

support of the new monarchs of the Orange dynasty, William and Mary. Unfortunately for Principal Fall, they were not sufficient to prevent his dismissal in November 1690 at the hands of the Commission of Visitation, charged with purging the country of 'nonjurors', public officials who refused to swear their allegiance to William and Mary. In the case of Principal Fall, he felt unable to comply because he had previously sworn allegiance to James II before the king's flight, rather than through a particular animosity towards the new regime.

Principal Fall was replaced by William Dunlop, a supporter of William and Mary, who was later appointed Historiographer Royal. Dunlop resumed the completion of the building works. An account of 1694 describes the purchase of materials for a large plastering exercise in the Hall, but the nature of the plasterwork (decorative or plain, ceiling or walls) is not clear. Decorative plasterwork ceilings, divided into geometric compartments, were common at this time. It seems likely that a grand fireplace was located in the centre of the long west wall, above the entrance to the College from the High Street.

When it was photographed in the 1860s the Forehall was panelled with dark oak, part of a replacement decorative scheme installed in 1740–45.[50] At the north end there was a large fireplace, which appears to correspond to details described by the carver, James Adams, in his account of May 1745.[51] These parts of the Forehall interior were reassembled at Gilmorehill after 1870 (see pages 72–73). The room was lit by candles in wall sconces. The Clerk's Press, a beautiful marquetry cabinet made in 1634 and used to hold the documents of the College, was kept in this room [FIGS 14, 15]. The original fireplace in the centre of the west wall (overlooking the High Street) had been removed by this date.

With the two quadrangles finally complete in the early 1660s, student numbers stood at about 200, an increase of two-thirds on the students recorded by Sir William Brereton in 1635.[52] From 1667 every student renting a room in the College was required to keep the fabric of the building in the same condition as they found it, on pain of being whipped and expelled for breaking windows or causing other damage.[53] The 'Glorious Revolution' of 1688, which brought about the accession of William and Mary as joint monarchs, resulted in more settled times for the town and University. Presbyterian governance of the Church in Scotland was reintroduced in 1690, and created a demand for the education of ministers. Numbers of Arts and Divinity students rose, bringing the student total to about 400 in 1702.[54] Apart from the local students, there were a number of sons of the gentry and aristocracy from across Scotland, numerous Irish students, and a small number from England.[55] The first student from North America was John Porter who came to study at Glasgow in 1703.

Chapter Two

Expansion at the High Street 1700–1845

16 Blackfriars' Kirk (The College Kirk) High Street, Glasgow
Mitchell Library, Glasgow

With the exception of the east range of the Inner Close, which was replaced by the Hamilton building in 1811 [FIG.32], the 17th-century buildings remained the core of the University campus until its removal to Gilmorehill in 1870. The dining requirement was dropped in 1694 and by 1704 only about forty students out of 200–300 resided in the College.[1] Internally, there were many changes in the 18th and 19th centuries, reflecting the increasing need for teaching rooms and the move away from the provision of residential accommodation for students. As the University expanded, new residential and specialist buildings were added around the core: professorial houses; a library; an observatory; a museum and classrooms.

BLACKFRIARS' KIRK (THE COLLEGE KIRK) 1699–1702

As well as serving as the College Kirk from 1572, the old Blackfriars' church, shown in Slezer's view [FIG.2], had been used as a hall for graduation and other ceremonies. In a deal to relieve the College of the maintenance burden of the much-decayed building, the Town Council took it on as a parish church in 1635, reserving some of the College's rights to seating and the burial ground.[2] On 29 October 1670 the old Blackfriars' Kirk was struck by lightning the 'like whereof was not heard in these parts; it rent the steeple of the said church from top to bottom, and tirred the sclattes [stripped the slates] off it, and brake down the gavills [gables] in the two ends of it, and fyred it, but was quenched afterwards by men'.[3]

Work only began in 1699 on a replacement building, the first new church in Glasgow since the Reformation [FIG.16]. This was completed with a contribution of £3,300 Scots from the College towards the overall £21,308 Scots cost in 1702.[4] John Aird (younger), the Dean of Guild, and William Barclay, Master of Work, who appear to have been the main 'manadgers' of the Blackfriars project, responded to the Presbyterian requirements and emphasis on preaching with a relatively plain rectangular meeting-house and ogee-domed tower.[5] Some of the materials were probably salvaged from the old building, but others, including the slates from Luss, were brought in by barge to the city's only harbour at the Broomielaw.

The City of Glasgow Union Railway Company purchased the church in 1875, and it was demolished in the following year. The remains from the College's burial plots were transferred to the Necropolis.

PROFESSORS' COURT 1722–1780

Until the early 18th century the only houses in the College complex were those of the Principal and the Professor of Divinity at either end of the High Street range. Three 'yards' north of the College were acquired and the whole estate enclosed within a high wall in 1685.[6]

In December 1722 the Faculty decide to build eight new houses for the professors in a court to be formed with the existing north ranges of the quadrangles.[7] By this period there were ten professors, all of whom lived in the town or in chambers in the College. Although a number of the College servants were female, the teaching staff and scholars were all male. College rooms were considered unsuitable for married staff. Greater student numbers also placed pressure on the remaining residential accommodation in the Old College closes, which were increasingly devoted to teaching rooms. The two junior and un-housed professors were to be compensated so that they could live in similar style in the town.

Further land was purchased in June 1723 and the architect, Alexander McGill, was selected in August.[8] McGill was one of the leading architects in early 18th-century Scotland. He worked on several country houses including Craigiehall near Edinburgh, Yester House in East Lothian, House of Nairne in Perthshire, Blair Drummond in Stirlingshire and Donibristle in Fife. He had a number of prominent patrons, including the Duke of Montrose, who was also the University Chancellor. While he is best remembered as the nemesis of Rob Roy MacGregor, Montrose was a discerning architectural patron, who had sought advice from James Gibbs, the famous architect of St Martin's-in-the-Fields church in London, and McGill on alterations to his Glasgow townhouse in the Drygate in 1718.

The professors' houses progressed as funds allowed, starting on the north side. Six houses were complete by November 1726. The house at the south-east corner was under construction in 1732, and a large house backing onto the High Street was built in 1749–51. The site at the north-west corner of the court was occupied by other buildings until at least 1828 and was probably only developed as a taller, narrower and grander house than its neighbours in the 1830s.[9] Various subdivisions, amalgamations and reconstructions occurred, and parts of the old Outer Close were included as houses, making a total of thirteen professors' houses by the mid-19th century, when there were twenty-six professors. The Principal's house remained at the southern end of the High Street range, but was completely rebuilt by Principal Leechman sometime after 1761 to designs by Allan Dreghorn.[10]

The north side of the court was a very early example in the city of the regularising and classicising tendency of Enlightenment urban planning that was to sweep through Scotland's towns and villages in the 18th and 19th centuries. In Professors' Court individual townhouses were marshalled by McGill's plan into terraces of unified design around a square [FIG.18]. Each house was 4 bays wide and 3 storeys in height with an attic and no front basement area. The doorways had classical cornices and 'lugged architraves', or surrounds with 'ears', and were divided from each other by rusticated vertical bands in the manner of pilasters. The windows had plain surrounds and the tall panelled chimneys were corniced. Behind, the arrangement was less regular, with stables, a hen house and even a byre for a cow belonging to one of the Divinity professors.

Terraces of stone-fronted, self-contained, classical townhouses were extremely rare in Scottish towns at this date, when tenement dwelling was the norm for most middle class and professional families. In the light of the ubiquitous terraced 3-bay townhouse design with basement area that dominated Scottish urban and suburban development for the next two hundred years, the design of the professors' houses with four bays and no front basement areas appears unusual to modern eyes. McGill is known to have been in London in 1717, and it may be that the design of the houses is derived from his experiences there, where the 4-bay format of terraced houses was common. Although the professors' houses were not quite on the scale of the little classical mansions built around Argyle Street by *nouveau riche* merchants from 1711 onwards, they were certainly some of the largest and most comfortable dwellings in the city of their time. Unsurprisingly, professorial squabbles over the occupancy of the houses were a feature of College life throughout the 18th and 19th centuries.

Maintaining the great length and regularity of the High Street frontage, which was one of the architectural glories of the city, proved to be a constant concern. The Professor of Divinity's request to replace the 17th-century windows and shutters of his house at the north end of the High Street range with sash and case windows was considered by the Faculty in 1730.[11] Care was also taken in the construction of the new house of 1749–51 to maintain the roofline of the High Street frontage. Dormers in a 17th-century style were added to the west (rear) elevation to match the adjoining range of the Professor of Divinity's house, Forehall and Principal's house. By March 1745 the king's arms over the entrance to the College were showing signs of decay, notably the unicorn, whose foot and ear required the ministrations of the carver James Adams. He also charged to 'Oil the King's Arms, and put up the 2 vases on the sides of the same.'[12]

A large pyramidal well-head and pump was set up in the middle of the court, although there may have been an earlier College well on the site or elsewhere in the complex. The proximity, convenience and free availability of the well were great luxuries, as other parts of the city depended on sixteen public wells, from which

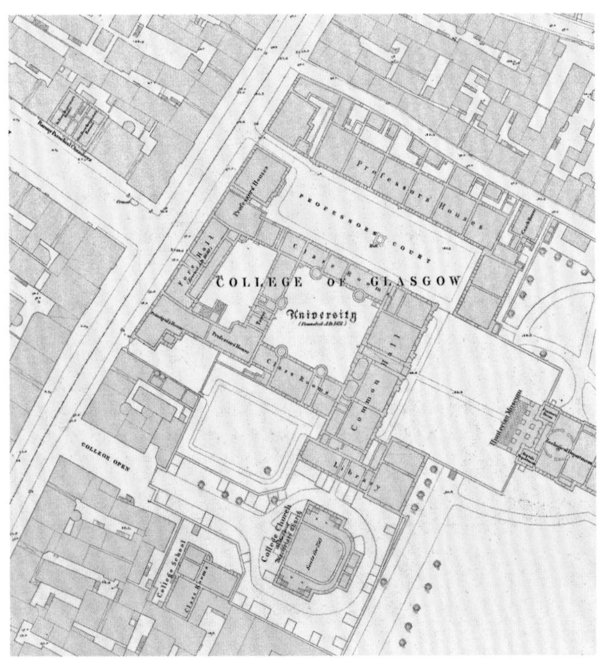

17 Ordnance Survey Town Plan, 1858
GULMOPS [OS Town Plan 1857–8, Sheet VI.II.12]

18 Professors' Court looking north-east, photographed by Thomas Annan, probably in 1864. The houses on the right-hand side were designed by Alexander McGill in 1723.
GUAS [Old & New 12]

water had to be carried. In the early 19th century the College spring water was replaced by a supply from a water company. It was not until the completion of the first phase of the Loch Katrine reservoir scheme in 1860 that the public wells finally disappeared. After the introduction of piped gas for lighting in about 1832, the pyramid was used to house the College gas meter.[13] The roll call of occupants of Professors' Court makes an impressive 'Who's Who' of the Scottish Enlightenment, from the philosopher Francis Hutcheson (1694–1746) and physician and chemist Joseph Black (1728–99) to the social philosopher and pioneer political economist Adam Smith (1723–90). Smith lived in the court in the 1750s and 60s with his mother and cousin, Jane Douglas.[14] It was commonplace for principals and professors to provide lodging for boarder students in the houses, a number of whom scratched their names on the glass of the windows.

THE LIBRARY 1721–1744

The more stable political conditions from the 1690s onwards saw an increase in the number of students to about 400 by 1702. New chairs in Mathematics, Greek, Humanity, Practice of Medicine, Law, Ecclesiastical History and Anatomy and Botany were founded between 1691 and 1718. The regenting system ended in 1727 and the professorial system returned to stay. There was an accompanying need for more books, storage and improved security. In 1691 some £770 Scots was spent 'lenthening the Library Room by taking away the Bibliothecarius his chamber, altering the presses [cupboards] where the books stand, making seven new presses intirely new, making wire casements to the whole presses' and 'painting all the casements and presses in the Library green and the wyre and inside reed'.[15] Coincidentally, the University's earliest surviving library catalogue also dates from this year. Thomas Morer's interesting account of various libraries in late 17th-century Scotland praises the use of wire-fronted cupboards, rather than chains, for security, and commends Glasgow: 'The Library is well digested, and the Books so order'd, (not as at Edinburgh, where they are Marshall'd and distinguish'd according to the benefactors), but as the Sciences direct 'em. And the Superscriptions serve only to shew what Books they are, and not who gave 'em.'[16] In spite of the librarian's sacrifices for the enlargement of the library in the Inner Close, new accommodation was required by the 1720s. Following the hospitality offered to his sons in 1720, James Brydges, 1st Duke of Chandos, gifted £500 to the College the following year. The Chancellor, James Graham, 1st Duke of Montrose, who was responsible for determining the use of the money, suggested waiting for accumulating interest to cover the cost of a new library.[17] By 1730 Montrose was agitating for progress, but a site had not been selected and there were no estimates.[18] A site at the back of the Common Hall (east range of the Inner Close) was finally identified.[19] Two local wrights, Allan Dreghorn and John Craig, submitted proposals for the new building in the first couple of months of 1732. Both men had successful businesses and appear to have collaborated on other projects. Dreghorn went on to design St Andrew's Parish Church in 1739, the most opulent and sophisticated of Glasgow's 18th-century churches. A mason from Stirling, James Adam, who had undertaken the professors' houses, was engaged to build the new library.[20]

The minutes of the Faculty's building committee in March 1732 suggest some hesitancy about the architectural quality of the project, with the members even resorting to consulting William Halfpenny's *Practical Architecture* of 1724, a builder's manual for fashionable Palladian details. The Professor of Oriental Languages, Charles Morthland, had particular concerns in relation to lighting of the basement.[21] With a degree of relief, John Loudoun, Professor of Logic, reported to the March 1732 meeting that 'Mr Ja. [William] Adam the Architect was at Hamilton. They judged it very proper to send for him in order to have his advice upon the plans for the Library before they proceed to any further directions to the matter'.[22] William Adam was by that time an enormously successful designer and entrepreneur, dubbed Scotland's 'universal architect' by John Clerk of Eldin. Amongst many other projects, Adam was working at Hamilton on the remodelling of Hamilton Palace and its vast landscape and the design of the spectacular banqueting house, or 'dog kennel', at nearby Chatelherault. Adam's connection with the College is not clear. It is possible that he was invited at the suggestion of the University Chancellor, the Duke of Montrose, who had met him in London in 1727 and invited him to Buchanan, Stirlingshire, where he intended to build a new house. Adam seems to have been at work on the design of a monument at the Montrose mausoleum in St Kattan's Kirk, Aberuthven, for the duke in 1732. Montrose's friend and 'procurator', or chamberlain, Mungo Graham of Gorthie, acted as the duke's main contact with the building committee, and liaised with Adam over the Aberuthven monument. Graham was also the Rector of the University between 1718 and 1720.

Typically, Adam lost no time in dismissing the earlier schemes and drawing up his own plans. Two characteristically engaging and persuasive letters survive in the University Archives from William Adam to an unknown member of the building committee, probably John Loudoun, whose new house faced the site of the Library.[23] By the time of the first letter of 20 April 1732, Adam had clearly viewed the site, met the building committee and was preparing the plans and elevations [FIG. 19]. The committee had raised a number of issues, to which Adam responded: it did not matter that the Library's north elevation was not in 'Compleat Symetrie' with the gable of Professor Morthland's new house at the south-east corner of Professors' Court; the library keeper and other visitors could be prevented from entering the forecourt and gardens by an arrangement of fences and gates; the entrance needed a handsome stair, portico and seat; and the Library should be entered from the north, rather than the long west wall, even if it meant having only one fireplace. Adam went on:

19 Design by William Adam for the Old College Library, 1732
GUAS [BUL 6/56/12]

What I have in view is not only Conveniency But a Magnificence Joined with Simplicity. I am not Affecting gaudy ornaments that would run to great Expence But that the Entrance to the room should be in the most Conspicuous place and where att the same time you have the eye satisfied with variety of Agreeable Prospects, And this can only be from the litle Parterr which ly betwixt the Design'd Library and the North Buildings … By entering att the end of the room you have the most Extended & graceful prospect of the room itself and the Chimney facing you in a right manner & at a right distance By which the height & Ceiling of the room has a noble Effect. Consider a litle and you'l see what a noble Effect the Gothick Churches have when you enter att one end, which you know was a Ceremony Observed in former days, And when you enter att the broad side of the same Church it has not near the same Appearance, And must be so in all buildings which are longer than broad if there is a fine height.

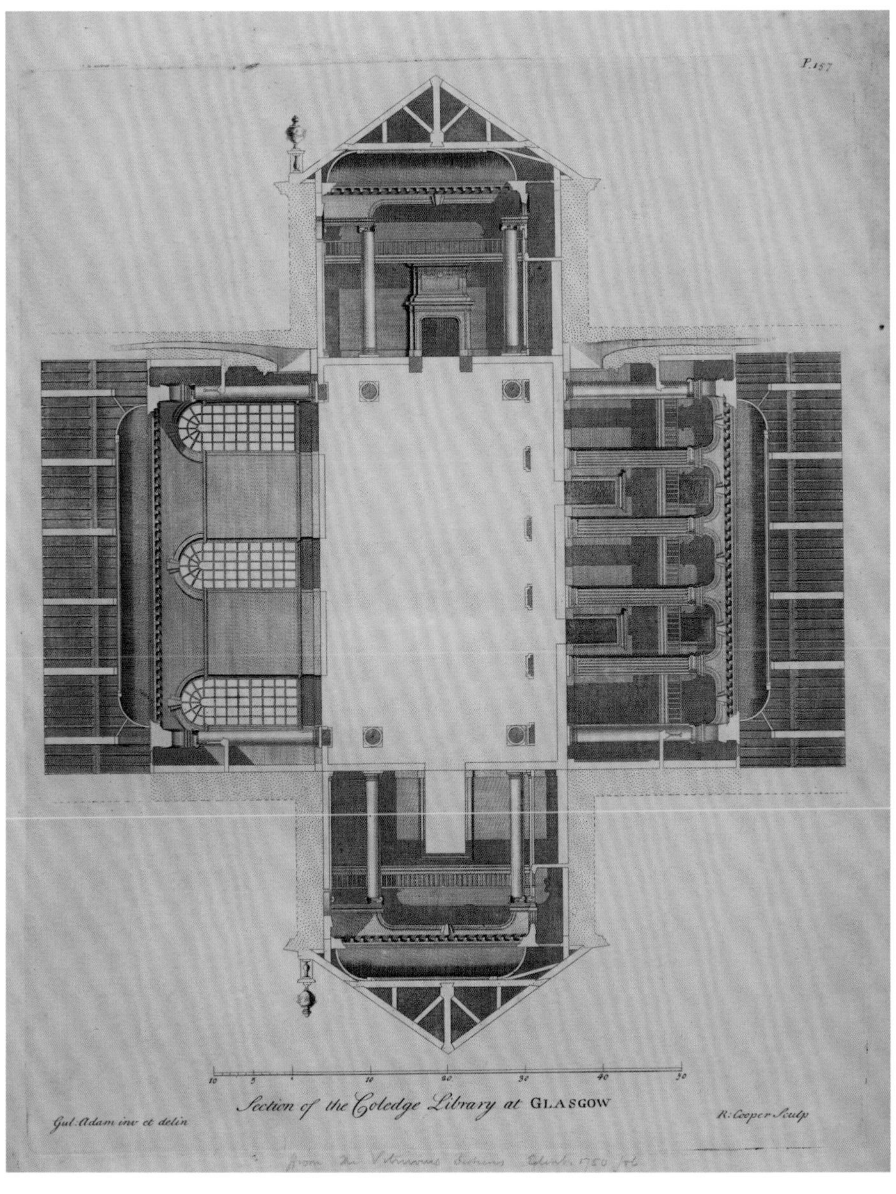

20 Design by William Adam for the Old College Library, published in *Vitruvius Scoticus*, 1812
GULSC [e11]

Adam's second surviving letter of 6 May 1732 accompanied the plans. In it he apologised for the delay and expressed the view that 'as I expect it will please so shall wish to have the satisfaction of seeing it exactly Execute. In which case you may reasonably Esteem it one of the best pieces of its kind in Brittain'. The Senate approved the Library plans on 9 May 1732.

The scheme was engraved for publication in William Adam's projected book of designs, *Vitruvius Scoticus*, eventually produced by his grandson in 1812 [FIG.20].[24] Although compact, the temple design was elegant and practical. In response to the difficulties of the earlier schemes, Adam provided a deep basement with two large teaching rooms, well lit by basket-arched windows and heated by stoves. Above, the beautiful 2-storey library room had a columned gallery around three sides. The fourth side, again amply lit by large round-headed windows, faced east over the gardens. The entrance was in the north side of the room and there was a marble fireplace in the south gable, as Adam insisted. Externally a grand perron stair led to a small portico flanked by statue niches in the north elevation. The corners and basement windows were rusticated. Carved swags hung over the statue niches and a series of urns decorated the roof balustrade of the east (garden) elevation. The pediment was intended to contain a deeply cut coat of arms of the Duke of Chandos, and a series of urns. A small room for the librarian and an internal staircase projected to the west.

Although the building was small, the project was plagued with practical and financial difficulties. Second-hand stones, left over from the Duke of Montrose's abandoned alterations at his Drygate townhouse, were to be purchased, but negotiations and payment were protracted. By June 1733 £670 Scots had been spent on the building, but more timber, wainscoting and glass were required. The roof was still to be put on, the great stair to be built, the coat of arms to be carved and the 'bullostrodes' [stone balustrade around the roof] installed.[25] Many of the contractors' accounts are in the University archives, including those of Dreghorn and Craig, who did at least get to supply materials.[26] Considerable care was taken over the interior, where James Adams, carver, supplied a fine veined marble fireplace and mahogany festoons.[27] The Library was eventually completed in 1744. Craig's heirs were only able to obtain the fee for his unexecuted designs following his death in January 1745.[28]

David Allan's painting of about 1761, and the subsequent engraving, of the Foulis Academy [FIG.21], which operated from University premises between 1753 and 1775, are often claimed to depict the interior of the Library on account of their representation of three round-headed windows. However, if Allan intended to show the Library, it is a very fanciful rendering. Apart from the exaggerated variance of scale in the figures, there are a number of differences between Allan's

21 Engraving of the Foulis Academy after David Allan. The scene is often thought to depict the Old College Library, but apart from the arched windows it bears little resemblance to the library as built.
GUAS/GULSC [MU23-y.27]

22 The Old College Library photographed by Thomas Annan probably in 1864
GULSC [B26]

depictions and the room as it is known to have been built: Allan shows no galleries; the fireplace in the south wall is off-centre; the glazing pattern differs; the windows do not reach the coving; and there appears to be a large opening to another room in the right-hand (north) wall.[29] Photographs from the 1860s show that the coat of arms was never carved [FIG.22]. The urns and statues were probably never installed and it is possible that the roof balustrade was also abandoned. There are later (undated) alternative drawings for the staircase in the University archives, which suggest that the original design was not implemented, or that it was replaced. A number of other alterations took place during the 126-year existence of the building, notably an extension to the west that linked it to the main east range of the Inner Close, and replacement of the portico and stone staircase with an ugly iron staircase.

THE MACFARLANE OBSERVATORY 1760

Astronomy had been taught at Glasgow since 1451, largely based on *Tractatus de Sphaera*, or *The Sphere*, a teaching text by the 13th-century scholar Johannes de Sacrobosco, or 'John of Holywood'. The study of practical astronomy developed significantly in Europe throughout the 17th century. By the middle of the 18th century the College owned a number of telescopes, including an 8-foot instrument of 1693.

In June 1754 the committee for astronomical instruments obtained permission from the Faculty to raise subscriptions towards a new observatory. Further stimulus to the construction of an observatory was provided by Alexander Macfarlane's legacy of astronomical instruments to his alma mater in 1755. Macfarlane died in Jamaica, where he had made his fortune as a merchant and plantation owner. The instruments suffered from exposure to salt water on the sea journey to Glasgow and James Watt, later the famous inventor, was commissioned to repair them in 1756. On the 8 April 1757 the Faculty approved the plan and expenditure of £400 on construction of a new observatory.[30] The author of the plan is not known for certain, but it is likely to have been Allan Dreghorn, who was contracted to build the structure on a site behind the College at Dowanhill.[31]

The foundation stone for the first purpose-built university observatory in Britain was laid on 17 August 1757.[32] Although the building survived well into the 19th century, and its size, location and ground-plan are identified, there are no known detailed images of the structure. However, it was described by Tobias Smollett in his novel, *Humphrey Clinker*, as 'well equipped with astronomical instruments'; and by the Revd W.M. Wade in his *History of Glasgow* of 1822: 'This simple little structure ... consists of a quadrangular centre with a projection also quadrangular and surmounted by a balustrade on the east and west'.[33] Allan Dreghorn ornamented the building with a globe and vases.[34] George II founded a chair of Practical Astronomy in 1760. It was first occupied by Alexander Wilson, a type founder and

23 James Adam's College Street development photographed in 1960
© Newsquest (Herald & Times) Licensor www.scran.ac.uk

scientific instrument maker, who was awarded the Gold Medal of the Royal Society of Sciences in Copenhagen in 1772 for his pioneering work on sunspots. His discovery of what became known as the 'Wilson effect' started research in solar physics that continues to be a major research interest within the University today. Some of the Macfarlane instruments are now in the Hunterian Museum. William Hershel visited the observatory in July 1792.

In 1813 John Brash added a small extension to the west wing.[35] By the 1830s the atmospheric pollution and construction of tall buildings around the College grounds were such that astronomical observations were impossible. At the instigation of the fourth holder of the chair, John Pringle Nichol, the College eventually purchased the observatory at Horselethill in the west end from the 'Friends of Astronomical Science in Glasgow' in 1841.

COLLEGE STREET 1792–1794

From about 1750 to 1790 the University gradually acquired the lands facing the College on the opposite (west) side of the High Street as far back as Shuttle Street. One of the plots was purchased in 1766 from Robert and Andrew Foulis, booksellers, printers to the University and founders of the Foulis Academy of Fine Arts. By 31 May 1792 the Faculty were considering how 'the whole ground opposite the College might be laid out or disposed of for the advantage and ornament of the College'.[36] The project committee determined that the most advantageous and ornamental way of dealing with the ground was to commission a plan from 'some Architect of Character' for a 'street with its centre precisely opposite the Centre of the College Gate, fifty feet wide at the least, having on the south side a Row of handsome Houses each occupying a space of 55 feet from front to back, back yard included, outside measure; and having on the north side a like Row of houses each occupying a space of 63 feet from front to back ...'[37] Two plans were drawn up in 1792 for creating the new street westwards from the High Street to Shuttle Street. Initially the committee approached the local architect and builder, James Jaffrey. However, after viewing his plans, they determined 'unanimously to employ Mr Adam (James Adam, son of William Adam) Architect at London, to make out also a Plan and Elevation of the same with all possible dispatch, as they reckon it a matter of great importance to have a Plan from an Architect of the first Reputation before proceeding farther in this Business'.[38] The reason for engaging James Adam is not explained, but unless there were continuing links through his father's work on the Library, the connection is probably via George Jardine, Professor of Logic. Glasgow Royal Infirmary was under construction in 1793 to designs by Robert and James Adam. Jardine was appointed by the College as their manager of the Glasgow Royal Infirmary and also served on the committee for laying out the ground opposite the College. The death of his brothers Robert, on 3 March 1792, and John, on 25 June, left James as the sole practising member of the great architectural dynasty. At the time of the College Street proposals James was busy with the completion of a number of other projects in Glasgow: the Tron Kirk, the Barony Church, the Trades' Hall and the Assembly Rooms.

The Faculty approved James Adam's scheme on 11 March 1793.[39] Part of the purpose of the ambitious project seems to have been to provide further accommodation for the University teaching staff, but also to generate income through the lease of 'handsome shops in the ground story suited to the street' and the duties from the feudal superiority of the land. However, the widespread political and economic consequences of the French Revolution reached Glasgow in the form of bank failures and commercial instability, which caused the Faculty to postpone its ambitious development proposals for a year [FIG. 24].[40]

A start was finally made on the 4-storey High Street buildings framing College Street in 1794, for which the builder Andrew Macfarlane was paid £3,500.[41] The long 5-bay elevations facing the High Street had advanced outer bays with giant Corinthian order columns and paterae, or circular decorative panels, at the attic storey; the short 3-bay pedimented elevations faced each other across College Street. Inside, the flats were generous, with six or seven apartments. The southern block was altered in the 19th century to provide four, rather than three, windows at the centre of the High Street elevation. The University quickly lost the appetite for its largely speculative development and sold off the southern block in 1803, followed by parcels of land for others to develop along College Street. The conditions for sale of the land continued to give the College oversight of the designs for buildings, but the Faculty's interest was limited to a general correspondence with the details of the James Adam buildings.[42]

THE HUNTERIAN MUSEUM 1797–1807

The proposal to create a permanent University Museum was first made in March 1769 by Professor John Anderson, who later fell out with his colleagues and bequeathed his fortune to found the separate 'Anderson's University' and Andersonian Museum.[43] However, in 1783 Dr William Hunter, an eminent London physician, antiquarian, bibliophile, art collector and alumnus of the University, left his entire collection to the Principal and Faculty of the College, along with £8,000 for the construction of a museum in which to house it. Despite a codicil to Hunter's will that delayed transfer of the collection to the College for 30 years, Robert Mylne, designer of Hunter's London house and school at 16 Great Windmill Street in 1767, and a member of the great Scottish dynasty of master masons and architects, almost immediately went to Glasgow with a view to designing the new museum.[44] However, it was some 15 years before the codicil was overturned (by mutual agreement between the trustees and the University), cataloguing of the collections was complete, and designs were sought.

Hunter had stipulated the approval of his trustees to the design of the Glasgow building, who ruled that it should have a distinctive separate identity from the other College buildings and be placed in a conspicuous location. The process of selecting a site and design began in earnest in May 1797 when the Professor of Logic and Rhetoric, George Jardine, approached the trustees of Hunter's will to determine the amount of accommodation needed to house the collections in Glasgow.[45] The trustees turned to Mylne for the information, which he supplied along with a renewed offer to design the building.[46] Undecided as to the location of the new museum, the Faculty commissioned its own drawings from at least two local architects, John Clarkson in 1798, and David Hamilton in 1799[47] :

These different [three or four] *sites, it was thought*

24 James Adam's College Street development. The huge and magnificent presentation drawing for the buildings is undoubtedly one of the high points of the golden age of architectural draughtsmanship. The scheme proposed a domed corn market building on Shuttle Street framed in the foreground by two grand neoclassical blocks of tenements and shops that stretched along the High Street and lined the new College Street. The blocks were demolished in 1974, long after they had been sold by the University.

Sir John Soane Museum, London [Adam vol. 38/12]

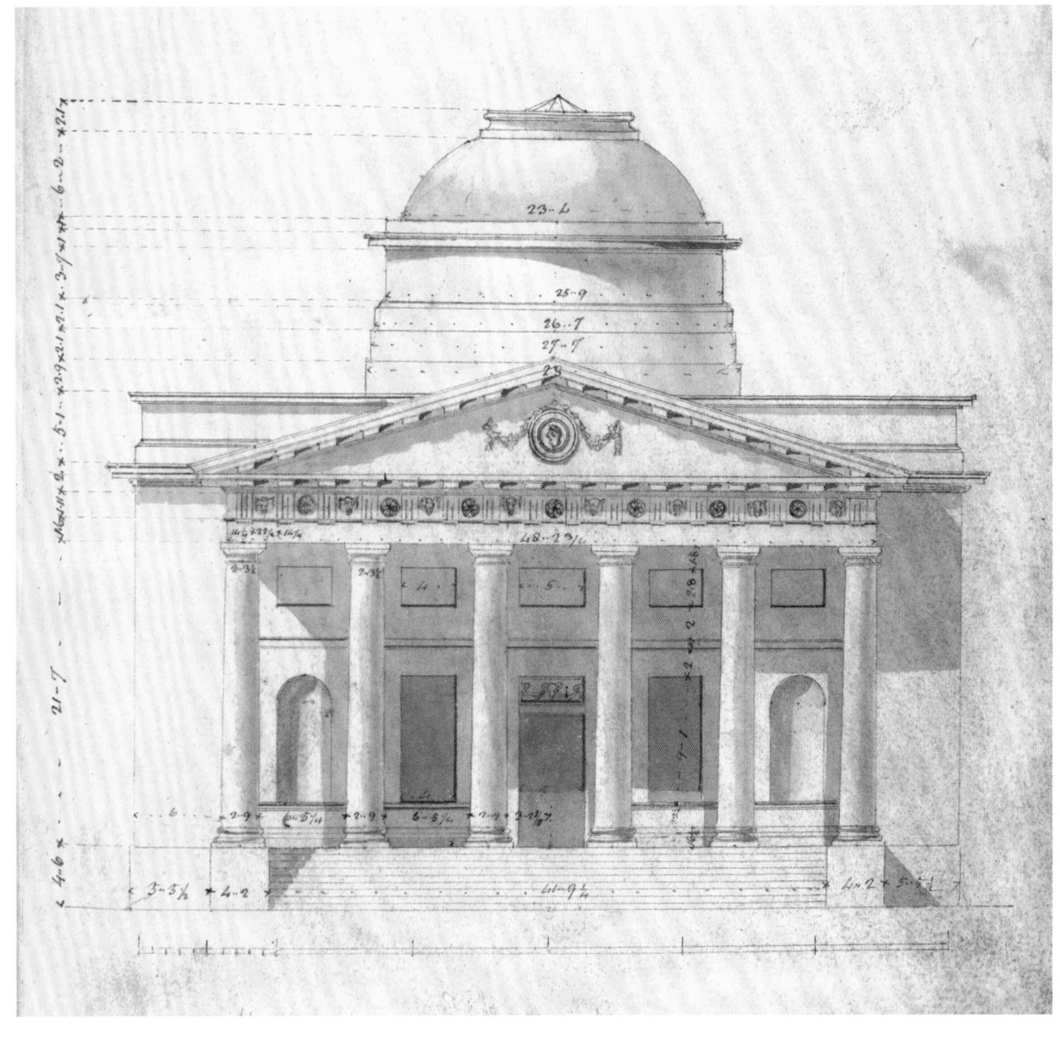

25 Design for the Hunterian Museum by William Stark, 1803. The annotated drawing forms part of Stark's 'Discription' book of annotated designs.

GULSC [MR574(S.4.19)]

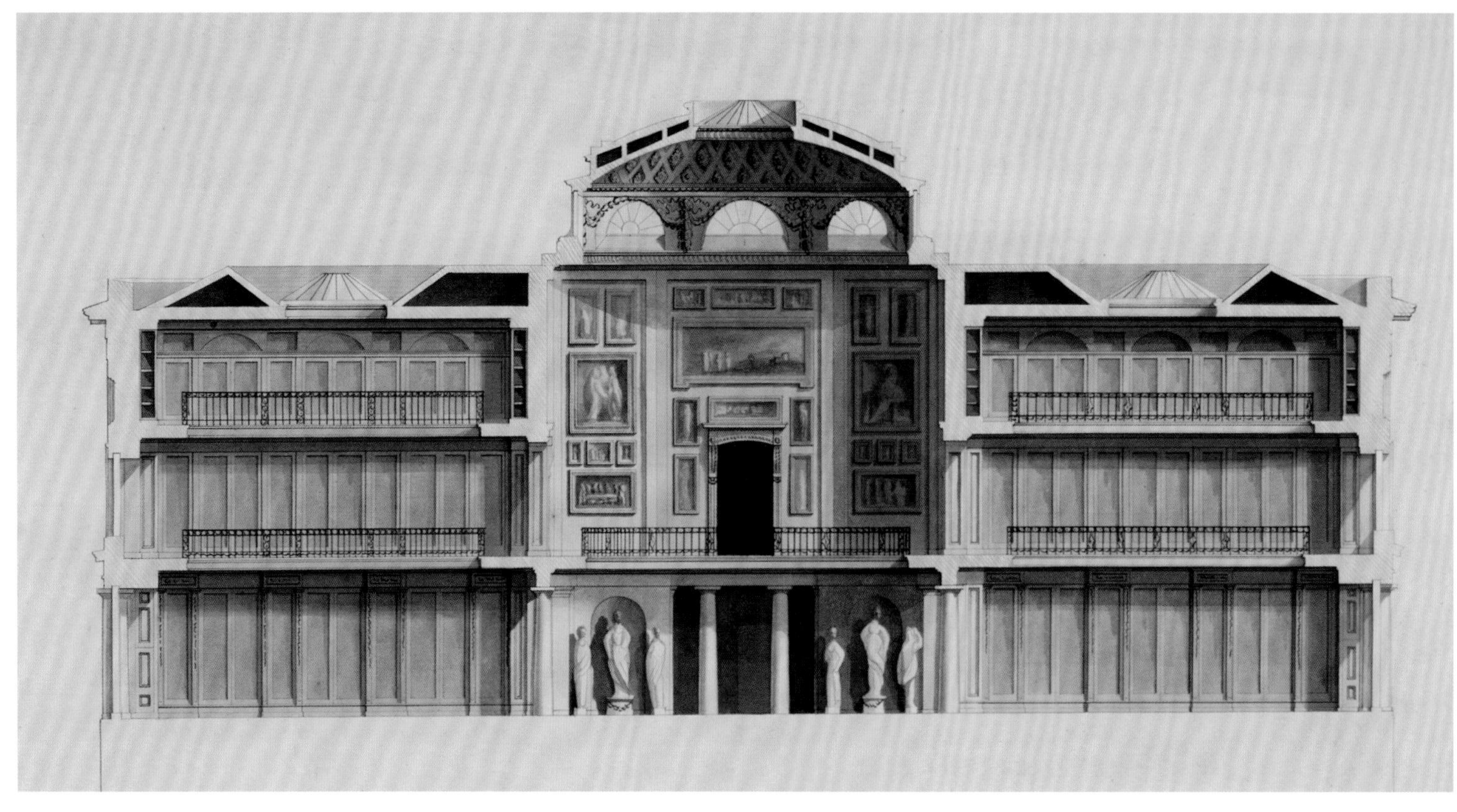

proper to examine minutely and to compare their advantages and disadvantages, for which purpose, Sketches of the intended Buildings accommodated to each of them was found necessary.[48]

From the survival of a £28 account for 'Sundrie designs for a Museum' in 1799 and a number of highly polished, but undated, sketch schemes in an album now owned by the Hunterian Art Gallery, it seems likely that David Hamilton was responsible for most of these 'Sketches'.[49] Clarkson, formerly one of Robert and James Adam's superintendents, ruled himself out of the running by succumbing to a fatal inflammation on 12 October 1798 at the age of sixty.[50] The David Hamilton schemes appear to be for a number of locations, including the eventual site of the Hamilton building (replacing the east range of the old College) and the freestanding site finally chosen for the Hunterian Museum (to the east of the old College). Some designs are just for a museum, and others include teaching accommodation, laboratories and even a chapel. Two of the drawings are annotated by the Professor of Anatomy, James Jeffray, who was largely responsible for supervision of the Hunterian Museum project.

In October 1799 Hunter's nephew and executor of his will, Dr Matthew Baillie, also an alumnus of Glasgow, sent proposal drawings by his friend Mylne to the Faculty.[51] Evidently these uninvited designs caused the Faculty some embarrassment, as it took them more than a year to decide how to respond to Baillie. A further mildly awkward exchange of letters took place, and eventually the Faculty settled a fifty guinea account from Mylne with some haste.[52] The reasons for the Faculty's dissatisfaction with Mylne are not recorded, but perhaps he was regarded as the trustees' man intent on meddling, or possibly it was a more practical concern about local supervision of the construction.

Having received Baillie's approval to use any architect they wished in December 1802, the Faculty appointed a special committee for the project and instructed them to bargain for detailed designs from Peter Nicholson (see the Hamilton building below) and David Hamilton.[53] Principal Davidson finally sent two schemes and estimates for Matthew Baillie to decide in April 1803: one by David Hamilton [FIG.26] and one by William Stark [FIG.25].[54] Davidson's covering letter asked Baillie to decide between the architectural schemes on the basis that no teaching rooms would be provided at the outset, but that they could be added easily at a later date. This instruction immediately favoured the Stark scheme, which was already limited to the museum function. Although Hamilton had previously provided sketches for a 'museum-only' option, his submitted scheme included teaching accommodation. Hamilton's ground plan shows an 'optional' teaching block at the rear of the building, but the other plans and elevations show the teaching accommodation as an integral part of the design.[55] Funding probably lay at the root of the problem: Hunter's bequest could be used for museum purposes, but not for the desperately needed teaching accommodation, which would have

26 Design for the Hunterian Museum by David Hamilton, 1803
GUAS [GUA 3495]

27 [opposite] The original Hunterian Museum from the south-west, photographed by Thomas Annan, probably in 1864
GUAS [Old & New 16]

28 Bucranium decoration which was above the entrance to the old Hunterian Museum in the High Street
RCAHMS [SC 1323710]

29 The saloon of the old Hunterian Museum, photographed by Thomas Annan, probably in 1864
GUAS [Old & New 17]

30 Design for the Hamilton building by Peter Nicholson, 1806
GUAS [BUL 6/56/35]

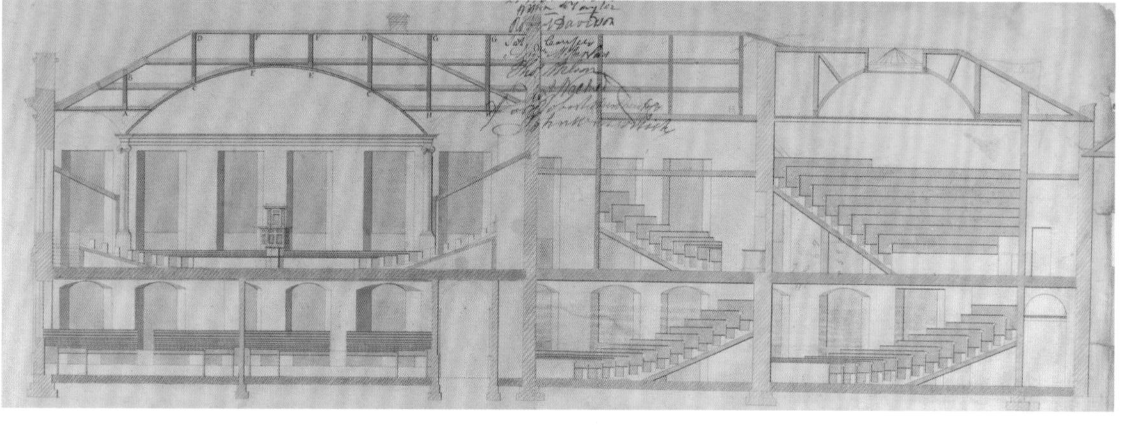

31 Contract drawing for the Hamilton building by Peter Nicholson, 1806. This cross-section shows the raked seating of the 'classrooms', or lecture theatres.
GUAS [BUL 6/56/30]

to be financed separately by the College. Not surprisingly, Matthew Baillie and the other trustees opted for William Stark's smaller, and presumably cheaper, discreet scheme. Stark was another talented and innovative Scottish architect, who had travelled widely in Europe and lived in St Petersburg in 1798. When Sir Walter Scott, Stark's patron for an extension to Abbotsford, heard of his architect's premature death in 1813 he commented that 'more genius has died than is left behind among the collected universality of Scottish architects'; and Lord Cockburn considered him 'the best modern architect that Scotland has produced'.[56] The foundation stone was laid on 2 August 1804 and a 'time capsule' of contemporary documents and coins was buried beneath it.[57] Scott's future son-in-law, John Gibson Lockhart, a student from 1805 to 1809, recalled the event:

I remember the people were busy about its [the Hunterian Museum's] foundation that gloomy morning when the news of Trafalgar was received by us all, men and boys, with more of sadness [at the death of Nelson], I think, at least of solemn and awful feeling than of joy and triumph. I shall never forget the face with which the celebrated John Young, professor of Greek, came out bare-headed with the newspaper in his hand to read the Gazette to the whole crowd of Togati [undergraduates].[58]

Although he had not been chosen to design the Museum, Peter Nicholson was appointed as the superintendent architect for its construction.[59] In view of its conspicuous location and use as a public building, the Faculty considered various enhancements to the quality of the masonry after the contract was signed with the builders, Galloway & Anderson. The most extravagant of these amendments, substitution of smaller Garscube quarry stones for the front columns with enormous single stones from Craigleith quarry near Edinburgh, was abandoned.[60] Omissions from Stark's plans, such as steps, paving and deafening for the floors, were added to the scheme.

The building was largely complete by September 1807 at a cost of about £10,500.[61] The 60-foot (18.2m) temple front faced west towards the old College buildings, while slightly longer side elevations stretched back into the College Green. Like Hamilton's rival scheme, the interior of the Museum had a strictly neoclassical plan based around a central domed space. The spaces were conceived for their intrinsic architectural qualities, rather than in particular response to the display requirements of each collection. There were no teaching rooms and the whole building was given over to the Hunterian collections, the Hunterian library and a house for the Keeper. On the ground floor were the Natural History 'Saloon', flanked by the mineral and coral rooms, and the Anatomical room stretching across the width of the east end. The main public starcase ran through the building in the north-west

32 The Hamilton building, photographed by Thomas Annan, probably in 1864

corner. The small staircases from the Anatomical room led down to the 'Hall of the Elephant', containing a stuffed adult elephant and a zebra presented to Hunter by Queen Charlotte. Beyond, to the south lay the 'Antique Room', home to Hunter's Roman stones, and to the centre and north the furnace room and Keeper's house. Lighting of the secure, windowless, top floor picture gallery, library and coin room, was achieved from above through rooftop cupolas and skylights. Looking back to ancient models such as the Pantheon in Rome, neoclassical architects frequently adopted such dramatic overhead natural lighting. John Soane used a similar toplit approach to the display rooms of the Dulwich Picture Gallery of 1818, the first public art gallery in the British Isles.

Stark's involvement was not limited to the construction of the building, but also extended to its decoration and fitting out, as is evidenced by his account for designing glass cases, cabinets, tables and presses (cupboards).[62] Glasgow's premier upholsterers, cabinet-makers and joiners, Cleland & Jack of Virginia Street supplied the fittings, carpets and other furnishings of the highest quality between May 1808 and September 1809.[63] Some impression of the rich colouring of the interiors is conveyed by Cleland & Jack's accounts for the Library and Saloon (central ground floor hall): 172 yards (157m) green baize and binding (presumably carpets, as an additional sum for tacks and laying were charged, but possibly for wall-covering, as was common in other exhibition spaces, such as the Royal Academy in London); fine green cloth and brass tacks for the front of the library shelves; green cloth coverings for the table tops; two green japanned library ladders; two mahogany writing tables with brass paw castors; and most spectacularly, eight 'Roman Chairs covered with fine Crimson Moreen [heavy woollen fabric], brass ornaments and strong brass castors' along with their crimson moreen cushions trimmed with black velvet.

The inventor James Watt designed the clever arrangement of warm air heating ducts supplied by a central stove, which was intended to reduce the need for maintaining dirty open fires in the galleries and for multiple chimneys breaking the purity of the monumental Roman Doric temple exterior.[64] The heating system proved ineffective almost immediately. Watt was recalled to advise Stark, and another local architect, John Brash, supervised alterations to the system and the installation of curtains and double-glazing of the dome to reduce heat loss.[65]

The collections were carefully packed over several months in 1807 and transported by ship to one of the Forth ports, then by canal barge to Port Dundas and onwards to the Museum by cart.[66] The coin and medal collection was considered too valuable to send by water, and six armed guards accompanied a wagon from

London to Glasgow. The objects in the Museum were 'well arranged on a scientific basis' according to David Murray, who had first-hand experience of the building and described it in his *Memories of the Old College of Glasgow* in 1927.[67] The building was already crammed with exhibits by the time everything was unpacked. Some ten thousand visitors flocked to Scotland's first public museum between August 1808 and June 1810.[68] John Brash prepared an enlargement scheme in January 1823 to create a range parallel to the Hamilton building, but this was not undertaken.[69] Instead, a long and low range was added on the back (east side) of the Museum to house the Zoology and Anatomy departments in 1829. The Museum was the first building to be demolished in 1870 after the University moved to Gilmorehill.

THE HAMILTON BUILDING 1806–1811

Between 1800 and 1806 the number of undergraduates doubled, and then trebled in the following seven years. The failure to acquire teaching space in the new Museum left several subject areas in desperately cramped conditions in the old buildings, notably the Humanities, Chemistry and Anatomy, of which the last two were in need of specialist equipment and spaces. Since 1763 the Chemistry laboratory and classroom had been sited in a small separate building adjoining the Physic Garden to the south-west of Blackfriars' Kirk.

It was determined to replace the old east wing of the Inner Close with a new, larger building in a Greek Doric classical style facing the Roman Doric temple front of the Hunterian Museum. On this occasion Peter Nicholson (a London architect who had moved to Glasgow in 1800) was chosen. Nicholson built the large terraces of townhouses in Carlton Place, Glasgow, and, as has been previously noted, supervised the construction of the Hunterian Museum, but is best known as the author of the *Builder & Workman's New Directory* of 1823. The new building [FIGS 30, 31, 32] was to be named after Robert Hamilton, merchant in Canton, in honour of a bequest. The College sought an interest-free government loan to cover the period between the construction of the new range and the receipt of the bequest (which was not received until 1823).

The Faculty minutes record the submission of two sets of plans by anonymous architects in March 1804, possibly including one set by Peter Nicholson.[70] In any event, Nicholson was invited to examine a further sketch by the Professor of Astronomy, James Couper, and turn it into a third set of plans.[71] This design was approved on 7 April 1806 subject to detailed costing and specification, including high-quality Possil or Garscube sandstone for the frontage facing the Hunterian Museum [FIG. 27].[72] Nicholson invoiced for the drawings in October 1806, but the Faculty only approved them for construction in May 1810.[73] The proposal involved the demolition of the 17th-century east range of the Inner Close. In order to provide a deeper building on the same site and maintain the access from Professors' Court to the gardens, the eastern ends and stairtowers of the 17th-century north and south ranges were also removed. The old east range had contained the common hall, initially a dining hall, and the 17th-century library. Observers were alive to the picturesque qualities of the old building, and there was some disquiet about the loss of the 'primitive Gothic air' of the Inner Close and the jarring modern style of the replacement range.[74] The new building was to house a large common hall and classrooms for Latin (374 students), Greek (350), Logic (300), Chemistry (320), Anatomy (student numbers are not shown) and Medicine (160).

The old common hall had served as a chapel and ceremonial hall for a number of years, and the new hall reflected that function in its raked seating arranged around a pulpit. For the first time in the history of the University, the classrooms also had curved or horse-shoe rows of raked wooden benches and desks arranged around a podium or demonstration area: in the case of Anatomy, a dissection table. A circular rooflight, or cupola, lit the Anatomy classroom from above. In their size and arrangement these 'classrooms' were the forerunners of modern lecture theatres. A staircase served each room on the upper floor and book storerooms were provided for all the classes. The whole building was heated by open fires in each room. A vaulted open corridor ran through the middle of the building connecting the Inner Close with Museum Square. The visible frontages of the new building were symmetrical, but in fact the new building extended southwards to connect to the western wing of the Library. From about 1854 one of the classrooms was converted to form an annex to the Library.

CHEMISTRY BUILDING, SHUTTLE STREET 1831

In 1831 a new Chemistry laboratory block was constructed on the north-west corner of College Street with Shuttle Street for the University's first practical Chemistry course, taught by the new Regius Professor of Chemistry, Thomas Thomson. It had leased shops at the ground floor to help fund the project, with two floors above of offices and teaching rooms and a large laboratory on the top floor [FIGS 33, 34]. The block replaced the classroom in the Hamilton building.

33 Shuttle Street Chemistry laboratory photographed in 1957. It was sold when the College moved to Gilmorehill, and demolished in the 1970s.

34 Interior view of Shuttle Street Chemistry laboratory in summer 1864. According to David Murray in his *Memoirs of the Old College*, it was 'esteemed one of the best and most complete of its time'.

GUAS [UP5/520]

Chapter Three

The Search for a New Site 1845–1863

35 Presentation drawing of John Baird's second scheme for the Woodlands site, 1846
GUHMAG [GLAHA 54352]

By the early 19th century, Glasgow was established as a major commercial centre and industrial city, and was expanding rapidly. In 1791 the population stood at about 66,000, but by 1831 it had reached over 200,000. Much of the industrial activity was concentrated in the east end and around the River Clyde. The commercial activity was more focused on the developing Merchant City. As the middle and professional classes moved westwards into the smart Blythswood grid-plan of elegant new tenements and terraced townhouses, the medieval and Renaissance buildings clustered around the High Street, Trongate and Gallowgate, descended into a slum of overcrowded workers' housing, with little sanitation or fresh water. Apart from constant outbreaks of typhus and cholera, poor health conditions were further compounded by appalling atmospheric pollution from the many coal-powered factories. By far the worst of these was the giant St Rollox Works, to the north of the High Street, then the largest chemical plant in the world, which spewed out smoke from 30,000 tons of coal a year. The Glasgow Police Act of 1800 was an attempt to improve the cleanliness and sanitation of the city, but it was ineffectual against the industrial pollution.

To some extent the confines of the College provided a haven from the surrounding slum, but here too soot blackened the buildings, trees and grass, and the stench was carried by the wind. The Molendinar Burn, which ran through the College grounds, was a toxic semi-enclosed sewer. Cholera affected a number of professors and students. There was also evidence of local resentment against the College for the luxurious accommodation of its professors, the relative wealth of its students and their perceived aloofness in their distinctive scarlet gowns, or *togati*. New chairs in Surgery, Midwifery, Materia Medica (Pharmacology), Theory of Physics (Physiology), Forensic Medicine, Botany, Chemistry and Civil Engineering and Mechanics were founded between 1807 and 1840, and student numbers increased accordingly. While there were relatively recent buildings, some of the older structures were not in good order. Against this backdrop in the 1830s and 40s, there was considerable discussion under Principal Duncan Macfarlan of a move to a more salubrious and spacious location.

On visiting in 1845, the College's London parliamentary lawyer, John Richardson, described the appalling scene of the High Street: 'From what I saw even walking up the High Street to call upon the Principal, indicative of vice and destitution and misery in its most abject form, I have concluded an opinion of the impropriety of the present situation of that great institution which I have no words to express.'[1] In August 1845 the Glasgow, Airdrie & Monklands Junction Railway Company (GAMJRC) made tentative enquiries about purchasing

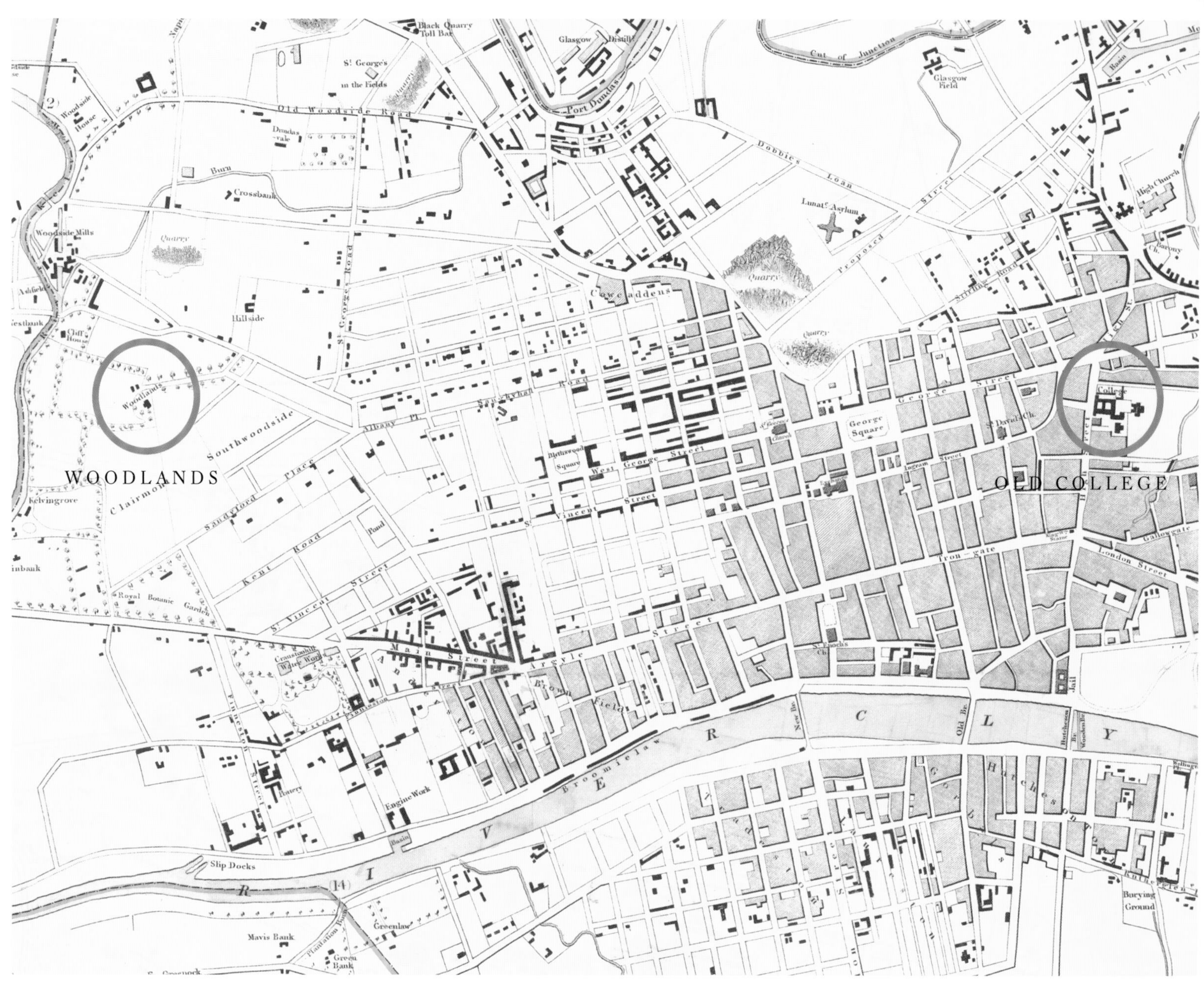

36 Great Reform Act map of 1832, showing Old College in the east (right) and the Woodlands estate in the west (left)
National Library of Scotland, Edinburgh [Map.m.557.8]

an area of ground 100 yards wide on either the north or south side of the College grounds in order to form a terminus in the High Street.[2] Recognising the potential of the railway company's interest in the site, the Principal and Advocate Professor of Laws, Alan Alexander Maconachie, pursued a more radical deal to remove the College from the High Street altogether. By November 1845 the railway company had agreed to purchase a new site and construct new College buildings in exchange for the High Street site.

WOODLANDS SCHEMES 1845–1850

Although the complicated story of the prolonged, and ultimately abortive, project to move the College to Woodlands in the west end of Glasgow is told eloquently elsewhere, no architectural history of the University of Glasgow would be complete without some account of the three schemes prepared for the Woodlands site.[3] Some of the finest British architects of the age were involved, valuable lessons were learnt, and in many ways the proposals formed the prototypes for the successful project further west at Gilmorehill.

The GAMJRC moved quickly to identify a potential site for the relocation at Woodlands [FIG.36]. Once a part of the great Blythswood estate that surrounded Glasgow on the north and west, Woodlands had been detached as a small rural estate of 23 acres (9.3 hectares) and purchased by the University alumnus and editor of the *Glasgow Courier*, James McNayr, in the last years of the 18th century. McNayr constructed a Gothick castle on the highest and most prominent part of Woodside Hill, where the gardens of Park Circus are now located. Although named 'Woodlands', the house was known as 'McNayr's Folly' because of its perceived distance from the town.[4] Even by 1845 the development of the city's second grid-plan as far as St George's Cross was incomplete, and much of today's west end still consisted of similar small rural estates. Some lands were laid out for housing, but building was slow until the second half of the century. The failure of the Woodlands scheme can be largely attributed to the length of time it took to get approval from the various interested parties. By the time agreement had been reached, the railway company was in financial trouble and could no longer meet its obligations in constructing the new buildings. During the approval process, three designs for new buildings on the Woodlands site were drawn up.

WOODLANDS SCHEME 1

In accordance with the initial heads of terms between the College and the railway company, an architect was appointed by the GAMJRC. The surviving College records suggest that the choice of the Glasgow architect, John Baird, was left largely to the railway company. It is likely that the company selected Baird because they needed plans in a hurry. He had a reputation for accurate costing, and he already knew the ground well through his 1830 layout and designs for housing on the adjacent lands of Clairmont (Claremont) and South Woodside.[5] Although stylistically conservative, Baird was versatile and well-regarded. He was a pioneer in the use of cast-iron, notably at Gardner's Warehouse in Jamaica Street, and employed the young Alexander 'Greek' Thomson as an assistant. GAMJRC sent the Faculty a ground plan and elevation by Baird on 17 December 1845.[6] These hurried drawings are not known to survive, but probably formed the basis of a surviving set of drawings of June 1846, approved by the Faculty as part of the agreement with the railway company and the College Removal Act of 24 August 1846. Members of the Faculty contributed to the development of the plans and reviewed them following submission. However, there were clearly some misgivings about the plans, and possibly about the architect too, at an early stage.

The root of the Faculty's uneasiness lay in a number of issues. Firstly, the Faculty quickly found that they were to a large degree at the mercy of the railway company in the design process, and that the railway company's interests were not necessarily those of the College. There was little time to consider all the College's requirements, and probably also a lack of understanding and poor co-ordination of the design process amongst the Faculty members. There was also a sense of being out of their depth in architectural matters. Thirdly, the quality of the new buildings was regarded as a primary concern and a matter of public interest in obtaining parliamentary consent for the removal. Any concerns about the design quality could be used to thwart the parliamentary approval. Finally, there were practical worries: the space provision for the library and museum seemed inadequate; the proposals lacked a separate chapel; they also lacked a hospital and the site was far from the Royal Infirmary, where much of the medical teaching took place. In addition, there was the usual bickering over status and accommodation amongst the professors, with the Professor of Divinity demanding a larger house to match his superior accommodation in the Old College.

On the advice of the Rector, Andrew Rutherfurd, on 12 January 1846 Principal Macfarlan asked the College lawyer to write to the railway company to request them to pay the costs for him and Baird to consult with the eminent Edinburgh architect William Henry Playfair 'in case evidence of a professional man be required' for the parliamentary process.[7] Playfair was experienced in designing large educational buildings, such as the completion of Robert Adam's Old College for the University of Edinburgh (1817–26), the remodelling of Heriot's Hospital (1828–30), and the construction of Donaldson's Hospital (1842–54). He was also a friend of Rutherfurd and architect of alterations to his house at Lauriston Castle in 1845. Unfortunately, for unknown reasons, Playfair quickly declined the invitation to assess the proposals.

The Faculty then requested 'That they [the GAMJRC] should without loss of time instruct Mr Baird their Architect presently to submit and explain his plans to Mr [pencil margin note 'Decimus Burton or Mr Edward Blore'], who is to be ordered to put himself into communication with and to report upon them to the College and to prepare himself for examination before a Parliamentary Committee and that the plans, which Mr Baird has stated to be at present imperfect, should as soon as possible after the revision aforesaid be put by him into a more completed form and again tendered by the Railway Company to the College.'[8] Burton and Blore were both major London architects with connections to Glasgow. Burton had designed the initial layout of housing developments on the Kelvinside estate in 1839–40 and Blore was consultant architect to the Office of Works on the 'restoration' of Glasgow Cathedral from 1846 to 1849. There is no evidence that Burton was approached, but Blore was to play a significant part in the final Woodlands design.

The first design envisaged an E-shaped plan with the main range facing south-east towards the city and the wings stretching north-westwards to form two open-ended courtyards.[9] A separate terrace of professors' houses was proposed to the west behind the main block. The central arm of the plan was to comprise the library on the ground floor and the Hunterian Museum above. The remainder of the building was dedicated entirely to teaching rooms and offices. Significantly, no living accommodation was to be provided. The revived 'Jacobethan' style of the proposal, using a variety of features common to buildings of the reigns of Elizabeth I

of England (Gothic elements) and James VI of Scotland (classical Renaissance elements), was heavily indebted to Playfair's Donaldson's Hospital and the remodelled Heriot's Hospital in Edinburgh. However, some of the details, such as the purely decorative window pediments may nod towards the College's own buildings in the High Street [FIG.37]. The site layout indicates building stances along the approach roads to the new College, which were presumably to be sold on to developers.

WOODLANDS SCHEME 2

In addition to approval by the Faculty and Senate of the College and the GAMJRC, the College Removal Act introduced a requirement for a final set of plans and specifications to be approved by the Lords Commissioners of Her Majesty's Treasury and a new body of commissioners for the College removal, who included the Chancellor, the Principal, and the Rector (also the Lord Advocate, Andrew Rutherfurd). To add to the already complicated approval process, the Lords of the Treasury appointed their own specialist architectural advisors and the site of the chapel was to be approved by the Commission of Woods and Forests.

The ink was barely dry on the College Removal Act before Baird's office began work on a second set of plans to address the concerns about the space provision.[10] This time Baird took the precaution of providing room plans and explaining them to the Faculty in person.[11] The library and museum wing was extended by transepts into a T-plan and linked to lower ranges that enclosed the north-western sides of the two courts. A self-contained chemistry block was added to the north corner of the complex, in part to remove the noxious fumes and danger of fire from the main building. The more lively elevations were overtly rooted in the Scottish Renaissance idiom of Heriot's Hospital and the surviving 17th-century buildings of Glasgow and elsewhere in Scotland. The square towers with polygonal domed upper stages, tower pavilions with 'pepperpot' corner turrets, buckle quoins (corner stones in the shape of buckles), and tall chimneys on the gable over the entrance are all to be found in Scottish 17th-century models. Other elements, such as the large windows and *porte cochère* (covered carriage entrance) owed less to historical precedent, but were more practical [FIG.38].

On 17 February 1847 the Lords of the Treasury sent on the plans of both Baird's first and second schemes to their advisors, Charles Barry and Augustus Welby Northmore Pugin, the architects of the new Houses of Parliament, which were then under construction in London. Barry and Pugin's response was not favourable on several grounds: cost, circulation and artistic merit.

37 East (main) elevation perspective of the first Woodlands scheme by John Baird, June 1846
GUAS [BUL 6/57/9]

38 East (main) elevation of the second Woodlands scheme by John Baird, December 1846
GUAS [BUL 6/57/29]

The first scheme was considered lacking 'in purity of style and was not of a high class of art or in any respect very meritorious'. The second set fared little better: 'In other words the revised plans are very similar to the original set and are consequently open to the same objections; therefore apart from consideration of the additional accommodation which they afford we consider the arrangement of them as a whole more objectionable than that of the original design.' Baird travelled to London to discuss the report with Barry in April 1847, and Barry even volunteered to draw up the elevations if Baird would revise the floor plans.[12]

WOODLANDS SCHEME 3

The ever-obliging Baird revised not only the floor plans, but also the elevations, to take account of Pugin and Barry's objections. Major alterations were made to the plan in extending and moving the library and museum to the rear range and omitting the central wing to create a large single court [FIG.40]. The side ranges were extended by 30 feet (9.14m) and the professors' houses relocated to two terraces lining the approach to the College. In the event Baird also revised the elevations, probably taking Barry's comments into account, but not involving him in the drawing. Parts of the design were simplified, the *porte cochère* removed, the height of the corner pavilions reduced, elaborate pediments added to the pavilions and further decoration added to the plinth. In fairness to Baird, there were now so many fingers in the architectural pie that it was impossible to produce a satisfactory result. These revised elevations were probably the least successful of Baird's three designs. The Treasury immediately instructed the Faculty to send them on to Edward Blore for revision in August 1847. Little progress was made on the project for a year while the Faculty searched for a site for the hospital. Finally, in September 1847, when the Faculty informed the GAMJRC that a site had been found, the railway company responded that so much time had passed since the College Removal Act that they had abandoned any prospect of acquiring the College lands in the High Street and that they had no intention of funding construction of the new College buildings at Woodlands, or the hospital.[13] The Faculty tried to force the issue by employing Blore directly to finish the elevations and obtain final approval from the Treasury.

One of Barry and Pugin's major concerns had been Baird's cost estimates. Baird was renowned for the accuracy of his estimates and had bent over backwards to demonstrate that Glasgow tradesmen could construct the building within budget. However, the Treasury were still swayed by their professional experts, who had not seen the site and were unfamiliar with the Glasgow building trades. Blore's revisions therefore concentrated on simplifying many of the decorative elements of the elevations to reduce costs. One notable increase in decoration was the addition of elaborate pediments, like those of the High Street elevation of the College, to all the windows. As a result, the final design was competent, but rather flat and dull in comparison to Baird's second scheme. After a further round of negotiations over cost, the Treasury eventually gave approval on 27 March 1849.[14] By this time the financial position of the railway company had deteriorated to such an extent that it was simply unable to fulfil its promises. The College received £12,700 from the GAMJRC in compensation in December 1850, but it was to be another twenty years before another scheme came to fruition.

CONTINUING DECLINE OF THE HIGH STREET BUILDINGS 1850–1863

The collapse of the Woodlands project did not dim the enthusiasm of the Faculty to seek a new site for the College. The professors were asked to report on the provision of accommodation in Old College. Unsurprisingly the responses in January 1852 were highly critical.[15] In December 1853 the Principal and professors of the University presented a 'memorial and petition' to Queen Victoria setting out the dire condition of the College buildings:

That owing to the progress of knowledge and the addition to the University, by your Majesty's Royal predecessors, of nine new professorships, without any accommodation being provided for them, the buildings of the College have long ceased to be adequate in point of extent, to the requirements of modern instruction in literature and science as now taught in the University. That this evil has at last become so great as to render it necessary that two, and in some instances three, classes should successively receive instruction in the same room, a state of things always objectionable from the impossibility of maintaining the air in a healthy condition in rooms occupied during so many hours by large bodies of Students, and especially inconvenient in the case of those Sciences which are taught by means of illustrative specimens and apparatus.

That the inadequate accommodation which does exist is antiquated, inconvenient and altogether unsuited to the improved methods of instruction now generally adopted, and that most of the objections apply to the buildings which contain the Museums and Libraries not less that to those in which the classes are taught.[16]

The memorial set out a number of other issues that were to form the basis of subsequent negotiations with the government. Firstly, it noted that the population of Glasgow had quadrupled since 1800 and doubled since 1833, generating 'an atmosphere impregnated with the effluvia arising from the filth'.

Glasgow now contained a one-fortieth of the population of Great Britain, yet the city contributed a thirtieth of the United Kingdom's revenue. Since 1800 every other college or university in Scotland had renewed its buildings at some degree of public expense, but Glasgow had received no government assistance. All the College sought was for the government to purchase the High Street site at a price that would cover the removal costs. Effectively, the government should guarantee the College's ability to move immediately, but would hopefully recoup all of their expenditure, or even make a profit, on resale of the site at a later date. A counter memorial was sent to the Lords of the Treasury by six of the nine Regius professors, who did not form part of the Faculty and were not housed in Professor's Court.

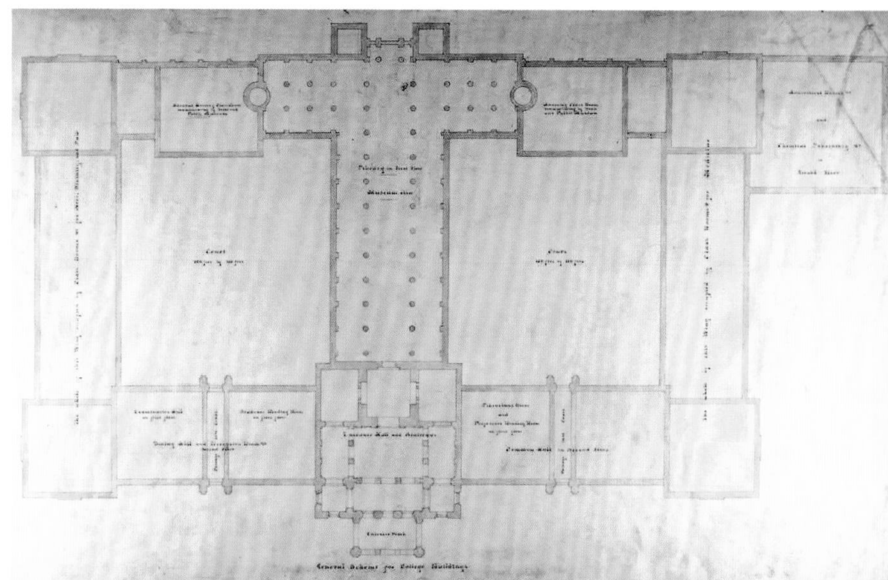

39 Double quadrangular plan of John Baird's second scheme for Woodlands, October 1846
GUAS [BUL 6/57/32]

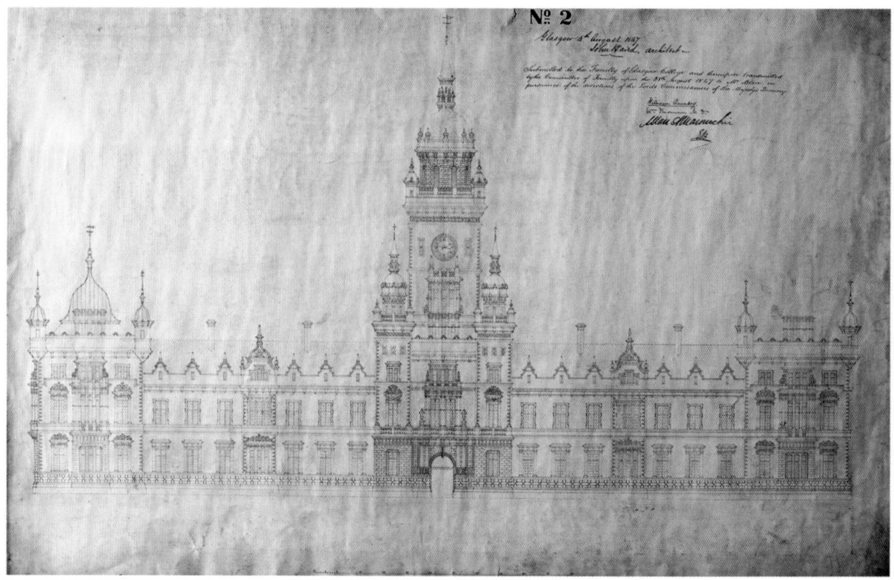

40 East (main) elevation of John Baird's third scheme for Woodlands, 4 August 1847
GUAS [BUL 6/57/19]

41 The College Green and the rear of the College buildings, photographed by Thomas Annan, in about 1870
GUAS [Old & New 15]

They pointed out that the memorialists stood to gain most from being re-housed in the fashionable west end of the city, and that there was plenty of ground on the convenient High Street site for the construction of new buildings.[17] The Universities (Scotland) Act of 1858 abolished the requirement for a clergyman as Principal, removed the distinction between Faculty and Regius professors, and set the framework for the modern governance structure of the University, establishing the Court as an appointments, disciplinary and appeal body for the Senate, re-ordering the Senate and introducing the General Council of graduate students. Effectively, the Faculty ceased to exist and matriculation became compulsory from this time. Under the Act of 1858, commissioners were appointed to investigate and regulate (by ordinance) administrative rules, financial affairs, powers and elections of office bearers, foundation of new professorships, admission, courses of study and examinations for degrees in the Scottish universities. Regular grants of money from the Treasury, including funding for the pensions of principals and professors, were, for the first time, established under the Act.[18] In spite of a promise by the Prime Minister, Lord Aberdeen, to investigate the 1853 memorial, there was still no government action on the College removal by 1859. The death of the veteran Principal Duncan Macfarlan at the age of eighty-four in 1858 and appointment of Thomas Barclay brought a renewed vigour to the removal campaign. A further memorial was presented to Queen Victoria on 7 February 1859 requesting her to use powers under the Act of 1858 to direct the new commissioners to investigate the state of the High Street buildings. This time the buildings were examined for the commissioners and condemned as inadequate by Robert Matheson, the Assistant Surveyor for Scotland in the Office of Works.[19] Matheson found even the more recent classrooms of the Hamilton building badly lit, poorly ventilated and inadequately heated by single stoves or fireplaces beside the professor's platform. Although Matheson considered that the Museum and Library could be improved, any attempt to expand or adapt the old classrooms was thought to be pointless. The squalid conditions of the High Street again influenced the outcome of the commissioners' report, which placed a higher commercial value on the site than its practical value to the University.

The 1858 commissioners recommended the sale of the High Street site for £50,200, the Shuttle Street Chemistry building for £15,000 and the collection of Hunterian coins for £20,000. Along with the £12,700 compensation for the failed Woodlands project, the funds available to the College were considered almost sufficient to purchase a new site north of the River Clyde for £24,000, or a site south of the river for £6,000, and the construction of new buildings for £85,200 (the sum estimated by John Baird in 1848 for the plans revised by Blore). The commissioners' proposals generated particular controversy in respect of the

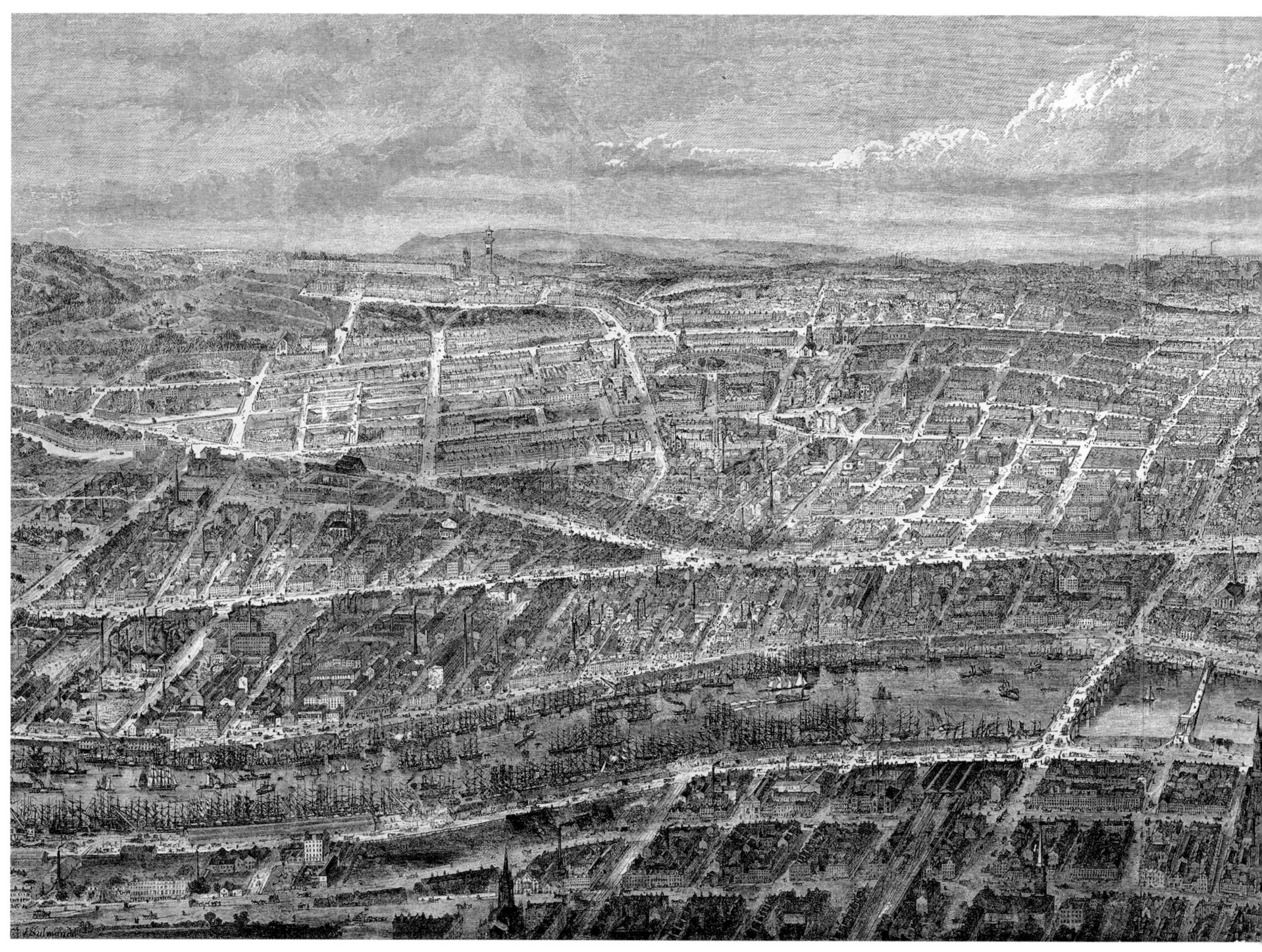

Hunterian coins, which formed part of the property of the separate Hunterian Trust, and were therefore not available for disposal by the University. The commissioners' estimates were flawed in a number of other respects: the value of the High Street and potential west end sites were underestimated, and the allowance for construction costs took no account of inflation since 1848.

From 1860 to 1863 the College made some plans for upgrading the High Street buildings, but used the 1858 commissioners' findings to press the government for funding to enable a move.[20] Deputations were sent to London, meetings were held with Viscount Palmerston, the Prime Minister (and Rector of the University from 1862 to 1865), and William Ewart Gladstone, the Chancellor of the Exchequer, and eventually a concession was wrung from the government that the Treasury would commit to contributing £21,400, half the estimated shortfall, when public subscriptions matched this figure.[21]

THE 'COVERED SHED' 1862–1863

On 22 December 1862 the students petitioned the University Senate for a 'covered shed' for use in wet weather.[22] Although the shelter is sometimes interpreted as one of the earliest modern sporting stands in the world, it seems more likely that it was intended primarily as a place for students to gather between classes.[23] The Senate accepted the estimate of £250 and a shelter in the style of a railway station canopy was erected against the wall of Blackfriars' Kirk in January and February 1863.[24] The designer is unknown. A photograph of the structure appears to show at least one long row of seating, which suggests at least a secondary use as a viewing area for sporting activities on the College Green [FIG. 41]. Certainly, it was used as a viewing stand for the Glasgow Celtic Society's Highland Games, which were held annually on the College Green from August 1862, and David Murray, the great chronicler of the University's history, mentions the shelter in his description of football on the College Green.[25]

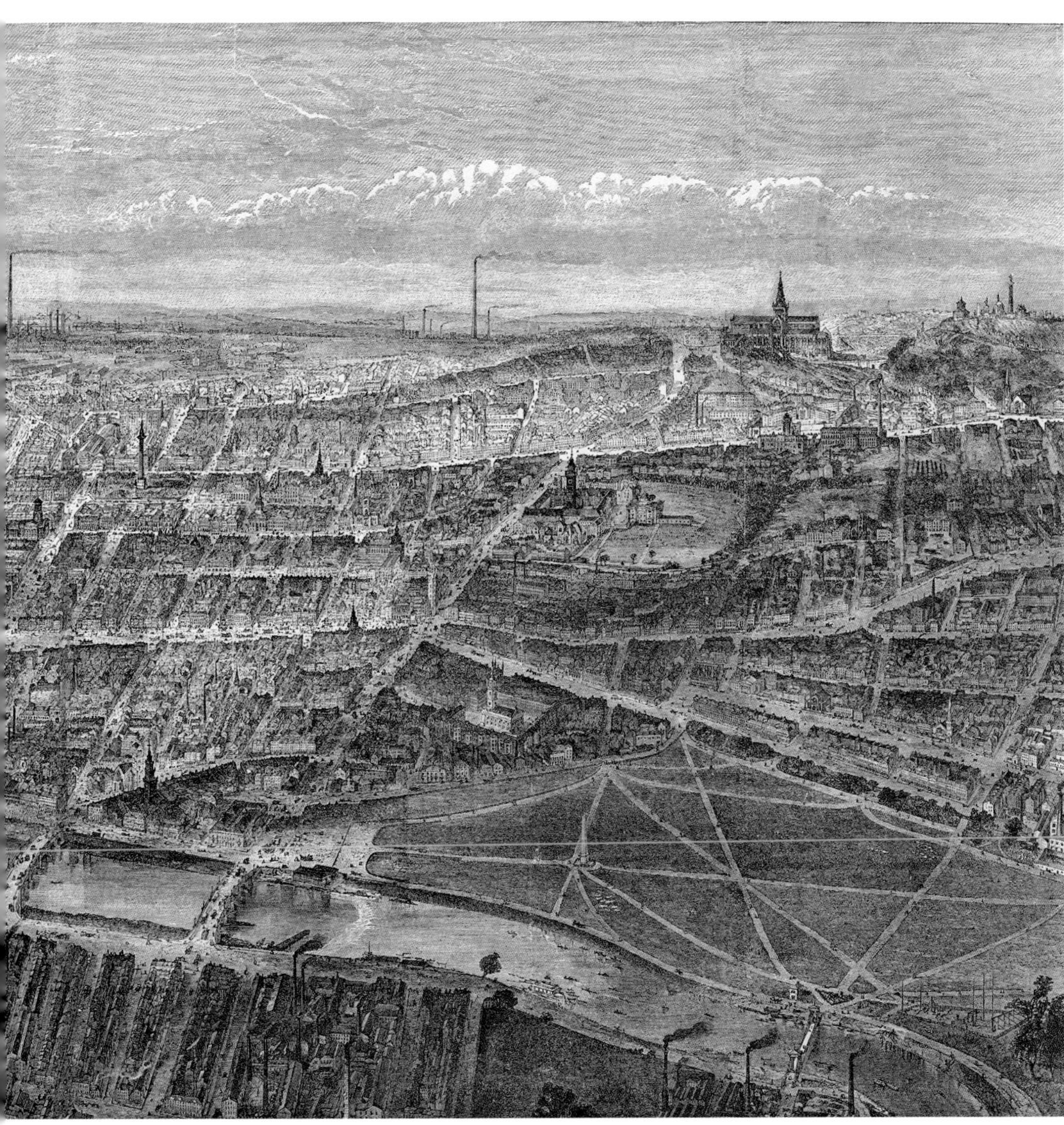

42 Panoramic view of Glasgow from a balloon, engraved by Thomas Sulman and published in the *Illustrated London News* of 26 March 1864. The view includes the Old College and College Green on the right-hand side and Gilmorehill House on the hill on the far left.
GULSC [MUI–a.I]

A wide variety of sports were played on the College Green, including bowling, archery and cricket. Football appears to have been played from the late 18th or early 19th centuries. It was certainly played every session from 1822 until the move to Gilmorehill in 1870: 'It was a rough and tumble game in which the contending sides swept across the low green from Blackfriars Street to the New Vennel and back again like the hordes of Attila.'[26] The sides were unlimited, and not necessarily equal in number, and the teams wore their normal clothes, or sometimes gowns. The leather-covered ox-bladder ball was kept by the College gardener. There were no goal posts.

OFFERS FOR THE HIGH STREET SITE 1863

The critical breakthrough toward a solution of all of these accommodation problems came in December 1863 when two railway companies, the City of Glasgow Union Railway Company and the Glasgow & North British Railway Company, served notice of their intentions to seek compulsory purchase powers for the College's High Street site.[27] The Senate must have had prior warning of the notices, as they had formed a College removal committee, on 27 November. Determined not to let the opportunity to relocate slip away again, the removal committee quickly began discussions with the Lord Provost and Glasgow Corporation to agree on the purchase of adjacent lands at Gilmorehill and Donaldshill for the new College buildings and hospital. At the same time, it started to develop a fundraising strategy, and appointed a commission to negotiate with the railway companies in London.[28]

Chapter Four

The Gilbert Scott Building 1863–1870

43 Detail of the design for the clock tower
GUAS [GUA 12464]

In order to deal with the various aspects of the complicated transactions and preparations, the removal committee formed seven sub-committees: Sites (purchase of sites and sale of leftover portions to Glasgow Town Council; Subscriptions; Finance (sale/purchase); New buildings (accommodation requirements); Library; Hunterian Museum; Hospital

The College issued dissent notices to both the railway companies, objecting to their compulsory purchase powers until an agreement could be achieved with one of them. After several lower offers, negotiations with the City of Glasgow Union Railway secured an offer of £100,000 for the High Street site on 5 May 1864 and a formal agreement was signed on 24 May. The Senate sought a simple cash offer, rather than the complicated land and buildings exchange arrangement of the failed Woodlands scheme. Taking into account the Woodlands experience, the College sought to reduce delays caused by parliamentary approval. Although government money was needed, the Senate removed the Treasury's power to meddle in design issues by vesting supervision of the purchase price in the Crown Agent (also the Queen's and Lord Treasurer's Remembrancer and senior legal advisor to the Lord Advocate).[1] The public interest in the transaction, of which the College authorities were acutely aware, was now safeguarded by a single person, rather than by the distant and obstructive Treasury Lords and officials.

On 29 July 1864 the City of Glasgow Union Railway Act received royal assent. The agreement between the railway company and the College was annexed to the Act.[2] Effectively the Act and its annex provided renewed parliamentary approval for the College to move from the High Street. The money was to be paid in four instalments over a four-year period. Corresponding releases of land extending westwards across College Green were scheduled until 30 July 1869, when the University was expected to vacate the Old College buildings completely. The Union Railway Company paid the first £25,000 instalment of their £100,000 in March 1865.[3]

PURCHASE OF THE GILMOREHILL, DONALDSHILL AND CLAYSLAPS SITES 1864–1865

Since the failure of the scheme for Woodlands, that site had been acquired by Glasgow Town Council and laid out in 1853 by Charles Wilson for high-quality housing and a park.[4] Work had begun on construction of Park Circus, again to Wilson's designs. In 1860 the College had investigated a number of sites including North Woodside Road, Great Western Road, Blythswood Holm, Gilmorehill, Yorkhill, Shields, Camphill, Overnewton and two sites at Hillhead.[5] Now the College focused on three sites: Gilmorehill, Donaldshill

44 Portrait of Sir George Gilbert Scott by George Richmond, about 1870

RIBA Library Drawings and Archives Collections

and Clayslaps, just to the west of Woodlands. These adjoining sites would not only allow the construction of the new College buildings on Gilmorehill, but also a new hospital on Clayslaps, and enable control of buildings on Donaldshill in the line of the prevailing wind from the west. The surplus lands were proposed for sale to Glasgow Town Council to form part of the 'West End Park', now Kelvingrove Park, and for controlled speculative development.

The Gilmorehill, or Gilmour Hill, estate had belonged to a series of Glasgow merchants from at least the mid-17th century.[6] In 1800 Robert Bogle Jr, a West Indies merchant, purchased the farmlands from Dr Thomas Lithan of Kelvinside, and about two years later he built a small classical mansion on the top of the hill [FIG.53]. There was also a lodge, which stood close to the site of the current Maggie's Centre on Dumbarton Road, a U-plan court of stables, located where the Bower building is now on University Avenue, and a large walled garden at the foot of the hill in the crook of the River Kelvin. Bogle 'laid off a large Portion of the Grounds in the Vicinity of the Mansion, in ornamental Plantings, Shubberies, and Walks, while extensive walled Gardens contained Grape, Peach, and Green Houses, besides other Accessories to a Gentleman's Country Residence'.[7] Bogle died in 1822. His son, Archibald, sold the estate to the Glasgow Western Cemetery Company in 1845. The cemetery company held a design competition for the layout, which was entered by at least two distinguished architects, John Dick Peddie and William Notman (under the pseudonym 'Alberti').[8] Three years later the cemetery company had become the Gilmorehill Company, a speculative development company, which held another popular competition for laying out the ground as housing.[9] Although the competition was won by the architect/engineer James Wylson, John Dick Peddie continued to develop his plan in a beautiful signed elevation of 1849, which survives amongst his papers in the National Monuments Record of Scotland [FIG.45].[10] The elevation shows severe Grecian terraces following the contours of the hill, after the manner of Playfair's Calton Hill scheme in Edinburgh. In spite of the designers' enthusiasm, the financial backers lost confidence in the speculative development scheme and let the house and grounds for various temporary purposes. Another housing layout was prepared by the surveyors Smith & Wharrie in 1863.

Donaldshill, another small estate to the west of Gilmorehill belonged to the Gray family of Dalmarnock, and was called 'the Brewlands' in the 18th century. There was no house, but fishing rights on the River Kelvin attached to the property. Robert Bogle Jr had bought the land in 1803, adding it to the grounds of Gilmorehill House. The remains of old quarries were located behind the Gilmorehill lodge on Dumbarton Road, and a large curling pond occupied a site to the east of Church Street. Sir Archibald Bogle retained Donaldshill when Gilmorehill was sold in 1845.

The small site of Clayslaps occupied the arc of land where Kelvingrove Art Gallery and Museum now stands, between the south bank of the River Kelvin and the new Dumbarton Road. The site was owned by the city's Incorporation of Bakers, who operated a large water-powered flour mill there. The open ground was to be sold, but the bakers were to retain the mill and the access and water-power rights. In consultation with Glasgow Corporation the University initially purchased Clayslaps as the intended site of the new hospital.[11] On 27 February 1864 the removal committee unanimously agreed that the West End sites were 'most eligible and suitable', and instructed offers of £65,000 for the lands of Gilmorehill House, £18,000 for Donaldshill and £17,400 for Clayslaps. Gilmorehill was secured for the offer price by June 1864 and Donaldshill and Clayslaps followed in January and February 1865.[12] The architect John Burnet (senior) was employed to prepare a ground plan of Gilmorehill, retaining some of the proposed speculative housing around the northern and western sides of the site.[13] In order to protect the University's interests on its northern boundary against speculative developers, the Senate also acquired Hillhead House and its grounds for £6,050 in November 1867.[14] By January 1875 the house and grounds proved surplus to requirements and were sold to a private purchaser, before being presented back to the University in 1917.[15]

SELECTION OF AN ARCHITECT, AUGUST–OCTOBER 1864

By September 1864 the question of an architect for the new buildings had become a matter of urgency. The Lord Provost was intent on recommending Sir Joseph Paxton, the famous gardener and architect/engineer of the Crystal Palace in London, to advise Glasgow Corporation on the 'proper arrangements respecting Gilmorehill & Donaldshill'.[16] For their part, the sites and sale sub-committee, comprising Principal Barclay, Allen Thomson, Clerk of the Senate, and Anderson Kirkwood, Professor of Conveyancing, were keen to appoint George Gilbert Scott of London – which in due course happened [FIG. 44].

Scott was born on 3 July 1811 in the parsonage designed by his amateur architect father, the Revd Thomas Scott, at Gawcott in Buckinghamshire.[17] He trained with the architects James Edmeston and Henry Roberts in London. His first practice with William Bonython Moffatt resulted in a number of austere workhouses. In his autobiography, Scott described how on a railway journey he was awakened by 'the thunder of Pugin's writings ... I was from that moment a new man. Old things [in his practice] had passed away, and, behold, all things had become new, or rather modernism had passed away from me and every aspiration of my heart had become mediaeval.'[18] This passion was fuelled by Augustus Pugin's persuasive arguments for the moral, romantic, artistic and practical benefits of Gothic – the 'national' style.

Gothic appeared to embody the very spirit of ancient woods, growing organically into great cathedrals and churches with their soaring pillars, arched roofs and sinuous window patterns. Each country's primitive Gothic architecture took on its own national form through local designers and craftsmen, and this was regarded as pure, native and Christian, in contrast with the supposedly invasive and pagan classical styles from Greece and Rome. The Gothic style was held also to be flexible and diverse in freeing the plans and elevations from the rigid unifying rules of classical symmetry: the exterior of the building could express the size and function of the interior spaces in an 'honest' manner without contrivance. Although a committed 'Goth', Scott was also a technophile, employing massive structural iron beams in his buildings to enable large floor spans and flexible internal arrangement of walls. Frequently the iron beams and columns were left visible, paradoxically in an honest, 'Gothic' manner.

In 1845 Scott won the international competition for rebuilding the St Nikolaikirche in Hamburg, which set him on a course for international fame as the most fashionable architect in the Gothic Revival style. The early years of his solo practice were mainly focused on new church buildings and the 'restoration' of England's great medieval cathedrals. Scott published his own architectural manifesto, *Remarks on Secular and Domestic Architecture, Present and Future*, in 1857. This set out Scott's belief that the Gothic style was as appropriate to secular buildings as to ecclesiastical ones, and that Gothic was not an antiquarian style that sought to revive everything ancient, but rather it was 'pre-eminently free, comprehensive, and practical'.[19] In the autumn of 1864 Scott was at the height of his career and led the largest architectural office in Britain. He had a reputation for being able to deliver large and complex projects in an efficient manner. Amongst a large number of jobs in design or under construction, he was midway through big projects at the Foreign and Colonial Office (1861–68) in London and Preston Town Hall (1862–67), and was working on the prestigious Albert Memorial (1863–72), also in London. Scott had some previous commissions in Scotland for a number of churches and had been appointed as architect for the Albert Institute (now the McManus Gallery) in Dundee in June 1864.[20] In spite of the Italianate classical style of the Foreign

45 John Dick Peddie's proposed development of Gilmorehill, 1849
RCAHMS [SC 669791]

Office, which was forced upon him by the Prime Minister, Lord Palmerston, Scott was ardent in his use of the Gothic style.

It is not known whether there was a direct connection between any of the University officials and Scott, or why his name arose. However, it is worth examining the discussions of the sub-committees for buildings, and for sites and sales, on the question of selecting an architect. The former recorded on 3 August 1864:

The Committee took into consideration the proper manner of selecting an Architect, and resolved that an open competition is inexpedient in respect experience has proved that it is unlikely that the best Architects would engage in such a competition. A conversation ensued on the subject of limited competition as compared with the appointment of an architect without competition, when opinion was in favour of the latter plan, and it was resolved to recommend Mr George Gilbert Scott of London.[21]

On 13 September, the sites and sale sub-committee minutes noted that:

... the members of Sub Committee had a full conversation on the subject of appointing an authority to guide them in the laying out of the grounds in the interest of the University; and from what they had heard of the eminent talent & taste of Mr George Gilbert Scott of London Architect they were unanimously of opinion that Mr Scott was the authority who should be employed for these purposes on behalf of the University.

The Sub Committee were of opinion that it would be of great importance that the same Gentleman who was to select the site of the new College & attend to the interests of the University otherwise in relation to the laying out of grounds should also be architect for making out the designs for the new College buildings in order that full effect might be given primarily to the position of these buildings in an architectural point of view. The Sub Committee were farther of opinion that not only to meet the arrangements with the Corporation, which were pressing, but to secure progress with the plans & details of the new buildings in regard to which it was necessary, under the provisions of the Act for the removal of the University from the present Site, that no time should be lost, the Architect to be employed in preparing these plans with the relative specifications & other details & superintending the erection of the new College should forthwith be appointed. And upon these grounds the Sub Committee agree to recommend to the Senatus Academicus that Mr Scott should be chosen by them as Architect for their new College ...[22]

From the recorded discussions it is clear that the committees were anxious to avoid the delays that had sunk the Woodlands scheme. By selecting Scott, the pre-eminent architect of the day and designer of the government's own Foreign Office, the committees perhaps hoped to neutralise government objections and interference in design issues. The lack of competition appears to have been brushed aside as an issue. Speed, simplicity and quality were the overriding concerns. Testimonials were sought discreetly from the College's parliamentary agents in London, Loch & Maclaurin. Mr Loch responded that although he did not know Scott personally, he knew people who did. Although Loch promised to enquire, he did report back the general view: 'perhaps you are not aware of his enormous occupation & of the common report that it is physically impossible that he can give personal superintendence to much that he undertakes'.[23] Without even discussion of his fee, on 30 September the Senate approved the recommendation of the buildings sub-committee to appoint Scott.[24] The following week Allen Thomson, convenor of the committee, wrote to Scott. The letter is interesting not simply as the beginning of a long and fruitful relationship between the University and the Scott family of architects, but also because it provides a useful summary of the requirements for the largest construction project in 19th-century Scotland.

8th October 1864

Sir

The University of Glasgow having occasion to remove from their present lands, and requiring new buildings to be erected on ground which has been acquired for the purpose in the Western part of the City, the Senatus Academicus at a recent meeting expressed their desire to obtain your services as Architect of the New Buildings, and they remitted to a Committee of their number, of which I am Chairman, to communicate with you on the subject.

I am authorised in the first place to make enquiry if it will be agreeable to you to accept of the appointment of Architect for the New University Buildings, and in the second place, should you receive this proposal favourably, to invite you to Glasgow at your earliest convenience in order to confer with the Committee and others with respect to the manner in which the work is to be carried on.

With a view to assist you in coming to a determination as to your answer to this communication I think it proper to furnish you with the following preliminary information.

The University of Glasgow is attended by about 1200 Students in the several faculties of Theology, Law, Medicine & Arts and has a Principal and Twenty-five Professors. The general University Library contains upwards of 100,000 Volumes and the Hunterian Museum of the University is a large and valuable

Miscellaneous Collection of Books and Manuscripts, Coins and antiquities, pictures, Natural History and Anatomical Specimens; all of which would require to be disposed according to the most approved methods of the time. Besides Lecture Rooms, Laboratories and other apartments connected with the several chairs, public halls for general meetings, committee meetings, examinations and reading rooms are required; as also dwelling houses for a certain number of the Professors and officers of the University. While ample accommodation is provided in the proposed buildings for the various objects now mentioned, the plans for their construction must be such as will readily admit of future extension.

For the erection of these buildings, which will obviously be of great extent, the funds at present available are, it is to be feared, somewhat inadequate, amounting it is supposed by the Committee, after allowing £32,000 for the purchase of the site, to be about £90,000, and great economy therefore will be necessary to obtain a building combining all the requisites of accommodation with sufficient elegance of design.

By the provisions of the recent Act of Parliament under which the present University Lands have been purchased by the Union Railway Company, the buildings now occupied must be vacated within five years from the 29th July last. Expedition therefore is equally necessary with economy in the erection of the new buildings. The Members of the Senatus or Committees appointed for the purpose will endeavour to furnish you with very full information as to the accommodation required in the several departments, and it need scarcely be mentioned that the Architect will carry out the directions of such Committees as may be authorised by the Senate to communicate with him.

I may mention also that in 1846 when there was a proposal to transfer the College of Glasgow to a new Site not far distant from that now contemplated, plans for the new buildings were executed with great care by the late Mr Baird, Architect of Glasgow, and after these plans were carefully revised and an improved elevation furnished by Mr Blore of London the buildings were contracted for. The drawings of these plans will be submitted to your inspection and may afford some assistance in judging of the extent and nature of the accommodation.

In order to obtain a suitable site, the University Authorities have found it necessary to purchase a much larger area of ground than they can afford to retain in connection with the new buildings. They have now in their possession about 60 acres of elevated and well-wooded ground bounded on the one side by the River Kelvin, presenting one of the finest sites for a large public building in the neighbourhood of Glasgow. They purpose retaining a space of about 15 acres as a recreation ground round the site which may appear best adapted for the new building, and from negotiations which have been going on they expect to be able to dispose advantageously of the remaining portion of the grounds to the City Corporation or otherwise with a view to its being added in part of the Western Park of the City, and in part disposed of for the building of dwelling houses. In this way the New University Buildings will be placed in a commanding situation with a large space of open ground surrounding them, and at the same time there will be an opportunity of effecting a great improvement in the extension of the City – both of which objects are likely to engage the interest of the inhabitants of Glasgow & west of Scotland.

I have to request therefore that you will inform me at your earliest convenience if you are disposed to be the Architect of this work, and if you are disposed to undertake it, how soon it will be possible for you to come to Glasgow to inspect the ground and give your advice as to its arrangement.

I am Sir, your obedient Servant
Allen Thomson MD
Chairman of the Removal Committee[25]

Perhaps not surprisingly, given the potential scale of the business heading towards his office, Scott accepted the commission by return of post on 10 October 1864.[26]

THE BRIEF, OCTOBER 1864

The first job for the buildings sub-committee was to supply a detailed list of the College's space requirements to their new architect in London. Although it was proposed to send the Baird/Blore designs as guidance to Scott, the intervening fifteen years had seen changes in the needs of the various departments. The committee members abstained from making remarks on the form and style of the accommodation, but provided some general guidelines and specific requirements for the Library, Hunterian Museum, public halls, classrooms and professors' houses.[27] At a general level, the sub-committee sought four things: provision for expansion; separate entrances and the grouping together of the classrooms belonging to the faculties of Theology, Law, Medicine, and Arts; arcades or cloisters to provide covered passages between the different parts of the building; and that at least one side of the buildings should be more private than the rest. The Library was to hold 20,000 square feet of shelving, enough to accommodate a further fifty years of collecting at the 1864 rate. For the first time, service rooms were to be provided for the Library staff: a delivery room for giving out the books, a fireproof room for the most valuable books, a committee room, a librarian's room, and 'arranging room' for holding unbound books. There should also be a cloakroom and toilets, and a reading room for a hundred readers, each allocated 10 square feet. The Hunterian curator produced a detailed report, from which the principal requirements were 18,000 square feet of floor space and proximity to the main Library and Anatomy and Medical departments. A new Common Hall should accommodate 2,500 and be capable of serving as a chapel. The Old College Forehall was to be 'reproduced as a Professors' Reading Room with such change in the elevation of the roof as may be thought proper'. Further public provision was to include an exam hall, a Senate room, committee room, fireproof record room, and registrar's room. A table of class room seatings was sent to Scott and general requirements: ceilings to be between 18 feet and 30 feet in height; each student should have a space 2 feet wide by 2 feet 9 inches in depth, including a 13-inch seat and 10-inch desk with provision for ink; each professor should have a retiring room; and the Anatomy and Chemistry departments should be located in outbuildings, with Anatomy in shade. Twelve houses of 64,000 cubic feet each were needed for the professors and one of 80,000 cubic feet for the Principal, along with houses for the janitor, chamberlains, Museum keeper and the gardener. The grounds were to include a 4–6 acre recreation field and a shed.

George Gilbert Scott came to Glasgow on 26 October 1864 to view the site.[28] He attended the Removal Committee meeting two days later, where he was introduced to the full Senate and made some remarks on the disposition of the new site.[29] The meeting resolved to form another committee to obtain 'photographic views of the existing College'. The purpose of the photographs is not recorded, but presumably since Scott was in attendance, they were primarily intended to help him with his designs in some way. It seems likely that the committee approached the Glasgow photographer, Thomas Annan, and the results are the series of twenty or so images bound in green buckram boards, several editions of which are now in the University's Archives and Special Collections.[30] A number of the images were later published by Annan in *Memorials of the Old College of Glasgow* in 1871, and a great many were published as individual albumen prints.

At some point on his trip, Scott appears to have stopped in Edinburgh to take notes on the College buildings there.[31] Baird's plans of 1846 were sent to Scott in November 1864 and there followed a flurry of letters amending the initial requirements, requesting a layout plan of the site and supplying a very detailed assessment of the necessary ventilation, heating and lighting of the new building.[32]

The mechanical engineering of the new building appears to have been a concern from the outset, as yet another sub-committee was formed to deal with that issue. The interest in the practicalities of ventilation, heating and lighting was possibly at the instigation of the Professor of Natural Philosophy, William Thomson, later Lord Kelvin, as the sub-committee's first report was sent to Thomson's brother James, Professor of Civil Engineering at Queen's University, Belfast. Perhaps sensing a spiralling list of demands and interference in his professional sphere, Scott returned a polite, but curt, note thanking the professors for their comments and suggesting that they employ a ventilation engineer in whom they had confidence.[33]

THE PLANS 1865–1870

A very large number of drawings, letters, telegrams, minutes, accounts and other records survive in relation to the construction of the Gilbert Scott building. The main collections are spread between the Glasgow University Archives Service, the Hunterian Museum and Art Gallery, the Royal Institute of British Architects (RIBA) and Peterborough Museum.[34] Very few of the drawings are dated, and all are unbound from their original volumes and disassociated from any accompanying correspondence, which makes piecing together the development of the design and sequence of revisions a matter of some speculation.

All drawings, even the largest and most highly finished pen and wash drawings (such as the 3.75m by 0.6m half-section of the tower [FIG.52]), were made in at least triplicate: one copy for Scott's office; one copy for the client; and a full set of tracings, which were supplied by the surveyor for the use of the contractors in the site office.[35] The earliest drawings seem to have been done in pencil to allow significant amendment. Later drawings are in pen and ink, sometimes with coloured washes and crayon, sometimes directly onto paper, and sometimes onto tracing paper backed with linen. The nine contract drawings, which were signed on 28 November 1868 by the University officials and the contractors, are all on thick wove paper, or *Vélin*, supplied and watermarked by the famous English papermakers, Whatman. By 1875 the University was in possession of over 840 drawings for the project.[36] It is certain that a number of people in Scott's London office were involved with production of the drawings, but none are specifically identified. Scott's long-term personal assistant, John Burlison Sr, made several appearances on site and in the correspondence before his death in 1868, but his role was more administrative than architectural, dealing with matters of finance and contract. When the first phase of the project was drawing to a close in 1871, Scott dispatched architectural assistants Joseph Maltby Bignell and George Wood from his office to examine the state of completion in detail.[37] It appears from this fact, and a number of items of correspondence, that these were the two assistants most closely involved in the

46 First scheme, March 1865. Initially the Chemistry and Anatomy wings were proposed on the west (left) side of the plan, but fearing the prevailing south-westerly wind would blow noxious smells across the campus, they were relocated to the eastern side of the building in the final scheme.
GUAS [BUL 6/1/24]

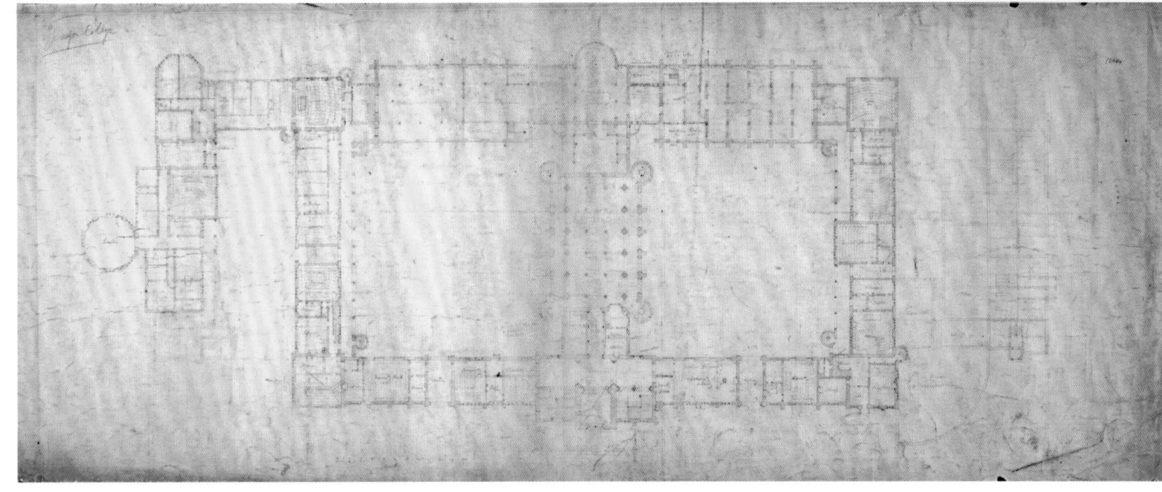

detailed design in London.[38] John S. Lee acted as Scott's quantity surveyor for the purposes of costing.

Scott's first small ground plan of the site was sent from London on 13 January 1865.[39] Within days the professors were suggesting amendments, worrying about the potential for expansion, questioning the layout of the commercial housing plots (that still remained on the north and west sides) and asking for cost estimates. This time Scott sent a stronger response, essentially telling the professors to back off until he could show them a completed design.[40] In the event the full proposal drawings were further delayed by the sudden death on 30 January of Scott's third son, Albert Henry, a student aged only twenty.

THE FIRST SCHEME, MARCH 1865

Scott's initial drawings were ready for the Senate towards the end of the same month. These appear to be the sketch elevations that were photographed by Thomas Annan, and two associated room plans. The first scheme was similar to the one that was built, but with the room arrangement reversed: the science classes, laboratories and Museum were proposed around the western quadrangle, while the Arts, Law and Divinity classes and Library were to occupy the eastern quad [FIG.46].

Scott's plans retained the monastic/collegiate symmetrical double quadrangle layout proposed by John Baird for the Woodlands scheme, but considerably expanded in dimensions to 540 feet (165m) long by 300 feet (91m) wide. The long range faced south with a 300-foot central tower and spire. The Museum and Library were located in the north range and the range dividing the two quadrangles contained a Common Hall over an open cloister. The Library, Museum and Common Hall were always intended to be capable of opening into each other via a reading room to allow large functions. William Henry Playfair's interconnecting layout of the Library and Natural History Museum at the University of Edinburgh possibly influenced this arrangement. The Library and Museum were also intended to be capable of later expansion by the addition of 'transverse wings projecting to the north'.[41] Cloisters were proposed for the west and east ranges facing into the quadrangles.

As was expected, the design was in a muscular Gothic Revival style. Rather less predictable was the almost classical symmetry and arrangement of the layout and the barrel-vaulted glass and cast-iron roofs of the Library and Hunterian Museum [FIG.48]. Scott himself described the style:

> *The design is in the style of the early part of the 14th century, and the treatment of that style is an attempt to harmonize it in some degree with the National characteristics of Scottish domestic and secular architecture – This harmonizing process is rendered necessary by the fact that we have few remains of secular architecture in Scotland in a sufficiently perfect state (castles excepted) which date from so far back, so that the salient characteristics of secular architecture in Scotland are to be learned from works of later date, though easily susceptible of being translated back into the earlier style.*
>
> *The early French examples when viewed relatively to those in England afford much help as they have many features differing from the English works, but bearing strong resemblance to those which are so characteristic of Scottish architecture though of a later period.*[42]

Scott's convoluted and implausible justification for the style suggests that he was well aware of the sensitivities of awarding the design of such a prestigious building to a London architect without local competition. In fact Scott's concessions to '*National characteristics*' were largely drawn from the 17th-century Baronial aspects of the Old College buildings in the High Street, such as the conical-roofed stair towers and crowstepped gables. The overall concept seems to have owed more to the celebrated Oxford University Museum of Natural History of 1855–60 by the Irish architects, Dean & Woodward.

The Oxford University Museum not only housed the University's natural history and other scientific collections, but also brought together previously scattered teaching and research facilities for Astronomy, Geometry, Experimental Physics, Mineralogy, Chemistry, Geology, Zoology, Anatomy, Physiology and Medicine. Each department had a lecture room and a private room in one of three ranges in a U-plan around the museum court. The frontage took the form of a Flemish cloth hall and the museum court was famously constructed as a modern 'cathedral for science' with a cast-iron structure and a vaulted glazed roof. The Chemistry department occupied an octagonal structure, known as the Abbot's Kitchen after the 14th-century original at Glastonbury, which was isolated from the main building to avoid noxious fumes. Stylistically, the front of the Oxford Museum owed much to the appearance of medieval Flemish civic buildings, such as the Ypres Lakenhal (Cloth Hall), with its extended range and central tower/spire. Scott had used a Ypres-type tower and spire in his winning, but unbuilt, scheme of 1856 for the Hamburg Rathaus (Town Hall) and at Preston Town Hall of 1862. The tower/spire of the Midland Grand Hotel, St Pancras, London, also designed in 1865, was derived from the same example. Scott himself compared the style of Glasgow University to his earlier Albert Institute (now McManus Galleries) of 1864 in Dundee, which was in a medieval Flemish-Baronial style '*which I may call my own invention*'.[43] The design for the Common Hall element of the Glasgow complex had particular similarities to the Albert Institute and Preston Town Hall.

Scott may also have seen the first phase (1861) of the Museum of Science and Art (now the National Museum of Scotland) by the engineer Francis Fowke in Chambers Street, Edinburgh, which also had an aisled arrangement, a soaring cast-iron internal structure and a largely glazed roof.

THE SECOND SCHEME, OCTOBER 1866

The plans evolved through 1865 and 1866 to a finalised scheme that was approved by the Lord Advocate under the terms of the railway company Act on 3 October 1866. The amendments to the plans were driven partly by practical considerations that arose through the detailed site survey and partly through the emerging requirements of the professors, but also in response to the lack of funds. Stylistically, very little changed. The two major adjustments were the reversal of the science classrooms and laboratories to the eastern side of the complex and the removal of the western range. The practical benefits of the reversal were increased light for the demonstration laboratories, shelter from the prevailing wind (which might have blown noxious fumes into the quadrangles), and the greater potential for expansion of the buildings westwards if necessary. This alteration also entailed swapping the positions of the Library and the Museum, the latter of which was to contain the natural history collections and needed to be placed adjacent to the Natural History (Zoology) classroom. The replacement of the western range with a covered walkway was a cost-saving measure.

The dark, damp, cold and smelly conditions of the Old College continued to influence the professors in their insistence that adequate light, heat and ventilation should take precedence over stylistic considerations. Scott reassured the building sub-committee that the window mullions would not have a material effect on the amount of light. However, the prime victims of the light and cost considerations were the attractive cloisters and covered walkways around the quadrangles.[44] Access to the rooms on the eastern side of the east quadrangle

47 Sketch of the proposed south front. The right-hand pavilion includes an oriel window, part of the Principal's Lodging in the first scheme of March 1865.
GUAS [GUA 2210]

48 First sketch proposal for the Hunterian Museum, which includes a glazed roof, March 1865
GUAS [GUA 2210]

was now to be provided directly from two circular stairtowers. At the insistence of the professors, who were keen to have command of their own territories and keep the student entrances separate for each subject area, there was now very little lateral internal connection between the various parts of the building. Only the three great public spaces, the Library, Museum and Common Hall, encouraged circulation.

In spite of the insistence on light and air, the proposed glass roofs were considered unsuitable for the Library and Museum.[45] There may have been practical maintenance or conservation considerations for the books and museum objects behind the professors' decision to drop these features, but there was possibly also an element of architectural snobbery. Glazed roofs had connotations of railway sheds, which were considered pieces of utilitarian industrial engineering rather than architecture fit for an educational institution. The disastrous collapse of the glazed roof during construction of Dean & Woodward's Oxford University Museum in 1858 is also likely to have played on the professors' minds.[46]

Perhaps in view of the disquiet about Scott's appointment as architect for the main building, the sub-committee decided in May 1867 that a local man would be appropriate for the new hospital. Ostensibly the decision was made because construction, operation and maintenance of the hospital depended more on local funding and it was envisaged that it would need to be expanded to a uniform plan from time to time. As John Burnet Sr had already provided advice and assistance with regard to the planning of the hospital, the building sub-committee proposed that he should be given the job without competition.[47]

CRITICISM OF THE DESIGN

Although there was widespread dismay in the architectural community of Scotland at the appointment of Scott without competition, the fiercest public criticism of the designs came from Alexander 'Greek' Thomson in his astonishingly frank and persuasive lecture to the Glasgow Architectural Society on 7 May 1866. The lecture was entitled *An Enquiry as to whether the Character and Purposes of the University can be fully expressed in Medieval Architecture – and whether the merits of the proposed Plans have justified the University Authorities in going from home for an Architect*. When the lecture was published in shortened form in *The Builder*, omitting the more trenchant criticism of Gilbert Scott, it was given the only marginally snappier title, *An Inquiry as to the Appropriateness of the Gothic Style for the Proposed Buildings for the University of Glasgow, with some remarks upon Mr Scott's Plans*.[48]

Thomson's rage was probably fuelled by his own involvement in the failed Woodlands project. As John Baird's chief draughtsman, Thomson is likely to have put considerable effort into the magnificent drawings for the various Woodlands schemes, and he presumably also shared his employer's frustrations with the constant changes and the ultimate collapse of the project after four years. The railway company's failure to pay Baird, and the subsequent effect on Baird's health may also have contributed to Thomson's animosity towards the appointment of Gilbert Scott. There is some evidence that Thomson tried to intervene directly with the University before delivering his public lecture. A letter of 2 February 1866 from Scott to Dr Allen Thomson, convenor of the building sub-committee (and no relation of Alexander Thomson) thanks him for 'your letter to Mr Thomson'.[49] Later in the year the building sub-committee minutes record that 'Dr. Thomson's letter to Mr A. Thomson [was] referred to' in relation to discussions about the Chemistry, Anatomy and medical laboratories.[50] Unfortunately Alexander Thomson's letter and Allen Thomson's response are not now traceable.

Whatever the personal background, Thomson argued on professional grounds that Gothic was not appropriate for a variety of reasons:

It is not associated with learning in any way; that it is not national; that the Christianity which it expresses was not of the purest type [i.e., it was Roman Catholic]; that it was the product of uneducated men; and that it does not teach us the higher principles of architectural art; that it is inconsistent with the best examples of sculpture and painting.

While there is some likelihood that the lecture was to some degree a satire on the polemical publications of Scott's Gothic hero, Augustus Pugin, Thomson's fundamental points were serious ones: neither the Gothic style, nor Scott's interpretation and implementation of it, were good enough for such a prestigious commission. Above all, Thomson argued, Scott had a sausage-factory approach to design and did not understand or care about the appearance or context of his mongrel building with its classical plan in Gothic clothing. The great achievements of Scottish Enlightenment art and architecture were founded on rational and ordered classical principles of refinement, which were the very opposite of Gothic:

The sentimental conceit of reproducing in effigy the architecture of a rude age, and distorting our habits to fit into its sinuosities, is, as I have already said, a mere fashion which has come in of late, and by-and-bye will go out again, leaving this great pile of nonsense to be a laughing stock to succeeding ages.[51]

The audience at Thomson's lecture included some of

Scotland's most prominent architects and designers, including Campbell Douglas, John Honeyman, James Boucher, Horatio Bromhead, Alexander Watt, P. Daniel Cottier, William Leiper and Thomas Gildard. According to the *Proceedings of the Glasgow Architectural Society*, an interesting and prolonged discussion followed. Scott, who was rarely slow to respond to criticism, was unusually silent when the lecture was reported and published. Thomson was not the only critic to go into print. John James Stevenson, an alumnus of the University, former apprentice and advisor to Scott on the Gilmorehill stone, and a founder of the Society for the Protection of Ancient Buildings, who had campaigned for retention of the Old College tower and reconstruction of the Forehall at Gilmorehill, also set out disparaging comments in his *House Architecture* of 1880:

These Edinburgh High Street houses illustrate also a method of building common in Scotland, and almost peculiar to it, which arose from the peculiar character of the sites which were chosen. Scotch castles were usually placed on the edge of a steep hill, enclosing a courtyard on the top of it. The side of the building to the court was of moderate height, but that to the outside founded down the steep hill had as many stories looking out to the open, under the level of the inner court, as it had above it. It is this practice which gives to many Scotch castles their appearance of height and grandeur, the lower stories to the outside, used frequently merely as cellars and showing outside as solid walls forming a grand base for the building.

The same practice was followed in building towns. They were commonly built along the ridge of a hill, the street running along the top of the ridge, with the houses on each side. The High Street in Edinburgh is built in this way. The entrance of each building, or 'land' as it is called, was at the level of the street from which the stair descended to as many floors below as there were above.

It is to be regretted, I think, that this feature of Scotch architecture was not followed in the new buildings of Glasgow University. These occupy the summit of a hill, of which the top was cut down to make a level platform for a long low building, the height of which is further lessened by a wide terrace in front, which buries a great height of foundation wall. Had the old Scotch plan been followed, all this useless under building would have been available for admirably lighted rooms, commanding an extended view; the hill, instead of being flattened, would have gained in height and the building would have been grander.[52]

Possibly in response to the lack of competition, John Thomas Rochead, another notable architect in Glasgow, produced his own design for the new College buildings.[53]

[opposite]

49 A watercolour perspective from Kelvingrove Park of the proposed new College buildings at Gilmorehill, after designs by Sir George Gilbert Scott. The perspective was drawn by Robert Edgar and hand-coloured by John Burbridge. This appears to be one of the earliest of the surviving series of large watercolour perspectives for the Gilbert Scott building, probably dating from late June 1865. The design of the Abbot's Kitchen (Chemistry laboratory) is altered in the later views. Unfortunately the watercolours have been damaged by exposure to direct sunlight, possibly resulting from their original display in the Old College Forehall and at the Glasgow Royal Exchange.
GUHMAG [GLAHA 54347]

50 Robert Edgar and John Burbridge's watercolour perspective of the proposed new College buildings at Gilmorehill, after designs by Sir George Gilbert Scott, August 1865. The view is from Mr Graham-Gilbert's property at Yorkhill, and includes the old mills at Clayslaps in the foreground on the right-hand side.
GUHMAG [GLAHA 54351]

51 Robert Edgar and John Burbridge's watercolour perspective of the proposed new College buildings at Gilmorehill, after designs by Sir George Gilbert Scott, November 1865. This view from the south-east was engraved for various purposes including newspaper articles and a receipt book.
GUHMAG [GLAHA 42452]

FUNDRAISING

It became clear at a very early stage in the design process that the funds from the railway companies and the Treasury grant would fall far short of what was needed. The convenor of the building sub-committee, Allen Thomson, estimated the overall cost of the sites and buildings at £239,000 in May 1865, towards which £100,000 would need to be raised in public subscriptions.[54] Recognising the scale of the task, and appreciating that alumni of the University and citizens of Glasgow would form an important part of the fundraising effort, a joint sub-committee of the Senate, General Council and 'gentlemen unconnected with the College' was formed. It first met on 17 May 1865 under the chairmanship of Principal Barclay.[55] The result of this meeting was a very large and well-organised campaign that sought contributions from as far away as Canada, the United States, India, Shanghai and Singapore. The main effort, however, was reserved for Glasgow and the West of Scotland. Through the joint sub-committee members, each city Ward was allocated a supervising fundraiser, who was to organise door-to-door collections. The Lord Provost of Glasgow and the provosts of the west coast burghs and county sheriffs, were asked to promote the cause, along with present and former Rectors, Deans of Faculty and members of the University Court. Other targets of the campaign were the nobility, gentry, heads of public bodies, parents of students, merchants, manufacturers, doctors, clergymen, writers (solicitors), shopkeepers, accountants, bankers, engineers, ship-builders and tradesmen.

In order to promote the campaign, images, events, literature and stationery were needed. Contacts with the press were also to prove important. The *Glasgow Herald* of 27 April 1865 reported positively on the exhibition of Scott's first scheme sketches in the Forehall of the Old College.[56] Small booklets of the sketches were produced for distribution. The parallels between the University's 17th-century fundraising and the new campaign were drawn in the creation of a facsimile booklet of benefactors to the Old College and a reproduction of Slezer's engraving. A *conversazione* with the architect was held on 22 March 1866 in the Corporation Galleries.[57] Scott himself recommended production of a large perspective drawing for display purposes. The English architect Robert Edgar was responsible for producing perspective views of the building [FIGS 49, 50, 51] from Scott's drawings and photographs of the site, probably by Thomas Annan. John Burbridge, an architectural presentation draughtsman and watercolourist in London, who had worked extensively with John Dick Peddie and Charles Wilson amongst other Scottish architects, was commissioned to colour the perspectives.[58] Photographs were taken of the perspectives and the originals placed

52 Design for the clock tower. The tower was only built to the turret stage in the first phase of construction to 1870. The spire and clock, which were similar in design to those at the Grand Hotel, St Pancras, London, were never built at Gilmorehill. Scott's son, John Oldrid Scott built a stone spire to a different design in 1888.
GUAS [GUA 12464]

on display in the Glasgow Royal Exchange. Engravings were prepared for reproduction in the *Illustrated London News*. This weekly newspaper, with a circulation of 600,000 copies at home and abroad, was regarded as the most efficient means of spreading word of the campaign. *The Builder* magazine also requested a copy of the perspective photograph in October 1868.[59] A more detailed prospectus was produced in 1866 in the form of a 'Statement by the Subscription Sub-Committees with Reference to the Proposed New Buildings & Hospital'. This reproduced lithographs of the perspective drawing and a plan, and outlined the history of the University. It also set out the proposals for the new building. Beautifully printed receipts for subscriptions also included the perspective view [FIG.53].

Scott suggested that the University might try to get interested parties to sponsor specific parts of the new building. An early success in this respect was to persuade the widow of the long-serving Professor of Humanity, William Ramsay, to contribute towards the construction of the Latin classroom. Other fundraising tactics included publication of benefactors' names and a royal ceremony for laying the foundation stone. A sub-committee for laying the foundation stone was formed. Initially, it was hoped that Queen Victoria would perform the ceremony on her way to the Highlands in May 1868. This proved impossible and a new date in August was set. The explosive attempt to free Richard Burke from Clerkenwell Prison in December 1867 had stirred up popular panic and Irish Nationalist 'Fenian fever' in London. There was considerable fear for the personal safety of the Queen. Rumours and hoaxes abounded, including reports of a plot to kidnap the Queen on the way to Balmoral and a sensational report of a planned attack on the Queen on her trip to Lucerne on 18 August 1868. The Prince and Princess of Wales finally laid a foundation stone each on 8 October 1868 in front of a crowd of some 20,000 people [FIG.54]. A list of subscribers was also buried in bottles beneath the two foundation stones. Following a highly successful day, during which the Prince and Princess received the freedom of the city and the Prince accepted an honorary degree, the University banked a subscription of 100 guineas from the Prince and £500 from his mother.

By March 1866 the subscriptions had reached an impressive figure of £67,000, but unfortunately the cost estimates had risen to £344,000. Even taking into account the railway company money and other reserves totaling £117,000 as well as the Treasury grant of £21,400, the University was still far short of the money needed to complete the project. The fundraising continued, the non-essential elements of the building were put on hold, and a new approach to the government was made. This time the University had a stronger hand, with building

£

GLASGOW

Received from
the Sum of
being payment of the instalment of his Subscription of £
towards the funds required for the erection of new College Buildings for the University of Glasgow, and a Hospital connected therewith, payable said Subscription in
yearly instalments, commencing 1st February 1866.

[left, top to bottom]

53 Subscription receipt incorporating the engraving from Edgar and Burbridge's perspective of the College buildings at Gilmorehill
GUAS [GUA 3310]

54 Engraving of the foundation stone ceremony on 8 October 1868 from the *Illustrated London News*
GUAS [GUA 9719]

55 Photograph of the construction of John Thompson's grandstand for the foundation stone ceremony in October 1868. The roofing of the east range is in progress and the south range has reached wallhead height.
GUAS [PHU 1/105/8]
By kind permission of the Faculty of Procurators, Glasgow

[right]

56 Gilmorehill House in use as the site office during the construction of the University buildings, photographed by Thomas Annan. The south range, behind the house, is advanced, but not roofed, suggesting a date of about 1869.
GUAS [PHU 1/104/1]

work underway, a deadline to remove from the High Street, and strong public support demonstrated through the subscription scheme. A huge deputation including the Duke of Montrose (Chancellor of the University), the Lord Justice-General and Gilbert Scott, went to meet Lord Derby, the Prime Minister (and former Rector of the University) and the Chancellor of the Exchequer, Benjamin Disraeli, at Downing Street on 4 May 1867 in an attempt to get the government to match the private subscriptions.[60] The arguments centred around the fact that Glasgow was the only university, apart from the lavishly endowed Oxford and Cambridge, not to receive substantial public money. Eventually the Treasury relented and an additional grant of £120,000 in six annual installments was voted through Parliament in 1868.

CONSTRUCTION 1866–1870

In terms of governance of the project, the Senate granted full powers of superintendence of the construction works to the building sub-committee, convened by Dr Allen Thomson, Clerk of the Senate and Professor of Anatomy.[61] They also authorised co-operation with the subscriptions sub-committee, which included external members, such as the city's Dean of Guild, Archibald Orr Ewing (also an alumnus). James Mitchell was appointed as solicitor to the building sub-committee.

The vast and complicated building operations [FIG.57] required for the new College buildings were largely co-ordinated and regulated by Scott's London office at 20 Spring Gardens. Arthur B. Thompson, Scott's personal assistant kept the great man's correspondence and diary in order. To ensure that things ran smoothly on the ground, a temporary Clerk of Works, Mr Finlay, was appointed by the College for the excavation works. An early decision was taken to retain the old Gilmorehill House as a site office during the construction process [FIG.56]. Such was the urgency of preparing the ground that a separate contract was let to Alexander & John Faill in June 1866 for levelling the top of Gilmorehill, before the designs were even complete. Two hundred men began work immediately and a policeman was appointed to guard the site. Scott sought the advice of his friend and former assistant architect, John James Stevenson, who lived nearby in Oakfield Terrace, about the nature and quality of the stone on the Gilmorehill estate.[62] Stevenson responded that the local free stone was not good-looking, but it was fine for building walls. The building sub-committee instructed the removal of 100 tons of free stone in preparation for building works. A small railway was constructed from the quarry beside the Dumbarton Road to the site on the top of Gilmorehill.[63] As a precaution against running out of funds and being unable to occupy any part of the complex, Scott was instructed to divide up the plans into discrete units that could be completed: *Division 1* The South and East Ranges and the Library/Reading Room; *Division 2* The tower/spire above second floor level; *Division 3* The Museum and adjacent lobby; *Division 4;* The octagonal Chemistry laboratory and adjacent low buildings. The Common Hall range dividing the quadrangles, and the professors' houses were to be omitted from the first phase of building.

Comprehensive specifications were drawn up for each element of the project, identifying general requirements and detailed materials, measurements, treatment and standards of workmanship. Different systems of quantity surveying applied in England and Scotland, so Scott's English measurements were also supplied using the Scottish system to provide a level playing field for local contractors. Tenders were sought for both the whole job and individual trades, in case that was cheaper. In the end the contracts were awarded to a combination of a comprehensive contractor (John Thompson) and individual trades:

Excavator, waller, bricklayer and mason John Thompson, Peterborough; *Slater* John Morrison, Glasgow; *Carpenter, joiner and ironmonger;* John Thompson, Peterborough; *Smith and ironfounder* John McElroy, Glasgow; *Plasterer* James Darion, Glasgow; *Plumber* Wallace & Connell, Glasgow; *Glazier* C. & J. Malloch, Glasgow; *Painter* Anderson & Carlton, Glasgow

Thompson's tender was not the lowest for the overall job, but the references for the cheapest contractor proved unsatisfactory. References for Thompson were supplied by George Gilbert Scott and were very positive.[64] The noted designer and decorator, Daniel Cottier, tendered for the painting contract, but was eliminated from the process as being by far the most expensive.[65]

Thompson's of Peterborough was a family building and contracting firm. The 1851 Census shows John Thompson Sr at the head of a master builder's firm employing thirty-five men, including John Thompson Jr (1824–98) as a builder's clerk. By 1861 Thompson Jr was running the firm, which he built up into one of the largest contracting firms in Britain. Thompson later became a Justice of the Peace and also Mayor of Peterborough four times (1881, 1882, 1888 and 1889). It is clear from the presentation of a gold watch and pencil case to Thompson on his forty-fifth birthday in February 1869 that he was very highly regarded by his employees at Gilmorehill. The magnificent accompanying 'address', listing almost 1,000 of the Gilmorehill workmen, details his 'calm demeanour and kind disposition' and mentions his establishment and funding of a Society for the Benefit of the Sick and Injured [FIG.58].

The selected local contractors were well-known figures in the west of Scotland building industry. John McElroy was a major ironfounder, railway contractor and property developer. The villages of Cove and Kilcreggan were formed on the south-west shore of the Rosneath peninsula in 1849 by the 8th Duke of Argyll as a speculative investment in holiday houses. McElroy was one of a number of Glasgow businessmen who took up the plots and built houses, including one of his own, Craig Ailey, Cove, designed by Baird & Thomson, architects (John Baird II and Alexander Thomson) in 1852. A permanent Clerk of Works, William Conradi,

57 Ground floor plan marked with red lines to show the extent of the divisions of the contract
GUAS [BUL 6/1/3]

58 Forty-fifth birthday greeting to John Thompson from his workers in February 1869. The star shape is filled with almost a thousand of their names.
GUAS [GUA 4058]

59 Photograph of the east range under construction, 1868
GUAS [PHU 1/105/31]
By kind permission of the Faculty of Procurators, Glasgow

60 Photograph of George Gilbert Scott (centre right, wearing a top hat) with the contractors on the day of the foundation stone ceremony, 8 October 1868
GUAS [PHU 1/105/26]
By kind permission of the Faculty of Procurators, Glasgow

was also appointed in January 1867, following an unsuccessful approach by the architect Robert Rowand Anderson, who was considered over-qualified by the building sub-committee.[66] Anderson had previously worked as an assistant in Scott's London office and supervised the construction of St James-the-Less in Leith. There was some suspicion about the approach by Rowand Anderson that Scott was trying to recruit a local deputy and that as a result the University would get less of the great man's time and attention.

As was usual in the period, heating and ventilation, gas-fitting and other services were designed and contracted for separately. Wilson Weatherley Phipson (1838–91) was selected as contractor for the heating and ventilation system.[67] Phipson was a great pioneering engineer of the later 19th century. By the time of the contract with Glasgow University, at the age of twenty-nine, he had already completed heating and ventilation schemes for fourteen major buildings including the Institution of Civil Engineers in London, Edinburgh University Medical Schools, the Birmingham Law Courts, the Marine Barracks at Woolwich, and the National & Provincial Bank in London, the last of which Scott examined prior to Phipson's appointment.[68] Amongst a huge number of later projects, he was to go on to work at the Royal Albert Hall, Alexandra Palace, Royal Holloway College, the Natural History Museum, all in London, and Mount Stuart, Castell Coch and Cardiff Castle for the Marquess of Bute.[69] Phipson used the patented 'Van Hecke' system at Glasgow, which drew fresh air down from shafts in the tower, pumped it through heated chambers and distributed it through vents near the ceilings of the classrooms and floors of the Library and Museum. Foul air was extracted through perforations in the steps to the raked seating in the classrooms. In summer the air was cooled. In the winter, a further stoker supplemented the normal crew of stoker and engineer for the boiler and steam engine. Unfortunately, it was impossible to regulate the temperature and airflow in individual rooms, so that classes full of students became unbearably hot. There were further problems in the Library, where the hot air system brought in Glasgow soot and dust and highly damaging moisture.[70] The system was gradually replaced with a hot water radiator system throughout the 1890s.

Work began on site in January 1867 and the first stone was laid on 4 April 1867.[71] Sheds for the masons, carpenters and smiths were constructed, but work on the ground was delayed by heavy frost. Problems with the quarrying caused delays to the progress of the massive foundations, which were on average 17 feet (5.2m) deep, but 24 feet (7.3m) deep beneath the tower. An increase in size of the basement beneath the Reading Room in the North Range, the addition of an access tunnel beneath the Common Hall to the boiler room, and the late incorporation of the heating/ventilation ducts added to the delays. In May 1867 another setback occurred in the form of a general strike by the masons' union of Glasgow over pay. Some 120 men took part at Gilmorehill. A number of the strikers had returned by July and others were replaced. Gradually the strike fizzled out. By February 1868 some 230 masons were employed, six steam-engines were in use, the foundations were largely complete and 42-foot (12.8m) iron girders were being laid for joisting the floors of the East Range with yellow Baltic pine [FIG.59]. Most of the Library and Museum iron pillars had been cast, but stored near the foundry until they were needed. Material excavated for the North Range foundations had been used to construct the approach roads and terraces under the direction of Smith & Wharrie, surveyors.[72] The proposed ornamental terrace wall was abandoned and Scott suggested a decorative railing could be substituted. As building progressed minor alterations to the internal arrangements were approved.

61 The upper hall of the Hunterian Museum, photographed by Annan and Sons, about 1890
GUAS [Old & New 32]

The introduction of a gas supply to the workers' huts had greatly increased productivity in the winter months, so the effects of the strike on progress were not disastrous. The positive response of the Treasury to the request for extra funding gave the building sub-committee confidence that all four divisions of the work could be completed. There was further good news in February 1868, when the Glasgow City Union Railway Company agreed to extend the date for taking possession of the High Street site by a year to July 1870.[73]

John Thompson designed and constructed a special stand for the laying of the foundation stones by the Prince and Princess of Wales on 8 October 1868 [FIG.55].[74] Rooms in Gilmorehill House were also prepared for the royal couple by Wylie & Lochhead, Glasgow's premier suppliers of furniture and furnishings. The day after the ceremony, John Thompson laid on an entertainment in the shell of the Library for between 1,300 and 1,400 contractors and their families and friends.

In February 1869 the Lord Advocate approved a second phase of works under the terms of the railway company Act.[75] These were to include the foundations of the central Common Hall, now termed the 'Great Hall' and the professors' houses. Estimates were sought from John Thompson and contracts were drawn up without competition. There was some concern that it would become difficult to get access to the Great Hall site if the surrounding buildings were complete and occupied. A similar concern prompted the sub-committee to approve a start on the second division of the contract, the tower and spire above the second floor. Thompson reported on the progress of the buildings in February 1869.[76] The East Range was most advanced, with the plastering and roofing work underway. Walls were at roof height on most other parts of the building, with the exception of the tower. Thompson estimated five months for general completion of the East Range, seven months for the South Range and nine months for the Library. The third and fourth divisions of the

62 The upper hall of the Library in the 1930s, photographer unknown
GULSC [A49/129]

contract, comprising the Museum and Anatomy and Chemistry laboratories, were in progress, but further behind. Work on installation of the bronzed cast-iron windows was also advancing.

With the deadline for removal from the High Street site only eight months away, the sub-committee began to press for more speed. Another progress report by Thompson in November 1869 detailed the practical completion of the East Range and the South Range as far as the central tower.[77] The aisles of the Library had been roofed, but the central 'nave' still awaited its roof. The Museum had reached parapet height and the tower had not progressed. All the other parts of the main building were nearing completion. The projected costs for approved works stood at £434,000 including the North, East and South Ranges of the main buildings, fixtures and fittings, the professors' houses, the roads and earth-moving, the quarry, the hospital, architect's fees and sundries like the foundation stone ceremony.[78] Furniture and equipment were not included in this total.

Sir William Thomson, later Lord Kelvin, the pre-eminent Professor of Natural Philosophy, was given charge of placing the lightning conductors in consultation with Scott.[79] By late 1869 attention was also turning to details such as the Library fittings, gas and water supplies, and the provision of locks and keys. The sub-committee were keen to avoid a proliferation of keys, so suggested a system of master keys. For the purpose of simplifying the lock system, the building was divided into three areas: the Library; the Museum; General Departments, which had a further subdivision of seven departments. A single grand master key was produced and a system of master and sub-master keys was established.[80] The records of the construction provide an interesting insight into the perils of a Victorian building site. While the safety record for the project was generally good, one man died when a crane broke at the professors' houses and three men were killed after the upper scaffolding platform in the Library collapsed. The cause of this latter accident was attributed to the labourers, who were in the habit of throwing building stones onto the planks in spite of instructions to the contrary.[81] John Thompson, the University and colleagues of the dead men subscribed to provide for their widows and families.

INTERIORS

Inevitably, as both time and money were running out towards the summer of 1870, the building committee directed the contractors to concentrate on finishing the construction work and other tasks essential to the occupation of the building:

In the autumn of the year [1870], it became obvious that the utmost effort would be required in order to have the buildings ready for occupation at the opening of the Winter Session at the end of October. All works, therefore, which were not absolutely necessary for this purpose, were for the time postponed; and such temporary arrangements were effected as were requisite to give free use of the parts of the Building necessary for University business, and at the same time, to provide for carrying on those parts of the work still requiring completion.

The result was that many of the interior spaces had a somewhat Spartan appearance when the students arrived in November 1870, with large numbers of rooms left as raw plaster. A review of the situation in 1871 found that greater time and outlay on fitting out and decorating the Library, Museum, classrooms, laboratories and halls was required than had been included in the contracts.[82]

UPPER HALLS OF THE HUNTERIAN MUSEUM AND UNIVERSITY LIBRARY (NOW THE KELVIN GALLERY), HUNTERIAN LIBRARY (NOW THE ENTRANCE HALL TO THE HUNTERIAN MUSEUM), AND THE LOWER HALLS (NOW THE HUNTER HALLS AND THE ADAM SMITH BUSINESS SCHOOL)

The Upper Library, Hunterian Library and the Upper Museum Gallery comprised the main suite of communal rooms in the first phase of construction. The upper halls of the Library and Museum form similar, impressive cathedral-like spaces, 129 feet long by 60 feet wide by 52.5 feet high (approximately 40m x 18m x 16m), with cast-iron colonnades, galleries and open timber roofs. The Hunterian Library, is a grand apsidal (round-ended) room set between, and at right angles to, the ante-rooms of the Museum and Library. Like the Museum and Library, it has an open timberwork roof. The lower hall of the Museum is a similarly large space, but lacks the height, light and grandeur of the upper hall. The lower hall of the Library has long been subdivided. Great attention was paid to the fireproof construction of the Museum and Library rooms. The structure included massive 60ft iron columns, a patent 'Fox & Barrett' floor of iron joists and concrete, and huge fireproof iron doors. The cast-iron columns rising through the building have different architectural treatments at each level: angular cluster columns at the lower hall level; cylindrical cluster columns at the upper hall level; and paired decorative columns at gallery level. The riveted wrought-iron beams of the structure are plainly visible in all of these rooms. The incomplete state of the building, without the Great Hall block, which was to include the principal staircase, meant that a temporary wooden staircase had to be constructed between the quadrangles to provide access to the upper floors of the Library and Museum.

The Library was the first of the main communal spaces to be fitted out when the University moved in, but even here the counter for giving out books and the fittings of the Rare Book Room were still in progress in November 1871. John Thompson estimated £2,590 for supply of the custom-made bookcases, but in the event another £980 was spent on additional cases.[83] The upper Library was designed to hold 65,000 ornamental volumes in fourteen bays off the central hall [FIG. 62]. Each bay contained a donated 'table' with further shelving below for oversize volumes. The lower Library was built for 80,000 volumes and a further 40,000 were to be accommodated in smaller rooms. Older volumes were placed according to the 1791 catalogue, while 19th-century works were re-catalogued and grouped according to subject.[84] Although the building work in the Hunterian Museum was complete in November 1870, it took several years to get the whole collection on display. In May 1871 the building committee was considering an estimate of £3,000 'To provide in the very simplest form cases and fittings for the Hunterian Museum', but there was still no progress by November 1871 and most of the collections remained in the attics.[85] Allen Thomson described the 1872 construction of the cases for the birds and mammals displays as 'a work of great delicacy and skill, in which able assistance was obtained from Mr James Weir and his foreman, Mr James Barr'.[86] Eleven specially designed cases 10 feet long by 5 feet 6 inches wide and 10 feet tall (approximately 3m x 1.68m x 3m), with a door and a space in the centre for access to the shelves, were assembled by Weir and Barr, glazed by the contractors for the building, C. & J. Malloch, and then painted by Andrew Wells, 'House & Church Decorator' and later co-founder of the prestigious firm of Glasgow art decorators, Guthrie & Wells.[87] These display cabinets were placed in the bays off the central space, where curtains controlled the light levels.[88] The larger skeletons and stuffed animals occupied the centre of the hall [FIG. 61]. Fifteen new 12.5 feet (3.81m) glazed 'table cases' were also constructed for the gallery, but a number of tables and cases from the old Museum were also pressed into use. The lower hall of the Museum contained smaller specimens in drawers,

63 Staircase in the south-west corner of the Gilbert Scott building

64 The vaulted ceiling of the Great South stair
GUPU [13-036-28]

such as insects, shells, minerals and fossils. Everything was re-catalogued and re-labelled by the under-keeper, John Young.[89] A system of bells and 'speaking tubes' installed by D. & G. Graham allowed the keepers and attendants to communicate between the different rooms and levels.[90] Even in 1875 the Museum curator was granted permission to employ a man for three months to assist with placing and cleaning the specimens.[91] The fitting out of the Hunterian Library also took some time to complete. Here bespoke bookcases to house 14,000 volumes were constructed around the walls, and free-standing book tables and display cabinets positioned in the centre of the room, along with the marble statutes of James Watt and Adam Smith and the collection of busts. The larger paintings from the collection were hung on the walls and on special stands along the middle of the room. Eventually the valuable coin collection returned from the Bank of Scotland in 1875 to be housed in new stone and iron safes.

A large number of alterations have taken place over the years, notably in the lower hall of the Library after the removal of the Library to the new Whitfield building in 1968, but the original spaces of the upper floor remain, and in the case of the Hunterian Museum the original use continues. The upper hall of the Museum underwent a major refurbishment in 2007 and the entrance hall in 2011. The Kelvin Gallery was refurbished and lighting/sound gantries and acoustic sails added in 1999–2001 by MkW Design Partnership. As part of the project Christian Shaw designed stained and painted glass roundels for the west gable, which are inspired by biological and electrical microscopic imagery. MkW was also responsible for the refubishment of the Hunter Halls. The most recent work in the subdivided lower Library hall was the formation of a Postgraduate Study Centre (now occupied by part of the Adam Smith Business School) by Page\Park in 2006–08. The Gilchrist Postgraduate Club in the basement was designed by ECD Architects in 2012.

GREAT SOUTH STAIR

Located to the right of the tower, entering from the south front, the Great South stair is a grand vaulted hall leading up to the old Court and Senate Rooms. Such was the state of the University's finances that even this imposing public space remained in its raw plaster condition until the summer works programme of 1873.[92] The Veitch and Sandford Memorials in their Renaissance frames were designed and added by John Oldrid Scott in 1896.[93]

COURT ROOM (NOW TURNBULL ROOM)

When the University relocated to Gilmorehill, the Senate was the pre-eminent decision-making body, but

65 The fireplace in the Senate Room (now the Melville Room), probably carved by James Adams in 1745. This was brought from the Forehall and installed at Gilmorehill in 1872.
GUPU [13-036-32]

66 The Veitch Memorial and its nearby partner, the Sandford Memorial, were designed by John Oldrid Scott and crafted by Robert Bridgeman of Lichfield in 1896 for the Great South stair and landing. The memorials are both in a Renaissance style and made of polished alabaster with decorative panels of 'Powell's mosaic' (painted glass tiles by James Powell & Sons) and a deep red marble inscription panel.
GUPU [13-036-25]

67 Sandford Memorial
GUPU [13-036-26]

[opposite top]

68 Practice of Medicine classroom, about 1976
GUAS [PHU 2/62]

69 Lord Kelvin teaching in his Natural Philosophy classroom in 1899
GUAS [GUSC 0209]

nevertheless the Court was provided with a small, but impressive, meeting room on the first floor of the tower. Although the room is only 7.3m square, the groin-vaulted ceiling extends to 10m high at the centre. Allen Thomson described the room as first fitted out by John Thompson in 1872:

[the room is] *fitted with presses and wainscoting constructed, as in the Senate Room, out of oak from the old College Forehall. The presses contain the Records and Documents of the University. From its construction, the room may be considered as almost completely fireproof.*[94]

In spite of its undoubted aesthetic qualities, the room appears to have presented long-term difficulties of heating, acoustics, lighting and comfort, as there have been numerous attempts to remodel and refurnish it over the years. John Oldrid Scott designed a suite of walnut table and chairs to complement the Gothic style of his father's creation.[95] In 1902 John Burnet & Son remodelled the entrance into a set of double doors, probably in an attempt to reduce noise from the corridor outside. The locomotive builder and steel manufacturer, Sir William Lorimer, made a bequest to the University, which was used to remodel and redecorate the room in 1933. T. Harold Hughes prepared two plans for this project: Scheme A, as executed, involved a relatively minor replacement of Gilbert Scott's fireplace (which was relocated to the College Club below the Chapel), the addition of new panelling over the fireplace, and some other repair and reconfiguration of the existing panelling; Scheme B was a much more radical proposal to reduce the height of the ceiling and classicise the room with round-arched windows.[96]

In 1969 an ugly gridded lowered ceiling and lighting rig designed by Ivor Dorward of J.L. Gleave & Partners was introduced.[97] This in turn was removed when MkW Design Partnership refurbished the room in 1991.

[above]

70 The Humanity classroom, endowed by the widow of William Ramsay, is the only large teaching room to survive in its original state. Ramsay's legacy enabled a higher level of decoration and ornamentation than in the other classrooms. As an Arts lecture theatre, the rake of the seats is shallow, and the professor's platform and desk are raised.
GUPU [13–036]

71 William Lang and J. Stanley Muir working in what was probably the private Chemistry laboratory off the main Abbot's Kitchen laboratory in March 1894
GUAS [PHU 80/54]

SENATE ROOM (NOW MELVILLE ROOM)

The Senate Room is a much larger, rectangular-plan room, to the west of the Court Room. Like its neighbour, it was fitted up by John Thompson in 1872 and incorporates elements from the High Street site. He noted that '[the] Senate Room [is] fitted up with wainscot lining made from the oak of the old College Forehall, in which the carving over the fireplace forms a conspicuous part'.[98] The fireplace and overmantle are probably those carved by James Adams in 1745 [FIG.65].[99] The oak panelling in the rest of the room has a consistency of colour, texture and tightness of jointing that is unlike the old oak panels in the Turnbull Room, suggesting, perhaps, that it has been re-cut or significantly repaired or replaced at some point.

CLASSROOMS (LECTURE THEATRES)

Although Allen Thomson admitted that the fitting out of the classrooms, with the exception of the Latin classroom, had been 'of the readiest and cheapest materials which could be obtained, and many of the materials have been brought out of the old College', the design of the rooms had been very carefully thought through: 'In all class rooms, however, the principle of a gradually increasing elevation has been followed, so as to give each successive tier of the audience an equally clear view of the Professor's table, and thus avoiding the disadvantages attending the old system of equal rises.'[100] The classrooms seated between 100 and 320 people, with an allocated area of 3¾ square feet per student. All classrooms were lit from both sides, or from two adjacent sides in the corner blocks, leaving a blank wall for blackboards behind the professors. The design of the seating and professor's platform and bench varied according to subject: scientific and medical classrooms had steeply raked seating and a low platform and bench to enable students to get an elevated view of demonstrations; arts classrooms had less steeply raked seating and the professors' platforms/benches were higher so as to place them above or on a level with their audience [FIG.68]. The classrooms were fitted out to a standard design of long and curving tiers of fixed wooden benches with angled writing desks, similar to church pews. At the front of the theatre was either a desk or a demonstration bench mounted on a podium. Usually there was a doorway from the relevant professor's office on one side of the podium. Students entered either from anterooms at the front or directly off the staircases from the rear. The desks had blind Gothic arches in the sides. The largest theatres had a central stair in addition to the standard side stairs. A committee on small classroom furnishings controlled additional purchases.[101] Not all the rooms worked perfectly at first: there were complaints about heating and ventilation generally, and an echo in the English classroom. Initially few of the rooms were painted. When painting did take place, it appears to have been of a utilitarian nature: remnants of the paint scheme in the Natural Philosophy classroom suggest an olive green dado with a cream colour above.[102] Perhaps the two most significant classrooms were those dedicated to Humanity (Latin) and Natural Philosophy. In the first of these, and in recognition of the generous benefaction of the widow of the late Professor of Humanity, William Ramsay, an oriel window was added to the design to commemorate Ramsay, and the room was fitted out in a more luxurious style, with granite columns, carved stone capitals, panelled timber dado and decorative platform railing [FIG.70]. This room remains as the only classroom in its original configuration. In the second case, special consideration was given to the needs of Sir William Thomson, later Lord Kelvin. By the 1860s he was the University's undoubted star academic as Professor of Natural Philosophy, and internationally pre-eminent in many fields of early modern physics and engineering such as electricity and thermodynamics. Although the financial circumstances were extremely tight, he was given an unusually generous suite of rooms to the left (west) of the tower in the South Range. The laboratory was located on the ground floor, linked via a stair to the apparatus room and classroom above. The classroom had an especially wide platform for illustrating experiments and ample lighting from an oriel window and a large octagonal cupola some 40 feet above the platform (for experiments requiring height).[103] The laboratory and classroom became some of the earliest teaching rooms in the world to be lit by electricity in 1881 [FIG.69].[104] The process of adapting and changing the classrooms in the Gilbert Scott building for the modern era began in earnest after the Second World War. The architectural firm of John Keppie, Henderson & J.L. Gleave was particularly active in the 1950s, carrying out alterations for the departments of Mathematics, History, Political Economy, and Geography and Geology.[105] In 1953 the sculptor Hew Lorimer designed a memorial to James Dalrymple, Viscount Stair (1619–95), who set out the foundations of modern Scots law in his *The Institutions of the Law of Scotland* (1681).[106] The memorial, now located in the lobby at the foot of the Great South Stair, was first unveiled in the Scots Law classroom by Lord Cooper, the Lord President of the Court of Session on 29 June 1953.

A number of the lecture theatres survived into the 1960s and 70s with very few alterations, apart from larger blackboards or the addition of projector boxes in the centre of the student seating. Since that period there have been significant changes to all the major classrooms apart from Humanity. Ivor Dorward of J.L. Gleave & Partners converted Kelvin's Natural Philosophy apparatus room and classroom into the Carnegie and Senate Rooms in a major project funded by the Carnegie Trust in 1966–69.[107] John Cochrane & Co., the specialist joiners responsible for the woodwork in the Chapel, carried out the timber acoustic grids, panelling and fixed furniture.[108] The Carnegie and Senate Rooms were again stripped back to a shell and refurbished as the Senate Suite in 2010 by MkW Design Partnership with consultants New Acoustics.

PROFESSORS' SQUARE (NOW 'THE SQUARE')

As with all matters relating to the professors' accommodation, there were endless discussions and disagreements about the location, number, size, finishing and allocation of the new houses [FIG.73]. Instead of expanding the professorial accommodation to house all the professors, the decision was taken to limit the housing to the same number of houses at Professors' Court in the High Street: 'It is contemplated to build thirteen houses for the Principal and Professors, and the Architect is required to lay out his plan in such a manner as may admit of others being built on the ground. Each house, excepting the Principal's to contain not less than 64,000 cubic feet – The Principal's not less than 80,000 cubic feet ... It is contemplated also to build three houses of four apartments and kitchen each for Janitor, Chamberlains and Museum Keeper and a lodge for the Gardener.'[109] Scott's initial layout for the professors' houses placed them in two blocks on the north side of the main building along what is now University Avenue. A gap in the terraces was intended to allow views of the new buildings. However, in order to obtain sufficient space for the houses, the College buildings needed to be moved further south. The site survey indicated that this was impractical, so eventually in March 1866 Scott determined the layout of the houses on the west side of the main building at an estimated cost of £24,000.[110]

72 The professors leave the Old College for the last time, led by Bedellus Lauchlan Macpherson (carrying the University mace) and Principal Thomas Barclay (with the long beard), on 29 July 1870. Apart from being ceremonial bearer of the mace, the Bedellus played an important role in maintaining the University buildings, attending to the heating, and being 'in perpetual and watchful attendance at the College Gate, day and night'. GUAS [UP 9/5/1]

73 Professors' Square, 1890s GUAS [PHU 3/3]

The building committee and professors subjected the detailed designs to particular scrutiny. The first scheme, at £2,700 per house, was deemed too expensive, so Scott prepared a second, more pared-back, design.[111] One of the difficulties of reducing cost still further was the need to have dressed stone on both the front and back of the buildings because of their location. The four houses in the northern terrace and the six houses in the western terrace were all designed to the same generous 3-bay specification. The larger and more elaborate pair of houses on the south side of the square were allocated to the Principal (no.12) and Professor of Divinity (no.13).

A contract for the houses, separate from the main building contract was drawn up between the Senate and John Thompson in November 1868, by which time the costs were £30,200.[112] The agreement also required the separate approval of the Lord Advocate under the provisions of the City of Glasgow Union Railway Act of 1864. The Senate finally signed the contract on 10 February 1869 and work began immediately.[113] The specifications are interesting for the variety of stone and wood used for different functions in a standard late 19th-century house. All rubble and interior stone was to be be sourced from Gilmorehill, dressed stone was to be Giffnock, external steps and landings and internal hearths were Arbroath, and the basement floors to be of Caithness stone. Scott was to select the carver for decorative work. The wood was to be the best seasoned Memel (Klaipeda, Lithuania), Riga or Danzig fir, American red deal, and English oak, free of sap and knots. The mouldings were to be of 'Gothic' character. The front windows were specified to be of large square plate glass, and the remaining windows of 21oz sheet glass.

The north and west blocks of the professors' houses were roofed and the Principal's Lodging was at ground floor level by November 1869.[114] The Principal's Lodging was delayed to allow continued use of the temporary railway from the quarry to the main building. Apart from the Principal's Lodging and the Professor of Divinity's house, the terraces were completed as promised in summer 1870. The houses were allocated to professors with accommodation rights, allowing the most senior by appointment date to choose their house. The professors were responsible for furnishing their own houses, except for the Principal, whose house had £300 of furniture provided by the University.

Although 11 The Square looks just like the other houses on the outside, it occupies a unique place in the history of domestic architecture as probably the first house in the world to be entirely lit by electricity. On 22 December 1881 its occupant, Sir William Thomson, wrote to his friend Dr John Hall Gladstone in London:

I am on the point of beginning to light my laboratory, lecture-room, and house with Swan and Edison lamps. As an auxiliary for night lights and dark winter mornings, I shall have about 130 cells (round) of the Faure battery, on the original pattern, which I made here last June and July. Many of them are bad, but on the whole I expect they will give the result I require, although not with perfect economy. I have got my house completely wired from attic to cellar, and I mean to have no gas and no candles. The gas-engine I am going to use will be in my laboratory ...'[115]

Large numbers of changes to all the houses have taken place over the years, particularly as they have been adapted from domestic to departmental or administrative use. In the post-war years the houses were menaced with demolition to accommodate more departmental buildings, but other sites emerged and the threat passed. Perhaps the biggest change to the Principal's Lodging occurred in 1962 when W.N.W. Ramsay reconfigured numbers 12 and 13 and created a new doorway facing The Square.[116] The Principal's Lodging alone remains in part-residential use, but the larger part of the house is given over to hospitality and corporate events.

REMOVAL, NOVEMBER 1870

The theft of an elephant tusk from the old Hunterian Museum on 5 December 1869 galvanised the Museum sub-committee into considering the security of the Hunterian collections, particularly the valuable coin collection, during the removal to Gilmorehill. Eight specially constructed iron cases containing the trays of Hunterian coins and some precious stones were riveted shut and deposited in the vault of the Bank of Scotland for the duration of the move. Although the new Museum was incomplete, the old Museum was the first building required for demolition by the railway company, so the Hunterian collections were moved for storage in the attics at the eastern end of the building at Gilmorehill from March to May 1870.[117] A watercolour by Jemima Blackburn, a popular illustrator and wife of the Professor of Mathematics, Hugh Blackburn, depicts the loading of carts bearing stuffed polar bears, lions, tigers, giraffes and other exotic animals before they set out on their bizarre cavalcade through the streets of Glasgow [FIG.74]. In March 1870 preparations began for winding down the borrowing of books from the Library.[118] The six-week process of transferring more than 100,000 volumes to the new building took place in the autumn of the same year. Remarkably, no damage was reported to either the Museum or Library collections.

The 1869–70 session closed on 29 April 1870, when the students met in the Common Hall of Old College for the last time. The Principal and professors continued to occupy Old College until 29 July 1870 [FIG.72]. The inauguration of the new buildings was marked on Monday 7 November with a general congregation of the University in the lower hall of the Hunterian Museum. Finally, on the night of Wednesday 9 November, the students celebrated the move to Gilmorehill by holding a torchlight procession:

They assembled at eight o'clock in the grounds of the old College behind the Museum, lighted their torches, sang 'For Auld Lang Syne' and then moved off in orderly procession by way of High Street, George Street, Buchanan Street, Sauchiehall Street, St George's Road, Woodlands Road and Gibson Street to Gilmorehill. Glasgow had been enveloped in fog for several days, but this had disappeared and the night was good.

Many spectators lined the route, and large numbers assembled in front of the Old College buildings. The procession was headed by a piper who played popular airs in which the students joined. A large crowd, in which the hooligan element was predominant, followed the procession and, although they were very provocative, the good sense of the students and the presence of a large body of police prevented any actual conflict taking place. The boundary of the city terminated at the Kelvin and the police force proceded no further. On reaching Gilmorehill, the students endeavoured to prevent the crowds from entering the College precincts, but were not successful. The procession moved up the hill to the eastern end of the new building where the present embankments were then in course of formation. Here the great assemblage of spectators which had already gathered loudly cheered the procession as it filed in. A circle was formed, and a bonfire started by throwing the torches into a heap in the middle. Meanwhile the noisy crowd which had followed the procession began to press upon and jostle the students and some fierce encounters occurred. The students fought to keep the crowd back, but the roughs were too numerous. A number of them went to the workmen's sheds and tearing down planks and laying hold of other timber threw all upon the bonfire. They also hurled planks and other missiles at the spectators and at the students.[119]

74 Watercolour by Jemima Blackburn showing the removal of the animal specimens from the old Hunterian Museum in the High Street in 1870

GUHMAG. By kind permission of Alan Blackburn and family

75 The first phase of building completed at Gilmorehill, photographed in 1872. The western side of the University quadrangles remained open to Professors' Square, and neither the Bute Hall nor the spire were started. Gilmorehill House had just been demolished, the lawns planted and fenced, but the old Forehall doorway from the High Street had not yet been re-erected.
GUAS [PHU 11/12A]

FACTS AND FIGURES

The figures assembled by Allen Thomson at the end of the first phase of the Gilbert Scott building make impressive reading [FIG.75].[120] The new building comprised 5.8 million cubic feet (164,238m^2), almost four-and-a-half times the size of the Old College. One million cubic feet (28,317m^2) of stone were extracted from Gilmorehill quarry and 235,000 cubic feet (6,654m^2) from other quarries, 1.9 million bricks were used, 94,000 tons of heavy materials moved, and 29,200 square yards (6 acres/2.4 hectares) of flooring laid. The North and South Ranges extended 540 feet (165m) in length and the East Range, 186 feet (57m). The two quadrangles were 180 square feet (16.2m^2). Room heights were 21 feet (6.4m) at ground floor, 29 feet (8.8m) at first floor, 35 feet (10.7m) at second floor (to the open roofs), and 10 feet (3m) in the attics. There were 25 classrooms and associated professors' rooms and 30 other teaching spaces, as compared to just 15 classroooms and 16 other teaching rooms in the Old College. An estimated 1,876 gas burners were installed, over 200 locks fitted by Charles Smith & Son, more than 3,100 feet (945m) of copper wire rope attached to the building as part of the lightning conductor system, and the display area under glass in the Museum was about 4,200 square feet (390m^2).

The total cost of the project in 1877, including the land purchases, was estimated at £427,856, of which the larger ticket items of construction were as follows: the 25 classrooms at £95,000; the Museum and Library at about £36,000 each; the Hunterian Library and the Student Reading Room below it at £21,000; the tower/administration block at £32,000 and the stairs and corridors at £30,000.[121] George Gilbert Scott's account for the first phase of works, including designs for unexecuted work such as the tower and central hall, amounted to £16,491.[122]

Welcome to the
UNTERIAN MUSEUM

Chapter Five

Completing the Gothic Campus 1870–1890

76 The Grand Staircase in the Randolph Buildings

The period from 1870 to 1890 was taken up with finishing George Gilbert Scott's great citadel of learning. The lack of finance and the great rush in which the first phase of the project had been undertaken left a large legacy of problems. At the same time, fundamental changes of approach in teaching and research, particularly in science, were beginning to manifest themselves in new university buildings around the world. Scott's creation, which had its origins in a scheme of the 1840s, was beginning to look outdated before it was even complete. Development of new subject areas and specialisms was constrained by the lack of space. Between 1870 and 1887 student numbers rose from 1,279 to 2,188, after which they remained relatively stable until 1904. These increased student numbers and the greater social and welfare expectations also put pressure on the facilities at Gilmorehill.[1] Students began to organise representative bodies and lobby for improved amenities in this period. The Glasgow University Athletics Club was founded on 20 April 1881 as the first organisation representing the student body as a whole.[2] The Union followed four years later, and the Student Representative Council a further year after that.

Beyond the campus, the city of Glasgow experienced difficulties too. The massive industrial, shipping and commercial expansion continued apace, but there was a significant setback, especially in the building sector, following the crash of the City of Glasgow Bank in 1878. In its new bucolic location the University was now more sheltered from the terrible overcrowding, health and social issues that continued to afflict tens of thousands of people in the heart of the city.

The Gilmorehill buildings were far from complete when the University moved in. A great deal of hurried finishing work continued as the first academic year at the new site got underway. A report by the committee on servants was prepared to ensure the smooth functioning of the incomplete buildings as far as possible.[3] A number of Old College elements were removed to Gilmorehill and stored until they could be incorporated there. The Lion and Unicorn Stair and the doorpiece of the old Forehall were constructed as a gateway from Professors' Square into the open side of the west quadrangle, probably in 1872, before being incorporated into the Chapel and Arts wing in the 1920s.[4] The Forehall fireplace was built into the new Senate Room (now the Melville Room) in the Gilbert Scott building, while panelling was incorporated into the Court Room (now the Turnbull Room). The marble bust of Zachary Boyd was restored by the sculptor, John Mossman, and built over the doorway to the Hunterian Museum library.

When the money ran out and work halted completely in May 1871, the tower lacked its upper levels and the Great Hall was complete only to ground

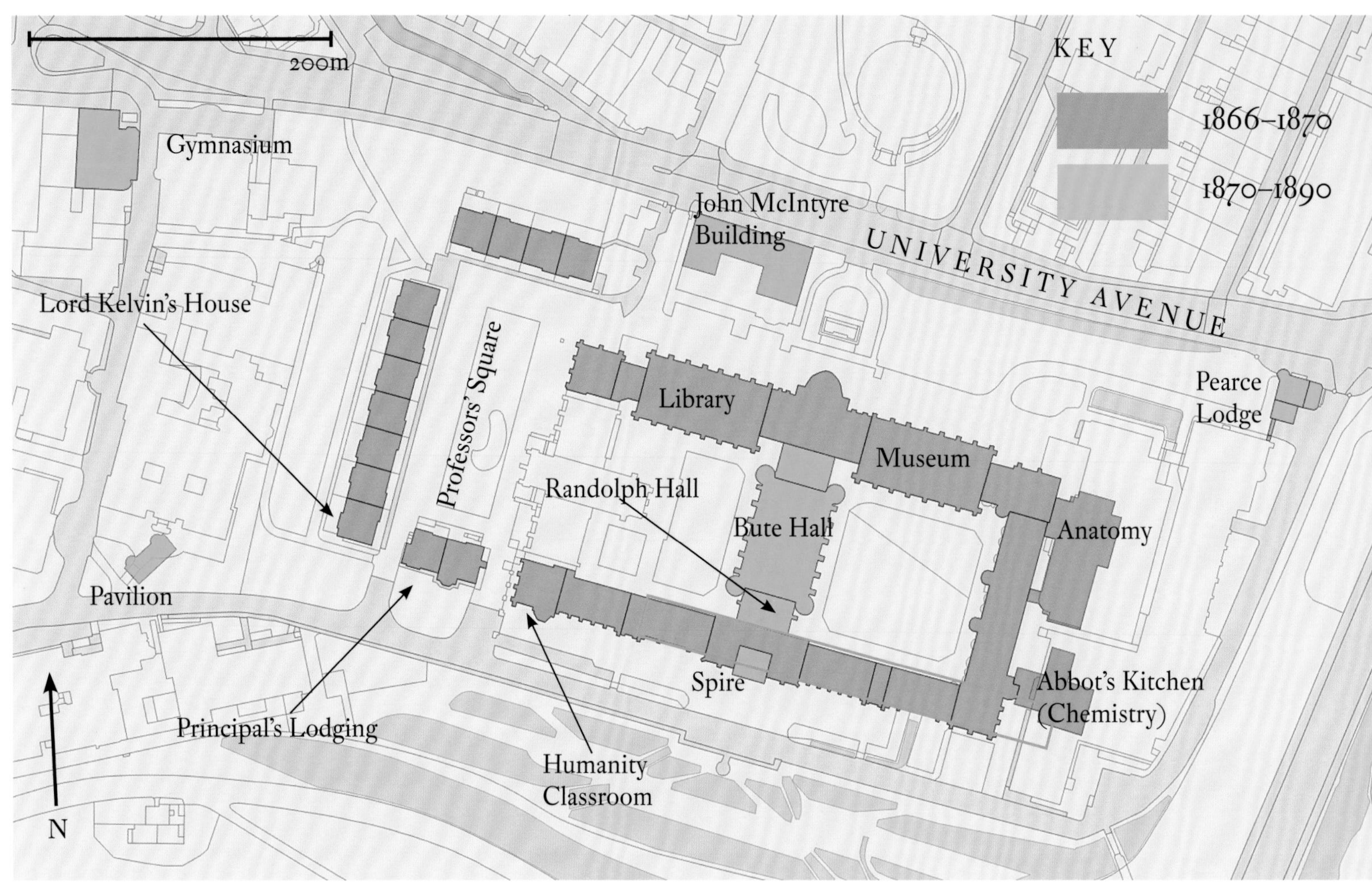

level.[5] Gilmorehill House remained, operating as a refreshment room and additional offices, until it was dismantled in the summer/autumn of 1872. With George Gilbert Scott's approval, the stones were used to build an enclosing wall along the west side of the west quadrangle, and the timber and lead were auctioned off.[6] Gradually the quadrangles were cleared of site huts and builders' debris until it was possible to sow the lawns with grass seed.

No start had been made on the associated hospital when the University moved to Gilmorehill. The delays were a result of negotiations between the University and the Town Council over its location. Initially, it had been intended for the Clayslaps (Kelvingrove) site, but eventually the Donaldshill site was selected. Medical students therefore had to be ferried to the Royal Infirmary in distant Castle Street by omnibus until the new Western Infirmary was opened in 1874. Much to the relief of the University authorities, a separate subscription and construction programme had been established for the hospital in 1871.[7] Various works continued on a small scale throughout the mid-1870s. Allen Thomson resigned his chairmanship of the building sub-committee in May 1877, just before major new funding arrived for the second phase of building, which included the Great Hall, Undercroft and principal staircase. The third and final tranche of money needed to complete Gilbert Scott's scheme in modified form was bequeathed for construction of the spire in 1886.

FATE OF THE OLD COLLEGE BUILDINGS

As the removal from Old College was taking place, the Union Railway's agents noticed that items were being 'wrongfully and illegally removed' from seven of the professors' houses, reducing them to a state of 'perfect dilapidation'.[8] The agreement between the College and the railway company allowed for the removal of fittings and furnishings, but not fixtures. Missing items included mantelpieces, press doors, baths and taps, a kitchen range, and in one case the whole plumbing system. Embarrassingly, several Professors appeared to have instructed the removals and sold the items for personal profit. The matter was resolved amicably by reminding the railway company of items that the College were entitled to remove, but were leaving in situ, such as the benches.

Not all the buildings on the High Street site were demolished immediately on relocation of the University to Gilmorehill in 1870. In spite of a proposal by the sculptor John Mossman to move the Hunterian Museum stone-by-stone to the new Queen's Park, it was the first building to be demolished on the transfer of

77 Development of Gilmorehill between 1870 and 1890.

its ownership to the North British Railway Company in July 1870. The Library, Hamilton building and Professors' Court followed soon after. The Senate received notification that the tower and 'certain of the Old College Buildings' were about to be taken down in November 1871 and arranged for careful removal of the carved and inscribed stones.[9] Parts of the Inner and Outer Closes survived a little longer in use for small businesses, including a brewery, and the High Street range was converted to house part of the new High Street railway station. The interred remains from the College's burial plots at Blackfriars' Kirk were removed to the Necropolis in 1878.[10] There was some hope that the range fronting the High Street might be spared, or even moved to Gilmorehill. The architect John James Stevenson was a notable campaigner for salvage of the Forehall and clock tower:

It is to be regretted that within the last few years these most interesting buildings have been destroyed. The progress of the city westwards made the site unsuitable, and it was sold for a railway station. But I thought at the time and endeavoured, ineffectually, to persuade others that, the removal of the college being decided on, it would not be impossible to remove the Fore Hall, with its staircase and cloisters and its noble front to the High Street, to the new site. I was informed, however, that the college authorities were advised that the architecture of the building was of a degraded character. The destruction of the tower, which was one of the land-marks of the city, seems needless. Railway stations need a clock-tower, and a little ingenuity could have made it a part of a new building.[11]

Hopes of a substantial rescue were finally dashed in 1887 by expansion of the North British Railway station complex, when all the remaining structures were flattened.

SURVIVING FRAGMENTS AND RECORDS OF THE HIGH STREET COMPLEX

Some of the more decorative stones from the High Street complex were incorporated into the Pearce Lodge at Gilmorehill. Other fragments, such as a 1656 dormerhead, a wooden panel, the movement of the College clock and part of a window sash, also survive in the Hunterian Museum collections. Various admirers of Old College removed still further decorative elements as mementos. Dormerheads appear to have been salvaged by Sir John Watson for re-use on estate buildings at Earnock near Hamilton.[12] One of the dormerheads from the 1650s building phase now forms the pediment to the Earnock Covenanters' Memorial in Hamilton parish kirkyard. A gateway also survives at North Biggar Road, Airdrie. Sir Michael Connal, the nephew of John Mossman, arranged for fragments of the Hunterian Museum frieze to be taken to his Stirlingshire house, where they still remain.[13] The decorative carved bucranium, or ox's head, which adorned the main entrance to the Hunterian Museum ended up in Campbeltown Museum, and has recently been presented back to the University [FIG.28]. Apart from the physical remains of the Old College, a number of drawn and photographic records were made. The University itself commissioned Annan's photographs, which were published as *Memorials of the Old College of Glasgow* in 1876. Several architects, including James Wylson, David MacGibbon, Thomas Ross, William Shanks, and Charles Rennie Mackintosh, made measured or sketched records at various times.

Although not using original materials from Old College, Robert Rowand Anderson's Pollokshaws Burgh Hall, completed for the benefactor (and son of the former Chancellor of the University) Sir John Stirling-Maxwell in 1897, was designed as a homage to the lost complex, incorporating strapwork dormerheads, crowstepped gables and a tower with a swept lead roof.

The High Street site of the Old College was investigated in 1984. The construction of the station basement in 1878 had obliterated evidence of previous structures from much of the site, but stone foundations of 17th- and 18th-century backlands buildings, pottery fragments

78 Pencil drawing of one of the Old College doorways by Charles Rennie Mackintosh, September 1886
GUHMAG [GLAHA 41425]

79 First sketch by Sir George Gilbert Scott of the exterior of the Common Hall in 1865. The building was later named the Bute Hall. The form of the building, as a medieval cloth hal[l] remained constant through its 1[3] year gestation period, but some details, such as the flèche (spire) roof ventilator, were dropped from the final scheme.
GUAS [GUA 2210]

80 Sketch by Sir George Gilber[t] Scott of the interior of the Common Hall in 1865
GUAS [GUA 2210]

and cess and rubbish pits survived to the south-west of where the College complex had been.[14]

BUTE HALL, RANDOLPH HALL, GRAND STAIRCASE AND UNDERCROFT 1865–1884

The wooing of John Crichton-Stuart, 3rd Marquess of Bute, for a contribution to the building fund began in 1868 during the preparations for the foundation stone ceremony. James Allen Campbell, chairman of the General Council's subscriptions committee wrote to Allen Thomson urging University representatives to attend an address by Sir James Fergusson of Kilkerran to the Young Men's Christian Association: 'our hopes of making a friend of Lord Bute depend very much on Sir James [his former guardian] on which account it would be good policy to begin with him'.[15] In the previous month, September 1868, Bute had turned twenty-one, the age of his majority, when he inherited a vast fortune based on land, coal and industry. He was a noted scholar, writer, bibliophile, traveller, philanthropist, and patron of art and architecture, with a passion for Gothic. The relationship with Bute took some time to cultivate, but in 1877 it finally resulted in an offer of £45,000 towards the construction of a common hall on condition that the University raise a further £25,000.[16] A Bute Hall committee was formed and convened by Hugh Blackburn, Professor of Mathematics.

Sketch proposals of the Common Hall had been made at the outset of the first phase of the project in 1865, followed by more detailed drawings in preparation for a start on the foundations in 1869 [FIG.79]. From the watermarks on drawings in the RIBA collection, it would appear that work continued on a third revision of the Common Hall drawings in 1870.[17] The next known watermarks are 'Whatman 1876', which are likely to relate to the fourth revision of the design, and were probably started as soon as Lord Bute announced his gift in the second half of 1877.[18] John Thompson signed this set of drawings and specifications in relation to his estimates on 25 March 1878.[19] However, disaster struck just two days later when Sir George Gilbert Scott died, aged sixty-six, after a short illness. He was buried in Westminster Abbey on 6 April next to Sir Charles Barry and beside the great nave pulpit of his own design.[20] There was certainly some feeling within the family that a deputation from Glasgow regarding the Bute Hall project had hastened the great man's demise. As George Gilbert Scott Jr wrote at the time:

On this day [Tuesday 19 March 1878] he kept his bed, but on the Monday he got up and had an interview in his study with two members of Glasgow University on the subject of the Bute Hall. He had acted against medical advice in leaving his bed while suffering as he was from the veins in his leg; and now, instead of returning to it, he decided to sit down to lunch with Dr. Allan [sic] Thomson and his companion. To his man, who ventured a remonstrance, he said, 'I feel perfectly well; why should I be mewed up here? I shall enjoy lunching with them, and it will do me good.'

There is reason to fear that this imprudence cost him his life, the exertion bringing about that disaster against which his medical advisers had distinctly warned him, the detachment of a blood-clot from the inflamed vein, and its passage into the circulation, and eventually to the heart. Still, although, as his man expresses it, 'done up', he was in good spirits.[21]

[opposite]

81 Contract drawing showing a coloured part-elevation of the Bute Hall. The drawing was signed by John Thompson and witnessed by George Wood for the Scott practice on 6 May 187[8]. The Principal and the Marquess of Bute added their signatures o[n] 10 May 1878.
GUAS [BUL 6/4/9]

82 Detail of the projected flèche that was dropped from the final scheme
GUAS [BUL 6/1/37]

83 Cross-section of an early scheme for the Common Hall, about 1870
GUAS [BUL 6/1/38]

Half Elevation of Great Hall
1/4 Scale
The portion of this Drawing within the Red lines
is that referr'd to in the accompanying spec-
-ification and my estimate dated Mar 25/78
John Thompson
43 Wood Street
Peterborough
May 6 1878
Half Elevation of Great Hall

Archives Services 00004398

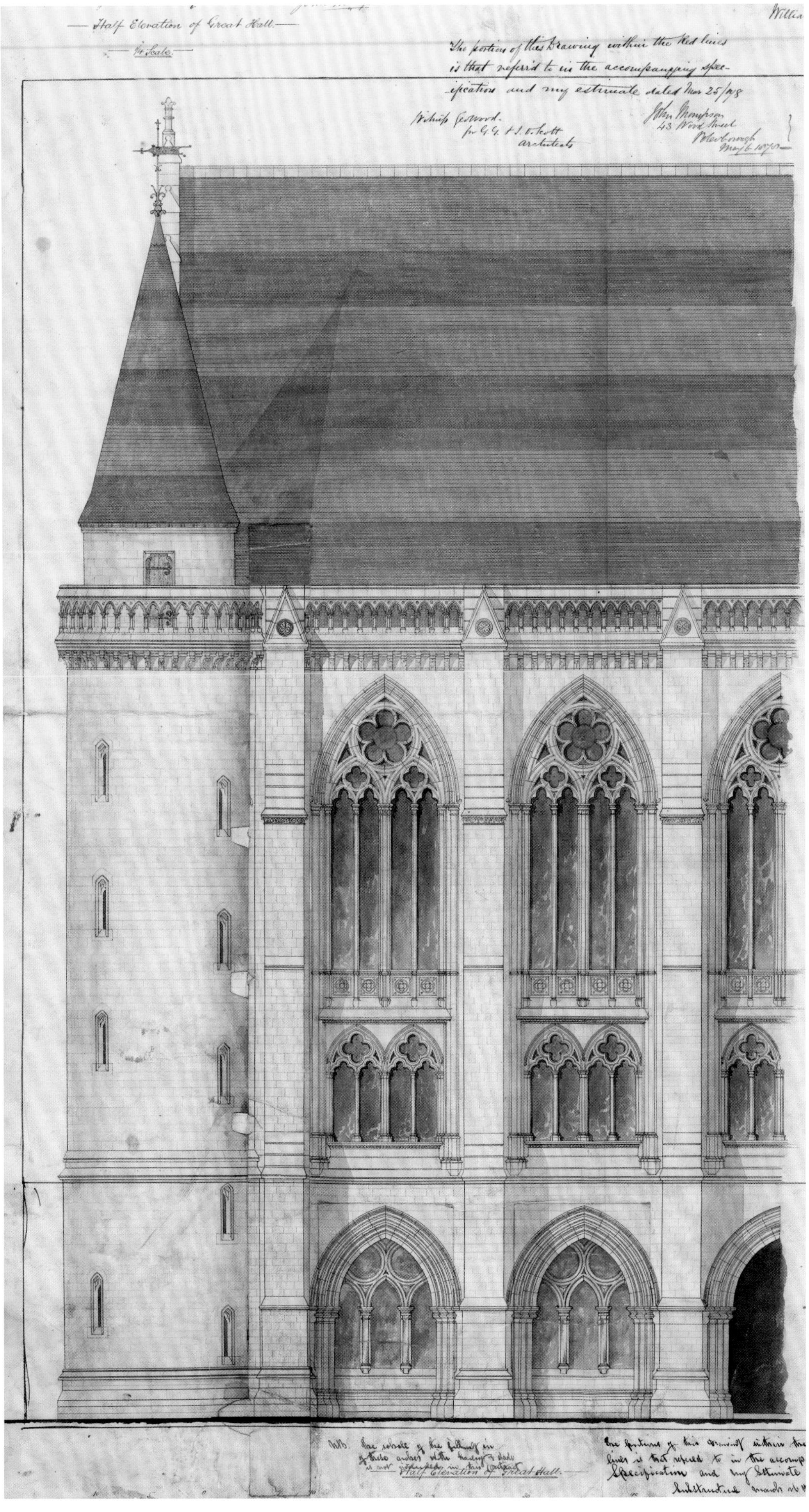

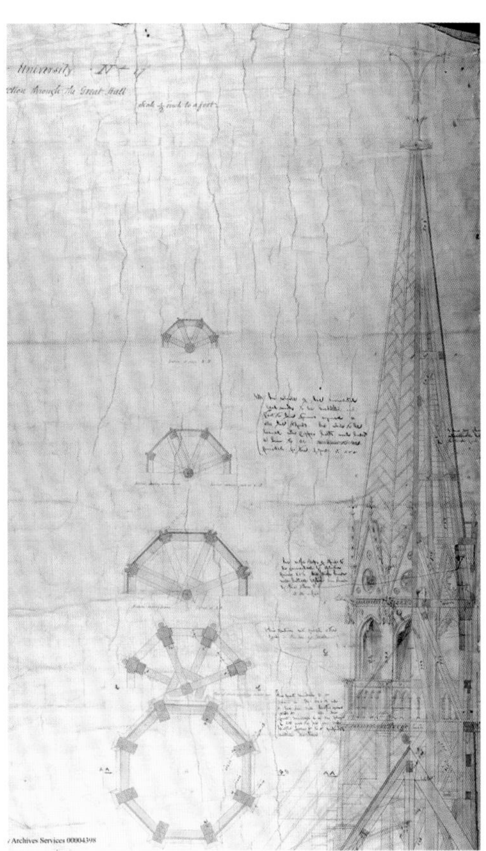

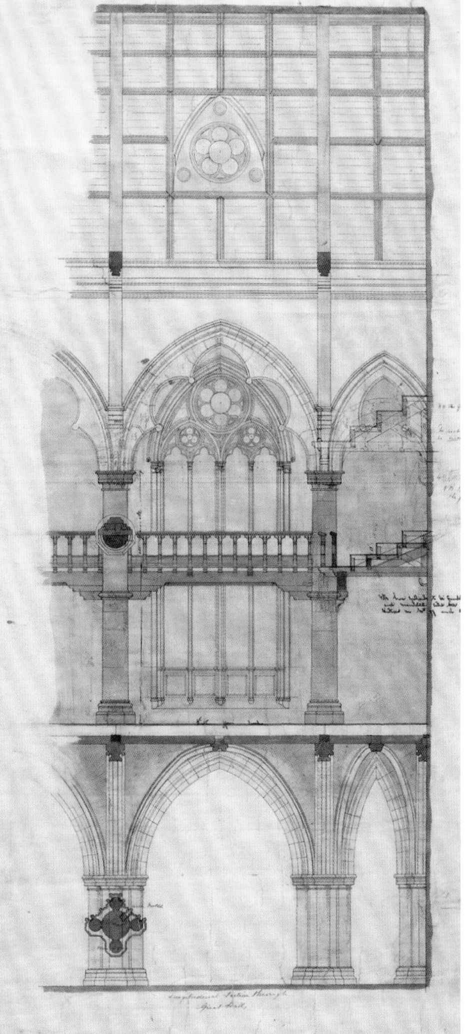

Scott's unexpected death plunged his enormous architectural practice into a state of confusion. His sons, George Gilbert Scott Jr and John Oldrid Scott, took over, but even seven years later there was uncertainty about what payments had been made to Sir George by the University.[22] Although both sons inherited the business, John Oldrid Scott took the lead on the Bute Hall contract, which was at an advanced stage by then. He appears to have been assisted on the Bute Hall project by George Wood, who acted as Clerk of Works for most of its construction, and who also signed some of the contract drawings on behalf of George Gilbert Scott Jr and John Oldrid Scott.[23] Late in the contract Edwin Morgan took over as Clerk of Works.

Lord Bute signed a minute of agreement with the University on 10 May 1878 [FIG. 81], setting out his requirements: the University should meet the whole cost of the substructure (Undercroft); the hall should be named the 'Bute Hall'; the building should be constructed for £44,748 (including architects' and clerk of works' fees, but excluding heating, decorating, lighting and seating) to the plans of the late Sir George Gilbert Scott and under the superintendence of George Gilbert Scott Jr and John Oldrid Scott; John Thompson of Peterborough should construct the building; the whole project should be completed within five years; and the Senate should maintain and uphold the Bute Hall 'in good and sufficient repair in all time coming'.[24]

An even larger sum, £60,000, was left to the University in November 1878 on the death of Charles Randolph, the founder of the Fairfield Shipbuilding & Engineering Company.[25] This second benefaction allowed the University to proceed with confidence on the most magnificent part of Gilbert Scott's scheme. The new 'Randolph Buildings' were intended to provide important circulation and functional spaces in a central south-north spine between the two quadrangles. Broad open cloisters at the ground floor, allowed staff and students to cross the quadrangles under cover for the first time, even if they were not protected from the cold and wind. They also served as somewhere for students to shelter between classes. The floor above contained the spectacular ceremonial rooms of the Randolph and Bute Halls. These completed the missing links in a grand processional route from the main south entrance gate and principal stair to the Library and Hunterian Museum in the north range. At the northern end of the Undercroft a new and sumptuous staircase finally connected the lower halls of the Museum and Library to their upper halls [FIG. 76].

In order to ensure that the conditions of the agreement with the Marquis Bute were met, a separate contract was let with John Thompson for the Bute Hall and substructure, and within that, separate accounting took place for work on the substructure and work on the hall.[26] John Oldrid Scott completely redesigned the Randolph Hall and Grand Staircase after his father's death, and further contracts were entered for the these parts of the complex in 1881. Once again, Wilson Weatherley Phipson was contracted to supply the heating and ventilation. The contracts provided for best white Giffnock stone for all the dressed stonework, Bannockburn stone for the 'plinths, strings and weatherings' of the buttresses, Chapelhall stone for the steps and landings, and unspecified local stone for the non-visible walling.[27] The opening of the buildings was celebrated formally by a *conversazione*, held by the Principal and Professors on 1 February 1884.[28]

84 Details of the chevron patte[rn] on the Randolph Hall ceiling
GUPU [13-036-29, 13-036-30]

RANDOLPH HALL

The University's brief to George Gilbert Scott in

1864 envisaged a reproduction of the Forehall in the Old College, which served as the Professors' reading room. George Gilbert Scott's initial proposals for the exterior of the Randolph Hall made it look like a simple link between the south range and the Common Hall. However, the arrival of Charles Randolph's legacy enabled a rather grander treatment in the final design. Huge traceried windows break through the wallheads into crowstepped gables on the east and west elevations. A further large traceried window punctures the south gable. Internally the hall is short in length, but tall with a timber vaulted roof, providing a soaring quality to the space. It is also richly decorated with parquet flooring, walnut and mahogany wainscot panelling, marble fireplaces, decorative carved stone corbels, and a vibrant painted chevron pattern between the roof timbers [FIG. 84]. Initially the walls were hung with the University's collection of professorial portraits.[29] Oldrid Scott's design for the walnut and mahogany screen between the Randolph and Bute Halls survives in the University Archives.[30] It is thought that the Randolph Hall was first lit by gas. Incandescent lamps were fitted in 1897, and Joe Gleave designed the four oak standard lamps and uplighters as part of a major redecoration and refurbishment in 1950.[31] The side windows retain their original clear leaded glazing. The Gilmorehill Centenary stained glass window in the south wall of the Randolph Hall was designed by Gordon Webster in 1970 to mark the centenary of the move from the High Street. The design comprises the forty-five heraldic arms of former Rectors of the University from the 1690s to the 1850s. Dr Charles Hepburn, an alumnus and whisky blender, presented the window.

A further major refurbishment of the Randolph Hall in 1986 removed the acoustic wall-tiles and restored its original colour scheme, based on paint analysis, and added a stenciled pattern of red fleur-de-lys to the gable wall.

BUTE HALL

The brief to George Gilbert Scott in 1864 required that 'the Public or Common Hall should accommodate in all 2,500 persons, that a floor of 8,000 square feet should be provided, and the remainder accommodated in Galleries. The platform should accommodate conveniently about 50 persons.'[32] The University's main ceremonial hall was intended to double as a chapel, but it has taken on many other roles during its existence, including an exam hall, a venue for theatre productions and a concert hall, notably hosting the great Austrian virtuoso violinist, Fritz Kreisler, in 1929.[33] Scott clearly took a great interest in the designs for the common hall at the core of his university complex. The first sketches of the interior and exterior were used to promote the project to subscribers in 1865, and it seems likely that the highly finished contract drawings for the revised scheme helped to secure the agreement of the Gothic-mad Marquis of Bute in 1878. The revisions to the scheme retained the medieval Flemish-Baronial style and casket-like shape, but as an economy measure the delicate flèche (spire), gabled dormers and elaborate painted ceiling were omitted. Oldrid Scott's input to the building after his father's death was mainly restricted to refining the interior detailing. As built, the Bute Hall is 108 feet (30m) long by 70 feet (21m) wide by 75 feet (23m) high to the top of its magnificent barrel-vaulted roof. Instead of placing the pulpit and platform against the long west wall, Oldrid Scott re-oriented the arrangement to locate the Principal's chair [FIG. 86] and platform in front of the screen to

85 Design by John Oldrid Scott for the screen between the Randolph and Bute Halls
GUAS [BUL 6/4/10]

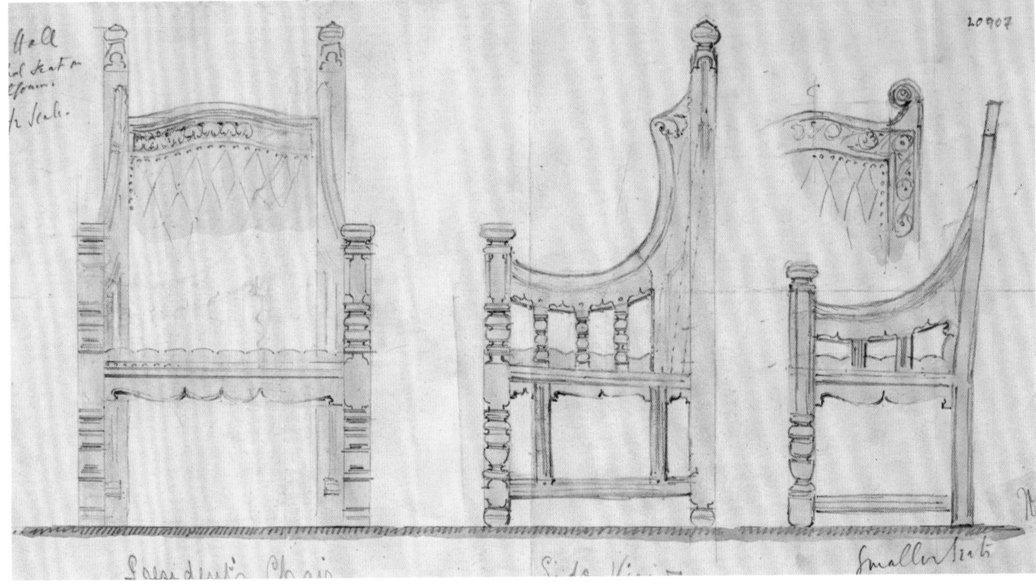

86 Design for the Principal's chair by John Oldrid Scott
GUAS [BUL 6/4/26]

the Randolph Hall. This allowed the formation narrow galleries along the length of the outer 'aisles'. The aisles are created by arcades of tall pointed arches supported by slender iron cluster columns. Empty niches adorn the spandrels between the arches. The tracery in the windows appears to be derived from the clearstory and triforium at Lincoln Cathedral.

Paint analysis in the mid 1980s established that the original paint scheme of the columns was based on the heraldic colours of the Marquis of Bute: blue (azure), red (gules), silver (argent) and gold (or). Oldrid Scott intended a painted heraldic scheme for the panelled ceiling, much reduced from his father's proposals, but this was never carried out.

Oldrid Scott designed all the furniture for the Bute Hall, including the Principal's chair, the pulpit, the professors' stalls and benches.[34] Although he also designed a magnificent organ case, it was not until 1904 that an offer to fund an instrument by Andrew Carnegie enabled the Court to commission the leading London organ builders, Lewis & Co.[35] The same firm built the Kelvingrove Art Gallery and Museum organ in 1901. Hill, Norman & Beard largely rebuilt the Bute Hall organ in 1962. A design by Scott for a gasoliers and early photographs suggest that the lighting was by gas at first, but this was augmented in 1897 by six Jandus arc lamps.[36]

When the building opened in 1884 [FIG.87], the windows were all of clear leaded glass with coloured margins. Over the years five stained glass windows have been added to further enrich the decorative scheme. The first, of 1893, a memorial in the centre of the west wall to Alexander McGrigor LLD of Cairnoch, Dean of Faculties (1876–79), was controversial because it was felt that the low colour key of the design by Sir Edward Burne-Jones and Henry Holiday interfered with the lighting of the hall.[37] However, the figurative design of the window, depicting great writers, set the pattern for later windows. Opposite, John Henry Dearle of Morris & Co. took philosophers and theologians as the theme in his 1901 memorial window to Principal Caird. Scientists and more writers pay tribute to John Pringle Nichol, Professor of Astronomy (1836–59), and his children, John Nichol, Professor of English Language (1862–89) and Agnes Jane Nichol (1837–1901), in the south-west window of 1903 by Henry Holiday.[38] Douglas Strachan designed the Janet Galloway memorial stained glass of 1914 for the window in the west wall next to the organ. Strachan was also responsible for the memorial stained glass to Principal Robert Story in the east wall nearest the Randolph Hall.

87 The earliest known photograph of the Bute Hall by James Valentine of Dundee, looking south towards the Randolph Hall, about 1884. The windows are all of clear glass, and there appear to be no light fittings.
Vivacity Peterborough Culture and Leisure [PAS/JTA/1/44]

[opposite]

88 Engraved design for the interior of the Bute Hall by John Oldrid Scott, 1878
GUAS [Accn 3659]

[below]

89 Stained glass window by Douglas Strachan in memory of Janet Galloway, 1914

THE BUTE HALL GLASGOW UNIVERSITY

90 A figure from the lower tier of the Nichol memorial window of 1903 by Henry Holiday

91 Robert Burns depicted in the upper tier of the Nichol memorial window

92 A Pre-Raphaelite figure from the McGrigor memorial window of 1893 by Sir Edward Burne-Jones and Henry Holiday

The re-wiring and supply of alternating current to the main building in 1948–50 created an opportunity for re-lighting and re-decorating Bute Hall and Randolph Hall and their respective staircases. Graham Henderson and Joe Gleave of John Keppie, Henderson and J.L. Gleave advised on the redecoration and attempted to address some of the longstanding problems with lighting and acoustics.[39] New pendant lamps were designed in the form of the head of the University's 15th-century mace and lit by an array of vertical fluorescent tubes.[40] A model was constructed and sample paint schemes tested. Acoustic tiles were applied to the ceiling and patent coatings added to the wood and stonework. The BBC were even asked to advise on a loud speaker system, but with little success in improving the acoustic quality of the room.

A grant by the predecessor body to Historic Scotland enabled a major refurbishment scheme designed for the Bute and Randolph Halls by Valtos Architects in 1984–86.[41] Extensive research identified and reinstated the original colour scheme, to which a stencilled thistle motif was added on the north gable wall and a gold fleur-de-lys motif on the columns. The project also removed the acoustic tiles, which contained asbestos.

UNDERCROFT

The Undercroft [FIG. 93], as part of the substructure of the Bute Hall, were funded by subscription and some of the Randolph legacy. Five substantial arches lead from the quadrangles into a dark and dramatic stone-vaulted space supported by four further rows of parallel columns. For many students, staff and visitors, the ancient collegiate atmosphere evoked by the Undercroft is one of their abiding memories of the Gilbert Scott building. Over the years various measures to provide more shelter from the wind have been attempted, but all with unsatisfactory visual results.[42] The McGill Memorial in the Undercroft was made by the sculptor George Herbert Tyson Smith in 1948 to celebrate the Glasgow alumnus, James McGill, whose bequest in 1821 founded the Canadian university that bears his name.[43]

GRAND STAIRCASE

The magnificent staircase hall [FIG. 75] at the north end of the Undercroft replaced the temporary stair that had served to link the lower and upper halls of the Library and Hunterian Museum. The 'dog-leg' form of the stair wraps around three sides of a generous hall and rises to a broad landing, which connects the Bute Hall to the Hunterian Museum. As its name suggests, the Grand Staircase is lavishly decorated, from its patterned 'marble mosaic' floor, decorative wrought-iron work, red and white marble stair facings and leaded windows to its coved and coffered painted timber ceiling. Like his father, John Oldrid Scott left the riveted wrought-iron beams exposed to view as part of the staircase's modern Gothic structural 'honesty'.

Undoubtedly the great glory of the Grand Staircase is the decorative wrought-iron balustrade. This extraordinary lattice with swirling foliate panels was designed by Oldrid Scott and manufactured by the leading Gothic Revival art metalworker, Francis Alfred Skidmore of Coventry.[44] Skidmore had worked extensively with George Gilbert Scott, notably on the choir screens for Hereford, Lichfield and Salisbury Cathedrals and on the Albert Memorial in London. The 14,000 elements of Skidmore's Hereford screen (removed from the cathedral in 1967) have recently been repaired and reassembled in the Victoria and Albert Museum in London.

Adjacent to the columned doorway to the Bute Hall is a bronze portrait memorial plaque to the Sir William Ramsay (1852–1916), recipient of the 1904 Nobel Prize in Chemistry, who discovered the noble gases. The plaque was designed by Sir John James Burnet and sculpted by George Henry Paulin.

THE GYMNASIUM, UNIVERSITY PLACE 1870

The first addition to the Gilmorehill complex was the Gymnasium [FIG.94], now part of the estates' department building, on the site of the old Gilmorehill House stables. A petition requesting the construction of a gymnasium had been signed by 565 students, and was considered positively by the Senate in February 1870.[45] By July plans had been obtained from Archibald MacLaren of Oxford.[46] John Thompson, the contractor for the main building, had supplied an estimate of £2,000, against which £1,600 had been raised by subscription. A further £500 was to provide a house for the superintendent. Although described as an architect in the Senate minutes, Archibald MacLaren was in fact the most famous teacher and author of physical education books of his day.[47] Born in Alloa, and educated at Dollar Academy, MacLaren went to Paris at the age of sixteen to study fencing, gymnastics and medicine.

The pioneers of modern gymnastic exercise were Friedrich Ludwig Jahn in Prussia and Per Henrik Ling in Sweden. In 1811 Jahn created the first gymnasium of the modern era, equipped with parallel and horizontal bars, and pommel and vaulting horses. Ling pursued a more scientific and medical approach to gymnastics, adapting routines to the needs of each participant. A Spanish colonel, Francisco Amoros, set up a public gymnasium in Paris in 1818 aimed at schoolchildren. His *Manuel d'éducation physique, gymnastique et morale* of 1830 promoted the 'healthy body, healthy mind'

93 The Undercroft, designed by Sir George Gilbert Scott and constructed under the supervision of his son, John Oldrid Scott in 1878–84. The ecclesiastical form of the Undercroft may be intended to evoke the University's earliest origins in the crypt of Glasgow Cathedral.
GUPU [13-036-1]

approach to education and military training that swept Europe in the 1830s and 40s.

In the 1840s MacLaren returned from Paris to Oxford, where he constructed the 'university gymnasium' on the corner of Bear Lane and Alfred Street in 1859. In addition to the usual equipment, it contained a trapeze, safety nets, climbing ropes, rope ladders, climbing-frames and dumb-bells. MacLaren published his own books, *Training in Theory and Practice* (1866) and the best-selling *A System of Physical Education, Theoretical and Practical* (1869) to promote his training regimes. MacLaren's pupils included the artists William Morris and Edward Burne-Jones. Burne-Jones drew a set of illustrations for MacLaren's *The Fairy Family: a Series of Ballads and Metrical Tales Illustrating the Fairy Mythology of Europe*, which was published in 1857.

The success of MacLaren's Oxford gymnasium was such that he was employed to design another for the army training school at Aldershot in 1861. MacLaren's system was officially approved by the army and adopted in all suitable military gymnasia. MacLaren subsequently obtained commissions to design gymnasia at a number of public schools and at least twenty-two army depots including Curragh, Dublin, Chatham, Woolwich and Sandhurst. The architectural style was generally Italianate on the exterior, with round-arched windows. Internally there was always a large central space with a padded floor. This open space could be easily supervised for safety, and it was lit by a large octagonal 'lantern' that also provided ventilation. Students were measured and assessed on enrolment and exercises modified to their ability.

According to a subscription prospectus of February 1871, 'Gymnastic exercises properly regulated do not merely increase the muscles, they brace the whole system, give force and healthy action to the vital organs, and maintain the proper equilibrium between mental and bodily exertion'.[48] In view of his ongoing role in the design of the main University buildings, George Gilbert Scott was invited to approve MacLaren's designs for the Gilmorehill Gymnasium. Scott took the opportunity to revise the elevations, which presumably involved the replacement of the original window design with Gothic designs and cast-iron glazing bars to match the main building. However, it was the architect of the adjacent hospital, John Burnet Sr, who supervised the construction in 1871–2, and the local firm Hunter & Marshall who provided the joinery.[49] The contents and form of management of the Gymnasium were described by the secretary, Walter E. Lee, in a letter to the Glasgow Herald on 29 October 1886:

The gymnasium was fitted up according to the most improved models, at a cost of £2500, and contains every appliance for safe and useful bodily exercise and training. It has been described by a Government contractor in London as a 'magnificent gymnasium, and more perfect than any about London.' There is a thoroughly competent instructor in the person of Mr Arthur Benson, under whose careful supervision there is no chance of injury from over-exertion. The fees, both for students and non-students, are the cheapest in this country for such a gymnasium.

Glasgow already had a private gymnasium, run by Messrs Foucart in West Nile Street, but it had a more medical bent, specialising in 'Preventing and Correcting Bodily Distortions'.[50] By 1886 this private gymnasium was defunct and the University Gymnasium was also struggling for both student and non-student members. The building was extended, probably by John Burnet & Son, by the addition of fives courts in May 1896.[51] A new locker room was added in 1908–9. The building continued in use until 1946, when the fives courts were demolished and the gymnasium was converted to house

94 Design for the proposed Gymnasium at the University of Glasgow, from the fund-raising prospectus of 1870
GUAS [GUA 2198]

95 The recreation ground, pavilion and tennis courts, viewed from the Western Infirmary, about 1900
GUAS [PHU 1/46]

the University workshops. Later it was altered again to form administrative offices.

SPORTS PAVILIONS, 1879, 1892 AND 1905

Access to outdoor sporting facilities at Gilmorehill took much longer to achieve. The students appear to have been allowed to use the 'College Green' to the west of Professors' Square for athletics for the first time in 1874 under the strict supervision of two of the Professors.[52] In March 1879 the Senate agreed to a petition by the newly-formed Glasgow University Association Football Club to allow them equal rights with the earlier rugby club in respect of the recreation ground. At the same time approval was given to the construction of a 40-foot (12m) by 16-foot (5m) covered shed with a small room at either end for use by the students' cricket and football clubs.[53] The central part of the shelter contained fixed seats and pegs. It was constructed of timber with a corrugated-iron roof at a cost of £150 on a site at the south-eastern corner of the recreation ground, immediately to the south of the entrance to what is now the Kelvin building.

The Glasgow University Athletic Club held an appeal in 1883, which enabled draining and levelling of the field and construction of a cinder bicycle track and tennis courts.[54] Apart from racing, cycling was enormously popular as a means of transport, so much so that the first measures to curb undesirable 'cycles standing all over the University' were taken in 1899 with the construction of a 'bicycle stable' for 24 bikes.[55] Grandstands were constructed for sporting events staged during the Glasgow International Exhibitions of 1888 and 1901, when the recreation ground formed a temporary adjunct to Kelvingrove Park. William A. Makins designed a sturdier replacement pavilion in brick on the site of the first pavilion in 1892.[56] As a legacy of the 1901 Exhibition, the cycle track was upgraded to granolithic laid on concrete with a cinder running track lining the inside.

The old pavilion [FIG. 95] was demolished when the Kelvin building was built in 1903–06, and a new cruciform pavilion designed by Duncan & Copland was provided on a site to the south of the Gymnasium.[57] In June 1909 a 15-acre site was purchased for a new recreation ground at Westerlands, Anniesland.[58] The Gilmorehill field remained in use until the construction of the Zoology building in 1922. A further ground at Garscadden was purchased in 1933. Some of the Gilmorehill tennis courts survived into the 1940s, when the extension of the Kelvin building forced their transfer to the roof of Jack Coia's new boiler house.

DUMBARTON ROAD LODGE (NOW MAGGIE'S CENTRE) AND GATEWAY 1880–81

John Burnet Sr was responsible for the design of the pair of attached gate-houses on Dumbarton Road, which was shared with the Western Infirmary.[59] The gateway to the east was also part of the design. John James Burnet worked for his father at this period, and it is possible that he contributed to the red sandstone Baronial design. David Page of Page\Park Architects converted the building with its small crenellated tower to form a Maggie's Centre for cancer care in 2001–02. The University's (eastern) part of the building was largely removed behind the frontage to create a light and bright extension with views to Kelvingrove Park and the University. The garden includes a small landform and sculpture entitled 'DNA' by Charles Jencks, husband of Maggie Keswick Jencks, after whom the centre is named.

THE SPIRE 1886–1888

At the time the building work on the new College stopped in 1871, the tower stood as high as the sixth stage, where the turrets remained without their conical roofs. Practical priorities, such as completing the Bute and Randolph Halls, took precedence over the largely aesthetic and symbolic desire to finish Scott's tower. However, two new legacies from Andrew Cunninghame, Town Clerk Depute of Glasgow, and James Marshall, a partner in Walter MacFarlane's Saracen Foundry, finally enabled the University to consider completion of the spire in November 1886. The civil engineer and architect of the Pearce Lodge, Alexander George Thomson, was quick off the mark to offer a new design.[60] The Senate declined and firmly directed that John Oldrid Scott would be in charge of completion of the tower.

As part of his commission to finish the tower, Scott was instructed to examine the structural stability of his father's work. Internal cracks had appeared in various parts of the tower during the sixteen years of its incomplete state. Oldrid Scott reassured the Senate that the cracks were caused by inevitable different rates of settlement between the massive tower and the less substantial adjoining buildings.[61] Scott considered the settlement to be complete and not a cause for concern. While the professors appear to have accepted Scott's advice, they sought further reassurance on this issue at each stage of the project.

Such was Scott's conviction about the structural stability of the tower that he substituted his father's proposal with designs for a much heavier open stone spire. Scott explained his decision in practical terms:

As regards the material for the spire, I am strongly in favour of stone rather than wood. It is more dignified in appearance and idea. It is not in danger of fire. It is more permanent – for a stone spire requires very little repairing, while one of wood, covered with lead and slates, would be continually suffering from the weather. Another point of advantage is that an open spire, such as I have roughly

Photo-Lithographed & Printed by James Akerman, 6, Queen Square,

sketched, would offer comparatively little resistance to the wind – a point of no small importance in such a position.[62]

With regard to the unusual perforated stone design [FIG.96], Scott drew his inspiration from Continental models, notably the Marienkapelle in Würzburg:

It is my intention, if the Senate approves, to make the whole Spire of open Stone-work, excepting a few feet at the apex, and a portion 6 or 7 feet high at the base. There are many noble precedents for this treatment abroad which are justly admired, as at Cologne, Antwerp, &c. Galleries projecting from the spire are also to be found at Wurtzburg and elsewhere. They are very picturesque, and in this case would prevent the Spire having anything of a Church-like look, which is, I think, undesirable.[63]

Scott appears to have submitted two alternative designs, which the Senate forwarded to the artist, Sir William Fettes Douglas, for his comments.[64] He replied in favour of the taller of the two designs. Sir William Thomson, later Lord Kelvin, was to provide the specification for the lightning conductor.[65] The Senate suggested three local contractors to Scott, but by the time the tenders arrived the ubiquitous John Thompson of Peterborough was at the top of the list. Apart from supplying the lowest tender, Thompson's contractual responsibility for both phases of the tower was considered to be an advantage. A shortage of Binny stone from West Lothian led to the use of Dunmore stone from Stirlingshire.

Work had begun on the spire when the Senate requested an estimate for a clock mechanism and bells.[66] No clock faces were to be provided, but Sir William Thomson recommended that the mechanism should be strong enough to drive the hands of a dial if one were to be added at a later date. J.B. Joyce of Whitchurch, one of the oldest clockmakers in the world, supplied the mechanism and an 'Ellacombe Chiming Apparatus', and the famous bell-founders, John Taylor & Co. of Loughborough, cast one large 57¾ cwt (2934 kilos) hour bell and two quarter-hour 'ding-dong' bells.[67] Taylor's also bought the Old College main bell, presumably for scrap.[68] A smaller class bell from Old College, made by John Meikle of Edinburgh in 1703, was installed in the Gilmorehill tower in 1880. John James Burnet prepared a design to install clock faces in 1915–16, but the University was unable to obtain the necessary wartime permit from the Ministry of Munitions, and the scheme lapsed.[69] With the completion of the tower and spire, the huge scheme of construction planned by George Gilbert Scott and John Oldrid Gilbert Scott and built by John Thompson, finally came to an end in the summer of 1888. Queen Victoria, who visited the University in August 1888, noted 'with much interest the beautiful buildings in which the noble work of your ancient and renowned University is now carried on'.[70]

96 Engraving of the stone spire, designed by John Oldrid Scott to complete his father's tower in 1886. The engraving was published in *Building News* of 6 July 1888.
GUAS [Accn 3659]

97 Photograph of the low sloping roof and half-timbered dormers of the south (rear) elevation of the Student Union in March 1892, before they were hidden by the extensions of 1907–08, when new dining and smoking rooms were added, the debating hall was enlarged and the roof ventilator re-located
Mitchell Library, Glasgow

STUDENT UNION (NOW THE JOHN MCINTYRE BUILDING), UNIVERSITY AVENUE 1885–1886

As quickly became evident when the University transferred to Gilmorehill, very little thought had been given to amenities for staff or students in the planning of the new buildings. The Gymnasium and playing field provided for the physical exercise of the male students, but basic provisions like toilets, catering and meeting rooms for societies were woefully underestimated. Individuals and small groups lobbied the Senate on various issues, but there was no overall representative student body. The Senate minutes for 29 January 1885 record 'an application from several students for the use of the Bute Hall to hold a meeting of students belonging to the various College Societies with a view to establishing a Glasgow University Union'.[71] The Union was subsequently established, and quickly sought permission to build its own premises.[72] Stanley Baldwin was later to describe the Union as a place for 'rubbing your brains with those of other people', a particularly necessary function in a University with no residential accommodation.[73] The Senate's committee on the proposed Union building reported on 29 April 1886 that it had 'instructed Mr. Burnet, the Architect, to prepare sketch plans of a Building to cost not more than four thousand pounds, of such an extent and character that, if placed along University Avenue opposite the western division of the University Library, it would be in keeping with the University Buildings'.[74] John James Burnet's proposed north elevation was shown to the Senate, who devolved authorisation for the construction of the building to the committee if the remaining elevations were also in keeping with the Gilbert Scott building. A potential funder had been lined up in late 1885, but he wished to remain anonymous. The plans were complete by July 1886 and the contract let.[75] Progress appears to have been relatively slow, as the building was not ready for occupation until February 1888.[76] Architecturally, the Union's unusual style of long, low ranges with squat pyramid-roofed towers is characteristic of the Burnet practice of the late 1880s and 1890s. The initial phase of construction included a common room, a library, a galleried debating hall, committee rooms and a refectory arranged in a shallow U-plan. Like the exterior, with its mullioned leaded-light windows and great chimneys, the interior reflects an idealised Gothic vision of collegiate life, with trussed roofs to the debating hall and reading room, wainscot panelling, spikey Gothic chimneypieces and occasional splashes of colour in the clubbable gloom provided by stained glass. Part of the design included a gateway to the west of the Union, the dimensions of which were to match the gate at Dumbarton Road. The gates were made by the smith, George Adam of Partick.[77] The anonymous donation covered the construction, but not the furnishings or maintenance. As a result of a highly successful 3-day student bazaar in December 1889 and other fundraising activities, Burnet was commissioned to extend the Union at the south-west corner in 1893.[78] A further dining hall/billiard room extension of 1907–08, again by Burnet, in which the southern end of the debating hall was also reconstructed as a 'lesser hall' and the exotic ogee-domed roof ventilator relocated, created a central court filled with a 'Pennycook' glass-roofed smoking room.

The building remained in use for male students until 1930 when the current Union was opened at the corner of University Avenue. The following year it was remodelled by T. Harold Hughes as the Queen Margaret College Students' Union.[79] The debating hall was converted to a dance hall, the lesser hall became a drawing room, and the smoking room served as a buffet and tea room. In 1969, when a new Queen Margaret union building was constructed in University Gardens, the building was converted for use as the headquarters of the Student Representative Council. The building is now named after Dr John McIntyre, the initially anonymous donor, who gifted £5,000 for its construction.

PEARCE LODGE, UNIVERSITY AVENUE 1885–1887

The fate of the High Street buildings continued to haunt the University authorities after the move to Gilmorehill. Their concerns would lead in due course to the creation of the small gate lodge that would become known as Pearce Lodge, named after its funder [FIG. 98]. By the middle of the 1880s plans were advanced for the Glasgow City & District Railway Company to demolish the last surviving part of the Old College, the magnificent 17th-century range facing the High Street, for a new goods station. A 'Removal of Old College Front Committee' was formed by the professors in the light of an offer by Sir William Pearce, chairman of the Fairfield Shipbuilding and Engineering Company, to fund the relocation of significant elements to Gilmorehill.

Some urgency was added to the Committee's deliberations in June 1885 by news of demolition of part of the High Street frontage.[80] A special meeting of the Senate resolved to appoint Alexander George Thomson, civil engineer and architect, to design a small lodge that would incorporate decorative stones from the frontage. Thomson had previously campaigned for retention of the High Street frontage and had already prepared alternative designs for its salvage. Sir William Pearce viewed and approved one of the designs on site and the local builders Morrison & Mason (also contractors for Glasgow City Chambers) were selected from four tenderers.[81] The design attempted to reuse as many of the decorative 17th – and 18th-century stones as possible within the much smaller gate lodge format, but not to replicate the High Street frontage. The contract between the University and Morrison & Mason of August 1885 specifies the works that were to be carried out:

Previous to demolition of old Building in High Street, the Contractor for Gateway Buildings shall cause all the quoins [corner stones], *mouldings, escutcheons, vases, door & window & dormer-heads, chimneyheads, clubskews* [stepped stones on the gables] *and finials to be figured with white paint, and diagrams of same to be painted on planed boards, for the guidance of the workmen when re-erecting stone detail. He shall also find careful men to watch and assist in taking down the stone detail and prevent damage and shall provide necessary appliances.*

The contractor shall have means of conveyance in readiness to at once remove the stones & deposit them safely within [the] *shed previously prepared at site of new erection in University Avenue, properly classified.*[82]

The stones to be removed from the High Street were itemised as follows:

1 Great sculptured Escutcheon [royal arms over gateway]
1 Sculptured Pediment [over arms]
2 Sculptured Vases [flanking arms]
2 enriched pedestals [flanking arms]
2 enriched consoles [strapwork]
16 Corbels [brackets for the two balconies]
2 moulded cornices on slabs
[flat stones forming balconies]
2 string courses
1 moulded skew – principal front
10 square chimney shafts over
1 Cornice and cope to ditto

98 Pearce Lodge, University Avenue. The centrepiece of the Old College is wrapped around the north-east corner of the lodge in Alexander George Thomson's reinterpretation of the High Street frontage.
GUAS [Old & New 35]

99 Pearce Lodge, detail of one of the balconies from over the entrance to the Forehall building in the High Street. The Town Council granted a licence for the balconies to project out over the street on 24 February 1660. They were probably designed by the mason-architect, John Clark, and originally featured swirling wrought-iron railings in a rinceau pattern.

100 The royal arms of Charles II, added to the High Street frontage after the Restoration of the monarchy in May 1660

101 A scrolled dormerhead from the High Street frontage incorporating thistle motifs. As with many buildings constructed during the Protectorate of Oliver Cromwell, the iconography of the decoration appears conservative, in the tradition of monarchical emblems. The Irish harp, Welsh fleur-de-lys and English rose appear on other pediments and dormers form the Old College.

102 One of the replacement urns that flanked the royal arms, carved by James Adams, who charged to the College to 'Oil the King's Arms, and put up the two vases on the sides of the same' in 1745.

6 Club skews [sets of crowsteps]
36 Window or Door finishings including jambs, sills, lintels & cornices
36 Carved ornamental Window heads
PRINCIPAL ARCHWAY re-erected on north front
2 Jambs [principal archway]
1 Lintel [principal archway]
1 Main cornice [principal archway]
1 Plinth [principal archway]
2 Window furnishings with pediments
2 Doric pilasters re-erected on S front
[from arcade below Fore Hall]
50ft Rusticated outband and inband quoins at angles of building

It is clear from the contract for the salvage work that more decorative stones were recovered than could be accommodated in the new Lodge. New stone was to be matched to the High Street stone and all the joint mortar tinted to match the colour of the stonework. Thomson also designed the unusual pinnacled gatepiers and railings adjoining the Lodge. Although Thomson designed an extension of the stone piers and iron railings along the length of University Avenue in 1892, it was not until 1900 that the railing alone (minus stone piers) was installed by George Adam.[83]

The main part of Pearce Lodge was used to house the Naval Architecture department, with a large classroom for drawing at the top of the building. The University's sub-janitor occupied the adjoining single storey house from its completion in May 1887.[84] Most of the High Street stones survive intact, although a number of the chimney stalks have been rebuilt in new stone. Internally the main surviving features are the spiral staircase in the tower and the attic classroom with a braced trussed roof.

The old Forehall doorpiece that stood at the top of the lion and unicorn stair appears to have been rescued at the same time.[85] It was reunited with the lion and unicorn (which had been removed in 1870) as a freestanding gateway between Professors' Square and the open west side of the western quadrangle.

Chapter Six

The Age of Applied Science 1890–1914

103 The general laboratory in the new Natural Philosophy building designed by James Miller in 1902–03, and photographed by Henry Bedford Lemere in 1909. The spacious laboratory area with freestanding benches and stools was intended for classes of undergraduates to conduct practical experiments. RCAHMS [Bedford Lemere Collection, SC 1140633]

By the 1890s the city of Glasgow had become the Second City of the Empire and was at the peak of its wealth and industrial might. The 1891 Census recorded a population of 565,839, which rose to 761,709 in 1901 and 784,496 in 1911. Opulent and exuberant mercantile, retail, commercial and civic buildings continued to replace the restrained classical townhouses at the core of the city's grid-plan, while new genteel suburbs of high-class tenements and villas sprang up on the outskirts. The patronage of rich merchants, industrialists and commercial traders encouraged a flourishing artistic and architectural community with distinctive Glasgow characteristics. In art, this period saw the emergence of The Four (Margaret MacDonald, Charles Rennie Mackintosh, Frances and Herbert MacNair), the Glasgow Boys and the Glasgow Girls. Architecture too developed its own 'Glasgow Style', typified by the use of red sandstone, bold sculptural treatment and sinuous Art Nouveau forms.

At the University, the provision of new science facilities in the early 1900s saw another expansion in numbers to almost 3,000 students before the First World War. The Faculty of Arts attracted more than half the matriculations before 1895, but the burgeoning Faculty of Medicine and new Faculty of Science (1893) swung the balance away from the Arts until 1914. The Divinity and Law Faculties remained relatively small and stable in their percentage share of the students. By prevailing standards, Glasgow had a relatively diverse social and economic mix of student backgrounds with about a quarter of students coming from working class backgrounds by 1910.[1] Undergraduate courses were generally three years long. The degree of Bachelor of Science was first established in 1872. Higher degrees came under the regulation of Commissioners under the 1889 Universities (Scotland) Act. The first Doctor of Science degree was awarded in 1890.

The 1889 Universities (Scotland) Act marked a very significant shift in Scottish higher education by enabling the admission and graduation of women. The Association for the Higher Education of Women had been formed in Glasgow in 1877. Principal John Caird strongly encouraged the Association, which was incorporated as Queen Margaret College in 1883. A number of University professors taught at the College, and it acquired its own premises in 1884 through the gift by the shipbuilding widow, Isabella Elder, of North Park House in Queen Margaret Drive. The house had been designed in 1869 by John Thomas Rochead and completed in 1871 by John Honeyman as a display case for the art collections of the merchants, John and Matthew Bell of the famous Bell Pottery. A medical school was started in 1890 and an Anatomy Department building constructed in 1894–95 [FIG.107]. From the outset

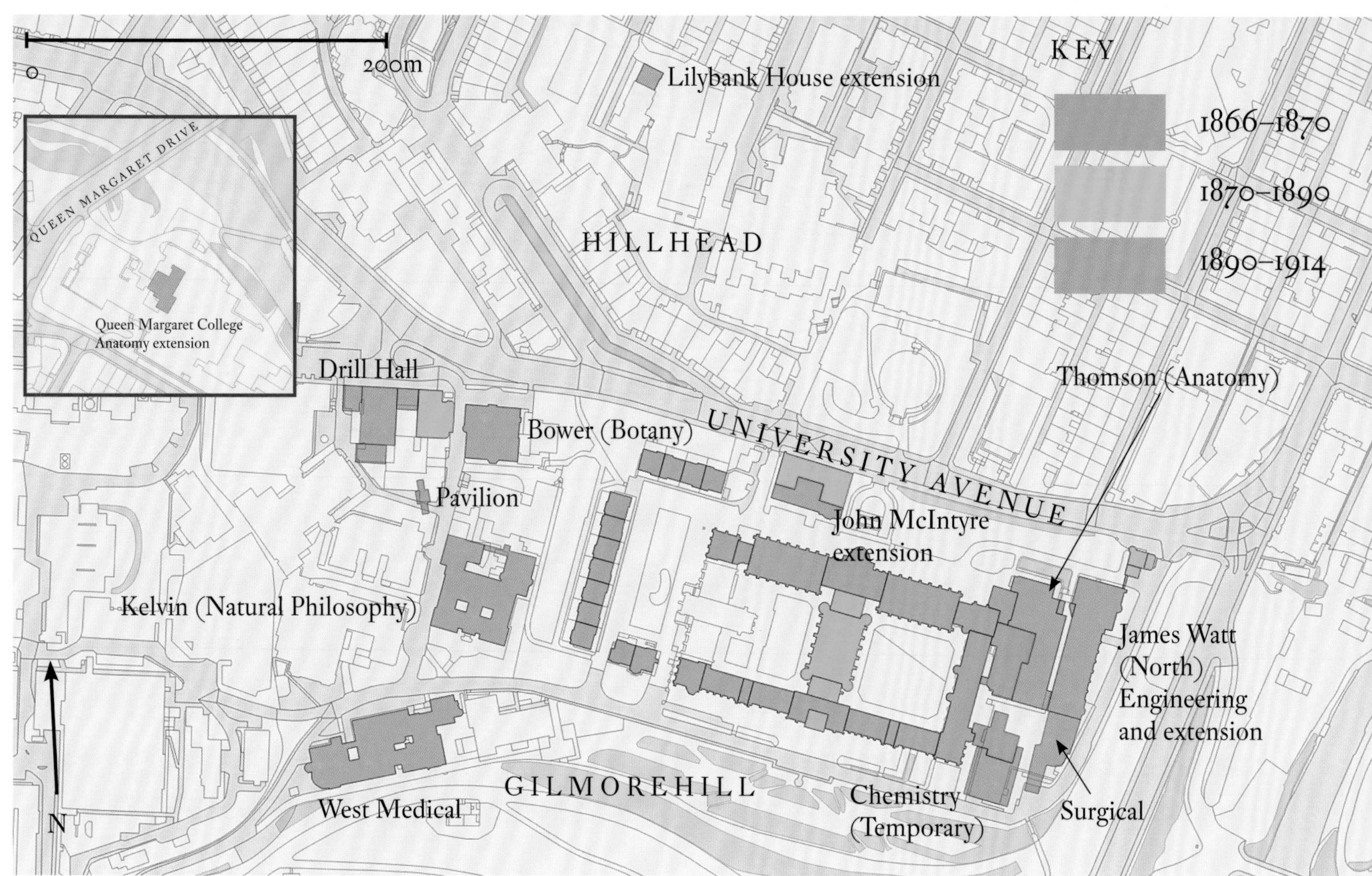

104 Development of the University between 1890 and 1914

the new College had its own management and separate existence, but aimed to provide teaching compatible with the standards of the University. Following the 1889 Act, the College Council decided to seek incorporation within the University. After merger in 1892, the buildings and endowments were to be kept separately for the teaching of women. However, mixed class teaching soon took place in the main University buildings. The first woman graduate of the University was Marion Gilchrist who was awarded a Bachelor of Medicine degree in 1894. By 1914 women formed almost a quarter of the full-time student population.

The 1889 Act also had a profound effect on the administrative structure of the University. The general management was transferred from the Senate to the University Court. The University collected class fees and paid assistants centrally rather than leaving these tasks to the individual professors. Endowments attached to individual chairs were pooled and staff salaries were regulated. Increased government funding and new endowments enabled new lectureships, assistants and the foundation of chairs in History, Pathology, Political Economy, Geology and Mining. The Commissioners under the Act also attempted to establish consistent admissions standards and guiding principles for an honours curriculum across the four Scottish universities.[2]

By the 1890s the applied sciences were requiring quite specific spaces and equipment for research and teaching. Much greater discussion took place between the client professors and the architects. There was now significant international experience in constructing and fitting out specialist laboratories and a growing technical literature on the subject. Perhaps the most influential of these publications was Edward Cookworthy Robins' *Technical School and College Building* of 1887, which examined international and domestic examples of laboratory buildings and equipment in universities, schools and colleges.

In 1908 a new ordinance was introduced that regulated the curriculum and conduct of Arts courses, dividing the academic year into three terms and setting out the qualifying requirements and numbers of subjects for ordinary and honours degrees.[3] Attendance at tutorials became part of the requirements for the first time and the frequency of classes was increased. Apart from the burgeoning staff required to implement the 1908 ordinance, the number of Arts subjects taught also swelled in the early years of the 20th century. New chairs included Scottish History and Literature (1913), English

Language (1907), Italian (1902), Celtic (1900), and Politics (1909).

ARCHITECTURAL ADVANCES

Growing professionalism in the business of architecture made study of contemporary developments in the provision of buildings for scientific study and face-to-face discussion with their designers and clients desirable. Improved long-distance transport made this more practical. The University Court required Honeyman & Keppie to visit Newcastle and Oxford to examine developments there before designing the Anatomy Department for Queen Margaret College in 1894. Two years later, John James Burnet went to the United States to study laboratory design in progress. The 1880s and 90s was also a period when advances in building technology and services really began to take hold. Steel, with its thinner profiles, lighter weight, greater strength and improved fire-proofing qualities, began to replace the old cast-iron technology. The use of concrete increased, and was no longer restricted to foundation footings – for example, it was used in the construction of the floor of the new Engineering laboratory. Glazed tiles and brick were important components in improved hygiene in laboratories.

Lord Kelvin's house in Professors' Square had been fully lit by electricity since 1881 and an electricity committee had been formed in 1888.[4] A telegraph wire to the Western Fire Office was installed in 1885 and a telephone in 1888.[5] In 1900 the University Court still instructed Burnet to provide for both gas and electric lighting in the new Botany building, but within a year a new mains supply had been laid by Glasgow Corporation and all subsequent buildings were fitted with electric lighting only.[6] The first American-style lift in the University was installed in the Engineering building in 1902.

Teaching equipment was also advancing in this period. The Edinburgh High School headmaster James Pillans is widely credited with the invention of the blackboard in the early 19th century. By the time of the move to Gilmorehill in 1870, blackboards made from large slates in wooden frames were fixed to the walls of some lecture theatres. In the later 1870s the Professor of Engineering, James Thomson, invented a system of counterweights to allow the position of the blackboard to be adjusted.[7] In 1902 the new Engineering building was fitted up with a 'lantern', or projector, and screen.[8]

EXPANSION AND LABORATORY SCIENCE

The research and teaching of science had been one of the University's great strengths for many years before the move to Gilmorehill. However, the provision of accommodation at Gilmorehill had been planned largely on the basis of a moderate expansion of what existed on the High Street site and a balancing of reasonable territorial claims between the professors. It reflected the then prevailing method of teaching science and medicine by lecture and demonstration, rather than by allowing students to undertake their own 'hands-on' experiments.

While there was more generous space provided for laboratories at Gilmorehill, notably in Anatomy and in William Thomson's world-famous Natural Philosophy (Physics) Department, the laboratories were not tailored for research, often being poorly lit and ventilated. Other research facilities were generally limited to the Hunterian collections and small departmental museums and libraries.

With the exception of the Chemistry department, the plans for Gilmorehill had almost completely ignored the developments in specialist laboratory buildings for scientific and technical teaching that were taking place internationally, most notably in Germany. The continental polytechnic systems not only invested in buildings and equipment, but in developing and exploiting scientific discovery through workshop practice and apprenticeships for industrial/manufacturing purposes. At the most advanced institutions laboratory space was provided for all students. The 1880s and 1890s were also years of extraordinary scientific and technological advances, during which the emphasis in teaching most scientific disciplines shifted to practical knowledge and skills in observation, measurement, experimentation and rigorous analysis of technical data. Research, too, changed from a largely theoretical approach to applied physical experiments. Subjects such as electrical engineering gained enormously in prominence during this period.

By 1888 the Professor of Botany, Frederick Bower, was complaining of the chronic lack of suitable laboratory accommodation, equipment and staff for his subject.[9] Bower sought permission from the Senate to approach John Oldrid Scott or another architect to remodel the attic floor of the East Range to provide en-suite accommodation for the Botany department. The basis of his argument to the Senate was the great advance in the subject in the previous fifteen years and the establishment of laboratory teaching as standard practice throughout the country. Dedicated space with proper lighting and heating was needed for advanced experiments and also for general laboratory teaching through physiological experiments. Associated rooms for preparation of specimens and a greenhouse were also essential.

While the provision for Botany was particularly poor, arguments for better accommodation based on huge scientific advances and the need for laboratory teaching also held true for all the other sciences and medicine.

Thus within a relatively short period of the construction of the new quadrangles at Gilmorehill, the accommodation for the teaching of science was considered outdated and inadequate. The symmetrical design and linear arrangement of the quadrangles made suitable expansion within the footprint of the Gilbert Scott buildings very difficult.

Principal John Caird, who was ailing for much of the 1890s, was supportive of the need for new laboratories and equipment, but was weak in the practicalities of delivering them. Even the regular and reasonable requests for new equipment and more space by Lord Kelvin, by then the most distinguished scientist of his age, were fobbed off by Caird in the Micawber-like hopeful expectation that some money would eventually turn up to pay for them. Bower and Archibald Barr, Professor of Engineering, belonged to a new generation of enthusiastic and dynamic professors, who were not prepared to sit back and watch their subject areas wither. They actively sought out funding, which bore fruit in the construction of new departmental buildings in the first years of the next Principal, Herbert Story.

Story quickly recognised the acute accommodation problems and began a fresh fundraising campaign in 1899, called *University Expansion & Better Equipment*.[10] Smaller class sizes and space for specialist research were essential. The importance of research and research postgraduates in drawing the best minds to the University and competing with international centres of science, medicine and technology was not lost on the new Principal.

Cautious of perceived government interference and mindful of the national preoccupation with the second Boer War, Story aimed his appeal at the citizens of Glasgow, especially through the pages of the *Glasgow Herald* in which he and other professors extolled the benefits of a first class university to the well-being and wealth of the city.[11] Story's approach proved successful, raising some £76,000 before his death on 13 January 1907. Legacies and trusts accounted for significant sums, but the campaign was also supported by industrialists, Glasgow Corporation and the Carnegie Trust for the Universities of Scotland. This latter trust, established in 1901 with an unprecedented gift of $10m by the Dunfermline-born American steel magnate, Andrew Carnegie, was to become a major benefactor to the University's various building programmes in the 20th century.

The architectural approach was to provide discreet or linked specialist buildings for individual subjects, as practised internationally, rather than by trying to adapt the quadrangles or complete the western side of the omni-purpose Gilbert Scott building. The sale of land for Kelvingrove Park and the Western Infirmary, and the provision of a recreation field, had left a site smaller than that at the Old College in the High Street. New building land at Gilmorehill was therefore relatively constrained by ownership and topography. These constraints pushed the new buildings to the perimeter of the University site. The first two buildings, Botany and Engineering, were planned from 1894. There was considerable discussion amongst the professors regarding the siting of the new buildings.[12] Various options were explored, but a compromise brokered by Lord Kelvin emerged in March 1898: the Botany department was to stand alone beside the Gymnasium on University Avenue; the new Engineering department was to be located to the east of the main buildings, but leaving enough intervening space for expansion of the Anatomy and Surgery departments.[13] The siting appears to have been determined on 'territorial' grounds by the professors, rather than on practical considerations such as noise and dirt, which, for example, influenced the location of the contemporary engineering building away from the main buildings at the University of Melbourne in Australia.

The remaining laboratory projects were prioritised in order of urgency in 1901: Anatomy; Surgery; Physiology, Materia Medica, Forensic Science and Public Health (these four to be grouped together in one building); and Natural Philosophy [FIG.106]. Chemistry, which pleaded urgent needs in 1902, was provided with a 'temporary' cheap brick engineering shed designed by John James Burnet around the old Abbot's Kitchen. Although all of the buildings were to be built separately as funds allowed, a masterplan governed the allocation of sites. Such was the determination to hang onto the recreation field and maintain the views to the Gilbert Scott building that even the terraces below the main building were proposed for a semi-subterranean range of laboratories for the Naval Engineering Department.

Eventually the Court recognised the restrictions imposed by retention of the recreation ground at Gilmorehill and purchased a new site at Westerlands, Anniesland, with the aid of a Carnegie grant in 1909.

JOHN JAMES BURNET, ARCHITECT

The stranglehold of the Gilbert Scott architectural practice and its associated main contractor, John Thompson, over the University's new buildings had begun to weaken with the involvement of the local architects, John Burnet & Son, in the construction of the Western Infirmary, Gymnasium, the joint Infirmary/University lodge on the Dumbarton Road, and the John McIntyre building. While John Oldrid Scott continued his father's influence over all architectural matters at the University, John James Burnet (the 'Son' in John Burnet & Son), took on an increasingly dominant role in the design of the

105 Photograph of John James Burnet taken for the artist members' portrait albums of the Glasgow Art Club, possibly by James Craig Annan, about 1893.
By kind permission of the Glasgow Art Club

new science laboratories. John Burnet Sr retired in 1889 or 1890 leaving his youngest son, John James Burnet [FIG.105], to continue the practice with John Archibald Campbell. Both John James and Campbell had studied in Paris at the Ecole des Beaux-Arts, and many of their buildings in Glasgow of this period reflected their academic classical training under Jean-Louis Pascal. Major Beaux Arts style commissions by John James in Glasgow included the Glasgow Institute of Fine Arts (1878), 2–10 and 14 University Gardens (1882, then known as Saughfield Terrace), the Clyde Trust Buildings (1882; extended 1905), the Athenaeum (1886), Charing Cross Mansions (1889), the Royal Faculty of Physicians and Surgeons interiors (1892), and the Glasgow Savings Bank headquarters banking hall (1894).[14] Burnet's flexibility in using other styles was demonstrated in the early pointed Gothic of Barony Parish Church (1886). By the 1890s he was producing innovative buildings of the highest quality, many technically advanced and a number influenced by great American architects such as Charles Follen McKim, Daniel Burnham and Louis Sullivan.[15] In 1891 Burnet moved house to directly opposite the Gilbert Scott building at what was then 18 University Avenue (now part of the University Estate at 70 University Avenue). He added the distinctive door and west library wing to the house in that year.[16] From this location he clearly had a good network of University contacts and an excellent view of what was happening across the road.

John Oldrid Scott and Burnet were commissioned jointly, and without competition, to design the Botany and Engineering buildings in 1894.[17] At the same meeting, the University Court decided to approach John Honeyman of Honeyman & Keppie Architects for the new Anatomy building at Queen Margaret College.[18] The Court left Scott and Burnet to sort out who did what. Their manner of co-operation was explained in a letter of 3 September 1894 from both architects to Alan Clapperton, Secretary to the University Court:

As regards the division of the work we have arranged that the design of the exteriors shall be made by Mr Scott and that the drawings connected with it shall at all stages be supervised by him, but that all office drawings shall be prepared by Mr Burnet in Glasgow. He will also communicate with the Professors as to all the details of the internal arrangements and will have full knowledge of and responsibility for all parts of the execution of the work. We are of opinion that the remuneration to the joint Architects should be 7½ per cent on the total outlay – travelling and incidental expenses being charged in addition in the usual way.

The Court's unusual approach seems to have been intended to give Scott control over the exterior appearance of the buildings in the context of his father's previous work. The relationship between the architects appears to have been amicable, but as might be expected, Burnet's presence on the ground gave him the lion's share of the work. When the designs for the Botany building were published, they were under the Burnet & Son name alone.

In 1896 Burnet travelled to North America to study engineering laboratory and operating theatre design and equipment in the company of Archibald Barr, Professor of Engineering, and Dr Donald James Mackintosh, a graduate of Glasgow University in 1884 and Medical Superintendant of the Western Infirmary from 1892.[19] In justifying his trip to the Senate in July 1896, Barr made clear his ambition of continuing the Engineering department's world-class status by procuring the best possible facilities, based on the most advanced recent examples.[20] The models chosen by Barr and Burnet were: the Columbia University Engineering Hall designed by McKim, Mead & White, then under construction as part of the new campus at Morningside Heights, New York; Winchester Hall at Yale University, built by Josiah Cleaveland Cady in 1892; and the Macdonald Engineering building at McGill University, Toronto, designed by Andrew Taylor and William Gordon in 1893.

Burnet's uncle George lived in the United States and his brother-in-law, James Marwick, had recently moved to New York. Marwick was to found the firm, Marwick, Mitchell & Company, which through various mergers has grown to become one of the four largest

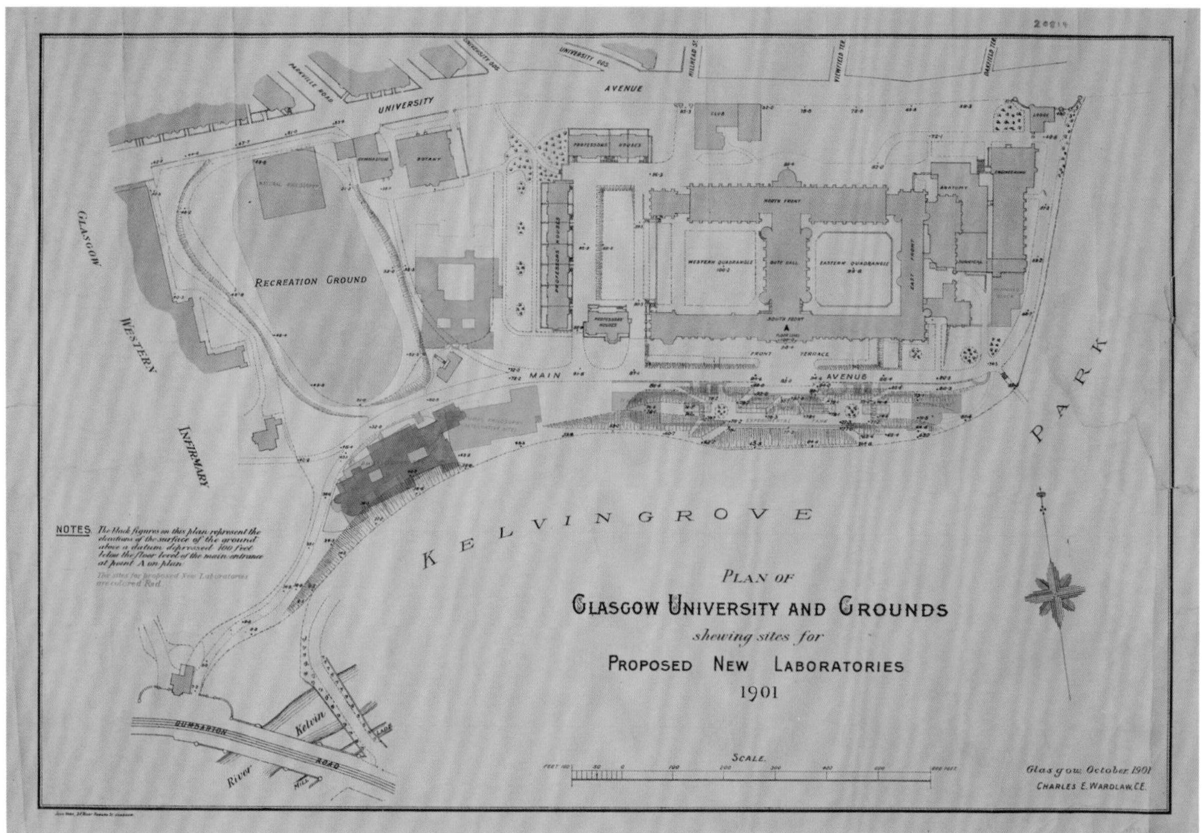

106 Plan of proposed new laboratories, 1901, drawn up by the civil engineer, Charles Wardlaw, with a coloured overlay in red of James Miller's Natural Philosophy and West Medical buildings
GUAS [BUL 6/9/11]

accountancy firms in the world, KPMG.[21] Burnet possibly already knew McKim through Ecole des Beaux Arts circles, but certainly became friends with him during the visit to America. Taylor trained in Scotland and practiced in London, so Burnet probably also knew him beforehand. The Professor of Architecture at McGill was Stewart Henbest Capper, who had worked at John Burnet & Son in 1884 and remained a close friend of John James Burnet.[22]

In 1903–04 Burnet was selected to design the Edward VII Galleries at the British Museum in London. This was to be a turning point in his career, leading to further major commissions and honours, including a knighthood in 1914. From 1905 Burnet spent the greater part of his time in the new London office of John J. Burnet, returning to Glasgow for only a few days a month. In spite of this, Burnet continued his close relationship with the University, receiving an honorary Doctorate of Laws in 1910. John Oldrid Scott died on 30 May 1913, leaving Burnet as the University's main architectural advisor.[23] In March 1914 Burnet began work on a masterplan for more new buildings on the limited Gilmorehill site.[24] The various surviving block plans show that Burnet intended to complete the western range of the Gilbert Scott building and develop a near-continuous front to University Avenue. The schemes continued the 1904 proposals for buildings in the terraces below the south front of the Gilbert Scott building. By this period, the most urgent accommodation needs were in the Arts Faculty and Zoology. The lack of a chapel was also keenly felt. The outbreak of the First World War in July 1914 put an end to immediate ambitions for construction, but Burnet continued planning and designing throughout the war.

THE ANATOMY BUILDING AT QUEEN MARGARET COLLEGE, QUEEN MARGARET DRIVE 1894–1895

Although the old College buildings in Queen Margaret Drive stand a short distance away from the main campus at Gilmorehill, the Anatomy building was an important commission by the University. It was the first of the new laboratory buildings to be built, it was the University's first major commitment to the provision of facilities for women, and Charles Rennie Mackintosh appears to have played a role in its design [FIGS 106, 107].

A medical school, initially funded by Isabella Elder (see page 97) was established at Queen Margaret College following the admission of female students to the Glasgow Royal Infirmary in 1890.[25] However, it was another four years before work began on purpose-built accommodation under the supervision of the lecturer in Anatomy and enthusiastic amateur archaeologist, Thomas Hastie Bryce. By this time the College had merged with the University. The new building was made possible by the award of a £5,000 capital grant by the Bellahouston Bequest Fund Trustees.

At the same meeting of the University Court that approved Oldrid Scott and John Burnet as joint architects for the Botany and Engineering buildings,

107 Queen Margaret College Anatomy building, designed by Honeyman & Keppie in 1894. Charles Rennie Mackintosh, who was a draughtsman at the firm and made this presentation sketch in 1895, may have been involved in the design.
Private collection [Academy Architecture 1895, p.70]

108 Floor plans of Queen Margaret College Anatomy building
Private collection [Academy Architecture 1895, p.148]

John Honeyman was selected to design the new medical department at Queen Margaret College.[26] Honeyman's appointment probably resulted from his connections with the existing buildings and key players at the College. Honeyman was responsible for the completion of North Park House, the main building of the College and he had designed the Necropolis monument to John Elder, Isabella's husband, in 1869. He had also laid out Elder Park for Isabella in 1883–84 and his firm designed the Fairfield Shipyard offices (1889–91) which still survive in Govan. In addition, he had carried out alterations to the University's Observatory on Dowanhill in 1862 and 1871–72; and, finally, Honeyman probably knew the Anatomy lecturer, Thomas Bryce, who shared his interest in archaeology, particularly that of Glasgow Cathedral.[27] Honeyman's firm had also had recent experience of medical buildings, having completed the Anderson's College medical school on Dumbarton Road, following the death of James Sellars in 1888.

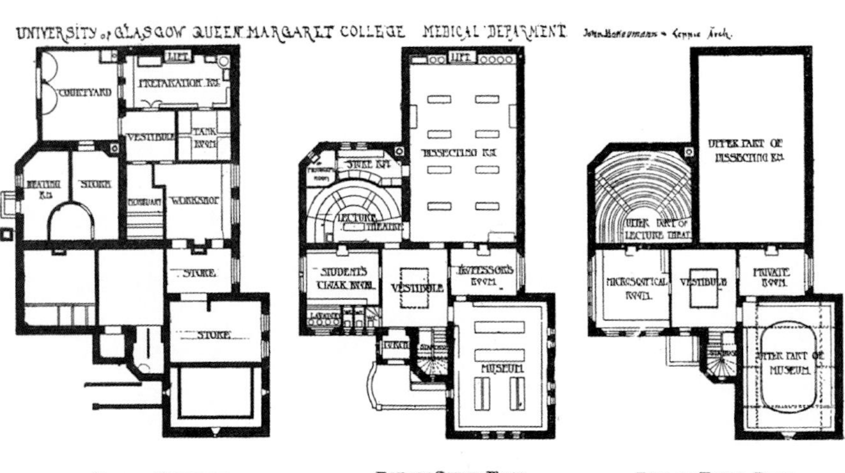

By 1888 Honeyman's architectural practice had almost collapsed and he had taken John Keppie into partnership to refinance the business. The firm of Honeyman & Keppie had then recruited a number of talented draughtsmen and assistants including Alexander McGibbon, Herbert McNair, Edward Whitelaw and Charles Rennie Mackintosh.[28] The University Court laid down an unusual condition of Honeyman's appointment. This was that he should examine two recent Anatomy buildings, one constructed for Professor Robert Howden (editor of *Gray's Anatomy*) of the University of Durham at Newcastle-upon-Tyne (1887–95, Dunn, Hansom & Dunn) and that built for Professor Arthur Thomson at Oxford. Thomas Bryce and John Keppie visited the buildings and commented favourably on Oxford, which had been laid out in functional units by Thomson and built between 1891 and 1893 in a free Renaissance style by local architect Harry Wilkinson Moore. The sketch plans submitted to the University Court in June 1894 reflected the Oxford arrangement in a number of aspects: the 2-storey scale; the polygonal stairtower; and the provision of a walled courtyard for discreet reception of cadavers.[29] The University Court approved amended designs in August and the city's Dean of Guild Court followed suit in September 1894.[30]

The separation (except for a hoist) of the preparatory areas in the basement from the teaching rooms on the ground floor was considered necessary to spare the female students from the unpleasant sights, sounds and smells of the preparatory processes.[31] Lighting of the double-height museum [FIG.109], lecture theatre and entrance hall were achieved by overhead glazed lanterns. In deference to its sensitive usage, the dissecting room had no windows and was lit by an industrial ridge-and-furrow northlight roof. The main south and east elevations were of Giffnock stone, but the west and north were of white-glazed brick, which provoked intense local criticism as the 'eyesore' and 'hideous firebrick monster' was constructed.[32]

As with a number of early Honeyman & Keppie buildings, there is some dispute as to the involvement of Charles Rennie Mackintosh in the design. In a letter of 1933 Bryce remembered Mackintosh on site with Keppie 'who designed the building'.[33] Apart from an attribution to Mackintosh in Charles Marriott's *Modern English Architecture* (1924), there is no documentary evidence of Mackintosh's part in the design. However, Mackintosh was responsible for the presentation drawing that was exhibited at the Royal Glasgow Institute of Fine Arts in 1895 and the Royal Scottish Academy in 1896, and published in the *British Architect* in the same year.[34] The stylised, elongated script on the sketch plans and Dean of Guild submission drawings also suggests his hand in those. Reviewing the building on 11 April 1895, the

109 The museum, Queen Margaret College Anatomy building
GUAS [DC233/2/2/2/2 p.10]

110 Stencil decoration of about 1864, probably to the designs of Alexander 'Greek' Thomson. The stencilled decoration was discovered in 2005 at Lilybank House.
GUPU [13-036-13]

Glasgow Herald commented: 'The design is appropriately simple and severe, but is not so remarkable as the drawing of it by Mr C.R. Mackintosh'. If Mackintosh was not the designer of the building as a whole, the stylistic evidence points to his possible authorship of a number of details, such as the sinuous decorative carvings executed by McGilvray & Ferris over the entrance, the Art Nouveau iron gates made by George Adam & Son, and the curved Japanese-style struts of the museum balcony supplied by James Maben & Son. Mackintosh had a deep interest in 17th-century Scottish Renaissance architecture, and it could be that a number of elements such as the ogee-roofed stairtower, chunky entrance balustrade, catslide roof over the porch, and window mouldings are loosely derived from his studies and sketches around Scotland.

By 1934 male and female students were all taught together at Gilmorehill and the Queen Margaret College site was sold to the BBC. Very substantial additions and alterations were made by James Miller in 1935–38. More additions and alterations followed between the 1960s and the 1980s before the BBC relocated to Pacific Quay in 2007. Many of the later accretions have been removed and the Anatomy building survives in modified form, minus the dissecting laboratory. Very few interior features remain.

The Honeyman, Keppie & Mackintosh firm made proposal drawings for a union hall and a hall of residence for Queen Margaret College in 1904, but it is not clear who commissioned the plans, or where the structures were to be built.[35]

LILYBANK HOUSE, BUTE GARDENS 1894–1896 AND 1908

The conversion of the mid 19th-century villa of Lilybank House to a hall of residence in 1894 is not strictly a project of the University of Glasgow, as it was undertaken for the quasi-commercial Queen Margaret College Hall Company Ltd. However, the occupants were all members of the University and the hall subsequently transferred to the University in 1923. It is now a departmental building, and forms a significant architectural landmark at the heart of the Hillhead campus.

The villa itself was built for Robert Allen, a Glasgow merchant, probably in about 1850. A small stable court adjoined on the north side. From 1857 the house was leased by John Blackie Jr (1805–73) of the publishing firm, Blackie & Son. Blackie bought the house in 1864. Both William Ewart Gladstone, Chancellor of the Exchequer, and Prince Alfred, Duke of Edinburgh, were entertained at the house during Blackie's period of office as Lord Provost of Glasgow from 1863 to 1866. Possibly for the purpose of these entertainments, Alexander Thomson was commissioned to remodel the house and build a new dining room and entrance wing to the south in the same period. The wing has a number of typical Thomson features, such as the Greek Ionic portico, tall and slim windows, grouped chimney flues and tall, incised chimneypots capped with floreate mouldings. Internal works in 2005 revealed the survival of Thomson's original richly coloured Egyptian-style stencil decorations [FIG.110]. The house was acquired as for conversion to a hall of residence for women students at Queen Margaret College in 1894. John Keppie is described in the share application document as the 'honorary consulting architect' to the company, and it was his firm, John Honeyman & Keppie, which submitted plans to the Dean of Guild Court for remodelling the house and north stable court into a hall in April 1895.[36] Although Charles Rennie Mackintosh was working for the firm at this time, there is no evidence that he was involved with this commission. Further minor alterations were carried out by the same firm in 1908.

BOWER BUILDING (BOTANY), UNIVERSITY AVENUE 1899–1901

The first of the major new laboratory buildings at Gilmorehill was the Botany building, now named the Bower building in honour of Frederick Orpen Bower, Regius Professor of Botany from 1885 to 1925. Bower was an energetic leader, teacher, researcher and author, who pushed for improved facilities from the time of his arrival at Glasgow in 1885. Under his direction the school won a world-wide reputation for morphological

111 The rear (south and east) elevations Bower building
Private collection [Academy Architecture 1900, p.119]

112 The opening of the Bower building by Sir William Hooker on 13 June 1901. Some of the teaching equipment is visible: long fixed blackboards and paper diagrams are on the wall; models of seeds can be seen on the benches.
GUAS [UP 9/20/1]

botany, the study of the physical form and structure of plants, and he pioneered the new field of palaeobotany, studying the relationship between modern and fossil plants. The building, which cost £19,000, was made possible through a grant of £6,000 from the Steven of Bellahouston Trustees and a £10,725 bequest from the estate of Charles Randolph.[37] The fittings in oak were to be supplied from a grant of £2,401 from the Robert Paterson Fund. The design was developed by Burnet from sketches by John Oldrid Scott in 1897. This dual authorship is perhaps reflected in the uncomfortable stylistic mix of classical Renaissance design with 'Scotticised' Baronial details such as the crowstepped gables, hood-moulds over the windows and the signature pepperpot turrets, derived from the main building design. Notably, all of the contactors, including the heating and ventilation engineers, were local.[38] The walls were of Bishopbriggs sandstone and the slates were Lancashire blue. Originally the building contained two large teaching laboratories, a herbarium (library of pressed plant specimens), a small library, a museum, a 213-seat lecture theatre, staff offices and a workshop. The object of the design was to provide a few first-rate rooms for elementary and advanced classes, rather than numerous rooms for individual research. Rather than fixed benches, the laboratories contained freestanding tables and chairs that allowed for flexibility of arrangement.

The building was opened as part of the University's 450th anniversary celebrations at 3pm on Thursday 13 June 1901 by the greatest botanist of his day, Sir Joseph Dalton Hooker, whose father William had been the Professor of Botany at Glasgow in the 1820s and 30s, a founder of the Glasgow Botanic Gardens and the first Director of the Royal Botanic Gardens at Kew.[39] The Stevenson Laboratory, a low, top-lit, Roman brick extension to the east followed in 1937 to the designs of T. Harold Hughes and D.S.R. Waugh. Following a serious fire in 2001 the building was almost completely reconstructed internally by BMJ Architects and re-opened in November 2005.

JAMES WATT ENGINEERING BUILDING (NORTH) 1899–1901

Although the Engineering buildings bear the name of the University's most famous engineer, the impetus behind their construction was provided by Professor Archibald Barr. As Professor of Engineering at the Yorkshire College, Leeds, Barr had been responsible for the construction and equipping of new engineering laboratories in1886. Barr was appointed to the Engineering chair at Glasgow in 1889, but continued to work with the Professor of Physics at Leeds, William Stroud, on optical rangefinders for weaponry.[40] Barr & Stroud became a limited company in 1912 and grew to be a famous supplier of rangefinders and other optical instruments to navies and armies around the world. The firm still exists under the name Thales Optronics Ltd.

Barr wrote a memorandum to the University Court in 1891:

It will be within the knowledge of Members of the University Court that I have been advocating the provision in the University of an Engineering Laboratory similar to those in other Engineering schools. So far as I am aware Glasgow University stands now absolutely alone among all the Universities & Colleges in the world in which Engineering Science is taught in having no provision for laboratory work in Engineering Science.[41]

Barr then persuaded local industrialists and charitable bodies to contribute £40,000 towards the construction of the new laboratories and £14,000 to equip them. He described the different type of design required for an engineering laboratory and remarked that 'the whole building has to be designed practically as a piece of apparatus, and this cannot be left to an architect whose work must be subsequent to that of the engineer'.[42]

Like the Botany building, the James Watt Engineering laboratories were the product of the unusual arrangement of John Oldrid Scott as architectural advisor/supervisor and John James Burnet as executant architect [FIG.113]. The result is more successful than in the Botany building, with the beautiful Renaissance details of strapwork pediments, carved panels and tall chimneys, all carved by William Shireffs, outweighing the weak Baronialism of the corner turrets.[43] The archway linking the laboratories to the Pearce Lodge, peppered with genuine 17th-century decorative stonework, strengthens the evocation of the old High Street complex in this corner of the Gilmorehill site. Burnet's drawings were approved by the city's Dean of Guild Court in September 1899 and immediately afterwards substantial earthworks were begun to prepare the steep site for the construction works.[44] The bulk of the teaching and office accommodation was formed in the 3-storey part of the building at the northern end of the plot, next to the Pearce Lodge. Because of the steep fall in the ground from west to east, there were two basement levels on the eastern side of the building. A very large single storey general workshop with a concrete floor, about 140 feet (43m) by 60 feet (18m), extended southwards and was lit from above by north-facing glazed panels in the steel-trussed roof. The industrial character of this roof was partly disguised by a high stone parapet along the wallhead.

While it is not clear that there were direct influences from Barr and Burnet's American research trip of 1896 (see page 101), the interior planning and servicing were certainly well-considered. For the first time in the long history of the Engineering department it had a spacious purpose-built mechanical engineering workshop that could accommodate all the students. In addition, there were workshop/laboratories for mechanical and electrical engineering, a lecture theatre, museum, classroom, demonstration room, technical drawing room, library, photographic and blue-print room, and, crucially, preparatory and storage spaces for equipment and materials, all fed from a central stair and corridor.[45] From the outset the building was designed to be lit by electricity. It was initially intended that the plant should also provide electricity to the rest of the University buildings. Another 'first' for an academic building at Gilmorehill was the inclusion of an 'Otis' elevator.[46] The building was heated from an enormous boiler in the first basement and a huge tank in the attic provided high water pressure for hydraulic experiments.

An additional sum, equal to one-third of the cost of the building, was spent on equipping it. By any previous standards of equipment at the University, the new kit for the Engineering department was lavish. The experimental boiler and engine were the two largest machines, but the general and electrical laboratories were equipped with all the latest devices for measuring material properties. A travelling crane for lifting heavy items ran along the length of the general laboratory. A 'flue' for testing the tensile strength of wires and a mercury column for measuring pressure were incorporated through three storeys of the building.

The building was opened by Lord Kelvin on Thursday 3 September 1901 as part of the International Engineering Congress hosted by the University.[47] The

113 Design for James Watt (north) building by John James Burnet, 1899
GUAS [BUL 6/6/30]

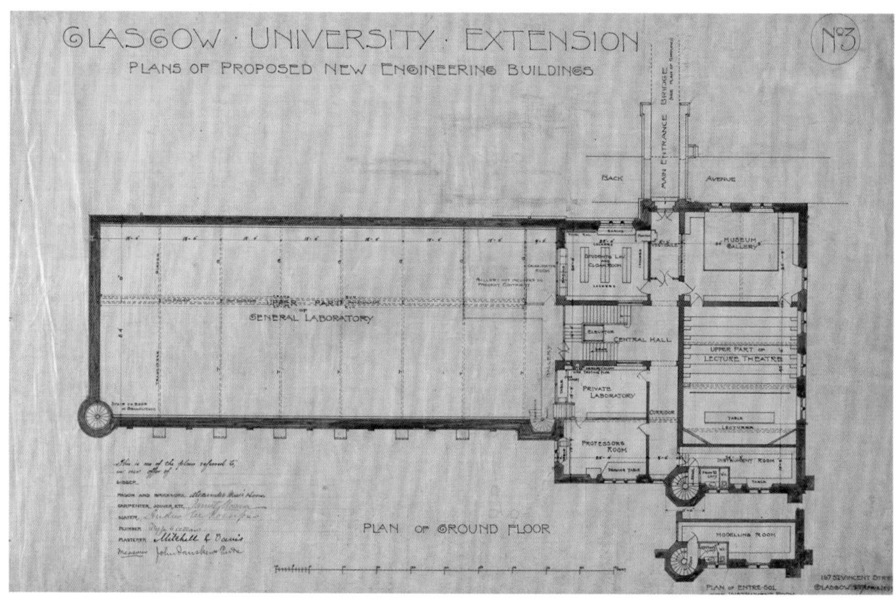

114 Ground floor plan of James Watt (north) building by John James Burnet, 1899
GUAS [BUL 6/6/20]

115 The Anatomy Museum designed by John James Burnet, 1899–1903
GUPU [13-036-19]

construction of the Engineering building straddled the reigns of Queen Victoria and Edward VII, both of whose monograms ornament the exterior. John Burnet Sr donated a run of *Proceedings of the Institution of Civil Engineers* from the library of his second son, Lindsay Burnet, a steam engineer, who had died aged thirty-nine in 1895.[48] Apart from the opening of the Engineering buildings, 1901 was a busy year for Barr as organiser of Scotland's first motor car reliability trials and vice-convenor of the Engineering and Electricity section of the Glasgow International Exhibition. The Burnet firm provided designs for additions to the building in 1908 and thanks to a Treasury grant raised the roof to create a new laboratory over the main workshop in 1920.[49] John Keppie, Henderson & J.L. Gleave removed this and added a 2-storey brick extension in 1959.[50]

THE THOMSON BUILDING (ANATOMY) 1899–1903

The Anatomy department extension was made possible by a legacy from James Brown Thomson of Kinning Park (1818–98), a quayside worker who had been left a fortune in 1887 by his two brothers, Thomas and John, both Glasgow merchants. Thomson's trustees distributed nearly £80,000 to educational and medical institutions in Glasgow. The largest sum, £13,000, went to the University and made possible the expansion of the Anatomy facilities.[51] The building was later named in honour of Professor Allen Thomson, convenor of the Old College removal committee and eminent anatomist and embryologist.

A design for a new Anatomy building between the main building and the Engineering building had been prepared by John Burnet Sr as far back as 1884, and the medical professors had subsequently made various representations to the Senate and Court about the inadequacy of their laboratory provision. A report of 1899 divided the medical facilities into those that could be expanded from the existing rooms in the East Range (Anatomy, Surgery, Medicine and Midwifery) and those that required completely new buildings (Physiology,

Materia Medica and Therapeutics, and Forensic Medicine and Public Health).

Planning for the Anatomy building began in earnest in 1899 as the Engineering building was finalised and the James Brown Thomson bequest was made.[52] John James Burnet was appointed as architect, this time without the oversight of John Oldrid Scott. The site and access were difficult, as it stands on a steeply sloping plot of ground. The new building had to connect into George Gilbert Scott's existing lecture theatre, which protruded from the East Range of the east quadrangle. Maintaining sufficient daylight for the adjacent Engineering building and also providing enough light for the Anatomy department were further complications. The University Court approved the plans on 14 December 1899. At the heart of the building is the 2-storey, top-lit, museum with a narrow gallery around the upper level [FIG.115]. Scott's lecture theatre was truncated to make room for the museum. The low front range, facing north, contained the museum keeper's house, offices for the professor and demonstrator and a laboratory for embryological research. The largest components of the extended facilities were the demonstration room and a practical anatomy laboratory. The external detailing of the modest north front includes Scottish Baronial and Renaissance motifs drawn from the adjacent Engineering building and Pearce Lodge. The grandest architectural flourish is reserved for the entrance to the keeper's house, now the CIDS Biomedical Incubator Unit, where Thomson's legacy is recorded in the Baronial panel over the doorway. Art Nouveau iron gates protect the door. Like Honeyman & Keppie's Anatomy building for Queen Margaret College, a discreet courtyard was provided for the reception of bodies. This was roofed as an extension by Dorward, Matheson, Gleave & Partners in 1977. Numerous alterations have been made over the years, including minor work by the architect Jack Coia for new cloakrooms in 1947.[53]

SURGICAL BUILDING 1900–1903

In 1900 Burnet prepared sketch plans of a new L-plan Surgical building to replace the existing temporary corrugated-iron sheds and wrap-around behind the Engineering and Anatomy buildings.[54] Construction of the Surgical building at an estimated cost of £10,540 was approved by the University Court the following March.[55] The main space was given over to an operating hall containing twelve operating tables (re-used from the old Surgical building). There was adjoining instrument, demonstration, examination, cloakroom and professorial provision, and an entrance hall, general research space and storage, including cold storage for bodies in the basement. The main entrance and 'frontage' was to the south, but this was quickly obscured by the temporary Chemistry building and then by its replacement, the James Watt Engineering building (South). Three large windows and rooflights lit the operating hall from the south (unlike Anatomy, which was lit by north-facing rooflights). Although this arrangement was at the insistence of the Professor of Surgery, Sir William Macewen, it proved necessary to introduce a sprinkler system to cool the glass roof in summer 1922.[56] The building has since been remodelled significantly, notably when the James Watt Engineering building (South) was added in the 1950s.

BUILDINGS FOR MEDICINE AND NATURAL PHILOSOPHY 1902–1907

For the first time on the Gilmorehill site the design of new buildings was opened up to competition in late 1902.[57] The planned Natural Philosophy and Medical departments [FIG.116] formed part of the first quinquennial grant programme of the Carnegie Trust for the Universities of Scotland, which awarded £20,000 to each building.[58] The remainder of the money came from the University's Ninth Jubilee Appeal of 1901.

The four architectural competition entrants, all Glasgow companies, were: Macwhannell & Rogerson; Honeyman, Keppie & Mackintosh; H.E. Clifford; and James Miller. Miller's plans for both buildings were selected on 8 January 1903 on the basis of reports into the practicalities of the buildings by the relevant professors.[59] Planning for the buildings continued in tandem and the same Clerk of Works (James Murray) and local building contractors were appointed for both projects.[60] Miller was assisted by James Carruthers Walker in developing the plans.[61] Unlike the other competitors, Miller also provided various alternative locations and a scheme for a single building containing both the

116 View by T. & R. Annan from the University tower towards the Natural Philosophy and West Medical buildings under construction, 13 July 1905
GUAS [PHU 2/115]

117 The Kelvin building (Natural Philosophy), view of the basement workshop, photographed by Henry Bedford Lemere in 1909
RCAHMS [Bedford Lemere Collection, SC 1140635]

Natural History and Medical departments in a linear arrangement with the main front of the Gilbert Scott building.[62] The constraint in the brief of maintaining the University recreation ground and cycle track in their existing locations to the west of Professors' Square presented serious difficulties in sensible planning of the new facilities. This restriction pushed at least one of the new buildings onto the steep slope down to Kelvingrove Park. Miller's alternatives were intended to improve the siting of the buildings by rearranging or scrapping the recreation ground, but the Court rejected these proposals.

Drawings for Macwhannell & Rogerson's bulky classical design and written descriptions of the other schemes remain in the University Archives, but the plans by Honeyman, Keppie & Mackintosh and H.E. Clifford are not known to survive.[63] According to a letter of 19 November 1902 from Charles Rennie Mackintosh to the German architect, Hermann Muthesius, Mackintosh was largely responsible for the firm's scheme:

120 Mains St, Blythswood
19th November 1902
Dear Mr Muthesius
I am very busy just now at two large buildings in connection with the Glasgow University competition of course – that makes eight competitions I have entered since the end of May and I have not got one of them so far. I have still another Town Hall to do before we come to stay with you in London.
With kind regards to you both.
I am
Yours sincerely
Chas R. Mackintosh[64]

Both the Medical and Natural Philosophy buildings were constructed of Giffnock sandstone to match the main buildings and roofed with blue Westmoreland slates. Internally, the fittings were made of high-quality exotic timbers, such as Kauri pine from New Zealand, teak and mahogany. They were also fitted with electric light and electrical power supplies for other purposes. A novel feature of both buildings was the 'Nuvacuumette' vacuum steam heating system supplied by Ashwell & Nesbit of Leicester. The company advertised that the benefits of the system were its controllability, efficiency, economy; and that 'rooms warmed by it do not become stuffy, the heat given off being mild and pleasant'.[65]

WEST MEDICAL BUILDING 1902–1907

The new Medical building was intended to house the three departments of Physiology, Materia Medica (Pharmacology) and Forensic Science and Public Health [FIG.120]. While the Honeyman, Keppie & Mackintosh scheme was the cheapest, Professor John Gray McKendrick (Physiology) found Miller's proposals 'convenient and well planned'. Stylistically, the building is a free mixture of Baronial, Renaissance and Baroque details, drawing on motifs in the existing Gilmorehill buildings by Burnet and the Scotts. The influence of the old High Street buildings continued to be felt in the strapwork pediments to the entrances and the gateway to the Materia Medica department. Maintaining the tradition of subject 'silos' in the main building, the three medical departments had their own separate entrances and there were no shared or connecting spaces within. At the centre of the intricate plan were two small courtyards, designed to bring light into the core of the complex. The articulation of the building in blocks of varying heights did not reflect the departmental distribution, but it did enable Miller to flood the buildings with natural light from all directions via the large numbers of windows and glazed roofs. In fact the level of daylight proved problematic and blinds were ordered. The department plans interlocked, with Forensic Medicine occupying the top two floors, Materia Medica inhabiting much of the first floor and Physiology taking up the remaining lion's share of the building.

The smallest department, Forensic Medicine and Public Health, had three large laboratories for toxicology, chemistry and bacteriology, a lecture theatre, class museum, library and balance equipment, preparation and store rooms. As might be expected, Materia Medica had a large pharmacy laboratory, a chemical laboratory, lecture theatre, museum, library and associated preparation rooms. Physiology had the magnificent horseshoe-plan lecture theatre with the domed cupola at the extreme west of the building, three enormous laboratories for histology, physiological chemistry and experimental physiology, a museum, library and centrifuge, balance, galvanometer (for detecting and measuring electrical currents) and other preparation and storage rooms. Specific rooms for research work were also provided. At this period all three departments undertook licensed animal experimentation, but insufficient housing was provided, so a brick animal house was added to the east of the building to serve the Materia Medica department.[66] Professor Diarmid Noël Paton, successor to Professor McKendrick in Physiology and pioneering researcher of metabolism and nutrition, planned the extensive fitting out and furnishing of the building. The Prince and Princess of Wales opened both the Medical and Natural Philosophy buildings on 23 April 1907.[67] Principal Donald MacAlister used the occasion to launch an appeal for funds to improve facilities for the Arts Faculty.

118 The lecture theatre of the Kelvin building (Natural Philosophy), photographed by Harry Bedford Lemere in 1909. The room was sub-divided horizontally in 1991.
RCAHMS [Bedford Lemere Collection, SC 683494]

The Medical building was much altered, particularly after the Second World War, when the departments of Public Health and Forensic Medicine left the building. Jack Coia made an initial investigation into increasing the seating in the Physiology lecture theatre in 1948 and the addition of another storey to the histology laboratory in 1949, and he converted the old animal house to a new human metabolism laboratory in 1953. However, Keppie, Henderson & Partners were responsible for a more thoroughgoing refurbishment and recasting of the building in 1968.[68] The large extensions to the east are considered in Chapter Eight.

THE KELVIN BUILDING (NATURAL PHILOSOPHY) 1902–1906

Built simultaneously with the Medical building, which is described above, the Natural Philosophy building had a more unified Renaissance design and near-symmetrical courtyard plan [FIG.119]. An access corridor ran around the courtyard, with rooms opening off it on the south, east and west sides. Professor Gray and Dr Caird of Natural Philosophy preferred Miller's scheme marginally over that of Macwhannell & Rogerson 'in point of arrangement of rooms for work, convenience

119 The main entrance of the Kelvin building (Natural Philosophy) photographed by Henry Bedford Lemere in 1909. As at the West Medical building, the decorative entrance and window pediments are intended to evoke the Old College buildings in the High Street.
RCAHMS [Bedford Lemere Collection, SC 683492]

120 The West Medical building photographed by Henry Bedford Lemere in 1909
RCAHMS [Bedford Lemere Collection, SC 683594]

of access, provision of light' and for the fact that they would not 'conflict glaringly with the designs of the existing buildings'. Miller's ample provision for research space, plant and appliances 'such as dynamos, secondary batteries, low temperature apparatus workshop etc.' was also a significant factor in his selection.

Internally, the huge building contained the following areas and related features. In the basement were: a mechanical workshop; a joiner's workshop; a dynamo and battery room; a room for electrical research; three research laboratoriess; three research rooms; male cloakrooms; and numerous stores. The ground floor contained: a large lecture theatre; an apparatus room; a general laboratory; a chemical physics laboratory; an electrical laboratory; professor's room and laboratory; preparatory, diagram and balance rooms; and female cloakrooms. On the first floor were located: a grating spectrometer room; a private electrical laboratory; magnetic, preparatory, photography, spectroscopy and special research rooms; a museum; and a small lecture theatre.

Notably, there was provision from the outset of both male and female cloakrooms. The Natural Philosophy building was the first at Gilmorehill to be equipped with the American Electric Utilities Company's 'Metaphone' system, an internal telephone network that could operate without a central switchboard.[69] The internal spaces were fairly basic in their finishing. A higher level of decoration was allowed for the public spaces and fitting of the professor's rooms. The entrance hall and stairs were panelled. The corridor was floored with 'terrazzo', a composite material resembling marble chips, and lined with white and yellow glazed tiles. Structural steelwork was left visible in places, especially in the roof of the main lecture theatre. One of the earliest experiments in the physical laboratory was to test the transparency of a Pilkington glass proposed for use in the new Edward VII wing of the British Museum, designed by John James Burnet.[70] Miller soon added a laboratory to the north in 1921–22.[71] Numerous further alterations to the configuration of the rooms have taken place over the years, but some of the original finishes survive. A new floor divided the 2-storey main lecture theatre in 1991. The extensions of the 1940s and 1950s are described in Chapter 8.

DRILL HALL, UNIVERSITY PLACE 1903

The University of Glasgow Officers' Training Corps (OTC) was formed in 1910 as a result of the Haldane reforms of the Army. In January 1911 the convenor of the military committee of the OTC, Dudley Julius Medley ('Deadly Muddly'), Professor of Modern History, submitted a request to the Court for permanent accommodation for the OTC and was allocated a site on the recreation ground beside the fives courts that then extended westwards from the Gymnasium. The Drill Hall, which was probably designed by David Barclay of H. & D. Barclay in 1911, has a mildly militaristic frontage of corbelled parapets and turrets facing University Place. It was then extended westwards by the successor to the practice, Colin Sinclair.[72] Apart from the Drill Hall itself, the building contained a miniature shooting range along its eastern side, an armoury, engineers' and infantry stores, orderly rooms, a cadets' dressing room, a lecture room and an officers' mess and library. Monro & Partners replaced the main Drill Hall behind the University Place frontage with a larger building in 1986.[73]

Chapter Seven

War and the Inter-War Period 1914–1945

121 Design for the Memorial Chapel by John Burnet, Son & Dick, with watercolours added by Robert Eadie
Glasgow University Chaplaincy Centre

Student numbers more than doubled from 1,921 to 4,727 between 1917 and 1920 as interrupted studies were resumed and new students enrolled. The shortage of space became chronic, particularly in the Medical Faculty (where the government paid the fees for returning servicemen). The Arts Faculty, Engineering and Zoology were also badly affected. Teaching staff in the Arts Faculty had increased from seven to fifty-three since the move to Gilmorehill, but the accommodation remained unchanged. Student and staff study and recreational facilities were similarly inadequate or non-existent. In 1919 the Chancellor of the Exchequer set up the University Grants Committee as a standing committee of the Treasury, under the chairmanship of Sir William M'Cormick. Its purpose was, 'To inquire into the financial needs of University Education in the United Kingdom, and to advise the Government as to the application of any grants made by Parliament towards meeting them.'

To begin to alleviate these accommodation problems by the erection of new buildings the Carnegie Trustees confirmed a grant of £45,000 over five years under their third quinquennial scheme starting in October 1913.[1] A committee on new buildings for Arts and Zoology was formed, and Burnet drew up a preliminary report and three alternative sets of plans in late 1913 and early 1914, for which he was paid £100.[2] Although the Court expressly reserved the right to select an architect by competition at a later stage, in fact they allowed Burnet to develop the second of his initial plans to such an advanced stage that if they had appointed another architect it would have caused severe embarrassment.[3] Burnet's proposal was to construct a new Zoology building to the west of the Natural Philosophy building and complete the western side of the west quadrangle with a chapel, staff facilities and classrooms for the Arts Faculty. Space freed by the removal of Zoology was to be converted into an examination hall. The University began to acquire a number of properties on the north side of University Avenue in this period, for example Hillhead House was gifted to the University by the family of the Glasgow merchant, Walter MacLellan of Blairvaddick, and 1 University Gardens was bought for the Women's Union in 1922.[4]

Initially, the outbreak of the First World War in July 1914 had had relatively little effect on the University, but gradually the loss of students and staff to military duties increased, student fees fell, and the impact was felt strongly. However, the impact of the Second World War was much more immediate and the physical effects much greater. The Principal began preparations for war in October 1938, when he ordered sandbags, timber and scaffolding, and had a large water storage tank installed in the west quadrangle for fire-fighting purposes. Air

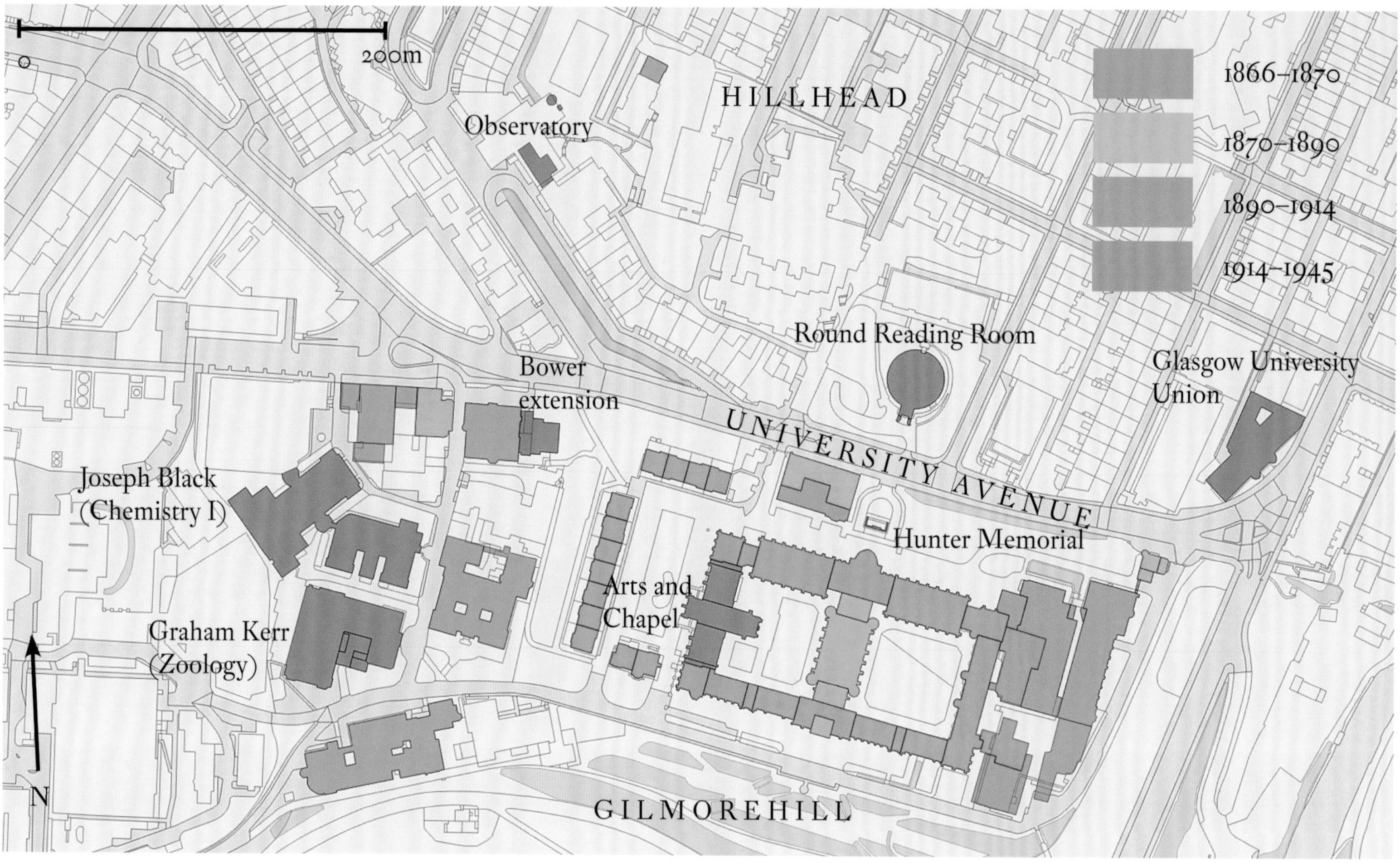

0 200m

1866–1870
1870–1890
1890–1914
1914–1945

HILLHEAD
Observatory
Round Reading Room
Bower extension
Glasgow University Union
UNIVERSITY AVENUE
Joseph Black (Chemistry I)
Hunter Memorial
Arts and Chapel
Graham Kerr (Zoology)
N
GILMOREHILL

raid shelters were created from rooms below the Cloisters and the West Range. The University buildings sustained no direct hits during the Clydebank bombing raids of 13 March 1941, but the Pearce Lodge chimney-heads and most of the windows on the south sides of the Gilbert Scott, West Medical and Zoology buildings were destroyed.[5] It was the end of 1946 before the firm of Hughes & Waugh could supervise permanent repairs.[6]

SIR HECTOR HETHERINGTON, PRINCIPAL OF THE UNIVERSITY 1936–1961

Hector Hetherington's tenure as Principal spanned six generations of students during a period of enormous upheaval and change [FIG.123]. He had been a student at the University from 1905–10, then a lecturer in Moral Philosophy from 1910–14, before moving to Sheffield in 1914 and his first professional appointment at University College, Cardiff in 1915. In 1920, at the exceptionally young age of 32, Hetherington became principal at University College and transformed its fortunes. He returned to Glasgow in 1924 for a three-year stint as Professor of Moral Philosophy before taking up the post of Vice Chancellor at the University of Liverpool. Here Hetherington again transformed the University's finances and estate, commissioning the Harold Cohen Library from the architect Harold Dod in March 1936. He was knighted at the beginning of the same year, before returning to Glasgow as Principal in the autumn. The charismatic Hetherington brought a dynamism and energy to the job that contrasted with his weary and ill predecessor, Robert Rait. There were numerous problems to tackle, particularly annual deficits,

122 Development of Gilmorehill and Hillhead between 1914 and 1945
© Crown Copyright 2013 Ordnance Survey [Licence Number 100021521]

123 Sir Hector Hetherington by David Abercrombie Donaldson in 1945
GUHMAG [GLAHA 44226]

demoralised staff and the serious under-investment in the University's estate. Gradually improvements in the University's finances and staffing were achieved. Recognising the need to plan capital investment properly, Hetherington set up a committee on building policy.[7] Hetherington's ambitious building programme started before the Second World War with the huge Joseph Black building (Chemistry) and the Round Reading Room, but continued with equal vigour after the war at the Kelvin building (Natural Philosophy), James Watt Engineering (South), the Alexander Stone building (Modern Languages), the Stevenson building (Physical Education) and the Davidson building (Biochemistry), along with a whole host of repairs and upgrading of infrastructure. He took a great personal interest in continuing the scheme of stained glass in the Chapel. Although he retired before the sudden and great expansion of the University in the 1960s, Hetherington was responsible for acquisition of the Garscube site and the appointment of Joseph Lea Gleave, the architect who planned the Hillhead campus.

BUILDINGS 1914–1945

THE GRAHAM KERR BUILDING (ZOOLOGY) 1913–1924

John Graham Kerr, Professor of Zoology since 1902, had long been a passionate advocate of improved facilities for his department, which inhabited a dark labyrinth of basements and cellars beneath the Hunterian Museum. His proposal was to locate a new building along University Avenue in front of the Hunterian Museum, so that the department would still have use of the Museum collections. The removal of the recreation ground to Anniesland in 1909 now allowed a more expansive site away from the vibrations of the road to the west of the Natural Philosophy building. Kerr finally had agreement to his new building in 1914, but war put a stop to all building activity.[8] With some exasperation he described conditions in his class in 1917:

The class room, built I am told for 150 students, has now to accommodate 270. Chairs are crammed into every available corner and every morning some students have to sit on the floor and others to stand. The atmosphere gets into such a state that twice when about halfway through the lecture it has become impossible to work on the blackboard through the moisture condensed on it and I have had all the windows open. The laboratory accommodation is still more inadequate.[9]

The scheme proposed was revisited between 1920 and 1922,[10] contracts being signed in November 1921.[11] Although John James Burnet provided the overall scheme, he continued to be busy at his semi-independent firm in London, Sir John Burnet & Partners, so much of the drawing was done by the Glasgow office draughtsmen, Walter K. Knight and James Napier.[12] Norman Aitken Dick, partner in Burnet's Glasgow firm from 1907, undertook the detailed work and construction supervision.[13] The building was designed to an extraordinary level of detail, down to the cupboards and laboratory benches, which were custom-made with single pieces of seasoned teak 3ft (0.9m) wide by 20ft (6m) long.[14] The building opened for the beginning of term in October 1923, but work continued into early 1924 [FIG.125]. Graham Kerr was an exacting client, demanding instant rectification of quite minor details. The finished building reflects his strongly held views on the teaching of natural history, with an emphasis on microscope laboratory work and the study of museum artefacts. To encourage its use, the museum was placed centrally between the main lecture theatre and the elementary laboratory.

The building marked a radical switch from the Renaissance and Baronial clothing of the firm's other work at Gilmorehill to a far more inventive and original design. The different functions of parts of the building are expressed externally through massing and detailing. On the south side, the large lecture theatre and museum are distinguished by the monumental quality of the deeply channelled Northumberland stonework and Baroque details such as the broken pediment and domed roof ventilator. By contrast the north elevation is highly glazed to provide light and airy laboratory working space [FIG.126]. Where windows were required, they were located to meet the internal functional needs, rather than for decorative or stylistic reasons (e.g. the windows of the main lecture theatre are stepped to reflect the raked seating inside). Critical reaction to the building was largely positive, with the marine zoologist Sir Maurice Young describing the teaching laboratory as 'the most magnificent in Great Britain and perhaps Europe'. However, *The Builder* journal was unimpressed: 'The new Zoology Buildings, Glasgow University, by Sir John Burnet, Son & Dick, lack unity in design. The curiously unbalanced nature of the composition is probably due to the necessities of the internal arrangement.'[15] Given the dark and damp conditions in the old basements, the two main functional considerations of the new building were the lighting and heating/ventilation. The mainly unbroken walls of the south side of the building protected the museum and laboratories from direct sunlight, but the large windows extending into the roof on the north side and the glazed lantern over the museum enabled well-lit working conditions. A small courtyard enclosed the live animal houses and there were two large tanks on the roof of the museum for marine biology.

Although there have been numerous alterations over

the years, the building still has a very fine interior. A spacious entrance hall with a terrazzo floor by the Hamburg firm, Diespeker & Co., leads to a broad staircase [FIG.128]. The original glazed tiles appear to survive here beneath later woodchip wallpaper. The newel posts of the stair are decorated with carved lions' heads. The main lecture theatre has pine panelling and steeply raked curved seating. The original mechanism for the window blinds survives and was in working order until recently: this lowered the blackout blinds for the three different sized windows simultaneously, darkening the room for Professor Graham Kerr's microscope projector and cinematograph equipment.[16] The large 2-storey elementary practical classroom with roof-glazing in the north-west corner of the building has subsequently been divided horizontally. The benches were arranged in parallel lines to the great windows, with the partially glazed roof illuminating the back of the classroom. At this early date the standard light-source for a microscope was natural daylight reflected up through the sample via a mirror, so good lighting provision was essential. The other laboratories for advanced zoology, protozoology and experimentation were all sited on the north side of the building, also with large windows for microscope work and viewing the colours of specimens in natural light.

The most magnificent space is the museum, designed to house the Hunterian Museum's zoological collections. This was laid out in the manner of a Greek temple with a Doric *peristasis* (colonnade or row of columns) around the central top-lit display/working area and a surrounding outer *pteron* (aisle) for wall display cases. The natural top-lighting, distributed through a grid of glazed panels over a deep timber grid to prevent direct sunlight hitting the exhibits, was lost when an extension was added to the top of the museum. The surrounding aisles have also been lost to the construction of stores and offices. Graham Kerr had very strong ideas about museum presentation, which included a preference for black velvet backgrounds in the display cases and black descriptive labels with gold text [FIG.129]. A utilitarian brick extension containing further laboratory and research rooms was added to the west by John Keppie & Henderson in 1946, but this has been replaced subsequently. The large elementary laboratory was subdivided horizontally in 1959. Wylie, Shanks & Partners created a neuro-physiology unit, aquarium and animal house in 1964, and Keppie Henderson & Partners constructed a rooftop extension over the museum in 1968.[17]

ARTS BLOCK AND CHAPEL 1913–1929

Like Zoology, accommodation for the Arts Faculty had been in crisis for a number of years before the

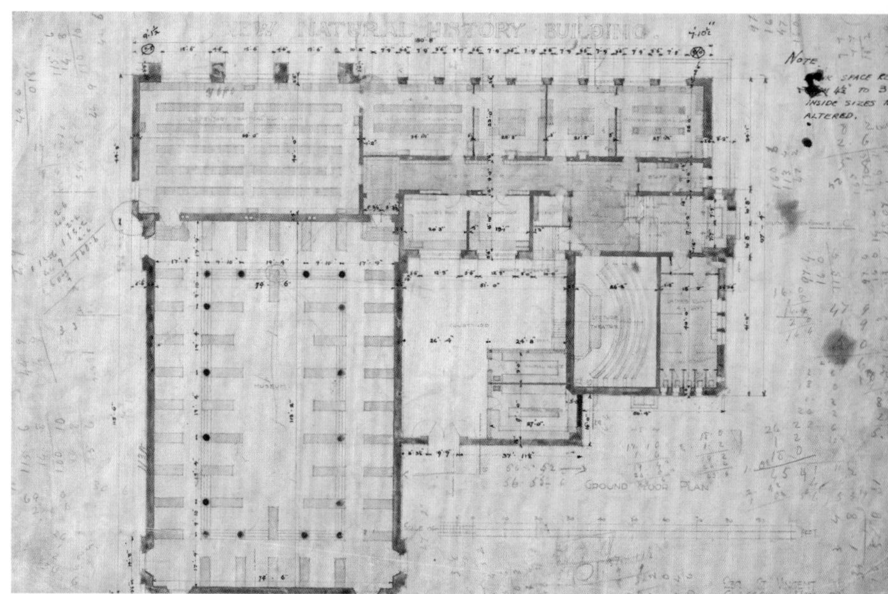

124 Ground floor plan of the Graham Kerr building (Zoology)
GUAS [BUL 6/16/9]

[right]
127 Professor Graham Kerr supervising practical experiments in the double-height laboratory. The benches are arranged parallel to the full-height windows on the right hand side of the image.
GUHMAG (Zoology)

128 The entrance hall and stair of the Graham Kerr building in 1924
GUHMAG (Zoology)

129 The museum of the Graham Kerr building, photographed after fitting out in 1924
GUHMAG (Zoology)

125 The entrance to the Graham Kerr building (Zoology), photographed soon after completion in 1924
GUHMAG (Zoology)

126 The great windows of the north front of the Graham Kerr building (Zoology), photographed soon after completion in 1924
GUHMAG (Zoology)

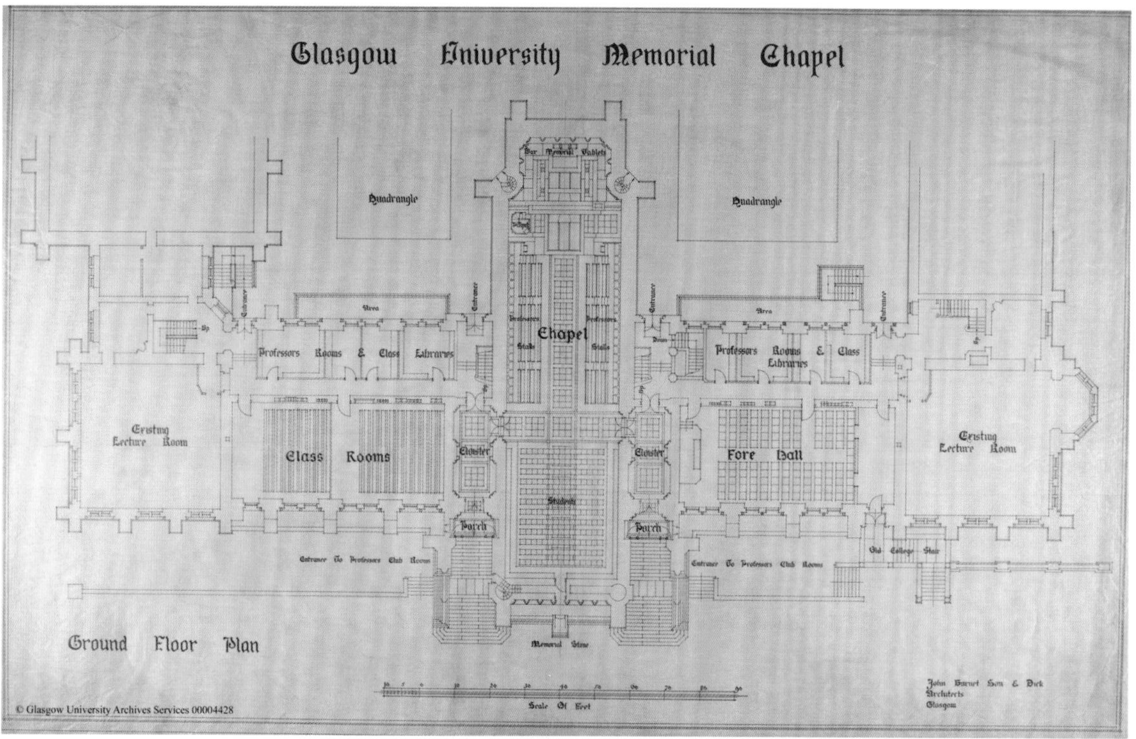

130 Ground floor plan of the Arts Block and Memorial Chapel, about 1922
GUAS [BUL 6/5/48]

First World War. Under Burnet's alternative schemes of 1913–14, the Arts Faculty would have been inserted between the northern row of professors' houses and University Avenue, with the Chapel adjoining to the south-west.[18] With hindsight, this would have enabled a much more practical plan for the Arts Faculty, but the professors were presumably not keen to lose their back gardens. Burnet first drew up detailed plans for the new building on the current site in the autumn of 1914, by which time the First World War had begun. These plans were revisited and revised after the war in 1919. By February 1922 almost £200,000 was in place for the new building as a result of Carnegie Trust grants and subscriptions to the Chapel, which was to form a memorial to the dead of the 1914–18 war.[19] Tenders were accepted in January 1923 for everything except the professors' stalls. Work continued until 1929. The site constraints on the design were a sharp slope between the quadrangle and Professors' Square and the new building needed to connect with the existing ranges of the Gilbert Scott building, structurally, functionally and aesthetically. The second of Burnet's three alternative designs proposed a cruciform plan with the ranges of Arts Faculty classrooms running north/ south between the Gilbert Scott pavilions and the Chapel, forming a short intervening east/west range at the centre [FIG.130].

Burnet was more heavily involved in the detailed design of the Chapel than with the Zoology building, but he still relied on Norman Dick to carry out much of the detailed supervision. He devised a compact plan and a soaring 13th-century French Gothic style with Scottish details and a beautiful open flèche (small spire), not dissimilar to his earlier Barony Church on Castle Street of 1886–90. The adjoining Arts Faculty ranges were more akin to Scott's collegiate Gothic style, even replicating the iron window pattern in steel. The unfortunate impression of these contrasting ecclesiastical and collegiate styles is that the Chapel has collided with the West Range. This effect is further reinforced by the disastrous internal plan, in which the Chapel cuts off any interconnection between the northern and southern teaching blocks of the range, except at basement level. The incorporation of the Chapel within the range effectively divided it in two, perpetuating Scott's separate vertical units of teaching rooms, and taking up

131 The Memorial Chapel under construction, about 1924. The steel frame and patent concrete floors are clearly visible, along with the more traditional masonry work of the exterior.
GUAS [PHU 11/4]

132 The Memorial Chapel

1914
1918
via veritas vita

133 Chapel interior, detail of carved stone angel

134 Pelican motif on the west front of the Chapel, possibly designed by Walter Gilbert

135 Owl motif, possibly carved by Archibald Dawson

valuable space with multiple sets of stairs.

In spite of the clumsy planning, the new range did provide significant additional space for the Arts Faculty: eight large classrooms, sixteen class libraries, sixteen rooms for professors, and a staff club including a common room, dining room, writing room and kitchen. Unlike the lavishly equipped Zoology building, the lecture theatres of the Arts building had simple chart hangers, blackboards and an occasional lantern screen. Toilet facilities were restricted to the staff club. A technical innovation was 'concealed electric light tubing', which was to be used everywhere apart from the tutorial rooms.[20] In order to close the west quadrangle of the Gilbert Scott building, it was first necessary to dismantle the Old College lion and unicorn stairs and Forehall doorway, which had formed an access from Professors' Square. Very detailed survey drawings were made and the stones were numbered for re-erection in a different arrangement as part of the new Arts building.[21] The stair had been rebuilt in its original arrangement in 1872 with a turn to the right, but the new building required a left turn in the stair. The decorative elements were to be re-used, including forty-two of the original forty-three balusters, but the steps and landings were to be reconstructed in York stone from Joseph Brooke & Sons and some additional balusters made. Although the West Range appears to be a traditional stone building in its construction, in fact it has a steel frame and patent concrete floors, which are totally independent of the walls. Burnet was keen to avoid the impact of delays in the supply of stone that had hampered the Zoology building, where the floors were dependent on the construction of the walls.[22] The two principal contractors by price for the building were Train & Taylor (masonry, £69,998) and John Cochrane (joinery, including the oak roof, £17,886).

A fireplace from the old Senate Room was to be installed in the professors' common room. The bell, from the Old College church, the Blackfriars' Kirk, first presented in 1643 by George Duncan of Barrowfield, and then re-cast in 1708, was presented to the University by Major Garroway during the war. The bell bears the incription: 'GEORGIUS DUNCANUS DE BYROFIELD ALMAE MATRI DICAVIT 1708'. It was originally destined

136 Detail of carved wooden figures on the Chapel stalls

for the main tower of the Gilbert Scott building, but the University was unable to obtain a construction licence. The bell was eventually hung in the flèche over the Chapel, but with an electric striking mechanism to prevent damage.

The undisputed glory of the scheme is the jewel-like interior decoration of the Chapel. Like its contemporary in Edinburgh, Robert Lorimer's National War Memorial at the Castle, the power of the Chapel interior derives from the simplicity of the space and the use of the highest quality materials and craftsmanship. An oak hammerbeam roof covers the rectangular-plan space with its geometric stone floor and tall lancet (pointed-arched) windows. The light fittings hang from carved beams representing the ten figures of the Wise and Foolish Virgins parable. The ornamentation started off as an allowance of £1,500 for stone carving in the 1922 contract, with provision for later detailed design and appointment of a specialist architectural stone carver. Although the original windows, designed by the Abbey Studio of the City Glass Company, were largely of small panes of clear glass with borders and simple decorative motifs, there was an early intention to replace them with a harmonious scheme of stained glass windows.[23] Much of the building work had been completed before attention turned to the detailed design of the decorative stone carving and timber fittings. In a letter of 26 April 1927 to Alan Clapperton, Clerk of the Court, the firm of Burnet, Son & Dick describe what they had in mind:

We have developed a limited scheme of carving for the exterior of the New Buildings, and we are in course of developing a scheme for the interior for the Chapel, which would be closely associated with the War Memorial, and the arrangement of the Stalls and the Organ. The Contract provides a sum of £1,500 for stone carving based on an estimate received from two Architectural Sculptors reputed to have some experience in Gothic Work.

On developing the models of the carving with these Sculptors we found they were not sufficiently appreciative of the type of work required, and were forced to obtain the assistance of a Sculptor of repute [presumed to be Walter Gilbert, co-founder of the Bromsgrove Guild who had previously worked with Burnet on the decorative elevator cage at the Edward VII Galleries of the British Museum and with Giles Gilbert Scott on the great reredos of Liverpool Anglican Cathedral] *who has done a considerable amount of work at Liverpool Cathedral. This Sculptor has given us several models which have been carved on the building, and a probable cost for the remainder of the external work and the internal carving.*[24]

In 1927 Lord Maclay, the shipowner, presented an organ by the great makers, Henry Willis & Sons, for which Burnet designed the casing.[25] The construction of the organ front, oak stalls, pulpit, communion table, lectern and memorial tablets required a separate tender in July 1928, which was won by the existing joiner, John Cochrane. However, there appears to have been some controversy surrounding the carved work, as Norman Dick seems to have instructed Cochrane's to subcontract it to another tenderer, Crawford. In the end much of the carving was probably carried out by Archibald Dawson of architectural sculptors, Dawson & Young. Walter Gilbert was responsible for the pulpit.[26] The electrical work, including the installation of Burnet's extraordinary Gothic electroliers, was under a separate contract awarded to Claud Hamilton.

In his last act as Principal, the ailing Sir Donald MacAlister presided over the dedication of the Chapel on 4 October 1929 in memory of the 750 students, staff and alumni of the University who had died in the 1914–18 war. The nine slate memorial panels were inscribed with the names of the fallen by Galbraith & Winton, marble cutters of Glasgow.[27] A further 404 names were later added to new memorial tablets for those who perished in the Second World War.

The remarkable collection of stained glass windows, which are now such a feature of the Chapel, were added from 1931 when Douglas Strachan was commissioned to create a series representing the efforts of the various branches of academia to understand the universe. The four lancets in the north wall completed by Strachan represent 'Theology', 'Law', 'Medicine' and 'Applied Science'. The 1937 'Alma Mater' window depicting the University buildings is also by Strachan, donated by graduates in New South Wales. Strachan left designs for 'History' and 'Literature' in the west wall, which were completed after his death by his pupil, Gordon Webster. Strachan described his work in the Chapel as 'an attempt to figure man's life, all life, as engaged on a spiritual enterprise'.[28] Strachan is perhaps Scotland's most celebrated stained glass designer of the 20th century. He also worked on the Bute Hall, the National War Memorial and St Margaret's Chapel in Edinburgh Castle, St Salvator's Chapel at the University of St Andrews and King's College Chapel at the University of Aberdeen. On the advice of the architect Joe Gleave of John Keppie, Henderson & J.L. Gleave, the Principal invited Sadie McLellan (Sally Pritchard) and Gordon Webster to produce competing designs for the last window, 'Law' in Strachan's scheme, in the north wall.[29] In spite of Gleave's preference for McLellan's originality, the Court selected Webster's design on the basis that it was more harmonious with the existing three windows by Strachan. The Court selected Webster again to design 'Literature and Art' and 'History' in the south wall in 1957.

In October 1958 Sir Hector Hetherington wrote to the architect Basil Spence for his advice on a stained glass artist for the three lights of the main east window, which were to be commissioned as the result of a £5,000 benefaction.[30] While acknowledging the need to maintain a harmony with Strachan's legacy, Hetherington clearly viewed the east window as an opportunity for a separate and more contemporary treatment. At that time Spence was employed by the University on the design of the Virology Institute on Church Street. However, it was Spence's experience as the architect of the rebuilt Coventry Cathedral that prompted Hetherington to seek his advice. The Cathedral is widely regarded as one of the architectural and artistic masterpieces of the post-war period. Spence responded with a shortlist of artists including William Wilson (who inherited much of Strachan's glass), Patrick Reyntiens, John Piper, Lawrence Lee, Geoffrey Clarke, Keith New and Margaret Traherne.[31] After much research by the Principal and Chapel Committee, Lee, Wilson and Carl Edwards (who designed the replacement windows for the bombed House of Lords) were invited to provide designs. Lee, the head of the stained glass department at the Royal College of Art and a collaborator with Spence

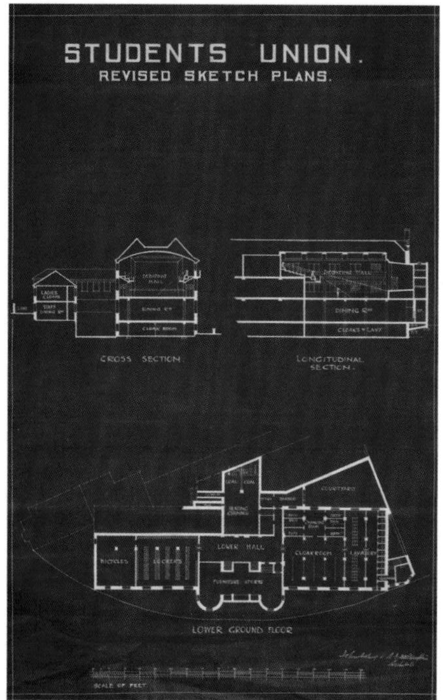

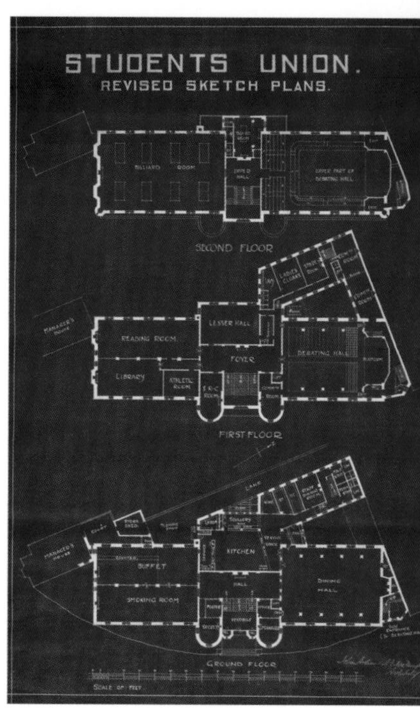

137 Blueprint sketch of Glasgow University Union
GUAS [BUL 6/18/12 and 13]

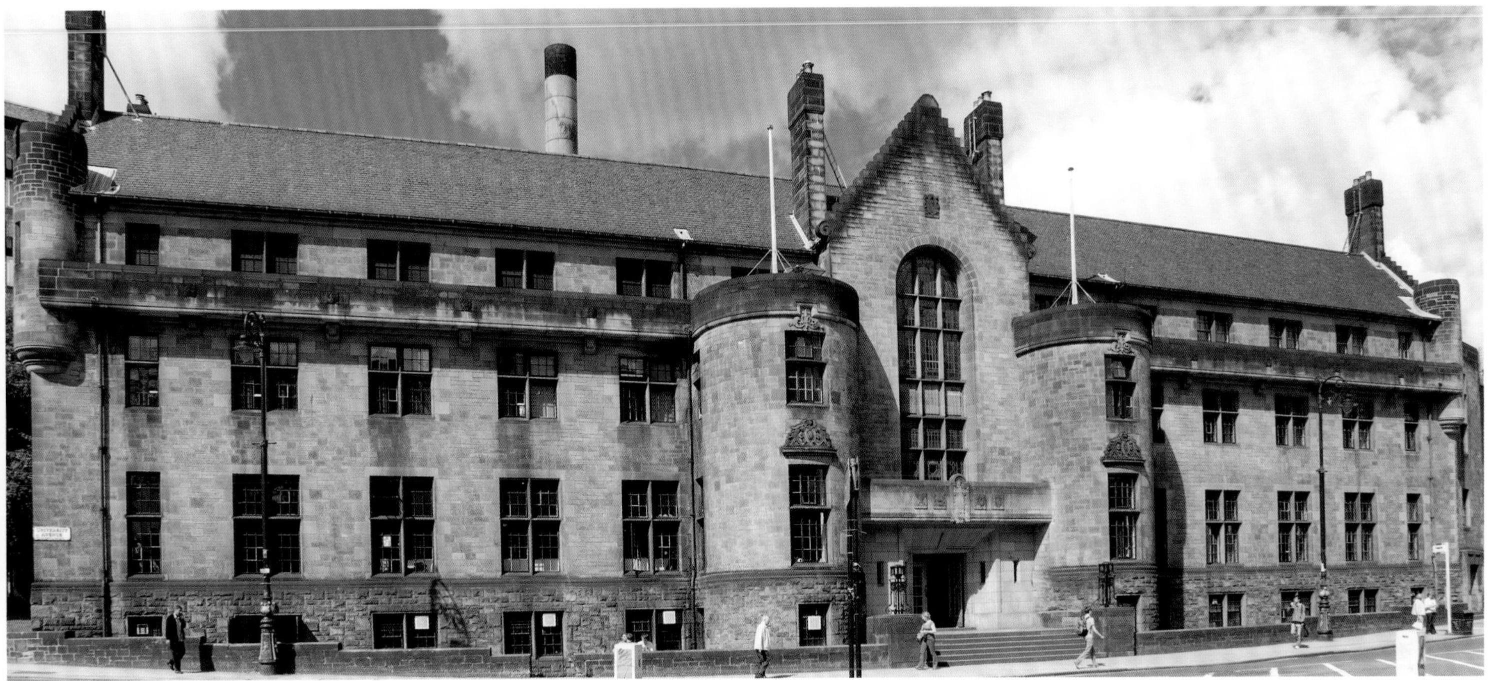

138 Glasgow University Union designed by Alan McNaughtan, a former assistant to John James Burnet, in 1928

on Coventry Cathedral, was selected and produced the spiky, angular 'Benedicite' window, which was dedicated on 13 May 1962.[32] Keith New, one of Lee's pupils and another contributor to the glass at Coventry Cathedral, made fresh designs for the remaining west wall windows, 'Science' and 'Philosophy', in 1966. More abstract designs by Alan Younger, winner of the Chapel 50th anniversary competition in 1979, fill a further two lancet windows in the south wall.[33] The original external lamps were replaced in 1953 by David M. Tyre & Sons, art metal workers.[34] The architect Ian G. Lindsay prepared a new scheme of lighting and raked seating at the west end of the Chapel in 1967, but this does not appear to have been carried out.[35]

WILLIAM AND GEORGE HUNTER MEMORIAL, GILBERT SCOTT BUILDING 1897–1925

The proposal to erect a monument to two of the University's outstanding alumni of the 18th century, William Hunter (1718–83) and John Hunter (1728–93), had a long gestation. George Ritchie Mather, had published a biographical sketch of the brothers in 1893. William was the benefactor of the University's Hunterian Museum and John was a pioneer of careful observation and scientific method in medicine, and regarded as one of the leading scientists and surgeons of his day. He was appointed Surgeon to King George III in 1776 and Surgeon General in 1789.

Mather wanted a prominent memorial to the brothers erected in their native city. However, before plans could be made, he died suddenly on 29 November 1895. The Faculty of Physicians and Surgeons took up the case and requested the University of Glasgow and the City Corporation to join with them in commemorating the Hunters. A public meeting was held on 29 June 1897 and a fundraising committee formed. Mrs Mather appears to have kept the project alive until John James Burnet was asked to design the memorial for a space at the centre of the north front of the Gilbert Scott building in July 1915.[36] These designs took the form of a tall, slender cross below the Reading Room and a new lodge and arched gateways fronting University Avenue. The First World War prevented further progress until 1923, when the memorial was completely re-designed by Burnet, Son & Dick in the form of a cenotaph with long low wings embracing a raised platform. The sculptor was George Henry Paulin. At last, on 24 June 1925, some thirty years after her husband had first promoted the idea, Mrs Mather was able to unveil this tribute to the two Hunters.

GLASGOW UNIVERSITY UNION, 32 UNIVERSITY AVENUE 1928–1936

A student welfare scheme was set up in 1921 to reinvigorate student life. Funds from the scheme were used to build a new Men's Union to replace the cramped provision in what is now the John McIntyre building. A row of shops dating from the 1870s was demolished to make way for the building, which was the first new University building on the north side of University Avenue/Kelvin Way. The architect chosen through open competition, Alan McNaughtan (1878–1952) of the firm Arthur & McNaughtan, had been an assistant to John James Burnet from 1895 to 1901. Stylistically, the stone-faced building, which was begun in 1928, looked back to the pre-war period, with details reminiscent of Burnet,

Charles Rennie Mackintosh and Robert Lorimer [FIG.138]. Although the *Glasgow Herald* described the internal arrangement as being '*designed on the most up-to-date principles*', to modern eyes the interior seems rather old-fashioned for its date (the year of Le Corbusier's Modernist Villa Savoie at Poissy-sur-Seine for example).[37] Fireplaces abound and traditional craftsmanship is evident in the high-quality finishings such as the cedar dado panelling, oak parquet flooring, leaded glass, stone staircase and Austrian oak wainscoting, On the lower ground floor were large cloakrooms, a locker room, barber's shop and bike store, and above them the dining hall, buffet and two smoking rooms. The main first floor housed the galleried debating hall, lesser hall, library and committee rooms. Finally the board room and 12-table billiard room were located on the top floor. Perhaps the most modern aspect of the building was its servicing, which included extractor fans for ventilation and integral pipework for vacuum cleaning. The decline of the Scottish building stone industry now made it cheaper to source the stone for its construction from the huge modern Blaxter quarry in Northumberland, which also supplied stone for the Zoology building and the Chapel. The roofing slates came from Ballachulish in the West Highlands.

Stanley Baldwin, the former, and future, Prime Minister, performed the official opening ceremony on 12 December 1930.[38] Numerous politicians have begun their careers in the debating hall, including John Smith, Charles Kennedy, Menzies Campbell, Scotland's first First Minister, Donald Dewar, and current Deputy First Minister, Nicola Sturgeon.

After the Second World War temporary huts were constructed adjacent to the Union as a refectory, and remained until the new University Refectory was completed in 1966.[39] The extension at the north end, called 'The Hive', was designed by Keppie, Henderson & Partners in 1965. An addition to the interior was Fyffe Christie's mural 'West End Perk' in the James Bridie Memorial Room to commemorate Bridie's poem of the same name. The Walter Elliot Memorial Library was designed by William John Fairweather, the University's Building Officer, and opened by the Prime Minister, Harold Macmillan, in April 1963.[40]

THE JOSEPH BLACK BUILDING (CHEMISTRY) 1937–1954

A temporary brick Chemistry building designed by John Burnet & Son had been constructed around Gilbert Scott's old Abbot's Kitchen in 1902. By March 1934, when the University Court came to consider an application to the Bellahouston Trustees to assist with urgent accommodation needs, a proper building for the Chemistry department came top of the list of preferred options.[41] An initial estimated cost of almost £200,000 was based on the experience of the University of Edinburgh in constructing the scientific complex known as King's Buildings, designed by Rowand Anderson & Balfour Paul in 1919–24. Building prices had fallen since 1924, but Glasgow had additional space requirements for the teaching of chemistry medical and engineering students. Sufficient progress on fundraising had been made by June 1935 for an architectural competition to take place.[42] The invited shortlist comprised: James Miller; Thomas Harold Hughes; Colin Sinclair; and William J.B. Wright.

The competition entries were received on 7 March 1936 and the anonymised design by 'Priestley' was selected on 21 April.[43] The author of the scheme turned out to be T. Harold Hughes, who had worked for John James Burnet in the 1910s and married his niece, Edith, in 1918. Hughes had left the Burnet practice after a long period of fraught relations with Norman Dick to teach at the Glasgow School of Architecture, where he became professor and director in 1922.[44] Hughes also continued in private practice, undertaking a significant amount of work in Oxford for the colleges and university. Following a limited competition, Hughes had designed the Garscadden Sports Pavilion in Art Deco style for the University in 1936, the same year in which he won the competition for the Chemistry building.[45] Another teacher at the School of Architecture, David Stark Reid Waugh, joined Hughes in his private practice from 1937.

One of the first actions of the dynamic new Principal, Hector Hetherington, in October 1936 was to authorise a public appeal, not just for the Chemistry building, but for the wider University needs.[46] Hughes's scheme comprised a large 'Chemistry Institute' complex of four new specialist departmental buildings for Organic Chemistry, Medical Chemistry, Physical Chemistry and Inorganic Chemistry on the old recreation ground to the north of Zoology. On completion, it was the largest chemistry teaching and research building in Britain [FIG.139]. Demands on materials and labour for the national rearmament programme of 1936 had an impact on general construction costs, which rocketed 20% from the original estimates by the time tenders for the building work were received in July 1937.[47] Increases in the equipment provision, the addition of basement garages, extra under-building and expanded accommodation pushed up the price further to £243,333.[48] Work began immediately, but the Court decided to drop the most expensive element, the Inorganic Chemistry department, which had been costed at £90,000, from the immediate scheme.

The Chemistry Institute was by far the most ambitious inter-war project at Gilmorehill in terms of scale, cost and construction technology. In spite of

139 Bird's-eye view of the proposed Joseph Black building (Chemistry)
Glasgow City Council, Development and Regeneration Services, with the approval of D.G.H. Waugh

140 Plan of the Organic Chemistry department of the Joseph Black building (Chemistry Institute), 25 March 1941
GUAS [BUL 6/19/11]

141 View of the proposed Joseph Black building (Chemistry) from University Place
Glasgow City Council, Development and Regeneration Services, with the approval of D.G.H. Waugh

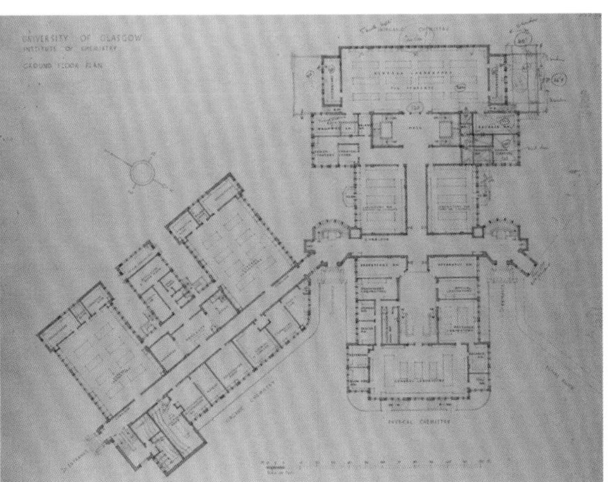

Hughes's vehement anti-Modernism, or the 'Bunkum of Modernity' as he described it in an address to the Royal Institute of British Architects in 1935, the design is a hybrid of contemporary styles. It was in part monumental classicism, with its near-symmetrical layout, stylised classical details and special slim 'Roman' bricks [FIG.141]. It also has elements of 'Art Moderne' (the term derived from the 1925 Paris World Fair *Exposition internationale des arts décoratifs et industriels modernes*) in its horizontal emphasis, flat roofs, butterfly plan, reinforced concrete structure, lying-pane metal windows, projecting glazed staircases, and zig-zag jazz railings.[49] Certainly the use of visible brickwork and cavity walling was a novelty at Gilmorehill. The vertical pointing mortar of the brick joints is flush, while the horizontal pointing is recessed to produce a slight shadow that emphasises the horizontality of the overall design. Band courses of fine concrete demarcate the different levels of the building. A hidden part of the horizontal design was the flat concrete roof with a coating of asphalt for waterproofing. The manufacturers of the Buckingham Palace gates of 1911, Bromsgrove Guild Ltd, produced the distinctive bronze lettering over the entrances. An incised frieze depicting animals runs along the southern range, which was reputedly added to placate the Professor of Zoology, Edward Hindle, who had lost his open views to the north on construction of the Chemistry Institute.

The butterfly plan, of three blocks linked by two full-height staircases, provided a practical arrangement of independent departments with some shared services in the central block, such as the enormous lecture theatre seating nearly 400 people, a staff common room, and a reading room. The Organic Chemistry department in the south-eastern block comprised four large, general laboratories, each with balance, combustion and demonstrators' rooms [FIG.140]. In addition there were central services and stores; a lecture theatre; a museum/tutorial room; and laboratories for more dangerous experiments. Medical and Physical Chemistry were to share the central block, but Inorganic Chemistry also occupied part of the ground floor until completion of its own north-western block after the Second World War. Cost-saving measures reduced the internal finishing to fairly basic levels. In spite of this, the communal spaces were well-detailed and contained features typical of the period: terrazzo flooring in the entrance halls and stairs; rubber flooring in the corridors; teak-block flooring in the laboratories and lecture rooms; timber doors with brass handles and glazed 'portholes'; wrought-iron stair balustrades; and steel plate clocks made by T.S. Cuthbert of Glasgow. The most spectacular spaces are still the two grand sweeping staircases between the blocks.

In-built services were an important part of the new facility. AC, DC and low voltage electricity supplies were provided throughout the building, along with gas, compressed air, steam and water at constant pressure. Two lifts supplemented the staircases. Like the earlier Natural Philosophy and the West Medical buildings, the heating and ventilation systems were designed and supplied by Ashwell & Nesbitt. The fumes from all the fume cupboards were collected and discharged from chimneys forming part of the entrance stairtowers. The garages in the basement were the University's first attempt to deal with the increasing problem of parking at Gilmorehill. Although the first two blocks were largely complete by autumn 1939, an official opening ceremony was abandoned following the declaration of war with Germany on 3 September.[50] One of the first consequences of war for the new Institute was the requisitioning of laboratories for use by the Admiralty.[51] The Court seriously considered camouflage measures for the roofs of the Chemistry Institute and Reading Room in June 1940.[52] Completion of the Inorganic Chemistry department and extension of the Junior laboratory were the University's top priorities after the Second World War. Ill-health had forced the retirement of Hughes in 1942, but the firm, under his partner David Waugh continued working to the original overall style and layout, preparing a new perspective, drawings and site plan in December 1946.[53] Detailed working drawings followed and tenders were invited in August 1947.[54] The project soon ran into difficulty when a wall collapsed into one of the many old coal mine-workings that

142 The main stair of the Joseph Black building
GUAS [PHU 12/5]

143 Stairtower at the Joseph Black building

144 Interior of the Round Reading Room, photographed before 1965
GULSC [A 49/119/1]

pepper the area. The civil engineers J.W.H. Ross & Co. investigated the site and a major underpinning exercise lasted until August 1950. The mine shaft remains accessible today from the sub-basement of the building for maintenance purposes.

The new wing formed a U-plan wrapped around a large, single storey, top-lit elementary laboratory. While the larger laboratories remained dedicated to teaching, there was now very significant provision for research in smaller laboratories and a high number of specialist equipment and preparatory rooms. A low-relief portrait memorial to Joseph Black, sculpted by Benno Schotz in 1953, was incorporated into the north wall. As the new wing was being constructed in 1953, faults in the pre-war buildings required attention: the flat roofs leaked, there were 250 panes of broken glass and the curved panes over projecting windows were also defective.[55] Gradually, many of the steel-framed windows in the older blocks were replaced with teak frames.[56] The entire Chemistry Institute was finally officially opened on 19 March 1954.

Alexander Wright & Kay designed the two phases of additional timber top storey laboratories, basement mycology unit and accommodation for the University's second computer, the enormous KDF9, in 1960–66.[57] The class library was extended into a new reading room extension in similar style in 1982, and a programme of refurbishment lasted between 1986 and 1993, during which the network of ventilation ducting sprouted from the laboratory windows. A further refurbishment scheme for the main lecture theatre and most laboratories was undertaken in 2004–6. The large Inorganic Chemistry lecture theatre was redundant by 2009, when Aedas Architects subdivided it into specialist research laboratories.

The building was re-named in 1997 after Joseph Black (1728–99), University lecturer in Chemistry from 1756 to 1766, who first identified carbon dioxide and carried out pioneering research on latent and specific heat.

THE MACMILLAN READING ROOM (THE 'ROUND READING ROOM'), UNIVERSITY AVENUE 1937–1939

In June 1937 Principal Hetherington submitted an urgent request to the University Grants Committee (UGC) for capital funding of a new 500-seat general reading room.[58] The UGC responded with the offer of a grant of £15,000 and the Bellahouston Trustees committed a further £7,500 towards the estimated basic construction cost of £20,000.[59] The main library at this period was still predominantly a reference collection as

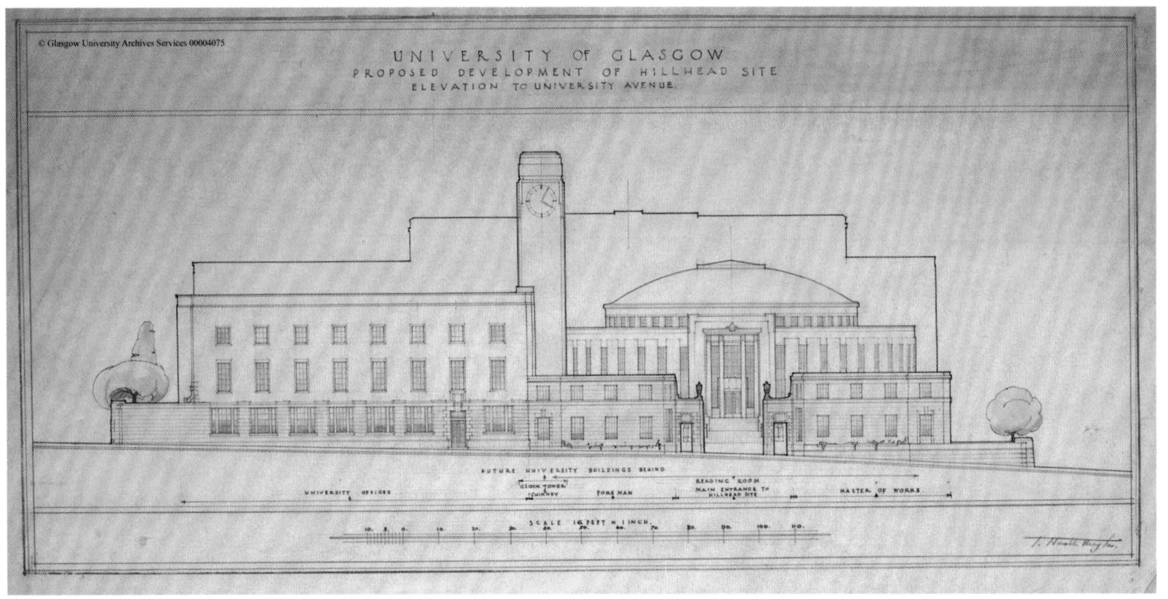

145 Design by T. Harold Hughes for the proposed University clock tower, offices and Reading Room on the site of Hillhead House
GUAS [BUL 6/22/11]

146 The Observatory, Universi Gardens, designed by Stewart Paterson, 1938
GUAS [BUL 6/23/10]

far as undergraduates were concerned, so its practical use was limited by the size of a supervised reading room. The majority of students lived at home or in rented accommodation, where there was little access to academic books or dedicated study space. Although George Gilbert Scott had designed a reading room on the ground floor of the North Range, and this had been expanded at various stages and new class libraries had helped the situation, student numbers had long since outgrown the space and book provision in the main building.

A site for expansion of the University, opposite the Gilbert Scott building on the north side of University Avenue, had been gifted in 1917 by the family of Walter MacLellan of Blairvaddick (1815–89). The property included New Hillhead House, a villa of about 1850 built by the muslin manufacturer and calico printer, Andrew Dalglish, and its spacious grounds. The Psychology, Russian and Celtic departments occupied the villa during the 1930s.[60] The Court now turned to Hughes & Waugh, who were already engaged on the Chemistry Institute, to lay out the whole site and work up more detailed plans for a reading room.

In January 1938 Hughes presented a number of alternative site layouts and a fully developed scheme for a circular reading room, which occupied the same axial position as the centre of the Gilbert Scott building in all his variants. All of the layouts involved a U-plan courtyard arrangement of potential future buildings around the south, west and north sides of the reading room, leaving the east side open towards Thomas Lennox Watson's Wellington Church of 1883–84. The University Avenue frontage was to incorporate a square clock tower. The University Court approved the Reading Room proposals, which envisaged a monumental circular domed building in a modern interpretation of the Pantheon in Rome [FIG.145]. The Brotherton Library, to a similar circular design by Lanchester & Lodge, had recently opened at the University of Leeds in 1936. The placing of a Roman-style temple immediately next to the decidedly Greek temple of Wellington Church was almost certainly an architectural in-joke by Hughes. New Hillhead House was demolished in mid-1938 and work on the Reading Room began immediately.

Hughes cited the easy supervision of the Reading Room with minimal staff as the prime reason for its circular plan [FIG.144].[61] A staircase leads down from the central issue desk to a large basement storage area. Specially-made curving oak desks form concentric patterns around the central hub. These are lit by electric globes hung from a circular gantry. The upper floor was designed to house fourteen departmental seminal libraries, each recessed behind a glazed screen and opening off the gallery. Like the Chemistry Institute, the Reading Room is constructed on a reinforced concrete frame with brick cavity walls. The bricks are of a hard, semi-engineering, quality made by J.C. Edwards of Ruabon, Denbighshire, and the Uxbridge Flint Brick Company. Continuing the Roman theme, the entrance doorway is constructed of Travertine stone, a form of limestone deposited by mineral springs. Internally the dome and walls were finished in a special cream-tinted plaster and the floors covered in 'battleship' linoleum. In 1950 the Reading Room won the Scottish Area RIBA Medal for work produced in the period 1936–49. It was renamed in memory of the University benefactors, Robert and Edith McMillan.

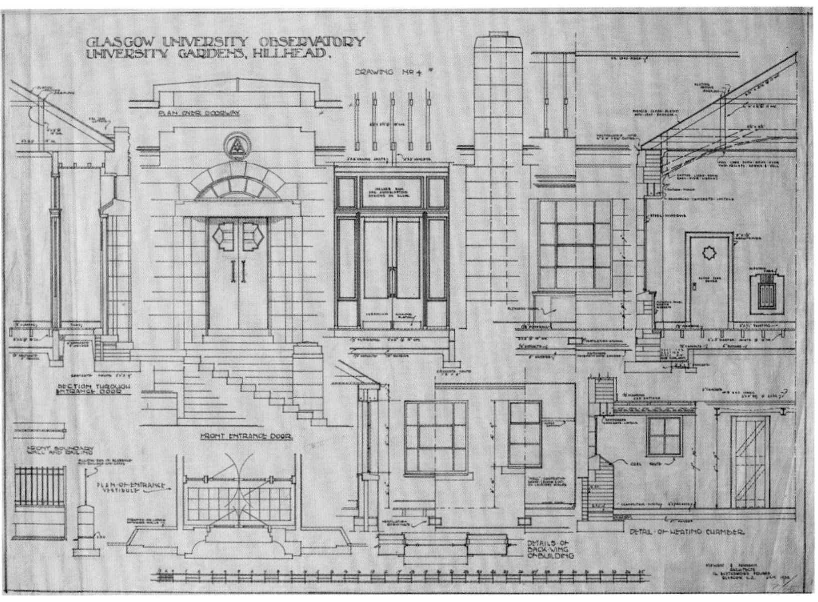

THE OBSERVATORY, UNIVERSITY GARDENS 1938 (DEMOLISHED 1966)

The University received an offer from the Trustees of Notre Dame Convent to buy the old Observatory building on Dowanhill in 1937 [FIG.146].[62] At the same time the University purchased a plot of vacant ground at the west end of University Gardens.[63] The old building on was in a poor state of repair and the encroaching city had made serious observation impractical. The incoming professor, William Marshall Smart, a researcher, writer and teacher of international distinction, recognised the need for new facilities and a new approach to astronomy at Glasgow. In a pragmatic and politically astute move, he re-focused the department on teaching and theoretical research in the emerging Hillhead campus, and largely abandoned advanced practical research. The new Observatory planned for University Gardens in 1938 was a relatively small (and it would be short-lived) building by Stewart & Paterson. John Stewart had been an apprentice in the Burnet, Son & Campbell office in the early 1890s, and George Andrew Paterson had been apprenticed to Honeyman & Keppie in the mid-1890s.[64] The pair had a prolific and diverse practice, but with a strong reputation in public/institutional buildings. Stewart & Paterson drew up plans for a new single storey building at the north-west end of University Gardens. It was a simple range with a rear wing and a mildly Art Deco doorway.[65] The structure was capable of upward expansion if necessary. Inside there was a large library, an instrument room, and rooms for Professor Smart and his assistant, T.R. Tannahill.[66] The 7-inch refractor telescope and transit circle (instrument for measuring the precise position of stars) houses were built separately at the top of the bank behind the Observatory.

Sir Arthur Eddington, the distinguished astrophysicist and early proponent of Einstein's theory of relativity, opened the building on 17 April 1939. After the Second World War the department flourished in its new location under Smart and his successor, Peter Sweet, to the extent that conditions were again cramped by the early 1960s and planning began for improved staff accommodation and undergraduate practical teaching equipment and facilities at the Garscube Eestate. The University Gardens Observatory was demolished in 1966 to allow the construction of the Queen Margaret Union. The department occupied temporary accommodation in Ashton Road from 1964 until a new observatory was opened at Garscube in March 1969.

BUILDINGS BEYOND THE GILMOREHILL/ HILLHEAD CAMPUS

Architects are noted in brackets.

1923–26	Westerlands Club House, Ascot Avenue (James M. Honeyman)
1936	Garscadden Sports Pavilion (T. Harold Hughes & D.S.R. Waugh)

Chapter Eight

Post-War 1945–1960

147 Detail of the exterior of the lecture theatre constructed in the second phase of the Natural Philosophy extension, designed by Basil Spence & Partners in 1956–57
GUAS [PHU 20/25]

The effects of the Second World War on Glasgow were profound and long-lasting. Apart from the physical and psychological damage to the city and its people during the war, the end of hostilities unleashed a whole raft of social and economic problems. Many of the difficulties, such as industrial decline, overcrowded housing and high levels of poverty, were not new, but the war had either masked them, or postponed a response. At the end of the war, Glasgow was still one of the most densely populated cities in the world.

In 1945 the city required radical action on social regeneration and industrial diversification. Glasgow Corporation's City Engineer produced the city's own extraordinary utopian plan, in the form of the two (Robert) Bruce Reports, which envisaged flattening the historic city and replacing it with a rational arrangement of futuristic homes, factories, offices, shops and ring and arterial roads. The aim of the reports was to create a strategy for a healthy and beautiful city. Central government produced a rival plan, the Clyde Valley Regional Plan, under its consultants, Patrick Abercrombie and Robert Matthew. Where Bruce proposed rebuilding within the city limits, Abercrombie set out a policy of displacement, relocating large parts of the population to new towns in the Central Belt. Apart from their social aims, the physical recommendations of both plans looked to new buildings, rather than regeneration of the existing stock, and both placed a new emphasis on planning for road traffic, particularly private cars. The plans were staggering in their scale and ambition. The tension between the two approaches played out in the political wrangling over detailed development planning and implementation. Glasgow Corporation was keen not to lose the political and financial power of its huge population by displacement. However, central government's resources and new national controls over healthcare, welfare, transport, industry, energy, utilities, housing and town planning gave primacy to the Abercrombie plan.

The Town and Country Planning (Scotland) Act 1947 came into force in January 1948, requiring the new planning authorities to draw up comprehensive development plans for approval by the Secretary of State for Scotland. National strategic planning, as advocated by the 1940 Barlow Report, became a reality for the first time. Planning permission, compulsory purchase powers and the compilation of lists of buildings of special architectural or historic interest were also authorised under this Act. The first City Development Plan for Glasgow under the requirements of the 1947 Act was published in 1951 and approved by the Secretary of State in 1954. It represented something of a compromise between the Bruce and Abercrombie plans with acceptance of Bruce's infamous 'motorway box' around the city centre and the designation of four enormous peripheral housing

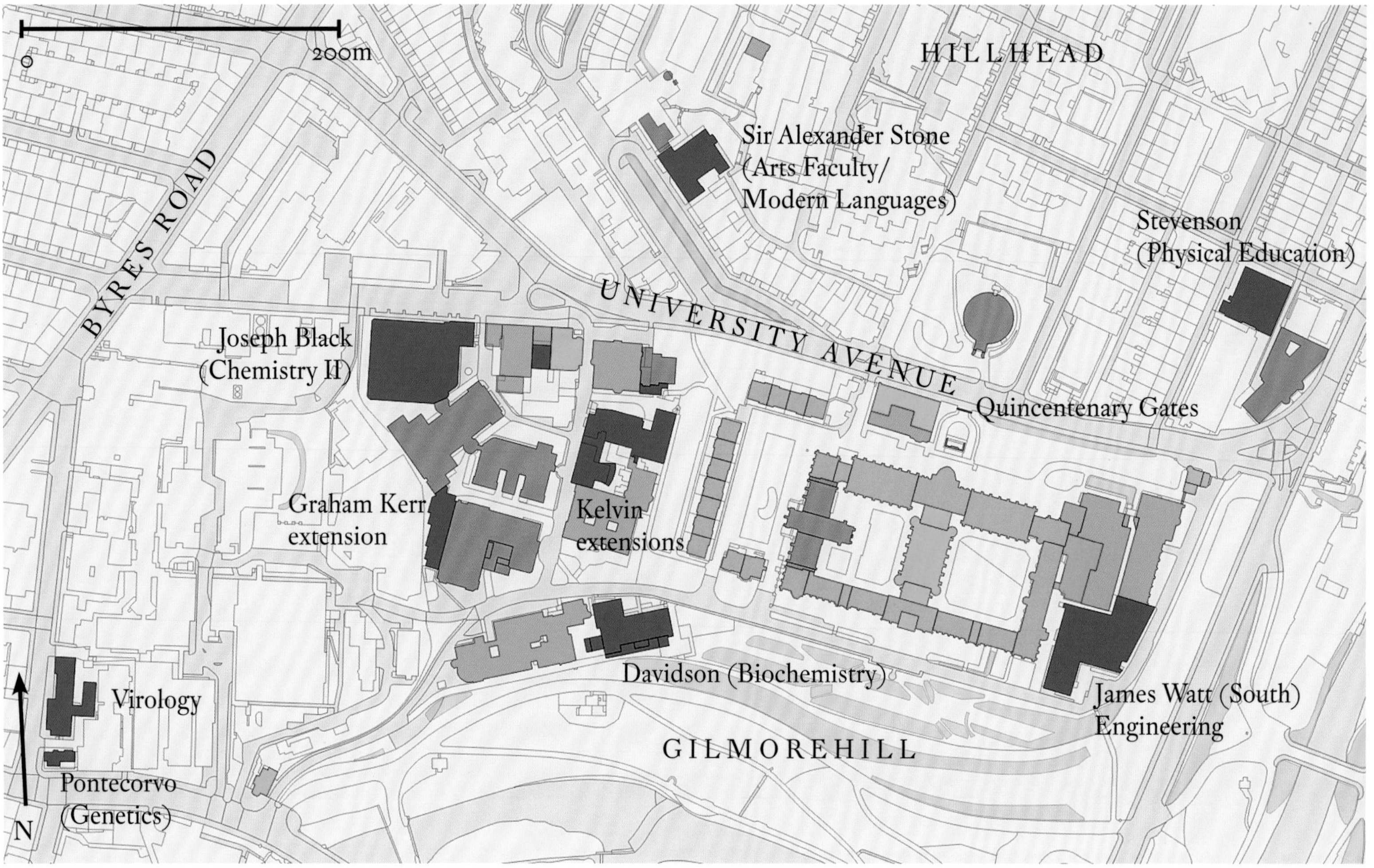

148 Development of Gilmorehill and Hillhead between 1945 and 1960

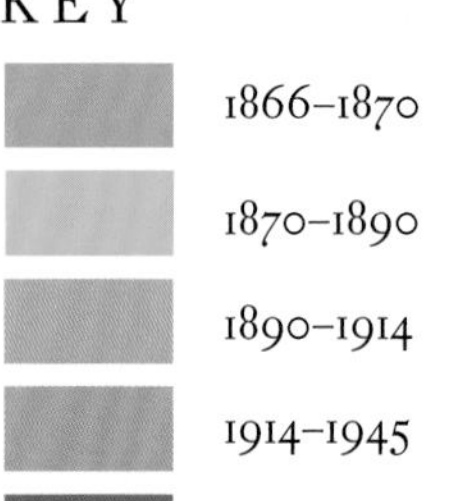

schemes at Drumchapel, Easterhouse, Castlemilk and Pollok within the city boundaries.

Throughout the late 1940s and early 1950s building materials were in increasingly short supply, delivery dates were prolonged even when the materials could be obtained, and prices rose dramatically. Steel was in particularly high demand and short supply, and licences from the Ministry of Works were needed for any construction or maintenance work until 1954. The main inflationary causes were the restriction of dollar imports and the devaluation of the pound sterling. Rationing, high prices, shortages of materials, disagreements over the strategic approach, and the economic crisis of the early 1950s delayed much construction progress until the late 1950s. Initially, the peripheral estates comprised low-rise tenements and some amenities, but by the end of the period, the urgency of the housing problem began to be met with high-density, high-rise blocks. There was some experimentation with pre-fabricated 'systems' and cheap, readily available materials such as timber, concrete, and sheet metal, but low-density construction proved slow and wasteful of land. Relatively little redevelopment took place in the city centre before 1960.

The influence of the architectural aesthetics of the inter-war years spilled over into the 1940s and early 1950s with the persistence of Art Deco and Art Moderne designs, motifs and materials. Where money and materials could be found, the 'Festival Style', derived from the hugely popular Festival of Britain of 1951, had a significant impact on architecture in the city. As an antidote to wartime austerity, jaunty balconies, spindly splayed railings, flying staircases, smooth white Portland stone cladding over rubbly base plinths, and occasional splashes of bright colour are typical of the Festival Style's brightness and optimism. The University was not immune to these powerful forces at work in post-war society, where renewal and regeneration went hand in hand with the massive expansion of education.

PLANNING FOR EXPANSION 1945–1960

By December 1944 the tide of the war had turned, and with the prospect of an Allied victory thoughts were already turning to what might be done when peace was achieved. The Works Committee of the University Court asked the Principal, Hector Hetherington, to draw up a list of buildings that he envisaged would be needed.[1] Hetherington presented a programme of sixteen projects:

- *Completion of the Chemistry Institute*
- *Extension of Engineering*

- *A new department of Anatomy*
- *A new department of Surgery*
- *More tutorial rooms for Arts*
- *A Fine Art building*
- *A Music room*
- *Storage space for the Museum*
- *Physical Welfare building for Men*
- *A Refectory (Students)*
- *Extensions to the Medical Science and Natural Philosophy buildings*
- *A Mathematical Institute*
- *More office space*
- *Hostels*
- *Possibly also Agriculture and Veterinary buildings*
- *Probably more library space, though the library committee has not yet asked for it*

The list appears to have been something of a 'back-of-an-envelope' exercise, and could not possibly have envisioned the huge expansion of higher education in the post-war years, but it did largely address the University's building ambitions for the next fifteen years.

Immediate construction needs were for permanent repairs to the windows of the buildings facing the River Clyde, which had been destroyed in the 1941 blitz.[2] It was the end of 1946 before the materials and permits could be obtained and the firm of Hughes & Waugh could supervise the work. The final reckoning of £43,670 for war damage and payment of the architects was only settled in 1960.[3] The Memorial Chapel once again became the focus of commemoration, with a new list of the fallen added to the chancel by the sculptor, George Herbert Tyson Smith (who provided the memorial to John Sampson, the first librarian of the University of Liverpool, when Hector Hetherington was Vice Chancellor there), and renewed efforts to complete Douglas Strachan's programme of stained glass windows.[4] Post-war plans for the student population centred on arrangements for returning service personnel and achieving a stable level of about 5,000 students. In fact the 'bulge' created by returning service personnel in addition to the normal intake, raised student numbers to 7,414 in 1949–50 before it sank back to about 6,500 in the early 1950s.[5]

Encouraged by a number of government working groups and increased funding through the University Grants Committee, growth and investment in staff, students and facilities were concentrated in Medicine, the Sciences, Engineering, and emerging Social Sciences. The expansion of the university sector and greater central funding inevitably required greater government involvement in co-ordination of subjects and the distribution of funds. In July 1946 the Chancellor of the Exchequer announced that the University Grants Committee would now 'assist in the preparation and execution of university development plans' in addition to its existing role of advising Parliament on the level of university funding. New subject area sub-committees were formed and detailed negotiations became the norm for the University's capital projects. Funding covered approved building work, purchase of sites, payment of professional fees and the initial furnishing and equipping of buildings.[6] By the late 1950s, the University Grants Committee had its own architectural department that assessed and advised on issues such as student to plot ratios and the minimum space for a faculty office.[7] Sir Frank Mears was employed to produce the University's first development plan in 1947–51 (see the Mears Plan below).

As a prelude to the introduction of the National Health Service in 1948, the far-reaching Goodenough Report of 1944 recommended a profound change in medical education that would make every medical school an integral part of a university. Glasgow began the necessary fundamental changes to the relationship between the University and the city's hospitals between 1945 and 1947. New chairs in Psychology, Psychological Medicine and Applied Physiology were founded, and increased investment in staff and facilities at the teaching hospitals was made. The University absorbed the city's two independent medical schools and their buildings, Anderson College and St Mungo's College, in 1947.[8] Similarly, all dental and veterinary teaching in the city was brought under the aegis of the University. The Barlow Report, *Scientific Manpower* of May 1946 recommended an ambitious doubling of science graduates from British universities within a decade. The government, recognising the important role of science and technology in the Allies' wartime successes, supported Barlow's conclusions and committed substantial new funding both to teaching and research. Hetherington had made a number of exceptional appointments before the Second World War, including the cancer research chemist, James Wilfred Cook, the eminent surgeon, Charles Illingworth, and the nuclear physicist, Philip Dee. These were followed after the war by further astute appointments, such as Norman Davidson, a distinguished pharmacologist, Bill Marshall, a pioneering engineer specialising in reinforced concrete, and Ian Donald, a leading obstetrician and developer of the first diagnostic ultrasound machine. These and other key figures attracted undergraduates, researchers and, critically, funding from the University Grants Committee and other external sources for Chemistry, Atomic Research, Engineering and Biochemistry facilities. Government capital funding for Glasgow rose from £13,400 in 1945–46 to £418,003 in 1950–51 and recurrent grants for teaching rose from £239,791 to £805,950 in the same period.[9]

Funding for Arts subjects was more of a struggle. However, the University Grants Committee favoured languages and the social sciences, which were then classed as Arts subjects. With help from the Rockefeller Foundation, a department of Social and Economic Research was founded in 1946. Sydney Checkland, an outstanding economic historian, was recruited from Cambridge in 1956. A new modern languages building was constructed in University Gardens from 1958.

Hetherington was a strong advocate of improved health, welfare and social services for students, but it was 1958 before sufficient funding was available to make a start on construction of a new physical welfare building (the 'Stevie'). Student residences were another area of difficulty: there was insufficient space or suitable buildings in Hillhead, and Garscube was too far away to serve Gilmorehill. Very little capacity was added during the period 1945–60.

Another important consequence of improved government funding was the money it freed up for the establishment of a professional central administrative team under Robert Hutcheson in support of the Principal and Court. Maintenance of existing buildings and management of tenders, contracts and other day-to-day construction issues were now administered centrally by dedicated full-time staff, which was to become the University's own Planning and Building Office. The administrative accommodation in the Gilbert Scott building was enlarged and improved for the new team.[10] Other central services, such as the boiler house serving the West Medical building, Zoology, Natural Philosophy and Chemistry, were also renewed and expanded.

Although the University had begun purchasing buildings on the north side of University Avenue before the Second World War, and continued to purchase more as they became available, the ownership was patchy. While an expansion into Hillhead remained an ambition, it was already clear that not all the University's needs could be accommodated there. A significant step in the University's ability to expand was the acquisition of a major new site. In October 1948 Sir George Campbell, of Succoth, presented Garscube House to the University, and over the course of the following months also sold a number of land parcels to the University.[11] William Burn had designed Garscube House in a Jacobean style in 1827, but by the time of the gift to the University, the Campbell family had lived at Crarae Lodge on Loch Fyne for a number of years. Although the land at Garscube was further away from Gilmorehill than Hector Hetherington had hoped when scouting for suitable expansion sites, it did provide more than ample space for the University's immediate and longer-term needs. Another country house estate, Cochno, in West Dunbartonshire, was acquired in 1954 for use as a veterinary field station, hostel and experimental animal centre.

The most important event of the period was the 1951 Quincentenary celebration of the foundation of the University.[12] This was marked in permanent form by the construction of new entrance gates in front of the Hunter Memorial. A mini architectural festival was held in 1954 to inaugurate the new buildings forming part of the largest university building programme outside London and Cambridge. In recognition of the government's £1.8m (90%) contribution over six years, James Stuart, the Secretary of State for Scotland was invited to open an extensive number of buildings and departments. These were: the Inorganic Chemistry block; the first phase of the Natural Philosophy extension; the Zoology extension; the Institute of Surgery (Western Infirmary); the boiler house; the Veterinary Hospital (Garscube); the research block for Mechanical Engineering (Spencer Street); and large-scale adaptations of the Anderson College (Dumbarton Road), the Veterinary School (Buccleuch Street), the West Medical building, Botany building and the University offices and Mathematics department (both in the Gilbert Scott building).[13] The next quinquennial allocation of capital grants by the University Grants Committee in 1952 was to prove more challenging. The economic crisis of the early 1950s was at its height, with high inflation, low production and a huge deficit in the balance of payments. Only minor works were given approval, so the three large projects for phase II of the Natural Philosophy extension, a new Arts (Modern Languages) building in University Gardens, and a large extension of the Engineering department were delayed until more favourable times prevailed in the later 1950s.

The University faced similar challenges for the funding of equipment. Planning for installation of Scotland's first university computer began in 1956, but it was not until February 1959 that Lord Halsbury opened a large room adapted for the purpose in the Chemistry Institute.[14] Even then, the University had needed to abandon its plans for a Ferranti Mark II in favour of a cheaper and less powerful Digital Electronic Universal Computing Engine (DEUCE) machine.

The Natural Philosophy extension marked a brief flirtation with 'big science', where a building was designed at Gilmorehill specifically to house a large and expensive piece of kit. As both the University and the University Grants Committee found quickly, such projects were phenomenally expensive for a single institution to purchase and operate. In commissioning the next generation of electron linear accelerator, a more strategic and collaborative approach was adopted, with the University investing in shared premises and equipment at the National Engineering Laboratory at East Kilbride.

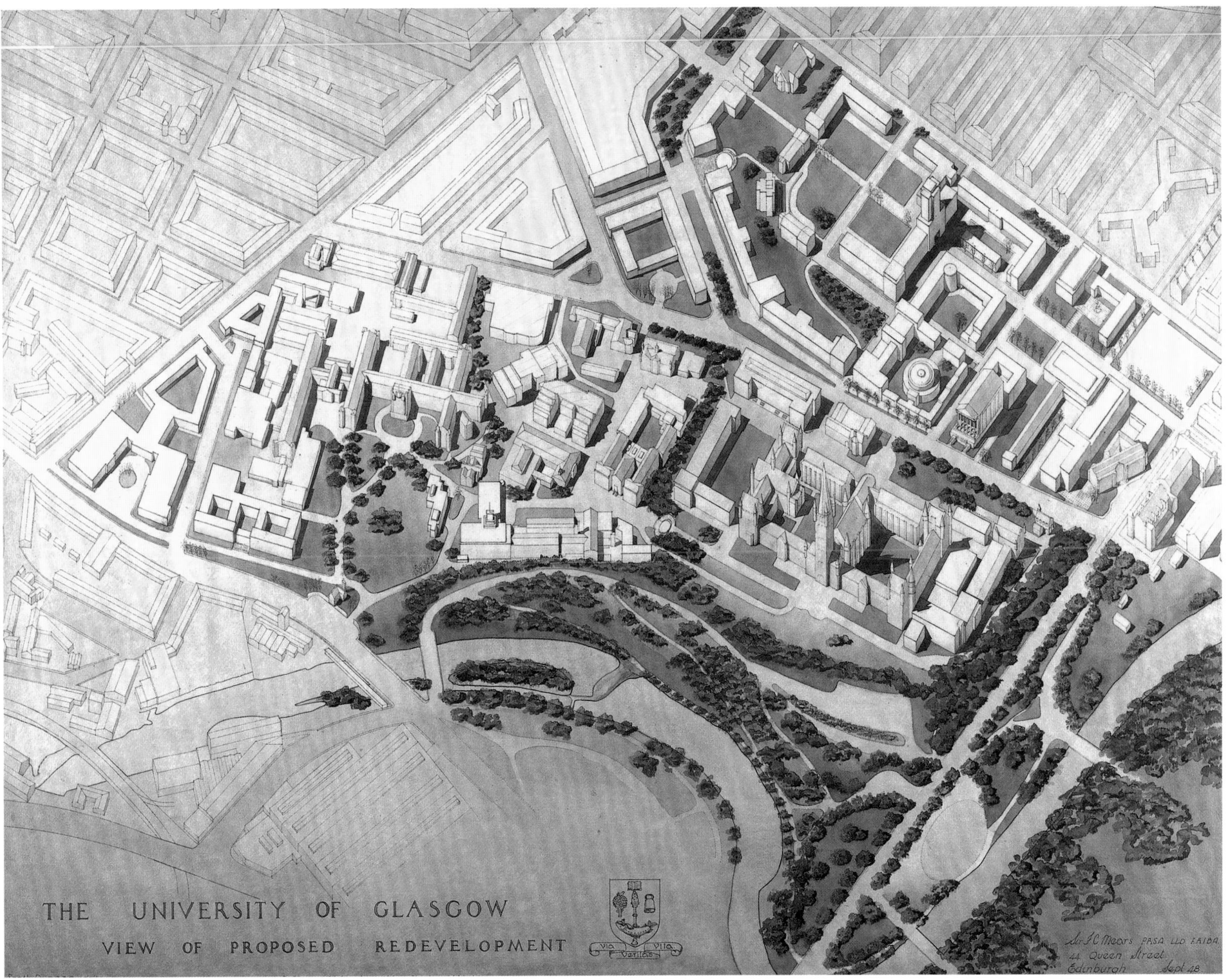

149 Bird's-eye view of Frank Mears's proposed first phase for the redevelopment of Gilmorehill and Hillhead, September 1948. This smaller area was bounded by the River Kelvin, Dumbarton Road, Byres Road and Great George Street.
GUAS [BUL 6/59/5]

When the Engineering extension was under consideration, the building was conceived mainly for teaching and small-scale experimentation. The large heat engine research was located at the University Mechanical Engineering Research Annexe at Anniesland.

THE MEARS PLAN 1947–1951

In late 1944 Hector Hetherington had written to the influential English town planner, Sir Patrick Abercrombie, who was then working with Robert Matthew on the Clyde Valley plan, regarding a suitable consultant for a University development plan.[15] Abercrombie responded suggesting Frank Mears, who himself was working on the equivalent plan for Central and South-East Scotland.

Frank Charles Mears (1880–1953) was a major figure in Scottish architecture and planning in the first half of the 20th century. He was articled to the Edinburgh architect, Hippolyte Jean Blanc from 1896 to 1901, won the RIBA's Soane Medallion in 1903, joined the practice of Robert Weir Schultz in the same year, worked with Ramsay Traquair from 1906, and was an assistant to the polymath and pioneer of town planning, Sir Patrick Geddes, from 1908 to 1910.[16] He finally set up his own practice in Edinburgh in 1910 and married Geddes's daughter, Norah, in 1915. Mears's early architectural career included a number of buildings and the layout for Edinburgh Zoo (entrance, tropical bird and reptile house, monkey house), several Highland bridges for the burgeoning trunk road network and the restoration of Gladstone's Land and Huntly House in the Old Town of Edinburgh. The University plan evolved over a period of four years. Mears presented an initial outline in February 1948, and then discussed detailed proposals with departmental heads.[17] In his initial zoning, prepared in July 1948, Mears envisaged three stages of ambitious northward expansion between Byres Road and the River Kelvin: the first from University Avenue to

Great George Street; the second to Great Western Road; and the third to Hamilton Drive/Lacrosse Terrace. A very important consideration was the ground condition of the Hillhead area, which like Gilmorehill, was known to be riddled with the remains of 18th-century mineral workings. A report by consultant mining engineer, J. W. H. Ross, identified underpinning requirements for new buildings and supplementary work on existing buildings.[18] The surveyors Kyle & Frew supplied levels for the Hillhead area.

In July 1950 the Ministry of Town and Country Planning issued a circular offering 'all possible assistance to the universities in connection with their requirements for land and developing it', effectively a promise to support the universities' development proposals through compulsory purchase powers if necessary.[19] In the end Mears's plan was submitted rather hurriedly to Glasgow Corporation in March 1951 for inclusion in their zoning proposals under the newly required City Plan.[20] The report was circulated to the *Glasgow Herald*, the *Scotsman* and the Mitchell Library a month later, and the first stage of Mears's zoning was adopted in the first City Development Plan of December 1951.[21] The plan also adopted a proposal to widen and designate Byres Road as a 50-foot wide 'sub-arterial' road.[22] The various schemes for this proposal were to impact on the planning of the western boundary of the University zone for the next twenty years.

Mears's plan covered an area bounded on the north by Great George Street, on the west by Byres Road-Ashton Road, on the east by the River Kelvin and on the south by Dumbarton Road.[23] Mears identified the constraints and problems of the Gilmorehill site, and set out a series of principles for new building work. The plan looked largely to a new campus on the north side of University Avenue, but included some new structures on the old Gilmorehill campus and the Church Street fringes of the Western Infirmary site. At Gilmorehill, Mears proposed extensions to the east and west of the Materia Medica building, an extension to the north of the Gilbert Scott building for Geology/Geography, replacement of the existing Botany building for a new Mathematics building, demolition of the Principal's house for a University clubhouse, demolition of the north side of Professors' Square for a new University library, and removal of the old Union building. Perhaps the most radical (as yet unrealised) proposal was to close University Avenue to traffic to create a Great Central Court between the Gilbert Scott building and the Reading Room.

On the north side of University Avenue, Mears proposed a new campus that respected the existing domestic road layout and scale of Hillhead, but would involve the demolition all the existing buildings. Here, quadrangles of low buildings were considered appropriately academic and minimised the need for deep piling in the difficult ground conditions presented by the old mineral workings. Views to the Scotts' tower were to be preserved, and there were to be 'no extremes of scale, colour and texture'.[24] Mechanical uniformity was to be discouraged by the appointment of various architects, who would be free to design organically within the overarching principles. These principles included the promotion of order and harmony, a limited palette of materials and colours, restrained use of sculpture, consideration of context, views and vistas, and integrated landscaping and parking provision. Notably, Mears proposed the retention of 78 Southpark Avenue, the former home of Margaret and Charles Rennie Mackintosh, the loss of which was to cause considerable controversy some twelve years later. Mears proposed clusters of buildings to serve related departments, and careful positioning of entrances and stairs to minimise wasteful corridors and circulation spaces. In promoting departmental clusters, Mears sought to end the territorial rivalry that beset the planning of the Gilbert Scott building and subsequent departmental buildings on the Gilmorehill site. This proposal reflected the beginning of a more collaborative academic approach between disciplines that was also

150 Sir Basil Urwin Spence by Lida Moser (detail). The photograph shows Spence in his Edinburgh office; his perspective of the Natural Philosophy extension hangs on the wall behind him.
Scottish National Portrait Gallery, Edinburgh [PGP 43.6]

151 Presentation drawing by Basil Spence for the Natural Philosophy extension, 1947–59
RCAHMS/© Crown copyright [DP 094022]

being promoted by the University Grants Committee.

With the exception of the Arts building in University Gardens, the Engineering extension and the gymnasium in Oakfield Avenue, little of the Mears plan was implemented. Shortages of materials and funding prevented much progress before Mears's death on 25 January 1953. The University continued planning on the basis of the Mears plan, but it was 1960 before another consultant was appointed to update the plan and advise on detailed architectural matters.

THE BUILDINGS 1945–1960

INTRODUCTION

The University had longstanding relationships with several firms of architects, which continued after the Second World War. The firm of T. Harold Hughes & D.S.R. Waugh had begun the Chemistry Institute in 1938, and were re-appointed to finish the job at the Inorganic Chemistry block. They also undertook the Institute of Surgery at the Western Infirmary in 1947–53. Another favourite firm was Keppie & Henderson, known as John Keppie, Henderson & J.L. Gleave from 1958. Various architects from the firm, including Andrew Graham Henderson, J.L. Gleave and Richard De'Ath dominated the design work at the University between the 1940s and the 1960s. Distinguished new recruits to the University's roster included Basil Spence, a rare interloper based in Edinburgh, who succeeded in interview for the Natural Philosophy extension in 1947, and Jack Coia, who began with small jobs on the West Medical building and graduated to design of the boiler house in 1948 and then the Veterinary Hospital at Garscube in the following year. Spence provided advice on the Chapel stained glass and returned to design the Virology and Genetics departments in the late 1950s and early 1960s. However, the construction of Coia's Veterinary Hospital proved problematic, and he did not work for the University again. Although there were also difficulties with the Arts block in University Gardens, Walter N.W. Ramsay had a more successful relationship with the University, continuing to work on the halls of residence at Bellshaugh Road, Belhaven Terrace West and Park Terrace and on buildings at Garscube into the 1960s and 1970s.

The post-war building programme relied on tried and tested construction methods, largely steel frames with stone cladding and in-situ concrete floors and roofs. Spence introduced bright white Portland limestone as the cladding for his Natural Philosophy extension [FIG. 151]. As one of the 1951 Festival of

Britain architects, it is not surprising that the style of the Natural Philosophy extension incorporated elements that were to become part of the 'Festival Style'. The largest and most expensive of the post-war buildings, Keppie, Henderson & J.L. Gleave's James Watt Engineering (South) extension, emulated this optimistic style, but perhaps on too ambitious a scale for the site. Towards the end of the period, Spence included a lecture theatre of in-situ cast reinforced concrete structure in the second phase of his Natural Philosophy extension. This allowed a much more daring and expressive fan-shaped form, cantilevered out over the internal quadrangle. After the disaster of the steel windows in the pre-war blocks of the Chemistry Institute, there was some wariness about metal windows. However, aluminium frames emerged as a relatively successful alternative to steel in the post-war buildings. As a mark of their modernity, all the new structures had flat roofs, although the covering materials varied from copper at the Natural Philosophy building to the proprietary 'Paropa' system of cement-screed slabs at the Arts building and Engineering extension.

The interiors of all the post-war buildings were necessarily constrained by cost and a need for robust finishes. Again, Spence's Natural Philosophy extension was perhaps the most avant garde and refined, with its monobeam stair [FIG.156], plywood-panelled lecture theatres [FIG.154], and tea bar [FIG.153], detailed right down to the flower boxes. As the provision of a tea bar suggests, more thought was given to shared social spaces in the new buildings. At the same time as providing new facilities, the University needed to update the utilities and services to the existing buildings. Much of the University still relied on Direct Current (DC) electricity supply in 1948, when proposals to convert the estate to Alternating Current (AC) were costed at £26,000.[25] A new double telephone switchboard required a room to itself in the Gilbert Scott building in 1948.[26] The centralised heating boilers and plant in both the main building and the surrounding departments were also very outmoded and required replacement.

Blackboards still predominated in the classrooms and lecture theatres, but many were now of the revolving type invented by William Brownie Garden in 1911. The lecture theatres were all equipped with projection screens. The main lecture theatre in the Engineering extension marked a departure from previous designs for the University in that it was without natural daylight and ventilated by mechanical means. Other aspects of teaching were also advancing. A typewriting pool was established for the Arts Faculty in 1947. Duplicators, such as the one Philip Dee ordered in the same year, enabled distribution of typewritten lecture notes.[27] Some aspects of technology remained relatively expensive: twelve calculating machines for the Mathematics department cost £1,380 in October 1947.[28]

KELVIN EXTENSION (NATURAL PHILOSOPHY) 1947–1959

Such was the international rush for technological advancement after the Second World War, particularly in nuclear and particle physics, that in January 1947 the government's Department of Scientific and Industrial Research offered to provide a 160-megavolt synchrotron, or particle accelerator, and a grant towards a high-voltage generator for Glasgow's Natural Philosophy department. This offer was the result of an application by Professor Philip Dee, an outstanding physicist, who had trained and worked at the Cavendish Laboratory in Cambridge under Ernest Rutherford and taught at the Oxford Clarendon Laboratory before the war.[29] Dee's work on radar during the war was an important factor in government recognition of, and support for, British physics in the post-war years. Developed from the cyclotron, the first electron synchrotron was built by Edwin McMillan at the Berkeley Radiation Laboratory

152 Basement plan of the Natural Philosophy extension showing the location of the circular synchrotron chamber, which was surrounded by thick concrete walls
GUAS [BUL 6/10/8]

153 Design for the tea bar of the Natural Philosophy extension
GUAS [BUL 6/10/288]

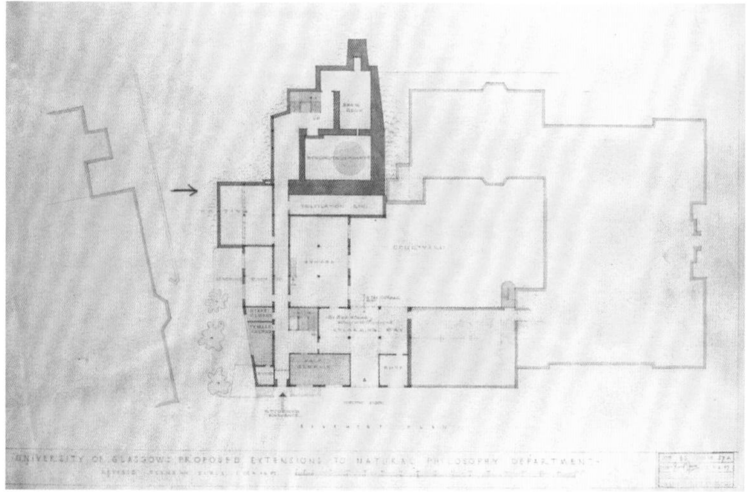

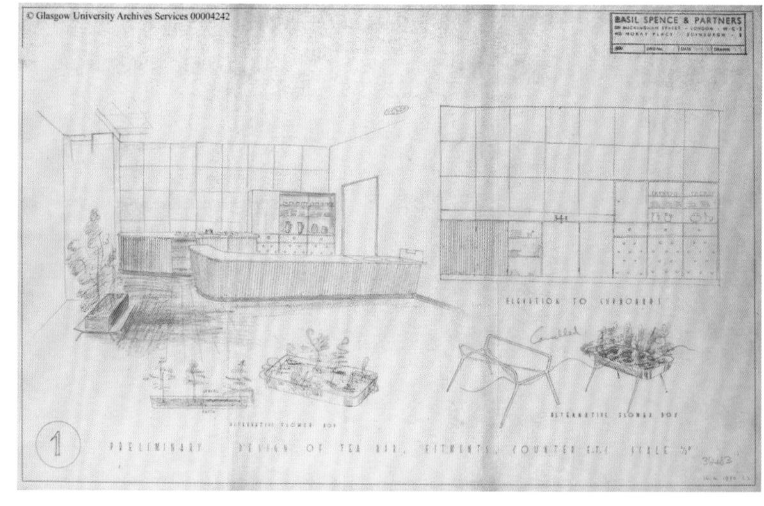

154 The exterior of the lecture theatre constructed in the second phase of the Natural Philosophy extension
GUAS [PHU 20/25]

155 Synchrotron chamber with its sliding roof, photographed about 1958
GUAS [PHU 68/17]

in California in 1945. The Glasgow machine was at the forefront of British technological research. It produced very intense pulses of light of many different wavelengths that allowed detailed study of matter at an atomic scale. This expensive equipment required a specially designed building to house it.

To this end, in January 1947 Dee interviewed Basil Spence (Edinburgh), Jack Coia (Glasgow) and Ronald Ward (London), and also consulted the London firm of Easton & Robertson, who specialised in university and medical buildings.[30] Spence was selected on the basis of the interview, and Dee met with him throughout 1947 for numerous discussions on the technical specification of the synchrotron chamber, beam room and associated service rooms.[31] It was to be the first of many of Spence's large-scale university projects in the Britain. The project was to be divided into two parts: an atomic research block opposite the Botany building on the very restricted site of the old tennis courts, which was to house the synchrotron, research rooms, lecture theatre, professors' rooms, class library and museum; and a teaching block with large laboratories linking the research block to James Miller's old Natural Philosophy buildings. The whole scheme would form a quadrangle attached to the north side of the old buildings. It was necessary to provide access through the building for heavy loads to the synchrotron chamber in the basement [FIG.155].

By December 1947 the structural plans were complete, and in May 1948 the scheme was sent for approval by the city's Dean of Guild Court.[32] Spence produced a number of attractive perspectives, including one that was exhibited at the Royal Scottish Academy. Spence's design cleverly acknowledged both the building's historic context and its futuristic purpose. The quadrangular plan and local roughly-dressed Blaxter (Northumberland) sandstone plinth provided the visual links to the historic surroundings, while the gleaming white Portland limestone facings, flat copper-covered roofs, strips and rows of flush or projecting anodized aluminium-framed windows, the completely glazed north wall of the entrance hall, concrete corner 'piloti' (supporting column), concrete balconies and oval stair cupola all pointed towards a new, brighter, technological age. Like the pre-war buildings, the frame was of steel and the outer brick walls were clad in stone. The University Court was cautious in its approval of the materials, accepting Spence's proposal for Portland stone cladding only on the condition that he demonstrate its cost effectiveness in relation to other potential facing materials.[33] As the design was worked out in detail, the estimated cost of the building soared from to £140,000 to £400,000.[34] Much of the funding for Stage I came from the University Grants Committee, who treated the project outside the normal round of grant funding in view of its national strategic importance.

The underground synchrotron chamber needed very thick walls and a massive 150-ton sliding containment slab roof to prevent vibration and radiation leakage and to reduce noise during operation. The deep foundations had to be carefully underpinned to take account of the old mine workings on the site.[35] The government priority for the project enabled the University to obtain the necessary building licences for labour and materials, especially steel, which was in short supply after the war and allocated to the universities through the University Grants Committee.[36] Some of the residents of Professors' Square tried to have the new building transferred to Garscube 'with a view to preserving the amenity of the University'.[37] When groundwork began, the residents quickly became concerned about the encroachment of the works into the gardens on the west side of the square, and legal opinion was sought.[38] There were also concerns about radiation leakage.[39] The synchrotron chamber was complete by June 1949, but it was 1952 before the Metropolitan Vickers machine itself was installed and the associated generator, condenser, control, electrical, ventilation, heating and other services were assembled.[40] The first operation of the synchrotron in 1954 was reported at the prestigious Rochester Conference in New York. However, following teething troubles, it was to be another six years or so before the machine reached its highest productivity levels.[41] While construction proceeded, Spence and his fledgling office produced reams of drawings for fitting out from balcony railings and laboratory doors to conference tables, light fittings and signage.[42] The result was a restrained, but beautifully detailed, interior. A number of the features still survive in the building. Perhaps the most spectacular is the monobeam stair (treads supported by a single central beam) that rises from the spacious and well-lit entrance hall. Another important feature that remains largely intact is the wedge-shaped second lecture theatre (similar to Spence's contemporary University of Southampton Engineering Faculty lecture theatre), cantilevered into the courtyard as part of the western teaching block added as part of Stage II in 1958. The distinctive expression of lecture theatres as wedge-shaped blocks became common after the founder of the Bauhaus art school, Walter Gropius, along with the English architect, Maxwell Fry, designed the radical Impington Village College, Cambridgeshire, in 1936 (opened 1939). While the main blocks of the Natural Philosophy building had steel frames, the lecture theatre was constructed of reinforced concrete and faced with vertical timber slats. At the ground floor, a glazed screen enables the heating and ventilation equipment to be seen from the courtyard. Internally the lecture theatre retains its light oak plywood panelling, cast-aluminium door handles and 'Race' tip-up seating with solid mahogany writing shelves.[43] Numerous alterations have been made to the building over the years, including the addition of a rooftop extension to the west range in 1966–68 by Basil Spence, Glover & Ferguson, and a more recent roof extension to the north range.

156 The monobeam staircase of the Natural Philosophy extension, designed by Basil Spence & Partners, 1947–52

JAMES WATT ENGINEERING BUILDING (SOUTH) 1948–1959

In March 1948 a special committee of the University Court setup to oversee a major extension to the old Engineering department drew up a shortlist of potential architects, which comprised Jack Coia, Basil Spence, Thomas Tait of Sir John Burnet, Tait & Lorne and

157 The 'Progress of Science' low relief on the James Watt Engineering building (south) by Eric Kennington and Eric Stanford, 1959

Andrew Graham Henderson of Keppie & Henderson.[44] With the exception of Tait, the other architects were already working on other projects for the University: Henderson on conversion of parts of the old Anderson's College for the Genetics department; Spence on the Natural Philosophy extension; and Coia on (unrealised) improvements to the Physiology lecture theatre.[45] Henderson was selected from the shortlist.

The site was challenging for a number of reasons, including its restricted size, the slopes, old mineral workings, its prominence in views of the Gilbert Scott building from Woodlands Hill, and the need to demolish Scott's old Abbot's Kitchen. The building needed to be substantial in order to accommodate increased student and staff numbers and cater for new areas of high-level research. Henderson experimented with a number of designs throughout 1948 and 1949, including an odd Art Deco design fused with Gothic details. By March 1949 the layout and Z-plan of the building was taking shape, but the stylistic treatment of the exterior remained unresolved. It was 1954 before a final design was decided, sufficient funding was secured and construction begun. Members of the department took experimental test readings on the behaviour of the steel frame as it came under load.[46] The curtain walling was hung from the roof to prevent the transmission of vibration. The design in a contemporary Modernist style reflected a little of the 1951 Festival of Britain spirit in its splayed plan, curtain walls with pale blue panels dividing the floors, Portland stone facings, spindly metalwork, concrete balconies and sculpted panel. However, the constrained resources and sheer scale overwhelm the details, particularly in views from the east, where even the enormous Gilbert Scott building is obscured by the structure. The extension contained new lecture theatres, tutorial rooms, a tutorial museum, offices, research rooms, staff rooms, laboratories, workshops and ancillary rooms, including dedicated space for Naval and Aeronautical and Fluid Mechanics engineering. Specialist spaces included a magnetic measurement room and a vibration room with independent foundations and floor slab for Electrical Engineering.

Although the new facility was opened to staff and students in September 1958, the low relief sculpture on the south elevation, 'the Progress of Science', was not begun until June 1959. It was designed by Eric

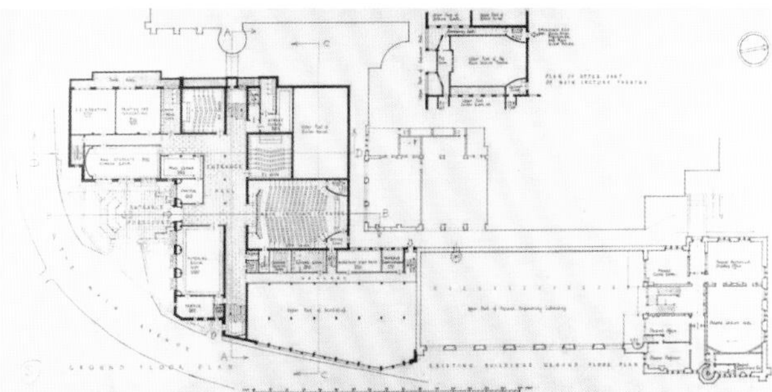

158 Ground floor plan of the James Watt Engineering building (south)
GUAS [BUL 6/24/26]

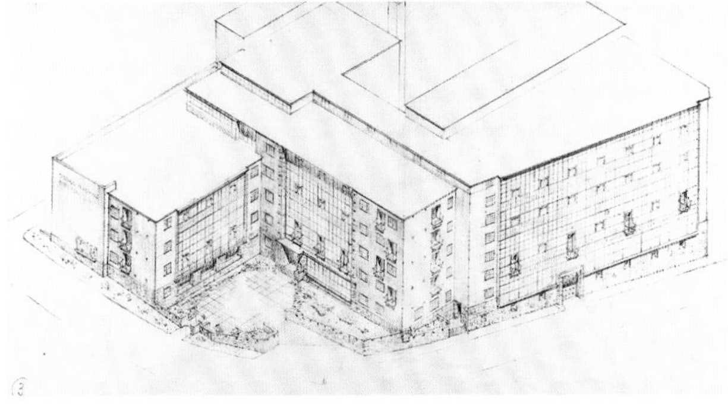

159 Axonometric of the James Watt Engineering building (south)
GUAS [BUL 6/24/36]

Kennington, a friend of Joe Gleave, who cut the pre-prepared stones in situ, and cost £3,000.[47] Kennington was initially a painter, but gained a high reputation as a stone carver in the 1920s and '30s. He designed the figure of 'Learning' on the new Harold Cohen Library at the University of Liverpool, when Hector Hetherington was Vice Chancellor there.[48] The James Watt (South) relief has an enigmatic cast of mythological and symbolic figures that inhabit the various engineering realms of sea, earth and sky [FIG.157]. The inscription reads: PER MARE PER TERRAS, SCIENTIA ET INGENIO, DISCE DOCE (By sea and by land, through knowledge and skill, learn and teach). Unfortunately Kennington became ill by October 1959, leaving his assistant, Eric Stanford, to complete the work.[49] Wylie & Lochhead, the well-known Glasgow furniture company, supplied all the blinds, curtains, chairs and carpets.[50] The building was inaugurated by Viscount Montgomery of Alamein on 4 November 1959. Some modest original features remain inside, such as the timber lockers lining the corridors and some early floor coverings. Much of the plan is intact, and the double-height workshops remain. The main lecture theatre and entrance hall have both been refurbished recently.

QUINCENTENARY GATES, UNIVERSITY AVENUE 1951–1952

The Memorial Gates were presented by the General Council on 18 June 1952 in honour of twenty-eight celebrated alumni from the first 500 years of the University, including Andrew Melville, Adam Smith, Lord Kelvin, James Watt and Isobel Elder [FIG.160]. They were designed by Joseph Lea Gleave of John Keppie, Henderson & J.L. Gleave and the original ironwork is by Thomas Hadden & Co. of Edinburgh.[51] Gleave was particularly proud of this project.[52] Two further escutcheons celebrating John Smith and Donald Dewar were added for the 550th anniversary of the University in 2001. The design symbolises the growth of a tree over 500 years, with each 'fruit' representing an alumnus or an alumna.

SIR ALEXANDER STONE BUILDING (ORIGINALLY ARTS FACULTY/ MODERN LANGUAGES), UNIVERSITY GARDENS 1952–1959

Hector Hetherington had identified additional tutorial space for the Arts as a priority in his list of projected building projects in 1944 (see pages 132–33). The immediate post-war shortages delayed further consideration of a new Arts building until 1952, by which time plans were crystallising around a centre for language studies located on a gap site on the north side of University Gardens, between the end of the 19th-century villas and the 1938 observatory. Selection of the architect was by a limited competition, to which the Glasgow Institute of Architects objected on the grounds that an open competition would be fairer.[53] The University pressed ahead anyway, inviting Jack Coia, Ninian Johnston, Basil Spence and Walter Neil Wilson Ramsay of C.J. McNair, Elder & Ramsay to submit proposals, with Andrew Graham Henderson of John Keppie, Henderson & J.L. Gleave to assess the entries.[54] In December 1952 Henderson judged his former colleague Ramsay's entry as the most sensitive to the site, best planned, and most closely aligned with the requirements of the brief [FIG.161]. All the entries were put on public display in the Randolph Hall the following month.[55]

By any standard, the site was challenging, with a sharp slope northwards towards Lilybank House and the potential for disturbing old mineral workings. Ramsay's ingenious design on a beamed and rafted foundation managed to integrate quite a large new structure within the restricted site without overwhelming the surrounding buildings. He envisaged a U-plan, with the range facing University Gardens maintaining the height, building line and sandstone frontage of the adjacent

[opposite]

161 Perspective for the Sir Alexander Stone building (originally Arts Faculty and Modern Languages) by Walter Ramsay in 1952
GUAS [BUL 6/26/1]

160 The Quincentenary Gates in 1952, designed by John Keppie, Henderson & J.L. Gleave
GUPU [13-036-36]

houses. The other ranges were taller, but built into the slope to maintain views from the Lilybank House site. Although there were tentative plans to redevelop the University Gardens houses and Lilybank House, the University recognised that these projects might take a long time to materialise, and that the Arts building should take into account both the current and medium-term context and the long-term potential for future linkages. Funding difficulties delayed construction work still further, until 1958. The project appears to have generated a number of niggling issues between the University and the contractors, but it was finally finished in 1959 at a cost of £200,000.

162 *Knowledge and Inspiration*

The design is economical and restrained in keeping with the times, but there are some fine contemporary features and occasional residual hints of pre-war Art Deco style, including the entrance with its splayed stair and parapet. Other features of this sort are the curved glass and black granite panel, the angled and strip windows on the west elevation, the projecting windows on the inner face of the West Range, and interior fixtures such as the doors and handles, thin metal stair balusters, and signage, all of which survive. After assurances that the materials would not stain the building, the Court commissioned the sculpture over the entrance, *Knowledge & Inspiration*, from Walter Pritchard (1905–77), head of the department of Murals and Stained Glass at the Glasgow School of Art, a respected stained glass artist, mural painter and sculptor [FIG.162].[56] Following his success in competitions for the University of Glasgow Faculty of Arts building and the University of Edinburgh Medical buildings on the north side of George Square (1951), Ramsay left his lectureship at the Glasgow School of Art to set up his own practice. He specialised in educational and church buildings. He maintained his relationship with the University, designing the large animal units at Garscube Veterinary Hospital in 1962, working on Queen Margaret Hall, Kirklee in 1961, Maclay Hall in 1966, the Dalrymple Hall conversion in 1966, and advising on the 1979 competition for stained glass windows in the Chapel, amongst a number of other projects.[57]

INSTITUTE OF VIROLOGY, CHURCH STREET, AND GENETICS BUILDING (NOW PONTECORVO BUILDING), DUMBARTON ROAD 1956–66

The University acquired the first of its offshoots at Dumbarton Road in 1947 when it merged with the old Anderson College of Medicine. The ornate building on the site had been designed in an eclectic free style of Italian and Scots Renaissance by James Sellars in 1888, but completed after his death in the same year by John Keppie of Honeyman & Keppie.[58] The large sculptural panel, by James Pittendrigh MacGillivray depicts the pioneering surgeon Peter Lowe (*c.*1550–1612), who was granted authority by King James VI to regulate medicine, surgery and pharmacy in the west of Scotland. John Keppie & Henderson carried out further work on the building in 1936. On inheriting the building, the University occupied it as departmental buildings for Bacteriology and Genetics, using the same firm of architects, by then known as John Keppie, Henderson & J.L. Gleave, for alterations in 1953–54.

By 1956 Hector Hetherington had determined to use the site to create a centre of medical excellence, based around the first institute of Virology in a British university and a purpose-built department of Genetics. The new Virology institute was aimed to entice Professor Michael Stoker from Cambridge, and the state-of-the-art Genetics facilities were intended for Professor Guido Pontecorvo, known as 'Ponte', one of the founders of modern Genetics.[59] On the basis of the success of the Natural Philosophy extension for the University, Basil Spence & Partners were selected to design the new buildings. Spence's stellar career was now in full swing, with major commissions for the Sea and Ships Pavilion at the Festival of Britain and Coventry Cathedral under his belt. Initially Spence sketched only the Virology institute [FIG.163], but soon afterwards, further designs of October 1957 conceived an integrated two-phase scheme for both Virology and Genetics.[60] This proposal would have involved the demolition of the old Anderson's College building, but, following discussions with the city planners, later revisions retained the old building and concentrated the Genetics accommodation into an adjoining nine-storey tower on the corner of Church Street and Dumbarton Road.[61] The scheme was worked up by David Rock in Spence's London office and then supervised by Peter Scott Ferguson from the Edinburgh office.

The Dean of Guild Court approved the Virology institute plans in September 1958, the tenements on the site were demolished, W. & J.R. Watson were selected as contractors, and construction began on 8 June 1959.[62] The Genetics department drawings were still under discussion with Professor Pontecorvo. The Virology institute comprises a rectangular-plan four-storey flat-roofed block facing Church Street with a single storey ancillary L-plan range behind. The structure is of reinforced concrete with steel cantilevers. Internally, the ground floor housed equipment rooms, including the projecting row of glassware and sterilising rooms, the second and third floors contained teaching, laboratory and office spaces, while on the top floor a recessed balcony is accessed from library, colloquium, or seminar room, and the Professor's office. Stairs and lifts are located at either end of the building. Externally, the building has not weathered well and the sculptural effects of the advanced and recessed planes of the Church Street frontage are hard to read. The once crisp bands of flush glazing and mosaic panels are much dilapidated, with many of the ceramic mosaic tiles failing to stick to their concrete panels from an early date. The gables are faced in a green Broughton Moor (Lake District) slate, as are the glassware and sterilising rooms, which project into Church Street.

After several revisions, the designs for the Genetics department were submitted for planning permission on 18 November 1960, and finally approved on 10 January 1961.[63] Like the Virology building, Genetics [FIG.165] has a reinforced concrete structure, designed with particular consideration for reducing vibration from the surrounding road network. On the exterior, mosaic panels face the main frontage to Dumbarton Road, and exposed aggregate concrete panels are used on the east and west sides. Similarly, these panels have not weathered well, and at the time of writing the building lies empty awaiting redevelopment of the site. The main south elevation is patterned almost abstractly with very small strips of windows, offset around pairs of staircase windows rising through the whole building.

163 Perspective of the Institute of Virology by Basil Spence, no date
RCAHMS [DP 012786]

164 Pontecorvo building (Genetics), designed by Basil Spence & Partners, 1958–60

165 The Institute of Virology in 1958
RCAHMS [DP 022944]

Only the upper level windows and the office windows to the north are of any size. The east and west elevations have no windows at all. The large wall-to-window ratio increased the cost per square foot above the normal level for the 21,000 square feet (1,951 square metres) of floor space provided. Internally, a Paternoster lift of constantly revolving compartments was selected over an express lift, again to reduce the potential for vibration transmitting to the surrounding laboratories. The Genetics building was re-named after Pontecorvo in 1995 [FIG.164].

STEVENSON BUILDING – 'THE STEVIE' (PHYSICAL EDUCATION), OAKFIELD AVENUE 1958–1961

The development of 'the Stevie' has a long history, dating back to at least 1937, when serious consideration was first given to the provision of medical and physical welfare services for the students. The University had acquired sites along Gibson Street between University Avenue and Oakfield Avenue, and now proposed to use part of the site for a medical centre, large gymnasium with space for two badminton courts, squash racquets and fives courts, swimming pool and changing rooms.[64] At this time the facilities were envisaged for male students only. The old gymnasium next to the Botany building was to be improved for use by female students. In early 1938 the Court appointed Graham Henderson of Keppie & Henderson to draw up plans.[65] The two houses on the site were demolished, but the advent of the Second World War put a stop to construction.

The proposal remained in the building programme after the war, but other priorities and lack of materials and money delayed the implementation for another thirteen years.[66] Henderson completely revised the design, which was conceived in tandem with an extension to the Men's Union, in 1958.[67] A photograph of the model was exhibited at the Royal Scottish Academy in March 1958.[68] Together, the two buildings were intended to form a U-plan around Oakfield Lane. However, only 'the Stevie' went ahead at this time in an L-plan arrangement, to be followed from 1961 to 1965 by the Union extension, redesigned by Richard De'Ath of Keppie & Henderson.

The new design for 'the Stevie' provided for both male and female students [FIG.166]. It featured state-of-the-art facilities including a 25metre swimming pool [FIG.167], built to metric instead of imperial measurements, to enable it to be used for Olympic training.[69] The pool was oriented with the slope of Gibson Street to minimise the requirement for excavation, and viewing windows were constructed below the water line. The ceiling was heated to avoid condensation and the pool water heated by electricity. The large gymnasium above the pool was panelled for half its 22ft height in guarea, a West African hardwood. It could be used for basketball, netball or badminton, or be subdivided into three smaller rooms by slatted wooden walls that descended from the ceiling. A smaller gym provided for boxing, judo and fencing. Two squash courts were built on the top floor.

Externally the steel-framed building continued the

166 Model of the proposed Physical Education building, later named after Sir Daniel Macaulay Stevenson, Chancellor of the University, whose trustees contributed towards the construction. The model is viewed from the north-west, looking towards the corner of Gibson Street and Oakfield Avenue.
GUAS [PHU 24/34]

167 The swimming pool in the Stevenson building, 1961
GUAS [PHU 24/24]

building line of the adjacent houses and was articulated by panels of gridded aluminium glazing that extended from the basement to the copper roof. Sandstone cladding divided the panels. Concrete balconies opened off the first floor level. The building was opened by the Principal, Hector Hetherington, on 9 January 1961 and named in honour of the merchant and benefactor, Sir Daniel Macaulay Stevenson (1851–1944), Lord Provost of Glasgow from 1911 to 1914 and Chancellor of the University from 1934 until his death. Stevenson's trustees and the University Grants Committee made significant contributions to the £260,000 building. 'The Stevie' was refurbished and reconfigured by the Holmes Partnership in the same year and given a post-Modern makeover that removed the balconies and flattened out the gridded glazed panels.

THE DAVIDSON BUILDING (ORIGINALLY BIOMEDICINE) 1948–1963

Following the submission of a report in October 1948 by the eminent heating engineer, George Arthur Rooley, on the poor state of the University's heating system, Jack Coia was commissioned to design a new central boiler room adjacent to the West Medical building and convert the old boiler room to an animal house.[70] The building was to be capable of upward extension at a later date to allow expansion of the adjoining Materia Medica and Physiology building. In the meantime, the length of the boiler house was to be extended to accommodate two staff tennis courts on the roof [FIG.168].[71] The scheme required collaboration between the various architectural firms working on the different buildings that were to be linked via underground ducts into the new heating system: T. Harold Hughes & Waugh at Chemistry, Basil Spence at Natural Philosophy and Keppie & Henderson at the Gilbert Scott building.

Coia's discreet and elegant boiler house was sunk into the slope above Kelvingrove Park and used the existing chimney of the old boiler house with a stainless steel flue inserted. On the north side facing the Natural Philosophy building, only the tennis courts were visible. The south side of the building was largely glazed with aluminium-framed windows facing Kelvingrove Park. The three boilers were initially coal-fired, but converted to oil in 1963 for improved cleanliness and handling.[72] The plan to build over the new boiler house remained an objective throughout the 1950s, but by the time a detailed design for a new Biochemistry building was required in 1958, Coia's reputation with the University had been dented by construction problems at the Garscube Veterinary Hospital.[73] As a result, Richard De'Ath of Keppie & Henderson was selected to design the new building [FIG.169]. The process of getting the plans through the assessors of the University Grants Committee, the City's Town Planning Department and Dean of Guild, and the Royal Fine Art Commission for Scotland took another two years.

De'Ath's design kept the main circulation spaces to the stone-clad stairtower at the eastern end and along spinal corridors between two parallel ranges of laboratories, research rooms and offices with single-glazed curtain walls. The Professor of Biochemistry, James Norman Davidson, celebrated for his work on nucleic acids, was concerned about solar gain from the outset, and expensive 'Louvredrape' (vertical) blinds, which were supposed to be better reflectors of heat than standard Venetian blinds, were installed on the south side of the building.[74] At a late stage in the design process, it was decided to install air conditioning, which involved redesigning the tower to accommodate the units. Double-glazing was also considered to assist with the retention of heat in winter, but ruled out on the grounds of cost. Work was far advanced in February 1962 when the main contractors, Crowley Russell

Ltd., went into liquidation. In order to avoid delays, the University offered to take over the subcontracts directly.[75] The building was finally occupied in September 1963 and officially opened by the eminent biochemist, Sir Rudolph Peters, in January 1964. It was named after Professor Davidson, who would be Professor of Biochemistry from 1947 to 1972. In 1994 it became home to the Biochemistry and Molecular Biology Division of the Institute of Biomedical and Life Sciences. Among the very few original internal features that remain are the corridor lockers, the entrance doors at the east end, stair handrails, seating (refurbished) and rooflight panelling in the main lecture theatre.

BUILDINGS BEYOND THE GILMOREHILL/HILLHEAD CAMPUS

Architects are noted in brackets.

- 1947–53 Institute of Surgery, Church Street (Western Infirmary) (T. Harold Hughes & D.S.R. Waugh)[76]
- 1948 Conversion of Anderson College, Dumbarton Road, to Genetics department and Anatomy and Physiology classrooms (A.G. Henderson of Keppie, Henderson & J.L. Gleave)[77]
- 1949–57 Animal Hospital, Garscube (Jack Coia)[78]
- 1949 Proposed conversion of Garscube House to staff flats (not executed) (Keppie, Henderson & J.L. Gleave)[79]
- 1954 Demolition of Garscube House
- 1958 Extension of Garscadden Pavilion (Alexander Wright & Kay)

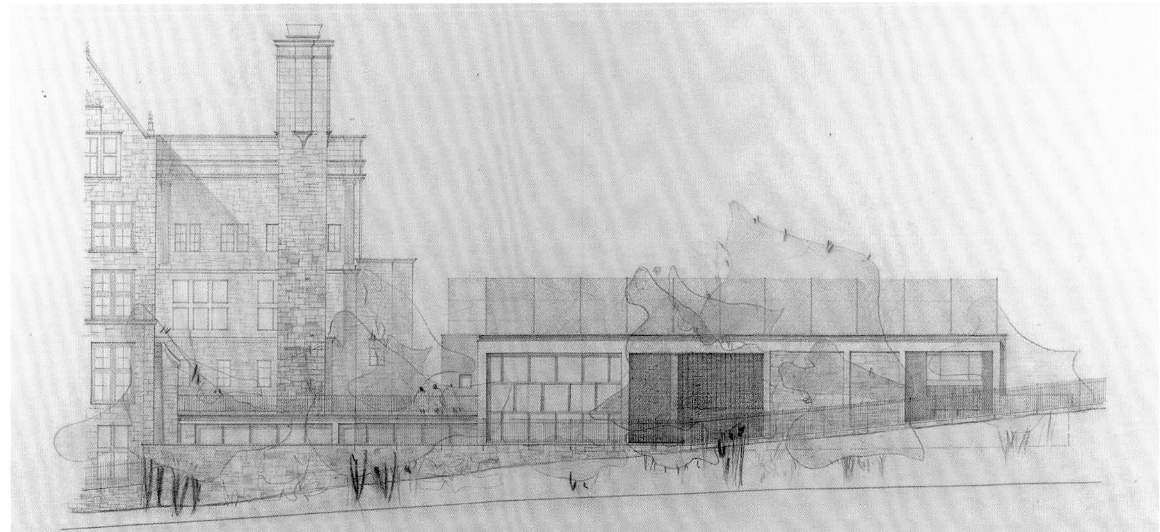

168 Jack Coia's boiler house and tennis courts, south elevation facing Kelvingrove Park, 1948. Variants on the design allowed for the rooftop tennis courts to be replaced by a departmental building.
GUAS [BUL 6/12/26]

169 The Davidson building (Biochemistry), designed by Richard De'Ath of Keppie Henderson & Partners, 1958
GUAS [PHU 8/3]

Chapter Nine

The Brutalist Campus 1960–1980

170 Detail from the presentation drawing by William Whitfield for the Library and Art Gallery, 1961
GUAS [GUA 78064]

This period is certainly the most controversial in terms of its architectural legacy, both in the city generally and more particularly in the University's Hillhead development area. Here, the leafy suburban hilltop is peppered in an apparently random manner with monumental blocks of Brutalist design that dwarf their domestic neighbours. In fact the random appearance of the buildings and the disjointed connections between them are the results of a series of hugely ambitious expansion plans that were never fully realised. The increasingly complicated political, financial, administrative, regulatory and architectural priorities all affected the way in which the buildings were planned, designed, constructed and used.

DESIGNING FOR THE FUTURE: MODERNISM TO POSTMODERNISM VIA BRUTALISM

As the level of criticism of insipid, backward-looking British university buildings of the 1950s grew in the architectural press, the universities and the University Grants Committee looked to new materials, new building methods and new architects to reinvigorate their campuses.[1] Architecturally, there was an increasingly international outlook to modern design, and an emphasis on rational planning, function, economy and speed of building over stylistic concerns. Reinforced cast-concrete skeletons, modular plans and 'systemised', and sometimes experimental, prefabricated elements allowed large and relatively cheap structures to be constructed quickly.

The Franco-Swiss architect, artist, designer and writer, Charles-Edouard Jeanneret (1887–1965), who adopted the pseudonym 'Le Corbusier' or 'the crow-like one', had an enormous influence on architects around the world. Throughout the 1950s, Le Corbusier and like-minded architects of the 'congrès internationaux d'architecture moderne' (CIAM; International Congresses of Modern Architecture) promoted the functionalist principles of the second phase of the Modern Movement. These were:

- rejection of historical and traditional styles;
- primacy of function and plan over form, or appearance;
- simplicity of form (removal of unnecessary ornament and detail);
- 'honesty' in structure (the structural components should be visible and form part of the architectural expression of a building);
- truth to materials (materials should perform a function, not disguise or act as decoration, e.g. stone cladding over brick);
- use of mass-produced materials and cultivation of the machine aesthetic over craft;

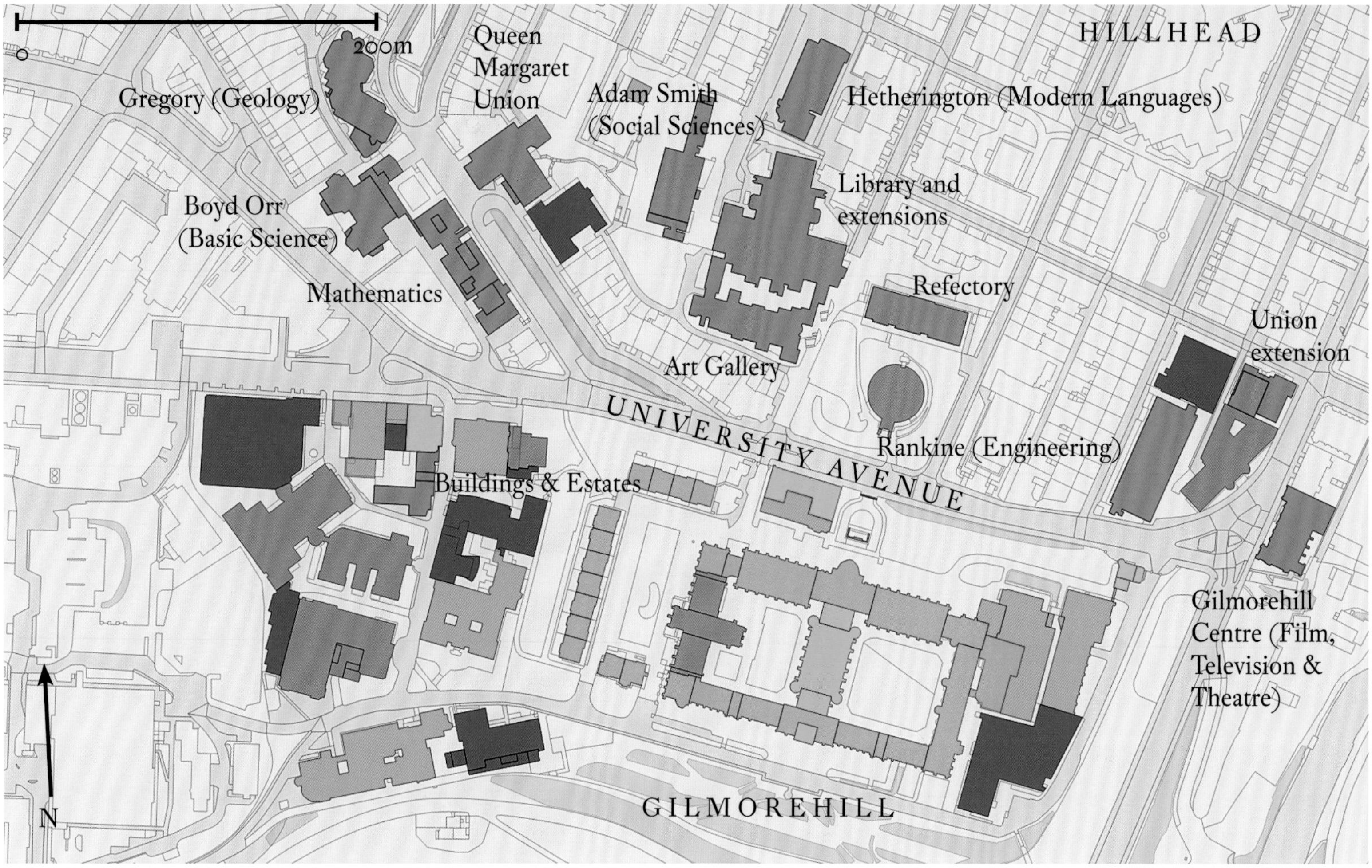

0 200m
HILLHEAD
Queen Margaret Union
Gregory (Geology)
Adam Smith (Social Sciences)
Hetherington (Modern Languages)
Boyd Orr (Basic Science)
Library and extensions
Mathematics
Refectory
Union extension
Art Gallery
UNIVERSITY AVENUE
Rankine (Engineering)
Buildings & Estates
Gilmorehill Centre (Film, Television & Theatre)
N
GILMOREHILL

- attention to the spaces between and around buildings: landscape and setting.

Apart from these principles, Modern Movement architects and architect-planners were frequently driven by social and/or socialist ideologies to create ideal communities of equality and opportunity. Buildings and landscapes were seen as mechanisms for encouraging structured and cohesive social behaviour. The test beds for these ideas were in the comprehensive planning or re-planning of cities and towns, and, on a smaller scale, institutions such as hospitals and universities.

In the university sector, the United States led the way with hundreds of new post-war university and college developments, including influential schemes at Harvard and the Illinois Institute of Technology by the great German expatriate architects, Walter Gropius (1883–1969) and Ludwig Mies van der Rohe (1886–1969). Major trends in American campus planning included: construction of a variety of flexible high-density buildings capable of extension and use by different disciplines; new concerns for lively, pedestrian-friendly 'urban centres' or 'precincts' and for the spaces between buildings; arrangement of buildings based on the natural pattern of pedestrian movements; exclusion of cars, or their segregation from pedestrians; zoning of functions.[2]

By the 1960s 'Brutalism' was rising as an architectural force internationally. It was a strand of the Modern Movement, broadly characterised by blockish, monumental structures with expansive, repetitive wall surfaces of *béton brut* (raw concrete) or other rough and raw surfaces including aggregate panels, brick and rough-hewn stone. Often the various parts and functions of the building were clearly expressed. For example, lift towers and machinery rooms were visible externally, rather than incorporated unobtrusively within the overall structure. While the terms 'Brutalism' and 'Brutalist' were used initially to describe the raw characteristics of buildings, they came to be used derogatively by critics and a public that found them ugly, overwhelming in scale, alien to their historic surroundings, often poorly constructed, and prone to weathering badly and to vandalism. By the late 1970s reaction to hardline Modernism and Brutalism had resulted in a new approach, 'Postmodernism', in which the blockish lines and modern materials of Modernism were replaced with historical references and a return to more traditional forms and materials.

Against the backdrop of this broader architectural context, the University Grants Committee established a specialist building sub-committee in late 1960 to oversee the increased spending on capital projects.[3]

171 Development of the University between 1960 and 1980

KEY

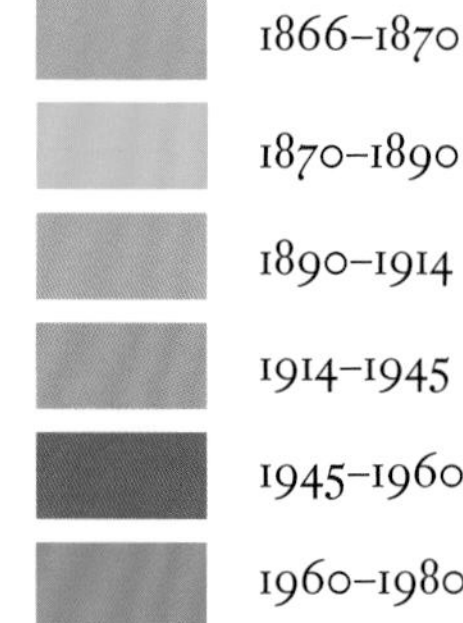

Throughout the 1960s the committee also became more engaged in supplying advice on design issues. It produced bulletins on design matters for specialist university building types and equipment, held seminars, encouraged the application of 'industrialised building techniques' (in particular the Consortium of Local Authorities Special Programme 'CLASP' system), and created links between universities and the National Building Agency.[4] The University Grants Committee's guidance on 'space norms' was particularly influential on the size and layout of buildings. The norms set out the standard dimensions of teaching accommodation expected per student. They were based on observations and assumptions about the teaching of students in different disciplines, such as the number of hours and type of teaching, staff/student ratios, and space types (e.g. lecture theatres, libraries, laboratories). Although the norms were always advisory, in practice most universities stuck to them closely in order to ease their capital funding applications to the Committee. Similarly, the Committee of Vice-Chancellors and Principals, which was chaired by Glasgow's Charles Wilson between 1964 and 1967, also set up a sub-committee on building and a university building information service, whose task was to promote good practice.[5] By the mid-1960s the planning of campuses and the design of university buildings were supported by a new range of specialist literature, for example, Richard P. Dober's *Campus Planning* (1963) and C.J. Duncan's *Modern Lecture Theatres* (1966). Although Britain did not possess American-style 'Educational Facilities Laboratories', groups of designers and equipment suppliers began to gather at conferences, such as the 1961 Manchester 'Designing & Equipping Modern Lecture Theatres Conference' to consider scientific principles for the layout of lecture theatres and other teaching spaces. Seating, acoustics, heating, lighting, ventilation, sound systems, projection equipment, teaching aids and technical administration of lecture theatres were analysed together for the first time in an attempt to define the optimum conditions for learning.

Another aspect of significant change in the period was the growing professionalism and organisation in the management of university estates and the procurement of buildings. The first annual 'Conference of University Building Officers' was held in 1959. The conference developed into the Association of University Directors of Estates (AUDE), which continues to promote excellence in the strategic planning, management, operation and development of Higher Education estates and facilities.

THE UNIVERSITY IN A CHANGING CITY

Slum properties, overcrowding and congestion in Glasgow still represented the major physical planning problems in Scotland in 1960.[6] Industrial decline continued and intensified to the point of catastrophe in places during the 1970s.[7] The exponential growth in road transport brought about major shifts in the freight and passenger transport infrastructure of the city away from river, rail and tram. Where the Corporation had struggled with the financial and practical implications of regeneration immediately after the Second World War, material shortages were easing and there was now improved political and financial backing for a profound transformation of the city. Both at national and local government levels, extraordinary efforts were made to address the housing problems, using a combination of the government's favoured scheme of overspill to the new towns, Glasgow Corporation's official policy of relocation of residents to twenty-nine proposed Comprehensive Development Areas (CDAS) within the city, and a rather less official crusade by the Housing Committee to utilise every available gap-site for high-density, high-rise blocks. A CDA was a designation under the Town and Country Planning (Scotland) Act 1947 allowing a local authority to acquire property in the designated area compulsorily, in order to re-plan and develop urban areas suffering from war damage or urban blight. In the cases of the new towns and CDAS, the method of planning the areas involved an idealistic all-encompassing approach to creating new 'utopian' communities from scratch on clear, or cleared, sites. From the outset the planning authorities favoured functionalist Modernist architecture and landscaping as the best way of expressing the newness and egalitarianism of the communities and their contrast with the crowded, unhygienic, hierarchical, fragmented, private developments of earlier centuries. The CDAS were slow and expensive to acquire and clear and the new towns were even slower to construct, leading to numerous difficult sessions on the issue for the government in the House of Commons, particularly for the Secretary of State for Scotland, John Maclay. The urgency of the housing problem favoured fast and cheap construction, which tower blocks provided in increasing numbers from 1962.[8]

Key figures in the dramatic reconfiguration of the city during the 1960s were the Lord Provost, Jean Roberts, and the convenors of the city's housing and planning committees, David Gibson and Bill (William Leonard) Taylor, along with the Housing Progress Officer, Lewis Cross and the Chief Planner, Robert D. Mansley. Jean Roberts was particularly interested in planning issues, and later became the Chair of Cumbernauld Development Corporation. In 1961 she led a study group of Glasgow councillors to the United States to look at comprehensive redevelopment, mass transportation and urban motorways in Washington DC, Baltimore,

Philadelphia, New York City, New Haven, Pittsburgh, Detroit and Chicago.[9]

A number of the University's architects also worked on some of the city's biggest housing schemes, for example Basil Spence at the Hutchesontown C scheme of 1960–66, Boswell, Mitchell & Johnston at Pollokshaws in 1961–71 and Woodside in 1970–74, Walter Underwood & Partners at Cowcaddens in 1968–71, and J.L. Gleave & Partners at Well Green, Pollokshaws, in 1968–75.

Unlike Edinburgh, which designated a huge Central Development Area (CDA) around much of the south side of the city for the development of its University, Glasgow's CDA efforts were concentrated almost exclusively on housing. The designation of a University zone in the 1951 City Development Plan provided the University with some security in its strategic planning of Hillhead, but it was far from the carte blanche represented by a CDA designation: properties could be acquired by the Corporation compulsorily on behalf of the University, but planning permission needed to be negotiated for each individual building and it proved difficult to integrate public roads and services within the design of the campus. The University zone was confirmed by the subsequent quinquennial review of the City Development Plan. The University's various plans of 1960, 1965, 1974 and 1978 for the Hillhead area are considered in further detail below.

Although the University was not directly affected by the CDA programme, the triangle of land bounding the Western Infirmary at Church Street, Byres Road and Dumbarton Road was included in the proposed Partick North Comprehensive Development Area. This triangle and much of the area west of Byres Road and south of Chancellor Street were planned for redevelopment with large blocks of flats in 1967.[10] Associated with the CDA programme was the city's Highway Plan of 1965, which envisaged a massive reconfiguration of the road network and creation of an inner ring road with connecting 4-lane 'expressways'.[11] The engineers, Scott Wilson Kirkpatrick, had begun detailed design work on the M8 urban motorway in 1960, and construction began in 1965. The scheme opened in phases from 1968, with Townhead I and Woodside I first, the Kingston Bridge in 1970, Woodside II in 1971 and Charing Cross in 1972. The University was more directly affected by the expressway proposals, particularly in the uncertainty surrounding a projected link between the Great Western (Road) expressway and the Clydeside expressway. At first various schemes were proposed for a route along, or parallel to, Byres Road on the western boundary of the University zone. By the 1970s consideration was given to moving the link to Bank Street at the eastern boundary of the University zone. In the end, the link on either route was abandoned. However, the protracted uncertainty about the link created difficulties for planning the University campus throughout the 1960s and 1970s. Other transport-related difficulties emerged when a Corporation deputation visited Hillhead Street in connection with its proposed closure for construction of the Library in 1966.[12] As a result of their concerns with the amount of student and staff parking on the streets, the Corporation demanded an overall University development plan showing car parking provision, and threatened to refuse future development applications. Car parking became an overriding obsession in the Corporation's voluminous correspondence with the University on planning matters after that date.

The Glasgow CDA programme was enormous in its conception and highly destructive in its execution. Whole communities were uprooted and moved to 'temporary' accommodation on the peripheries of the city. In most cases the process of acquiring all the properties for clearance took many years, during which the area was blighted and relatively little construction of new homes took place. Some commentators considered the effect on the fabric of the city to be worse than the wartime damage. The University of Edinburgh's destructive plans for the Georgian houses of George Square in the 1950s and 1960s provoked a powerful backlash that coalesced into the start of the conservation movement in Scotland. In Glasgow the height of the demolitions came in 1971, which was dubbed 'the Black Year of Destruction' by the historian and campaigner Frank Worsdall.[13]

The reaction against the destructive years was felt in the new planning regime that followed from the Town and Country Planning (Scotland) Act of 1972 and the reorganisation of local government in the Local Government (Scotland) Act of 1973, both of which came into force in 1975. Both Acts were intended to give more force to local communities and their needs and aspirations. Gradually, as the provisions came into effect, there was a move from the very rigid, centralised, comprehensive approach to a more flexible localised system. The city-wide development plan was replaced by 48 local area plans, including one for the west end, covering Gilmorehill/Hillhead, in the early 1980s. With the new high-density housing schemes creating fresh problems, Housing Action Areas were established from 1973 to rehabilitate existing buildings and areas. The CDA programme finally came to an end in September 1974, but the east end remained a persistent area of concentrated disadvantage, which led to the creation of the largest urban renewal project in Europe, the 8-year Glasgow East End Renewal (GEAR) programme, in 1976.

Measures for the conservation of historic buildings and areas also came into force in the early 1970s, and again these had an impact on the planning of the Hillhead campus. Statutory protection of listed buildings was finally implemented in Glasgow in 1970, and a conservation area was designated in 1972 covering a large part of Hillhead, including almost all of the University's new developments. The conservation area was expanded in 1983 to take in the Mathematics and Boyd Orr buildings, which had previously formed part of an excluded area around Byres Road. While a number of individual buildings were listed in Gilmorehill, no conservation area was designated there.

The University planners, who had previously enjoyed a high degree of independence from the wider city planning initiatives, suddenly felt the effect of the new provisions. There were now significant amenity and conservation constraints on development of the Hillhead area, even if money could be found to construct new buildings. Certainly, the days of monumental tower blocks and comprehensive planning were drawing to a close. Much of the planning discussion in the late 1970s related to the conversion of existing houses and tenements to University use. In 1976 the boundaries of the University zone were amended to omit Byres Road and to include an area bounded by Great George Street, Hillhead Street, Glasgow Street and Southpark Avenue.[14]

In relation to individual planning applications, the Royal Fine Art Commission for Scotland (RFACS), the government's advisory body on matters of public amenity or artistic importance, was increasingly influential. From the early days of the Commission a number of University-related figures had been appointed as commissioners and this continued after the war. Douglas Strachan, the stained glass artist for the Chapel, served from 1933 to 1947; Graham Henderson from 1948 to 1960; Ian G. Lindsay from 1953 to 1966; the University Principal, Hector Hetherington, served as Chairman from 1957 to 1965; Joe Gleave from 1960 to 1964; Frank Fielden from 1965 to 1969; Ivor Dorward from 1976; and Sir Robert Grieve, the University's first Professor of Town and Regional planning, also served as Chairman from 1978 to 1983. Through these contacts, the University had a good understanding of what was required of RFACS submissions, and emerged with generally positive endorsements of their proposals.

EXPANDING HIGHER EDUCATION: POLITICS AND STOP-START FUNDING

The period from 1960 to 1980 was one of convulsive change in higher education, architecture and planning. Although Scotland retained its distinctive higher education system, the government's financial allocations continued to be made in Westminster and distributed through the intermediary of the London-based University Grants Committee. An upturn in the economy enabled the 'one nation' Conservative governments of Harold Macmillan and Alec Douglas Home to loosen the purse-strings in pursuit of some of the immediate post-war political ambitions for greater social equality and educational opportunity. The expansion was fuelled not only by increased undergraduate access to higher education, but also by a broadening range of subjects and postgraduate research. The University Grants Committee began an unprecedented programme of investment in university buildings, which was described by the *Architectural Review* as 'somewhat similar to, and as exciting as, the cathedral building movement of the early twelfth century'.[15] Although university expansion and investment in the scientific revolution remained a core Labour policy, Harold Wilson's 1964–70 administration needed to tighten the fiscal policy to address the huge balance of payments deficit and threat of currency devaluation from 1965. The building programme was deferred and then cut back. By 1970 inflation was soaring, unemployment was rising, and industrial relations in the nationalised energy, transport and manufacturing sectors were deteriorating. Neither the Conservative government (1970–74) of Edward Heath, nor the Labour governments (1974–79) of Harold Wilson and James Callaghan, were able to sustain the university expansion programme. A letter from the University Grants Committee in January 1960 marked a turning point in the pace of new building at universities throughout the United Kingdom.[16] The Committee re-stated the government's existing target figure of 124,000 university students nationally, and for the first time recognised that the post-war 'baby boom' would require some 35,000 to 40,000 additional places (with an emphasis on science and technology) in the late 1960s. Critically the Committee had the support of the Chancellor of the Exchequer, Derick Heathcoat-Amory, in asking the universities to identify how they might expand and to revisit their building requirements for the years 1964–68.

In response to the increase in central funding of capital projects, the Carnegie Trust became concerned that their grants were tending to become unidentifiable supplements to grants from public funds. For the quinquennial distribution for the years 1962–67 it adopted a new policy of funding only projects that were not supported by the University Grants Committee.[17] In spite of this, the University managed to attract major funding from the Wolfson, Nuffield and Wellcome Foundations and direct grants from the Research Councils, so that the University Grants Committee's share of the quinquennial building programme dropped to just over a half.[18]

The 1963 report of the Committee on Higher Education, chaired by the economist Lionel Robbins, was a landmark in British further education. The Robbins Report, accepted by the Conservative government under Harold Macmillan, established the so-called 'Robbins principle' that university places 'should be available for all those who are qualified by ability and attainment to pursue them and who wish to do so'. The Report had two further fundamental recommendations:

- *The expansion should be carried out mainly by development of existing kinds of institutions—existing universities, the creation of new ones, the granting of university status to Colleges of Advanced Technology (CATS) and later to some Teacher Training Colleges (TTCS) and Regional Technical Colleges.*
- *All these university institutions, and the remaining TTCS* [which the Report proposed to remove from local authority control and associate with universities], *should be self-governing and financed by grants distributed through an independent Committee like the present University Grants Committee (UGC), with limited control by Government and accountability to Parliament.*[19]

To a large extent the recommended 68.2% increase in overall United Kingdom student numbers over a ten-year period (1963–73) reflected the government's existing provisions.[20] An emergency period of expansion was proposed to take account of the post-war 'baby boom' generation, which was now reaching the age for higher education.

The consequences of the Robbins Report were felt in the establishment of a new Education Ministry and the Universities (Scotland) Act 1966, which provided for a strengthened Court, and easier procedures for making ordinances, foundation of new chairs, introduction of new degrees, and increased involvement of non-professorial staff in the Senate and as assessors on the University Court. Perhaps the most significant development in Scotland was the doubling of the sector with the grant of university status to the University of Strathclyde in 1964, Heriot-Watt University in 1966 and the University of Dundee in 1967, and the foundation of the new University of Stirling in 1967.

The University of Glasgow estimated that it could reasonably accommodate a rise in student numbers from 6,000 in 1960 to 6,500 in the short term. The University's cautious reaction to the government's promise of new money overall weighed against Glasgow in the individual allocation by the University Grants Committee, as new institutions and those who promised a large increase in their intake benefited most. In fact Glasgow was left proportionately worse off than in 1958, and needed to rein in its building programme, most notably in the construction of student residences.[21]

In order to expand the student population on the Gilmorehill/Hillhead site, it was necessary to deal with some of the core accommodation problems, notably the Library, catering services, the student unions and the art collection. There was an ambition to provide student residences on site, but a recognition that academic and associated service buildings had to take precedence. On the academic side there was a long list of accommodation requirements

The University's building programme had no sooner got underway than the new Chancellor of the Exchequer, James Callaghan, imposed a blanket postponement of all government-funded building projects for which contracts were not signed, excepting housing, schools and hospitals.[22] Allocation of University Grants Committee funding for building projects dropped dramatically across Britain in 1966–67. In Scotland the amount dropped from £8.323m in 1965–66 to £2.87m in 1966–67.[23]

When the next quinquennial funding round began in 1967, the Glasgow programme was cut substantially to include only the completion of existing projects (the Boyd Orr Basic Science building at Hillhead and a number of buildings at Garscube) and a start on the Geology building and possibly the art gallery. In an emergency government announcement on the dire economic situation by the Chancellor of the Exchequer, Roy Jenkins, on 17 January 1968 all university capital projects were deferred for at least a year.[24] The Principal resorted successfully to special pleading with the University Grants Committee for the funds to make a start on the Boyd Orr building.

At initial meetings with the University regarding the 1972–77 quinquennial grants round, just three new buildings were identified for progression by the University Grants Committee:

- New Arts building (Hetherington)
- Extension of the Library
- Life Sciences[25]

Even these schemes and the existing Geology project were shelved indefinitely following the emergency moratorium on government-funded construction in December 1973. It was 1979 before funds could be found to extend the Library and construct the Hetherington building and Hunterian Art Gallery. In the same year the University Grants Committee decided not to fund the construction of further halls of residence.[26]

SIR CHARLES HAYNES WILSON, PRINCIPAL OF THE UNIVERSITY 1961–1976

Although planning for a major expansion began under Sir Hector Hetherington in 1960, the dominant figure in the detailed commissioning of buildings was his successor, Charles Haynes Wilson, who took over in 1961 and served until 1976. Wilson, a Glasgow alumnus and political scientist, taught Modern History and

172 Charles Haynes Wilson, Principal of the University from 1961 to 1976
GUAS [UP 1/3/87/2]

Politics at Corpus Christi College, Oxford in the 1940s, before moving to the United States in 1950 as the Visiting Professor of Comparative Government at Ohio State University. In 1952 Wilson was appointed Principal of University College, Leicester, and then became the first Vice-Chancellor of its successor, the University of Leicester, in 1957. During his tenure at Leicester, he assisted with the establishment of the University of Sussex (laid out by Basil Spence), and chaired the academic planning board of the new University of East Anglia (laid out by Denys Lasdun). Wilson was popular, dynamic, well-connected and ambitious for his academic charges [FIG.172].

Charles Wilson came back to Glasgow with experience of managing an expanding campus and commissioning masterplans and buildings. On the advice of the eminent English architectural historian, John Summerson, Wilson had appointed the highly influential former Chief Architect of the London County Council and lead designer of the Royal Festival Hall, Leslie Martin, to lay out the new campus at Leicester in 1956.[27] The individual buildings on the campus were designed by a variety of pioneering Brutalist architects including Martin himself, Denys Lasdun and the partnership of James Stirling and James Gowan. One of Wilson's last acts as Vice-Chancellor at Leicester was to commission the main social and refectory building, later named in his honour, from Denys Lasdun, in March 1961.

Wilson made the best of a brief window of relative financial ease at Glasgow to commission or plan most of the monumental blocks that now crown Hillhead. In terms of the scale of building expansion, Wilson compared the 271,300ft^2 (25,205m^2) of the original Gilbert Scott building with the provision of almost double that amount of new space (522,220ft^2/48,516m^2) in 1962–67.[28] It is clear that Wilson was aware of both the critical reaction to his building legacy and its symbolic value. As he remarked to the *Glasgow Herald*, 'Nobody has had his continuous expectation of what the university is like destroyed by expansion ... We lose no visible character by it – we make more marks in the sky and more monuments for people to associate us with, which is part of the folklore of identifying a university and fixing its position ... Our visible, known and expected character is not disturbed: there's just more of it.'[29] Wilson's successor in 1976, Alwyn Williams, was not so lucky in his political and financial circumstances. His tenure until 1988 was dogged by constant financial battles.

STUDENTS AND STAFF

A snapshot of statistics supplied to the University Grants Committee for the academic year 1960–61 shows that of the 6,223 full-time students, 74% were male and 26% female, 74% originated from within thirty miles of the University, and 73% lived at home, 20% lived in lodgings and just 7% lived in halls of residence.[30] There were 298 full-time research students. A further 7,000 students attended extra-mural courses of various sorts. There were 709 full-time teaching staff, including seventy-two professors, 190 part-time teaching staff, including six professors, and 1,257 full-time non-teaching staff.

An increase in recurrent funding by the University Grants Committee allowed a significant improvement in the staff/student ratio from 1964. By 1970–71 full-time student numbers stood at 7,969, 66% of whom were male, 34% female, and there were 368 full-time research students. On the teaching side there were 1,336 full-time staff, including 124 professors, and 439 part-time teaching staff, including two professors. Full-time non-teaching staff rose to 2,117.[31] The improved staff/student ratio allowed increased seminar and tutorial teaching provision, particularly in the Arts. The Arts Faculty almost doubled between 1964 and 1975.[32] The creation of the Social Sciences Faculty in 1975 brought the number of faculties to eight. A large number of new chairs were founded between 1960 and 1980 including Industrial Relations (1960), Veterinary Medicine (1960), Nuclear Engineering (1961), Microbiology (1964), Cell Biology (1965), Fine Art (1965), Architecture (1965), Management Studies (1970), Archaeology (1972), Medical Genetics (1973), Business Policy (1974), Cardiac Surgery (1974), Oncology (1974) and Accountancy (1975).

173 Joe Gleave's Arts, Communal and Pure and Medical Science zones, 23 April 1964
GUAS [BUL 59/24]

174 Second model of Joe Gleave's development proposals for Hillhead, 1962. This model includes William Whitfield's designs for the Library and Art Gallery.
GUAS [PHU 13/4/29]

DEVELOPMENT STRATEGY AND PLANS 1960–1980

Glasgow was keen to play its part in the national expansion of the higher education system, but the Court were cautious about promising to increase student numbers without appropriate facilities. The existing target of 6,000 students had not been met by 1960, and central facilities like the Library, staff rooms and residential accommodation were completely inadequate. The departmental needs were most problematic in the basic sciences, where a grounding in Mathematics, Chemistry and Physics was required to progress in these subjects and Engineering or Medicine. The Arts Faculty too was under pressure, lacking tutorial and seminar space, but Law and Divinity were considered capable of expansion. Recognising the constraints of the Gilmorehill site, the University considered two approaches:

The first is the acquisition at an early date of part of the present built-up area on the North side of the University. A considerable operation of this kind must be attempted in any event, since to meet certain existing needs which cannot be satisfied at a distance from our main campus, further adjacent sites must be acquired. A plan [Mears] *has been prepared and has been approved by the Corporation of Glasgow which, if confirmed by the Secretary of State, will have the effect of 'designating' (i.e. providing for compulsory purchase) enough land to meet our building requirements for the next few years. The plan also shows (without at this stage involving the 'designation' of occupied buildings) what would be possible in the next ten to fifteen years. That longer distance plan would provide accommodation for considerably expanded Faculties of Arts and Science, and make possible space for another 1,000+ students. But it has to be acknowledged that even if (as is probable) the Corporation were to support this programme, quite serious opposition is to be expected from the owners of affected property, and the expense will be formidable. On balance, assuming that an increased student enrolment in Glasgow is thought to be in the national interest, and always providing that the residential development keeps pace with the general expansion of student numbers, it seems that a slightly preponderant University opinion favours this local development.*[33]

The second approach was the establishment of a new campus, perhaps on the Ayrshire coast or at Stirling, which would be dedicated to teaching the first two years of the courses provided by the Arts and Science Faculties. The negative side of this proposal was the high set-up cost and the potential duplication of buildings and staff.

JOSEPH LEA GLEAVE, ARCHITECT

In 1948 Graham Henderson of John Keppie & Henderson invited Joseph Lea Gleave, then Head of Architecture and Town Planning at Edinburgh College of Art, to join the practice as a partner. Gleave had first come to prominence as the winner of the 1931 international competition for the Columbus Memorial at Santo Domingo Este in the Dominican Republic, a vast project encompassing not only the lighthouse, but a seaport, an airport, two bridges, a water gate and a

175 Wilson & Womersley's model of the Hillhead Campus from the south-west, 1965
GUAS [PHU 13/4/19]

hotel.[34] The competition was judged by the architects Frank Lloyd Wright and Eliel Saarinen amongst others. The Columbus Lighthouse museum/mausoleum was finally inaugurated in 1992, some twenty-seven years after Gleave's death.

Gleave made his reputation in Scotland as the designer of the innovative Vale of Leven Hospital in 1952–55.[35] He generally revitalised the Keppie Henderson firm. When he arrived, the practice was already heavily involved with new buildings and alterations of existing buildings for the University. These included the new Engineering extension; conversion of part of Anderson's College for the Genetics department; extension of the Zoology department and expansion of the Mathematics department into the old upper Forehall. The practice was also carrying out redecoration of the Randolph and Bute Halls, the upgrading of the heating sub-station beneath the tower in the main building, and proposals to subdivide Garscube House as staff flats.

The *Dictionary of Scottish Architects* records Gleave's habit of all-night working to meet deadlines, which was a cause of some friction with the more ordered Graham Henderson. The firm of John Keppie, Henderson & J.L. Gleave was eventually dissolved by mutual agreement on 31 December 1957.[36] Gleave set up his own practice at 10 Lynedoch Crescent, taking the commissions for the Queen Mother Hospital and the control tower at Prestwick Airport with him. Two years later, Gleave was appointed to the Royal Fine Art Commission for Scotland.[37]

THE GLEAVE PLAN 1960–1965

Glasgow Corporation wrote to the University Court in April 1959 requesting a sketch plan of the University's proposed developments in Hillhead.[38] The pressure for an updated development plan intensified following the University Grants Committee's letter of January 1960 regarding expansion of student numbers. The University Court approached several architects, including Frank Fielden, Ralph Cowan, Robert Hurd and Joe Gleave, to take over Frank Mears's role in advising on the Hillhead development. On the basis of the responses, they continued discussions with Gleave and appointed him formally for a period of three years from August 1960.[39] The appointment as 'general consultant for the Hillhead Development' was intended to be along the lines of a similar position at the University of Birmingham, which had been undertaken by Hugh Casson and Neville Conder in 1957.[40] The new Development Plan was intended to have a currency of twenty years. Gleave moved quickly to design an outline layout. Speed was important for the proposals to be included in the city's Quinquennial Review of the Development Plan and for consideration by the University Grants Committee. There was no time for detailed organisational proposals or time and motion studies, such as those that informed the widely-praised contemporary University of Leeds Development Plan by Joe Chamberlin of Chamberlin, Powell & Bon.[41] There appears to have been a written report in support of the Hillhead layout, but no copy has been located during the research for this book.[42] By contrast with the traditionalist Mears, Gleave was a committed Modernist in his concerns for expression of function and structure, rational form and flowing, flexible space. Although Gleave took the Mears plan as his starting point, he adapted it radically to form a long series of linked buildings between University Avenue in the south and Great George Street to the north, including a new Library, Art Gallery, Refectory, Mathematics department and Women's Union. In response to the growing concerns for traffic management and car parking, Gleave conceived the Hillhead site as a modish segregated 'precinct' development: cars at ground level and pedestrians at precinct level above. The Hillhead development was to be linked to the Gilmorehill campus by pedestrian bridges over University Avenue. To encourage both coherence and individuality in accordance with the recommendations of the University Grants Committee, the overall layout and design strategy was to be allocated to one architect (Gleave), while the individual buildings were to be designed by different architects. The area was zoned into three groups of buildings serving a similar purpose: the west end for Pure and Medical Sciences, with some commercial development at Byres Road; communal buildings, such as the Library, at the centre; and Law and Applied Sciences in the north-east. A number of the features of Gleave's plan, such as the precinct, zoning and the buildings interconnected by low links, suggest that he was aware of international trends in campus planning, particularly in the United States.

Gleave drew up a list of architects who might serve on a panel 'who would meet at intervals to discuss the whole planning of the area, and from whom, as a building was required, a suitable architect would be selected to carry out the work'.[43] The architects on his initial list and the proposed buildings were:

- Richard De'Ath (John Keppie, Henderson & Partners): Men's Union and Engineering extensions
- Walter Neil Wilson Ramsay (C.J. McNair, Elder & Ramsay): Mathematics
- David Harvey (Harvey & Scott): Social Studies (Adam Smith Building)
- Alexander Buchanan Campbell: Women's Union
- Frank Fielden (Professor of Architecture, Glasgow Royal College of Science and Technology): Fine Art
- Ralph Cowan (Head of the School of Architecture, Edinburgh College of Art): Refectory

The Mears palette of materials was updated to include reinforced concrete structures clad in pre-cast concrete panels with aggregate stone finishes.[44] No new development was proposed for the old Gilmorehill site. For the most part the proposed departmental buildings were tall, high-density blocks aligned north-south along the Hillhead ridge, and the smaller departments, service and linking buildings were to be lower and oriented east-west. Unlike the Mears plan, which took the Hillhead street pattern and scale as its starting point, Gleave's plan looked to the different alignment and larger scale of the Gilbert Scott building for its key. The Library, in the form of a large tower, was to form the focal point of the whole development and a counterpoint to the Scotts' tower and spire [FIG.174].

Gleave set out his intentions and suggested a number of eminent architects in a letter written on 30 May 1960 to Robert Hutcheson, Secretary of the University Court:

This building [the Library] *is a fine opportunity on an outstanding site and to a large extent will set the 'key' for other buildings. If possible, I think, the opportunity should be taken, from the point of view of both the town and the university, of making it rather a gesture. Do you think the Court would agree to us approaching Corbusier to see if he would do it. There is no doubt about Corbusier's position as the leading architect in the world, and there is no Corbusier building in Britain. He would, of course, require someone like me to deal with the actual building and so on in this country, and I would be very pleased to work on these lines.*

If not Corbusier, there is, however, Alvar Aalto of Finland and Arne Jacobsen of Denmark, but neither of these latter two would produce the originality of Corbusier. If none of these three could do it, it might as well be me.[45]

While the University Court generally welcomed Gleave's scheme, the proposal for Le Corbusier, Aalto or Jacobsen to design the library tower was quickly rejected as impractical. By October 1960, a block plan model had been made and photographed, and Gleave's outline proposals were sent to the Secretary of State for Scotland, John Maclay, for approval.[46] Building committees were formed for each of the major new projects.

By 1962, architects had been appointed for the Library, Museum and Art Gallery, Refectory, Queen Margaret Union, Men's Union extension and Social Sciences buildings. Another model was prepared for the Planning Committee of Glasgow Corporation showing the building layouts, access roads, circulation areas, public open space and facilities for car parking.[47] Planning permission for the Hillhead development was granted by Glasgow Corporation on 20 August 1963.[48] In early discussions, the Corporation's Chief Planning Officer, Robert D. Mansley, was keen to entice the University into an even more ambitious expansion to help redevelop Byres Road with shops and other commercial uses.[49] The scheme was part of a proposed remodelling of the city to link the Great Western Road (to be converted to an 'expressway') to the new Partick Comprehensive Development Area and Clydeside expressway.

Although relatively little of Gleave's scheme was

executed before his death on 16 January 1965, his plan guided the development of the Hillhead campus for the next fifteen years and his firm inherited the projects for the Mathematics Institute, the Boyd Orr building (Basic Science) and the Gregory building (Geology).

WILSON & WOMERSLEY PLAN 1965–1967

Gleave's premature death left the University without a consultant architect at a critical period in its development. The Principal moved quickly to appoint the influential Hugh Wilson of Wilson & Womersley Planning Consultants, the Secretary of State for Scotland's planning consultant for Irvine New Town and recent former chief architect of Cumbernauld New Town. Womersley was formerly the chief architect of Sheffield, where he oversaw the building of the infamous deck-access Park Hill flats. At about the same time as the Glasgow appointment, the firm also developed a new campus plan for the Victoria University of Manchester. Wilson & Womersley went on to work on major town plans for Northampton (1968–69), Cheltenham (1973), Liverpool (1974–77) and Manchester (1974).

Like Gleave, Wilson was a complete Modernist, and particularly influenced by planning developments in the United States. In the light of the University's decision to expand to 10,000 students with a greater proportion of research students, Wilson was commissioned to undertake a comprehensive review of the Hillhead development plan. Wilson's 'Hillhead Precinct Report Number One', which he considered as an 'interim statement', was completed in November 1965 and an illustrative model followed in December.[50] 'Report Number One' examined the existing conditions, previous planning proposals and the buildings under construction, and identified a number of principles for future planning. Two major criticisms of the Gleave scheme were that it did not take account of the surrounding city sufficiently and that the buildings were too closely spaced, leaving little amenity space or room for expansion. Wilson & Womersley set out five planning principles, which were:

- The University should develop in a precinct which is free from the noise, smell and danger of irrelevant traffic.
- The plan should accept the current and increasing high level of car usage. It follows from this that, in order to facilitate carefree and pleasant movement about the precinct, major vehicular and pedestrian spaces should be clearly defined and be segregated from one another as far as is practicable.
- The open spaces are as important to the environment as the buildings which define them. When a number of individual architects are operating in an area at different times it is essential that the spaces between their buildings should be designed carefully and coherently.
- The plan must be flexible and must be reappraised from time to time. This is particularly important now when academic organisation and development is so fluid.
- Maximum use should be made of the site through the twenty four hours. The introduction of some residential accommodation could contribute to the liveliness of the precinct. The provision of some commercial development could enrich the environment by its presence, and indirectly, by some alleviation of the financial problems inherent in the redevelopment of urban land.

'Hillhead Precinct Report Number Two' was completed in December 1967. Based on further studies and information, including a 40–50% increase in student numbers, 'Report Number Two' set out an overall development strategy for the land then zoned for University use. The Report envisaged a requirement for more detailed studies and proposals for different parts of the University Estate as they came to be developed. By this time, the funding brakes were beginning to be applied by the University Grants Committee, and the University recognised the likelihood that a number of buildings purchased for demolition would need to accommodate departments for the immediate future. In spite of the increasing financial constraints, 'Report Number Two' still envisaged an expansion of the University's site northwards to the Great Western Road by around 1975. In terms of building form, 'Report Number Two' recommended a continuous flow of new teaching and office space, constructed on a repetitive grid system, to enclose the existing core of free-standing communal buildings (Library, Refectory, Queen Margaret Union etc.) on the north and west sides along Great George Street and Byres Road. Such all-encompassing 'megastructures' were considered relatively cheap to construct and believed to be capable of flexible use and easy modification in response to developments in teaching, and shifts in the balance of subject areas. Wilson had used the megastructure approach in Cumbernauld town centre, and in the university sector similar 'teaching wall' concepts were then under construction on greenfield sites at the new Universities of East Anglia and Stirling.

In accordance with the principles set out in 'Report Number One', the movement of traffic and pedestrians played a large part in Wilson & Womersley's 'Report Number Two' proposals. Like Mears, Wilson & Womersley continued to push for the closure of University Avenue to through traffic in order to create a pedestrian precinct between the Gilmorehill/Hillhead campuses and to improve safety and amenity. While the Corporation was amenable, it wanted Ashton Road to be realigned at the University's expense as part of the scheme. This the University could not afford. University parking was to be rationalised to the periphery of the campus. A number of sites were put forward in 'Report Number Two', but in subsequent years more serious consideration was given to two multi-storey car parks: one in Lilybank Gardens; the other on the site of Laurelbank School on Lilybank Terrace.

Similarly important in the Wilson & Womersley plan were the proposals for the landscaping of the open spaces between buildings, which they regarded as the key unifying feature of the Hillhead development. Hugh Wilson drew up a separate document outlining landscape principles in September 1966.[51] The principles set out the need for a common vocabulary for various types of space and surface, predictable availability and cost of materials over a long period and high durability. There was also a need for low maintenance and 'timeless quality of design'. A number of unifying materials were suggested: stone setts or blue brindle engineering brick for parking areas, asphalt road surfaces and whinstone kerbs, precast concrete slabs for pedestrian areas with a mix of patterns and other materials for piazzas, setted edging to grassed areas, and boulders (rather than metal gratings) around the bases of trees. The lighting and signage were to be standardised.

Implementation of the Wilson & Womersley proposals was severely curtailed by the financial difficulties of the late 1960s and the 1970s. Of the projected building schemes, only the Hunterian Art Gallery and Mackintosh House, went ahead in accordance with the plan. The 'teaching walls' were never built and the spaces between the buildings were never unified by consistent design.

UNIVERSITY DEVELOPMENT PLAN 1971

By 1970, the University Development Plan of 1965 was considered outdated. Hugh Wilson expressed his concern that developments, such as the Geology department in Lilybank Gardens, were proceeding without a strategic context or understanding of Glasgow Corporation's most recent plans, particularly for Byres Road. The Corporation too was demanding to see a strategic plan for University development in Hillhead before approving individual planning applications. While the University continued to seek Wilson's advice on strategy, he was now based in London, and the Court felt the need for more local and immediate guidance on planning issues. The University appointed its own dedicated planning officer to update the University Development Plan in 1971.[52]

Citing the need for the Great Western and Clydeside Expressways to be opened before closure of University Avenue could be considered, the Corporation realigned University Avenue to form a larger junction with Byres Road and Highburgh Road in 1971.[53] On the western side of the designated University zone, the University recognised that it had no realistic prospect of being able to afford to purchase properties along the Byres Road frontage and develop above the subway tunnel leading to Hillhead Station, nor was there any great enthusiasm to participate in the Corporation's ill-defined plans for mixed academic/commercial development in the area.

The revised plan estimated an increase in the student population from 9,000 to 11,000 by 1976.[54] It described the Gilmorehill site as fully developed and also identified a number of constraints on developing the Hillhead sites more fully, including the newly protected listed buildings, Lord Esher's recommendation that Hillhead should be designated as a Conservation Area under the Civic Amenities Act 1967, the desirability of maintaining adequate amenity space, and the need to maintain the existing road network through the site. The University had been attempting to close the lower part of Hillhead Street to traffic since 1966, but the move had been fiercely resisted by local residents, culminating in a public inquiry in 1971.

UNIVERSITY DEVELOPMENT PLAN 1974

In a 1974 review of the University's expansion proposals, Glasgow Corporation noted increasing local opposition to expansion of the University in Hillhead and proposed that no further area be considered for re-zoning until the University produced a justification and details of its requirements.[55] In return for dropping its existing zoning for Byres Road, which was too expensive to acquire and develop anyway, the University had identified two new blocks of Hillhead as expansion zones. The first of these encompassed Great George Street, Southpark Avenue, Bower Street, Hillhead Street, and Cecil Street, while the second was bounded by Great George Street, Oakfield Avenue, Great Western Road, Otago Street and University Avenue.

The existing designated area was causing problems because the University did not have enough funds to progress schemes, and the undeveloped properties were blighted by their zoning for redevelopment. At that time the student population stood at about 9,000 and the ambition was to double that figure over the following twenty years. The building priorities at that time were identified in the 1974 Plan as:

- A multi-storey car park (northern end of Lilybank Gardens)
- Hetherington building, phase I (Bute Gardens)
- Library extension
- Refectory extension
- Computer Science (University Avenue, to the south-west of Mathematics)

176 The model by William Whitfield for the Library and Art Gallery, 1960
GUAS [PHU 15/26]

– Life Sciences (Lilybank Gardens, north of Queen Margaret Union)

At the same time, the Development Plan had to take into account the fact that the city's parking policy required the University to provide one parking space per member of staff and one space per ten students for all new developments.

UNIVERSITY DEVELOPMENT PLAN 1978

Cuts in the University Grants Committee's capital grants programme, a smaller increase in student numbers than projected, high inflation and changes in the city's planning objectives all combined to produce a major reassessment of the University's expansion proposals in 1978.[56] Following the 1974 Plan, Glasgow Corporation formally abandoned its plans to construct a bypass/service road along the lanes parallel to Byres Road. The University decided to redefine the western boundary of its development zone from Byres Road to a line down the centre of Great George Street, Lilybank Lane and Ashton Lanes in return for an expansion north of Great George Street to Glasgow Street, between Hillhead Street and Southpark Avenue.[57] The Secretary of State for Scotland formally approved the boundary amendment on 25 March 1976.

Of the six sites scheduled for redevelopment in the 1974 Plan, only four remained. The Refectory extension and Life Sciences projects were now omitted. The University's poor economic circumstances reduced the scale of the other developments except the Computing Science building. The multi-storey car park was reduced to a single level surface car park and the 3-block Arts building to a single block on Bute Gardens. The Library extension was reduced from a full-blown mirror image of Stage I to a much smaller stepped addition. In the event, the Computer Science building on the car park site parallel to the Mathematics building was also dropped as a project in 1980.[58] The remainder of the plan looked to the adaptation of existing buildings and conversion of terraced houses for departmental use, providing that the conversion works did not have a detrimental effect on the amenity of the neighbouring residential area. William Gillespie & Partners, landscape architects, were appointed to draw up an Environmental and Landscape Strategy, but again the dire financial conditions prevented much progress.[59]

THE BUILDINGS 1960–1980

INTRODUCTION

Joe Gleave was not only the University's preferred planner, he was also the key to the commissioning of architects for individual buildings at Hillhead. His own firm, J.L. Gleave & Partners, and its successors, worked for the University consistently throughout the 1960s and 1970s. Major projects included the Mathematics, Boyd Orr, Gregory and Hetherington buildings. Keppie, Henderson & Partners also continued their longstanding relationship with the University in the design of the Rankine building and Union extension in Hillhead, the Hydrodynamics laboratory and the Observatory at Garscube. They also carried out the conversion of Gilmorehill Church, amongst a number of other more minor projects on existing buildings.

Gleave suggested Frank Fielden for the Fraser building (Refectory), Harvey & Scott for the Adam Smith building, Raglan Squire for the Library and Art Gallery, and Walter Underwood for the Queen Margaret Union. Underwood went on to work on the first

177 View from the Gilbert Scott building of the newly built Refectory by Frank Fielden (middle ground, behind the Round Reading Room). The image shows the alignment of the Refectory and Reading Room with the Scott building, rather than with the street grid.
GUAS [PHU 22/21]

extension of the Library in 1979. Further afield, Basil Spence completed his scheme for Pontecorvo Genetics building on Dumbarton Road, and Walter Ramsay continued work on new buildings at Queen Margaret Hall and the conversion of listed buildings for Dalrymple and Maclay Halls. Building Design Partnership was commissioned for a number of buildings at Garscube in the early 1960s and drew up a separate development plan for that site in 1967.[60] Gleave set down the palette of materials for use at Hillhead, but each architect introduced variations, such as the size and colour of the aggregate in the precast panels.

An important part of the University's drive for more modern teaching methods and equipment was the development of a television centre at Southpark House. A director of the University's innovative television service was appointed in March 1965.[61] The equipment was used for a variety of purposes, including the teaching of psychiatric interviewing 'at the bedside', delivering lectures to a Geography 'overflow' classroom, and demonstrating autopsy techniques in the Pathology department at the Western Infirmary.

Automation of administrative records first began in 1966, with the transfer of enrolment information by means of punched cards to the huge and expensive new KDF 9 computer in the Chemistry building. The computer was then able to produce basic information, such as class lists, fee claims and a variety of statistics.[62] University Grants Committee grants normally only covered the initial furnishing and equipping of new accommodation, but in view of the expense of, and demand for, computers, provision was made on a 'regional' basis for some universities.[63] In 1970, the Minister for Education and Science, Margaret Thatcher, intervened directly to insist on a British-made replacement for the KDF 9, in spite of the University's preference for a more advanced and powerful IBM model.

THE FRASER BUILDING/THE HUB (REFECTORY), HILLHEAD STREET 1960–1966

Since the relocation of the University to Gilmorehill in 1870, catering for staff and students had proved to be a persistent problem. Before the Second World War the men's and women's Unions provided catering for their

178 The Refectory and Library towers in 1978
GUAS [PHU 23/11]

members and a gloomy basement room in the north range of the Gilbert Scott building catered for staff and students of both sexes. A temporary refectory was constructed at the men's union site after the war, but the increase in student numbers from 4,000 to 6,000 placed huge strains on all the catering facilities. In 1956 the University Grants Committee accepted Glasgow's case for grant-aiding the expansion of the catering and social facilities. The expansion of the University into the Hillhead House site created an opportunity for a centrally located refectory that could serve not only the old Gilmorehill buildings and the Round Reading Room, but also the projected Library, Social Sciences and other facilities north of University Avenue. The project was not without controversy however, as the two unions feared the provision of central University catering and social facilities would undermine their own offerings and impact negatively on membership fees.[64] Frank Fielden was appointed as architect for the new University Refectory in September 1960 [FIG.177].[65] Fielden had designed a number of buildings for the University of Durham before his appointment as Professor of Architecture at the University of Strathclyde. The plans, which were presented to the University Court for approval in March 1962, were the first from Gleave's masterplan, and the first to adopt the uniform of concrete and black flint/Creetown granite aggregate panels. The aggregates were chosen to look at their best in heavy rain.[66] Fielden proposed a long, low, symmetrical rectangular-plan range for a self-service refectory over a recessed undercroft that contained the kitchens.[67] Tall, narrow vertical windows punctured the austere horizontal composition. Fielden described the concept as 'a simple building ... with some rather heavy detail to keep pace with the Gilmorehill buildings and Wellington Church'.[68] The site was difficult, as the building needed not only to deal with the steep slope and potential old mineral workings, but also to modulate the geometry of the gridded street layout in Hillhead to the slightly different axial alignment of the Round Reading Room and the Gilbert Scott building. Fielden worked with the consultant engineers, W.V. Zinn & Associates, to resolve the structural issues. The Royal Fine Art Commission for Scotland described the result as 'quiet and well-mannered' and the Scottish Civic Trust awarded it a Class I Commendation.

Although by contemporary standards, the building was relatively sympathetic to its surroundings, a number of existing domestic buildings were to be demolished: 65 Hillhead Street and 74, 76 and 78 Southpark Avenue. The most serious of these losses was 78 Southpark Avenue, the former home of Margaret and Charles Rennie Mackintosh, which was listed provisionally at Category B. The University's Hillhead Development Committee, comprising the Principal, Sir William Robieson (Chancellor's Assessor), Alan Boase (Professor of French), Robert Gray (Rector's Assessor) and the University's consultant architect, Joe Gleave, were alive to the potential controversy surrounding the demolition, which had 'already caused some alarm in some quarters':

Mr Gleave pointed out that Mackintosh's work covered some internal alteration, interior decoration and furnishings, which if transplanted elsewhere would require a situation with similar lighting in order that its character be preserved. Externally the house was undistinguished as was the whole terrace of which it formed a part. There was general agreement with the view that at this juncture the University should refrain from comment on this aspect of the plans, as likely to lead to undesirable controversy.[69]

Initial discussion centred round recreating the Mackintosh interiors within the new refectory building, but eventually it was decided that incorporation within the new Art Gallery and Museum would be more practical (see below for more details of the new Mackintosh House).[70] The time limit on the grant by the University Grants Committee for the refectory meant that 78 Southpark Avenue needed to be demolished before a new home could be found for the interior work. The interiors were eventually stored in various nooks and crannies found for them by Andrew McLaren Young, the principal proponent of Mackintosh's work.

179 The Refectory, now known as the Fraser building, in 2010 after its refurbishment by Page\Park Architects

As originally constructed, the Refectory building contained two large dining rooms, a snack bar and a penthouse 'waitress-service' restaurant. The refectories on the main floor were linked to the lower level kitchens by ten food lifts in the blue brick and stainless steel servery core of the building. The main feature of the interior of the principal rectangular-plan refectory was a large mural relief, designed by Charles Anderson, who also worked with Fielden at the University of Strathclyde School of Architecture in 1965.[71] The in-situ poured concrete was left exposed to express the structure and both the refectories were lined with pine, fitted by John Cochrane & Co., the joiners for the University Chapel some forty years before. The building was intended to cater for up to 3,000 students every day, seating a maximum of 1,100 at a time. Construction began in 1963 and the building, which cost £283,000, was opened on 21 February 1966.[72] In return for their 25-year lease on the sole bank in the building, the Clydesdale Bank funded a £½m refurbishment in 1981–82, which included the provision of offices, travel agency, sport and clothing shop and insurance brokerage around a central concourse, with a snack bar on the floor above. The architect for this scheme was John M. Watson of Watson & Paterson.[73]

In 2007–09 Page\Park Architects undertook a further radical refurbishment and extension of the building, cladding the aggregate panels in bright blue and green glass curtain walling, building out the undercroft, and adding monumental stone-clad pavilions to either end [FIG.179]. Internally the top floor is entirely filled by the kitchens and large dining hall, which is divided into flowing, informal areas for sitting, eating, meeting and touchdown facilities. The old concrete frame remains exposed and painted black at ceiling level, while the new white plasterboard walls and colourful graphics form a light and airy backdrop to the oak and glass fittings. The bookshop, medical centre, careers service, welfare and other student services offices are housed at the lower level. A new grand stair and hard-surfaced piazza were created to the south. The refurbished building was renamed in honour of William Kerr Fraser, Principal of the University from 1988 to 1995 and Chancellor from 1996 to 2006.

The architects Walker & Cunningham produced a landscape plan for the ground south of the Refectory in consultation with Fielden.[74] The area was re-landscaped by the artist, Christine Borland, working with the landscape architects, Loci Design, in 2002. The benches with ceramic headrests were inspired through the long working relationship that Borland developed with the medical research departments within the University. The overall layout is also influenced by medieval physic garden designs, including an early proposal for a physic garden in the University, noted on the back of a page of the 1549 Fuchs edition of the *Historia* by the Revd Mark Jameson, a student who served as Rector's deputy in 1555.[75]

THE ADAM SMITH BUILDING, BUTE GARDENS 1960–1966

The Hillhead Development Committee noted in a minute of its meeting on 26 October 1960:

Of the Social Sciences Building, Mr Gleave said that it was essentially a 'background' building presenting few problems, calling for an architect rather efficient rather than brilliant. It would be an advantage if the architect were a local man, and one who would be ready to modify his design as might be required by the architect of the key Library building.

The Committee agreed to recommend the appointment of Messrs. Harvey & Scott, Glasgow, for this work, the early stages of which could well proceed, in Mr Gleave's view, without waiting for the final solution of the Library problem.[76]

The undeveloped site in the former garden ground of Lilybank House was relatively straightforward. No demolitions were required and a cellular raft foundation dealt with the potential problem of disused mine workings. Envisaged as the first part of a large linked complex aligned with the geometry of the Gilbert Scott building, the building stands at a slight tangent to Bute Gardens and Lilybank House. Apart from the unusual alignment, the failure to complete the adjoining buildings has left

180 The Adam Smith building from the south-east. The hanging stairtower was intended to link to a building that was never constructed.

181 Mosaic mural by George Garson in the Adam Smith building, 1967
GUPU [13-036-42]
By kind permission of the Estate of George Garson

an odd-looking fire escape staircase floating over part of what was intended to be an underpass for cars at the southern end of the building.

The 7-storey building was designed to accommodate 106 staff and between 800 and 1,000 students. The plan provided for various sizes of lecture/seminar/tutorial rooms, laboratories, computer rooms, common rooms and a library for Political Economy, Social and Economic Research, Economic History, Political and Social Theory and Institutions, Management Studies, Psychology, Social Psychology, Accountancy, Citizenship, Anthropology, Criminology, Industrial Relations and the School of Social Study.[77] A records store was provided beneath the Library for the Economic History department to house their rapidly growing collection of business records from the vanishing Clyde shipyards and heavy engineering workshops.[78] The Adam Smith building was the first of the University's multi-purpose blocks housing a large number of departments [FIG.180]. It was designed in two sections with an intervening link for stairs and a lift. The southern section is sub-divided into two blocks of teaching accommodation above the first floor (library) level, with the main staircase between them forming a U-plan; the staff offices are housed in the narrower rectangular-plan block at the northern end.

Although articulated sculpturally in blocks with different roof levels, the window strips in the teaching block and the landscape format of the office block windows serve to emphasize the horizontal planning of the building. A corridor runs through the length of the building. The intention was that the Adam Smith building would connect horizontally to further buildings in the complex. An open terrace, decorated with blue mosaic-tiled panels, wraps round the outside of the library at the first floor. Concrete and flint aggregate panels form the predominant external cladding over the reinforced concrete frame. Patent double-glazed aluminium units were specified for the windows, but perhaps fearing a repeat of the disastrous metal windows in the Chemistry building, timber units were substituted in construction.

The flint aggregate panels and blue mosaic tile panels continue into the main glazed staircase, creating an intermediate space between the exterior and interior. At the foot of the stair is a very fine mosaic mural by the head of the Mural Design and Stained Glass department at the Glasgow School of Art, George Garson [FIG.181]. Elsewhere in the building the finishes are more basic: painted brick corridor walls, plain plastered room walls and suspended ceilings. The main lecture theatre on the top floor is expressed externally by its floor-to-ceiling glazing, a feature that is more stylistic than practical when the room needs to be darkened for projection.

The building was named in honour of Adam Smith, economist and Professor of Logic and then of Moral Philosophy at the University from 1751 to 1764. Professor Sir Denis Brogan, the eminent political scientist, opened the building formally on 2 November 1967.[79]

THE LIBRARY, HILLHEAD STREET 1960–1968

Under the Mears Plan a new University Library was to be constructed on the site of the northern terrace of Professors' Square. In October 1959 the Library planning committee prepared an assessment of the spatial requirements of the Library for the next fifty years, in which it was estimated that some 18,500m² of floor area was needed. The committee recommended to the Court 'as a matter of urgency that efforts be made to find and to reserve for the Library a suitably-placed site capable when fully developed of accommodating a building with a total internal floor area of at least 200,000 square feet'.[80] When Gleave began work on planning the Hillhead development, he immediately allocated a much larger and more prominent hilltop site between Bute Gardens

182 Presentation drawing by William Whitfield for the Library and Art Gallery, 1961
GUAS [GUA 78064]

and Hillhead Street to the Library. Even at the early stage of planning the Hillhead development, Gleave conceived the Library as a monumental tower. The selected site had the benefit of proximity to the old campus and centrality within the new development area. It would meet the estimated internal space required for the immediate future and allow for expansion. The only drawback at the outset was that the University did not own the whole site: 1–2, 4–6 and 10 Bute Gardens needed to be purchased.

Having had his suggestions for the world's most famous contemporary architects, Le Corbusier, Aalto, and Jocobsen, rejected by the Court, Gleave turned his thoughts to eminent and committed British Modernist architects:

Mr Gleave spoke of the choice of architects for the new buildings in prospect. It seemed to him that the Library and Fine Art Building should be conceived as one entity, and that this building was the key to the development of the whole area. He suggested that the University should discuss its plans for this building with one or two of the few British architects whose known work could be said to have an international reputation. Alternatively, the University might consider some form of limited competition: this device might produce an imaginative solution from an architect of lesser eminence. He did not now recommend an appointment from outside the United Kingdom, as delays in communication were almost certain to impede the progress of the development.

The Committee agreed that an approach should be made in the first instance to each of three leading architects named by Mr Gleave viz. Sir Leslie Martin, Mr Raglan Squire, and Mr Frederick Gibberd.[81]

Martin and Gibberd were unavailable for the project, so Gleave suggested a further two candidates: Yorke, Rosenberg & Mardell and David du Roi Aberdeen & Partners.[82] The Committee on Hillhead Development met the three London architects, and in February 1961 unanimously recommended the appointment of Raglan Squire to the Court.[83] No full brief for the project was available, but Robert Ogilvie MacKenna, the University Librarian, had lots of ideas and hoped to travel to the United States to look at recent library buildings and seek guidance from people with experience of library construction.[84] MacKenna's main concerns were with 'simplicity of general plan, adaptability to changing needs and patterns of teaching and service, and capability of further extension after completion of the full original design'.[85] Raglan Squire (1912–2004) established Raglan Squire & Partners in London in 1948. The practice worked on industrial and educational buildings, but its most notable commission was the conversion of 100 townhouses to luxury flats in Eaton Square for the Grosvenor Estate. In 1952 Squire was commissioned to design the Engineering College at Rangoon University in Burma. Large commercial and industrial projects followed at home and abroad throughout the 1950s. William Whitfield joined Squire in partnership in 1961, but it was to be dissolved by mutual consent in October the following year. However, Whitfield would continue to work on the University Library and Art Gallery project in his new independent practice.

Whitfield trained at Newcastle-upon-Tyne under the pioneering town planner, Thomas Sharp (1901–78). He gained considerable experience of university buildings at Durham, where he was responsible for the students' union, refectory and debating chamber between 1960 and 1964, and for the Science library between 1963 and 1966. Whitfield had presented initial sketches and a model to the University Court, the Hillhead

Development Committee and the other architects involved on 13 July 1961.[86]

The reaction to the initial scheme was favourable, and Whitfield continued to develop the proposals, visiting a number of modern libraries with MacKenna. Several trips in 1964 took them to: the *Chalmers tekniska högskolas biblioteket* and the *universitetsbiblioteket*, Göteborg, Sweden; the statsbiblioteket, Aarhus, Denmark; the Universitätsbibliothek, Bonn, Germany; the Staats und Universitätsbibliothek, Hamburg, Germany; the Universitetsbiblioteket, Blindern, Oslo, Norway; Keele University Library, England; and the University of Reading Library, England.[87] MacKenna and the Library Planning Committee corresponded with other foreign libraries around the world and researched library planning in great depth.[88] The 1965 book, *Planning Academic and Research Library Buildings* by the Harvard University Librarian, Keyes DeWitt Metcalf, was influential in devising space allowances for various types of students and staff. Mackenna was particularly interested in the concept of open access for undergraduates, which had not been used previously at Glasgow.

Whitfield envisaged that:

the Library should consist of a glass-walled block within which the floors were free of all obstruction (other than supporting pillars), the block to be flanked by towers of irregular height and shape which would provide staircases, lift shafts etc. From the point of view of the Library's needs, the design had the merit of flexibility and would permit any desired arrangement of shelves. In relation to its surroundings the grouping of towers was more in scale with the existing architectural landmarks than a single massive tower. The design would allow of construction in two stages, the first being complete in itself. Provision was made for recreating the interiors of the Charles Rennie Mackintosh house on an alignment similar to that of 78 Southpark Avenue and without disturbing the interrelationship of rooms and landings. Externally this part of the plan would, of course, conform to the new style'.[89]

Apart from the functional requirements, Whitfield's approach to the design was determined by the need for the Library to act as:

- A building on its own
- A central feature in the Hillhead development
- An architectural complement to the University tower
- A feature in the Glasgow skyline

The architect attributed the design inspiration to Langley Castle, Northumberland, close to the village of Whitfield, from where his family originated. The castle had an open rectangular core with service towers around the outside. There are coincidental similarities with Louis Kahn's 1957–61 Richards Laboratories for the University of Pennsylvania, where the services are pushed to 'servant' spaces in external towers and the core forms a clear-span 'served' space for the laboratories.[90] This approach was comparatively rare at the time. Basil Spence's contemporary library for the University of Edinburgh, for example, had the opposite arrangement of a service core with surrounding functional spaces. The externalisation of services was later taken to extremes in international 'High Tech' buildings, such as the 1971 design for the Centre Georges Pompidou in Paris by Renzo Piano, Richard Rogers and Gianfranco Franchini with Ove Arup & Partners.

Over the next three years Whitfield developed the plans from the initial concept in consultation with the Librarian and Library Planning Committee. He generated the form from the plan and its functional requirements, with a book 'warehouse' and reading rooms at the centre and non-library or noisy activities, such

183 The Library under construction, 5 May 1967
GUAS [PHU 15/2]

184 The completed Library in February 1971
GUAS [PHU 15/28]

185 Hunterian Art Gallery and Mackintosh House to the left of the Library in 2009 before the Library re-cladding programme began

HUNTERIAN
ART GALLERY

as circulation and servicing, housed in the peripheral towers. While the peripheral towers were practical, they also had an aesthetic function as 'disruptive camouflage' in breaking up the profile of what was otherwise a 'lumpish cube'.[91] The potential effect on the Glasgow skyline was carefully considered from a number of key vantage points around the city. Like the other buildings masterplanned by Gleave, the Library was aligned with the geometry of the Gilbert Scott building rather than the Hillhead street grid.

In order to gain the approval of the building's main funder, the University Grants Committee, the scheme needed to be divided into two stages. Stage I comprised the core block and 2-storey western office annexe, both of which were built. Stage II was to be a mirror image adjoining to the north, but in the event this would not be built. The city's Dean of Guild Court approved the finalised plans for Stage I of the Library on 16 October 1964, the £969,615 contract was let, and work began on demolition of the Bute Gardens houses on 15 February 1965. Philip Sayer acted as the supervising architect. Whitfield's preferred structural engineer, Ove Arup, was unavailable, so Lowe & Rodin were appointed in his place.[92]

Progress was swift, but there were glitches such as the need for additional piling. By August 1966 the reinforced concrete frame had risen to ten storeys and by the following May the towers were reaching their full height and the cladding was being fitted [FIG.183]. The pre-cast aggregate panels were applied in upright format with intervening horizontal bands. Similarly, the narrow slit windows of the towers and the original opaque ridged 'Profilit' glazing of the core served to emphasize the vertical composition and disguise the building's essential 'blockishness'. Structurally the towers are isolated from the core to allow for differential movement.

In February 1968 the Library progressing committee selected a new Danish-manufactured cantilevered shelving system called 'Reska', designed by Rud Koreska.[93] With standard steel components and shelves, the system was extremely flexible, allowing different lengths, heights and types of free-standing shelving.[94] The Library was an early adopter of a system that is now widely used all over the world.

Work began on the huge task of removing, cleaning and transferring the 640,000 volumes from the old Library on 7 July 1968. A marker placed in every book indicated its location in the new building [FIG.184]. The floors were arranged to accommodate related subject groups. Special Collections and the Hunterian library were housed in the basement. Stage I of Whitfield's Library opened for use on 30 September of the same year, although building works continued into 1969.[95] For the first time open access to the shelves was available to all students, where previously junior undergraduates had needed to order books through the catalogues.

The final cost of Stage I was just over £1m.[96] Although Stage I was intended to be capable of operating without Stage II, in practice Stage I was immediately under pressure, most notably in housing only two unreliable lifts for an 11-storey building, and in provision of just 925 reading spaces for a student population of nearly 9,000. Failings in the weather-proofing of the hilltop building, which is battered by the prevailing south-west wind and rain, have been resolved only recently. The tight budget mitigated against cooling and humidity controls for each floor, resulting in a build-up of heat in summer.[97] The back wall of the building deteriorated quickly because it was intended to be internal, adjoining Stage II.[98] The initial inadequate budget, untested building materials, subsequent performance issues, the omission of the planned Stage II, and changing needs and technologies have all played a part in the large number of subsequent alterations to the original design. The most notable of these were: 1972–79 – new east-facing entrance in Hillhead Street (the original entrance faced south towards University Avenue) by Whitfield Partners;[99] 1979–83 – extension of the ground and first floors to the north by Walter Underwood & Partners to create a new 400-seat reading room;[100] 1986 – tiered addition on top of the 1982 extension, also by Walter Underwood & Partners; 1996–78 – the addition of a storey on the core block with a curved roof by the Holmes Partnership to house Special Collections; replacement of the opaque 'Profilit' glazing with blue-glazed curtain walling; removal of main stair and new entrance extension;[101] 2009 – new cafe extension/modification of the Underwood extension to the north by William Nimmo & Partners. Other internal refurbishments included the re-cladding, re-glazing, re-roofing and insulation of the towers in 2012–13. After considering a number of possible ways of dealing with the problem of the deteriorating original aggregate cladding, William Nimmo & Partners installed a new aluminium rain screen system over a layer of insulation

THE HUNTERIAN ART GALLERY AND THE MACKINTOSH HOUSE, HILLHEAD STREET 1960–1981

Andrew McLaren Young was the major driving force behind the creation of the new Hunterian Art Gallery and Mackintosh House [FIG.185]. McLaren Young had joined the University as its first lecturer in Art History in 1949. In 1965 he was appointed Richmond Professor of Fine Art. He was a notable scholar of the painter, James McNeil Whistler, and enriched the University's collections with numerous acquisitions and benefactions.[102] Throughout its long gestation the project was known officially as the 'Museum Extension', but in fact it was always intended to house the University's growing collection of paintings, drawings and other works of art. From the 1930s to the 1960s the collections swelled from about 300 works to some 10,000 items, with major gifts and a bequest by Whistler's heir, Rosalind Birnie Philip. There had also been gifts of prints from James McCallum, William R. Scott and A. Acland Allen, while important Charles Rennie Mackintosh drawings and furnishings had been gifted by Hamish Davidson, Cameron Davidson and Sylvan MacNair. A number of important paintings had also been gifted by Ina Smillie, W.A. Cargill of Curruth, Gilbert Innes, Charles Hepburn and Alec Macfie.[103]

An Art Gallery had first been proposed before the Second World War as part of T. Harold Hughes's scheme surrounding the Round Reading Room. In 1951 Frank Mears allocated a prominent site for the art gallery on the north side of University Gardens, linked to a theatre and music room. Mears's prediction that it would be some years before construction of an Art Gallery was possible proved to be correct. McLaren Young's enthusiasm and the increasing size and importance of the collection kept the ambition alive throughout the 1950s. Joe Gleave's initial model for the development of Hillhead showed a low Art Gallery linking the Library tower to the Refectory.

When the University Court approached Raglan Squire in connection with the Library, they included provision for the Art Gallery as an integral part of the Library scheme. McLaren Young's detailed requirements for the Art Gallery included not just space for display of the University's permanent collection, but also space for the Art History department.[104] In a bid to quell the controversy over the proposed demolition of Margaret and Charles Rennie Mackintosh's former home at 78 Southpark Avenue, relocation of the house interiors was also included in the brief. William Whitfield inherited the Art Gallery scheme when his partnership with Raglan Squire was dissolved in 1962.

Whitfield produced an indicative outline of the building as part of his sketch designs for the Library in July 1961, but it was not until 1966 that more detailed work began.[105] The development of the Art Gallery and Mackintosh House project was protracted and complicated by funding and planning difficulties. The building was ineligible for University Grant Committee funding, so that the money needed to be raised from the University's own resources and a variety of charities and grant-giving bodies.

By April 1970, when Whitfield presented his finalised plans to the University Court, the accommodation proposals for the Art History department had been dropped from the scheme.[106] The detailed designs therefore provided accommodation for:

186 The sculpture court between the Library (left) and the Hunterian Art Gallery (right). The lantern from the dome of Pettigrew & Stephen's warehouse, possibly designed by Charles Rennie Mackintosh in 1899, was moved to this location following the Glasgow Garden Festival in 1988.

187 Dhruva Mistry's 1990 bronze sculpture, *Diagram of an Object*, set against the backdrop of the Hunterian Art Gallery's 'concrete corduroy'

- the permanent collection of Old Master paintings
- the James McNeill Whistler collection
- the Charles Rennie Mackintosh collection
- the print collection
- temporary exhibitions
- a lecture theatre
- storage, workshops, photographic studios etc.

In addition, the enclosed space between the Gallery and the adjoining Library was to create an outdoor sculpture court [FIG.186]. Like the Library, the form the building took was developed from the functional and technical requirements of the plan. The only windows are vertical slits in the north elevation allowing glimpses of the sculpture court, otherwise the exterior is comprised of solid walls. Even more than its towering neighbour, the geometric shapes and variety of walling materials, colours and textures give the Brutalist building a distinctive sculptural quality.

One of the key sculptural effects is achieved by 'concrete corduroy' panels [FIG.187], a technique developed in 1962 by the American architect and Dean of the Yale University School of Architecture, Paul Rudolph. Vertical 'fins' are cast into the concrete using a plywood-backed mould. The edges are then knocked off the fins with a bush-hammer in alternating patterns when the panel is in situ. The removal of the edges reveal the warmer interior tones of the aggregate and the vertical fins suppress the subtle colour changes that are normally visible in smooth concrete surfaces.

By 1970 some £296,000 had been earmarked. One of the largest contributions, £102,000, was from funds bequeathed to the University, while the Carnegie Trust offered £20,000 towards the Mackintosh House and £140,000 towards the Art Gallery. However, when the tenders arrived in October, the difference between tender figures and the estimates was so great that a radical reassessment of the building requirements was needed, and the area of the lower floor was reduced. Shortages of steel and rampant inflation were significant factors in the cost increases. A number of

188 Detail of one of the four cast-aluminium doors to the main gallery designed by Eduardo Paolozzi and cast in 1976–77 © Trustees of the Paolozzi Foundation, licensed by DACS 2013

189 Detail of one of the doors to the main gallery, Hunterian Art Gallery, signed by Eduardo Paolozzi and dated 1976–77 © Trustees of the Paolozzi Foundation, licensed by DACS 2013

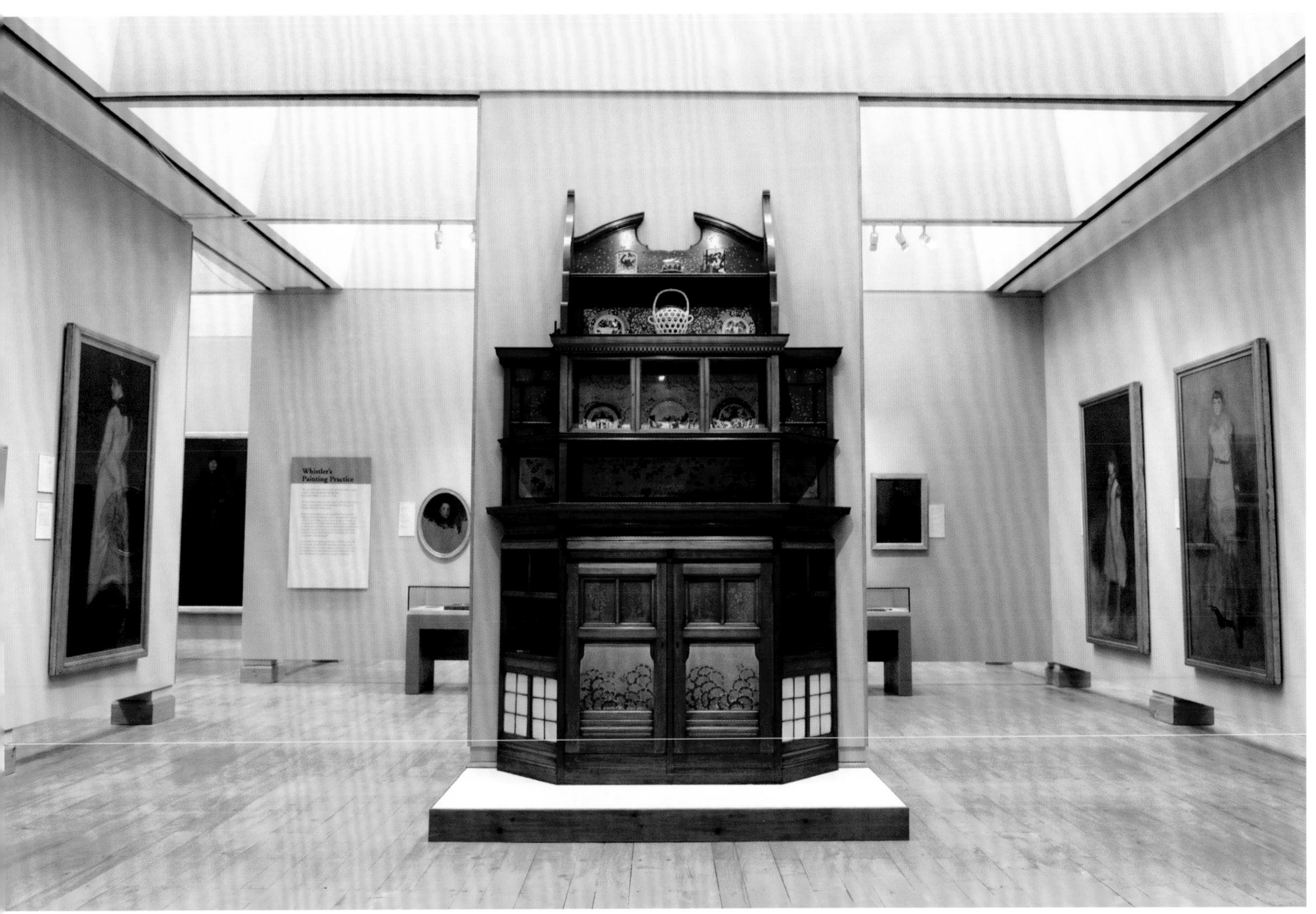

190 Main gallery, Hunterian Art Gallery, as refurbished in 2012
GUPU [13-036-4]

the grant offers were restricted by time limits, which raised concerns that the funders would withdraw if the delays persisted.[107] In the end the University accepted McLaren Young's pleas to proceed with the building before the costs rose further and deal with the shortfall of £30,000 during construction.[108]

The Corporation held up the grant of planning permission while car parking provision for the Hillhead development as a whole was discussed.[109] The construction of the Art Gallery and Mackintosh House also proved to be a very slow and rancorous affair, with long delays, bad weather, structural miscalculations, budget over-runs, contractual disputes and defective work.[110] Construction began in 1973, but it was June 1978 before the building was handed over by the contractors, and June 1980 before Sir Hugh Casson opened the Hunterian Art Gallery.[111] The Mackintosh House finally opened in 1981.

An appeal by the Principal, Alywn Williams, in 1980 had removed the need to proceed with the planned sale of eleven Whistler paintings in New York to cover the now massive deficit on the building of £320,000.[112] The National Heritage Memorial Fund made one of its first grants to the University in order to preserve the Whistler collection intact.

THE HUNTERIAN ART GALLERY

The Gallery complex is laid out from east-to west with links northwards enclosing a sculpture court at the foot of the Library. The main component is a single storey top-lit gallery that houses the permanent collection and the Whistler collections [FIG.190]. A cylindrical stair-tower adjoins to the east, providing a link to the 2-storey and basement block, containing the lecture theatre, shop (formerly a contemporary art display area) and temporary exhibition gallery. At the entrance to the galleries are four doors, each containing three cast-aluminium, low-relief panels designed by Sir Eduardo Paolozzi. The panels are typical of Paolozzi's graphic and sculptural work at this period, containing linear and abstract mechanical forms inspired by the syncopated rhythms of contemporary composers such as Charles Ives.

At the construction stage of the project in 1974, William Whitfield had discussed the general problem of sculpture in modern buildings with Paolozzi, who became enthusiastic about being commissioned to design doors for the Art Gallery.[113] Paolozzi had been a key figure, along with Alison and Peter Smithson, in the development of the New Brutalist architectural movement of 1953–56, and greatly admired Whitfield's proposals.[114] He was encouraged in the project for the doors by his friends and patrons, Gabrielle Keiller (widow of the Dundee marmalade heir, Alexander Keiller), and architect, Michael Spens, who had commissioned ceiling panels and hangings for Cleish Castle in Kinross-shire. Paolozzi himself waived his fee in memory of his friend, Andrew McLaren Young, who died suddenly in February 1975. William Whitfield also contributed towards the cost of the doors. In spite of his international reputation, the doors were Paolozzi's first public sculpture commission in Scotland, for which he was honoured with a Saltire Society award in 1981 [FIGS 188, 189].

The explosion of Dutch elm disease in the late 1960s led to wide availability and a drop in the price of the timber, which Whitfield exploited in specifying an elm floor and skirtings for the main gallery. Although there were initial problems with the elm floor lifting, it now gives a beautiful glowing quality to the space, which is lit naturally from the compartmental ceiling and north-facing skylights above. Elsewhere the finishing is restrained, with concrete or plaster surfaces and minimal detailing of fixtures, such as doorhandles and handrails.

The sculpture court currently contains Paolozzi's bronze *Rio* and a cupola by Charles Rennie Mackintosh from Pettigrew & Stephen's warehouse [FIG.186] in Sauchiehall Street, amongst other sculptural artworks.

THE HISTORY OF 78 SOUTHPARK AVENUE AND THE NEW MACKINTOSH HOUSE

The Mackintoshes lived at 6 Florentine Terrace (later 78 Ann Street, then 78 Southpark Avenue) from 1906 to 1914 [FIG.191].[115] The existing later 19th-century townhouse was immediately redecorated, furnished and modified in the Mackintoshes' own distinctive manner. Externally, the main changes were replacement of the front door and insertion of a horizontal strip of windows in the south wall to provide additional light and a view to the tower of the University [FIG.193].

The house was let from 1914, then sold complete with its furnishings to Mackintosh's patron at Windyhill, William Davidson, in 1920. In 1946 the University purchased 78 Southpark Avenue from William's sons, Hamish and Cameron Davidson, who had previously donated its contents. By 1949 the house was occupied by John Walton, Professor of Botany and son of E.A. Walton, but the poor condition of the plasterwork resulted in the replacement of the drawing room and entrance hall ceilings.[116] Further repairs and redecoration were undertaken in 1952.[117]

191 The former home of Margaret and Charles Rennie Mackintosh, 78 Southpark Avenue, is shown at the left-hand end of the terrace shortly before its demolition in 1963
GUAS [PHU 29/4]

192 Photographic record of the kitchen at 78 Southpark Avenue in May 1962. The kitchen was not recreated in the new Art Gallery, but the dresser now forms part of the Hunterian collection.
GUAS [PHU 29/9]

193 Photographic record of the drawing room at 78 Southpark Avenue in May 1962. The window was installed by Charles Rennie Mackintosh for Margaret Mackintosh in 1906, enabling views southwards to the University tower.
GUAS [PHU 29/58]

194 The floating doorway to the Mackintosh House, recreated as part of the Hunterian Art Gallery by William Whitfield, 1976–81. A terrace was planned to allow the doorway to be used, but it was never executed.

Under the Town and Country Planning (Scotland) Act 1947, the building was added to the provisional list of buildings of special architectural and historic interest at Category B in the surveys of 1956–58. The provisional list, intended to cover the period of compilation of the national list, had no statutory protection force.[118] It was not until 1970 that the list for the area became statutory. The Department of Health for Scotland, who were responsible for compiling the list, wrote to the University Court in November 1960, urging retention of the building, or at least salvage of its Mackintosh interior work.[119] The University were clearly aware of the interest of the interiors, but the 19th-century shell was of little or no significance and the site was needed for the construction of the Refectory. The reconstruction of the interiors in another location was considered a suitable compromise.

Whitfield visited 78 Southpark Avenue on Friday 26 May 1961 and 'spent a most interesting hour there in the afternoon'.[120] His enthusiastic initial reaction was to guide the Mackintosh project during the next twenty years:

Upon seeing the house it seemed to me that the significance of Mackintosh's work would be valid only if a reconstruction included indications of the original building as he found it, and the intimate scale of the house would become meaningless if the group of rooms did not occupy their present relationships. Whilst it is obvious that only the joinery, details etc need be transported, I think it will be necessary to recreate room sizes and heights and identical daylighting as existing. All of this is quite practicable and could be arranged in a way to allow further galleries to be built for those Mackintosh items which are not suitable for display in his own rooms. It will be necessary to do some research into the original appearance of the rooms, colour schemes and so forth, but I believe much evidence of this has survived.[121]

As the architect charged with incorporating the interiors into the new Hunterian Art Gallery, Whitfield stressed the need to examine, measure and record 78 Southpark Avenue carefully before its demolition. He recommended Fielden for the recording job since he had a local office and would be closely involved in any case with the demolition as the architect for the Refectory.[122] The survey was undertaken and key elements, including doors, door handles, fireplaces and fire surrounds, hearths, overmantles, skirtings, picture rails, window handles, and some of the earlier non-Mackintosh features (such as the staircase balustrade) were removed and stored prior to demolition of the house in 1963. Robert Cowper of the University Fine Art department made a photographic record in May 1962.[123] From the outset Whitfield's design envisaged a distinct entity for the Mackintosh rooms, located at the south-eastern end of the Gallery site fronting Hillhead Street. The building has a similar orientation to the original house in Southpark Avenue, ensuring that daylight fills the interiors in much the same way. The strip of casement windows in the south wall retains views of the University tower, as it did when Mackintosh installed it in Southpark Avenue for his wife. The Mackintosh House has a thoroughly Brutalist casing, but the Mackintosh features are set in harled panels that recall his work at Windyhill in Kilmacolm or the Hill House in Helensburgh.

Roger Billcliffe undertook considerable research on the house in preparation for the reconstruction of the interiors. The sequence and size of the principal spaces, the Mackintosh decorative scheme and a number of the 19th-century features were recreated as faithfully as possible on the basis of physical and documentary evidence and the accounts of visitors to the house. Principal spaces include the hall, dining room [FIG.195], stair, studio-drawing room and main bedroom. The rear kitchen [FIG.192], maid's room, guest bedroom,

195 The dining room of the Mackintosh House, recreated as part of the Hunterian Art Gallery by William Whitfield, 1976–81
GUHMAG

bathroom and attic of 78 Southpark Avenue were not reconstructed. The top floor gallery contains other (non-integral) Mackintosh artefacts including the recreation of the guest bedroom from 78 Derngate, Northampton, Mackintosh's last significant interior (1915–16) for Wenman Joseph Bassett-Lowke.

A curious feature of the new building is the height at which the front door is positioned above the street level. The doorway was placed here to open onto a series of terraces with steps and pedestrian ramps that were part of Gleave's masterplan, but they were never built [FIG.194].[124] The setted slopes at the wall footings are also a legacy of the unbuilt terraces. In keeping with the Langley Castle inspiration of the Library, Whitfield referred to them using the term 'glacis', which are banks of earth for military defence.

MEN'S UNION, 'THE HIVE', UNIVERSITY AVENUE 1960–1965 (DEMOLISHED 2013)

Plans for an extension to the Men's Union had first been considered as part of the scheme for the Stevenson building in 1958. However, only the physical education block proceeded at that time, and plans for the Union extension were scaled back. Keppie, Henderson & Partners were re-appointed in November 1960 on the condition that Richard De'Ath gave the project his personal attention.[125]

The building contained 1,100m² of additional space including a large hall, lesser hall, coffee room and other rooms and offices for general student use.[126] As a result of Glasgow Corporation's demands for increased off-street parking in the Hillhead development area, the extension has an integral 12-bay car park at the ground floor. While the plinth and centre of the north elevation are clad in concrete aggregate panels, the predominant material is dark brown facing brick. A projecting strip of glazing with stainless steel fins clasps the corner of Gibson Street and University Avenue. The extension opened in November 1965. A further beer bar extension by the same architects was opened in late 1969.[127]

GILMOREHILL CENTRE, UNIVERSITY AVENUE 1961 AND 1997

The former Anderston Free Church was purchased in 1960 with a view to dividing it laterally to provide exam rooms on two floors. The church was constructed in 1876–78 to designs by James Sellars, but the intended tower was never built. Keppie, Henderson & Partners made an initial investigation in October 1960, but found the building to be in such a poor structural condition that it would not support the proposed subdivision.[128] They suggested that it should either be demolished or reconstructed with a flat roof. The University Court asked the architects to consider what accommodation could be provided from the existing building without the expense of demolition or radical reconstruction. The Court agreed to lecture rooms in the halls, a temporary refectory and kitchen in the basement and an exam hall in the church itself.[129] In 1997 SBJ Keppie were once again engaged to convert the building to a new department of Theatre, Film and Television Studies. [130] The old floors were removed and seven new levels created within the shell to provide a 150-seat cinema, theatre and rehearsal space, television studios, sound recording booths, research facilities, teaching areas and offices. The 182-seat James Arnott Theatre is located under the original beamed roof and is lit naturally by the original stained glass south window and artificially by the first 'trampoline' lighting grid in Scotland. Pollock Hammond Partnership carried out further fabric and structural repairs in 2012.

QUEEN MARGARET UNION, UNIVERSITY GARDENS 1961–1968

In February 1961 the University Court invited their consultant architect, Joe Gleave, to design the new Women's Union building, but Gleave's other commitments prevented him from taking up the offer.[131] The site on the south side of University Gardens now occupied by Mathematics was selected initially.[132] On the basis of ease of working, Gleave recommended a shortlist of three local architects: Walter Underwood of Walter Underwood & Partners; Ninian R.J. Johnston of Boswell Mitchell & Johnston; and John Watson of Watson, Salmond & Gray.[133] On the basis of interviews, Walter Underwood was selected. David James Leslie was the partner in charge of the project .[134] The site continued to trouble the building committee, as it would involve the demolition of houses in use by various Arts departments. In June 1962 they asked Underwood and Gleave to consider an alternative site on the north side of University Gardens, where the Observatory then stood.

The brief for the £400,000 project envisaged a dining room seating 300, a coffee room, common room, 740-seat debating hall, games room, library, quiet room, magazine room, board room, committee and societies' room, secretary's suite and some sleeping cubicles for short stays.[135] The scheme was intended to double the size of the existing Women's Union accommodation in the old John McIntyre building.

The building has a reinforced concrete frame and concrete aggregate cladding panels and a sculptural concrete fire escape stair to the north. It is laid out in a T-plan in which the debating hall forms the short stroke of the T to the east, while the rest of the accommodation is contained in a taller and longer block running south to north into the slope below Lilybank House.

The debating hall structure is marked externally by the protrusion of the balcony cantilevered out over the pavement. The internal finishing has always been extremely basic, with the slatted wooden ceiling of the debating hall comprising the most notable feature.

The then Principal, Sir Charles Wilson, opened the building officially on 14 March 1968.[136]

MATHEMATICS, UNIVERSITY GARDENS 1964–1968

An assessment of the accommodation needs of the Mathematics department was first submitted in 1958. In 1964 the University Court asked their architectural consultant, Joe Gleave, to design the Mathematics Building [FIG.196] along with the adjacent Boyd Orr Building (Basic Science). Initial plans allowed for the construction of a Computer Science building parallel to the south of the Mathematics building and linking to the Boyd Orr building.[137] Following Gleave's early death in January 1965, the commissions fell to one of his partners, Ivor G. Dorward, and assistant, George Keith.

The combined site for Mathematics and the Basic Science building required the demolition of sixteen late 19th-century townhouses and the realignment of University Avenue. Like most of the Hillhead sites, old mineral workings were found and consolidated before work began. Planning permission was conditional on the provision of forty car parking spaces, some of which were accommodated under the building.[138] The Mathematics and Basic Science buildings were planned in tandem with shared landscaping, including a pond, and some shared services. The Mathematics building took the form of a linear complex of three linked units along the south side of University Gardens. The lecture block stands at the centre with an administration block to the west and a library block to the east. The functions of the three units are expressed externally through the window provision: no windows in the lecture block, lots of windows in the administration block and few windows in the library block. Similarly the structure is expressed externally in the concrete pilotis (columns) of the basement and beam ends. The composition is predominantly horizontal with vertical, dark aggregate panels and strips of windows marked by cream-coloured aggregate panels.

The interior finishing is utilitarian. The most distinctive feature is the double staircase that leads up from the entrance hall, but the confined scale makes it impractical for passing other users. The lecture block required large rooms with sloping floors of in situ poured concrete for tiered seating. The lecture theatres have all been refurbished.

The 1968–69 academic session had begun before the resolution of a strike by engineer and insulation workers. This delayed completion of the building until November 1968.[139] The final cost of the building and fitting out was £351,000.[140] E. M. Wright, Principal of the University of Aberdeen, opened the building on 19 May 1969.[141] On a sunny day, the Mathematics building is perhaps the most sculptural of the 1960s Brutalist buildings at Hillhead, with its geometric forms, recessed planes and projecting beams. The replacement of the glazing with flat UPVC frames has reduced this sculptural effect.

THE BOYD ORR BUILDING, UNIVERSITY AVENUE 1964–1972

The Boyd Orr building remains the most controversial of the University's post-war Brutalist developments, polarising opinion. On the one hand the Boyd Orr Building has its own Facebook fanclub, while on the other it is frequently cited as the ugliest building on the Gilmorehill campus. Love it, or hate it, the building is difficult to ignore, with its eleven storeys soaring high above the neighbouring late 19th-century tenements and terraces of Hillhead. It was named after the Nobel laureate, Lord John Boyd Orr of Brechin (1880–1971), who was Rector of the University from 1945 to 1947 and Chancellor from 1946 to 1971. Boyd Orr was a world authority on food, agriculture and nutrition.

The tower was conceived in 1963 as a general 'basic science' building to help manage a projected 50% increase in science student numbers during the late 1960s and early 1970s.[142] It was to accommodate about 1,500 first-year students in Mathematics, Chemistry, Natural Philosophy, Zoology and Botany, relieving pressure on the already congested parent departmental buildings. A small number of rooms were dedicated to more advanced teaching in Statistics, Botany and Biochemistry. In 1964 the University Court asked their architectural consultant, Joe Gleave, to design the building along with the adjacent Mathematics building. Following Gleave's early death in January 1965, the commissions fell to one of his colleagues, George Keith to complete.[143] However, it was not until September 1968, after the Principal's special pleading for exemption from a moratorium on major projects, that the University Grants Committee gave its approval for Glasgow to proceed with construction.[144] From the outset it was clear that a 'monster' building was required to meet the science teaching and other miscellaneous requirements of the University.[145] It was envisaged that 600 first-year scientists, 300 medical, dental and veterinary students, 250 engineering students and 200 other science students in later years of their courses and appropriate staff would occupy the building during term time. Large lecture theatres, smaller lecture rooms, seminar rooms, study rooms, laboratories, ancillary rooms, and even rooftop glasshouses were planned to serve these

196 Design for the Boyd Orr and Mathematics buildings by Joe Gleave, 1964. The two buildings were conceived together, but built consecutively.
Reproduced by kind permission of David S. Gleave

197 Photograph of the Boyd Orr and Mathematics buildings in 1972, shortly after completion of the tower. A Computer Science building was planned to run parallel to the Mathematics building, but it was eventually built to another design in a different location.
GUAS [PHU 10/10]

teaching needs. In addition the building was intended to provide a centre for conferences and vacation courses.

In the spirit of the age, Gleave looked to a tower structure as the cheapest, quickest and most efficient way of accommodating the urgent needs of the University [FIG.196]. Taking the opposite approach to the Library, where Whitfield kept the core clear and pushed the services and access to outer towers, Gleave chose a radial plan of three major blocks and a minor block around a central service/access core. The access core, with its three 'delay-proof' lifts, and the two staircases were generously proportioned to enable the large flow of students between classes.

The Boyd Orr has an in situ reinforced concrete frame with concrete floors and core walls to brace the structure against the strong lateral wind [FIG.197].[146] Externally, the finishes were in accordance with Gleave's overall development plan. Dark Whalley blue flint aggregate panels in upright format emphasise the vertical service elements and white marble chip Essno panels in horizontal format, alternating with strips of glazing, mark the floors of teaching accommodation. The copper clad roof area contained the ventilation and lift plant, while the boiler, electricity substation and telecoms equipment (all shared with the Mathematics building) were housed in the basement. The two main lecture theatres are expressed externally as cantilevered pods projecting from the ground floor level.

Servicing of the building, undertaken by Oscar Faber & Partners, was particularly complicated in response to the differing specialist needs of the various scientific subject areas. The Natural Philosophy laboratories on Floors 2 to 4 were divided into 'wet' (gas, water and some electric) and 'dry' (gas, and AC and DC electricity supply), while Chemistry, Botany and Biochemistry on Floors 4 to 6 needed compressed air, a vacuum system and steam generators, and Botany and Biology on Floor 7 required specialist hot and cold rooms.

Internally the finishing was always simple and robust in recognition of the anticipated heavy usage. Only the two main 550-seat lecture theatres on the ground floor were fitted out to more than a basic level. Here the walls were lined with vertical timber strips and the tip-up seats upholstered in beige leatherette.

The botanist Sir Eric Ashby inaugurated the building, which cost £1.25m, on 3 October 1972. The interior spaces have been largely refurbished, most recently the two main lecture theatres by crgp limited in 2009–10.

THE RANKINE BUILDING, OAKFIELD AVENUE 1964–1969

Keppie, Henderson & Partners were commissioned to design the new Engineering building in Oakfield Avenue in 1964.[147] The partner in charge of the project appears to have been Richard De'Ath.[148] The 1948–59 James Watt (South) extension of the Engineering Department occupied all the available space adjacent to the original James Watt building (North) on the Gilmorehill campus, so it was necessary to seek a new site as close as possible on the north side of University Avenue for the Civil Engineering and Electronics and Electrical Engineering departments [FIG.198].

As first built, the 8-storey building had sleek, crisp horizontal lines marked out in white aggregate panels, contrasting with strips of windows set in bands of Sievo ceramic mosaic tiles. Three of the eight storeys were below ground to reduce the impact of the building's height. The style appears to be influenced by the work of the Japanese architect, Kenzo Tange, whose famous

198 Model of the Rankine building by Keppie, Henderson & Partners, 1964–69
GUAS [PHU 21/1]

1958 Kagawa Prefectural Government Hall on the island of Shikoku included projecting double concrete beams after the manner of a traditional Buddhist temple.[149] The Rankine building's double beams express the divisions of the modular construction units of the reinforced concrete frame.

In spite of the metric 25metre pool in the earlier Stevenson building, imperial measurements persisted in the Rankine building. The design drawings are plotted over grids marked out in 1-yard squares, and each element of the building relates proportionally to the grid. The windows are mainly 1 yard square; the floor-to-floor heights are 3 yards; the stair towers are 4 yards wide; and the width between the double beams is 12 yards.

The long narrow plan incorporated a variety of teaching and research facilities including workshops and laboratories for acoustics, structures, traffic, materials, soil mechanics, concrete, cement, mechanics, high voltage, control systems, electronics, ultrasonics, microwaves, power systems, and PACE and SOLIDAC computers. Three lecture theatres for fifty, sixty and eighty students were provided in the sub-basement. Although there was no formal separation between departments, civil engineering uses were grouped at the northern end of the building and electronics/electrical to the south, with some overlap in the middle. Staff and postgraduate offices were arranged along the west front to the south of the entrance. Apart from the top and bottom floors, which have central spine corridors, all the offices and laboratories open from locker-lined corridors offset from the centre to the west. There was relatively generous provision for technical staff and support services, including a photocopying room, and student amenity in the form of a common room.

To modern eyes, perhaps the most curious component of the building is the open car park for thirty-three vehicles at the entrance level (effectively the third floor), accessed by a ramp from Oakfield Avenue. Planning permission for the new building was granted with the condition that there should be a pedestrian bridge across University Avenue from the Gilmorehill campus.[150] Three alternative designs for pedestrian bridges were produced by the engineers, Ove Arup & Partners, but eventually the planning condition was relaxed and the connecting space for the bridge in the south parapet wall of the car park remains unfilled.[151] The building was handed over by the contractors on 16 June 1969 and opened official by the Secretary of State for Scotland, Gordon Campbell, on 22 September 1970.[152] It was named after W.J. Macquorn Rankine, the University's second Professor of Civil Engineering, who played an important role in the design of Glasgow's water supply system from Loch Katrine.

While the Brutalist aesthetics of the Rankine building

were alien to its leafy context from the outset, the patina of age has not improved matters: the white aggregate is now weather-stained; the Sievo tiles have failed to stick to their concrete panels; and the flat UPVC replacement window frames have removed the subtle modelling of the window strips.

The abstract stainless steel wall sculpture on the southern stairtower was commissioned from local artist, Lucy Baird, to mark the 150th anniversary of the Regius Chair of Civil Engineering in 1990.

UNIVERSITY WORKSHOPS AND OFFICES 1965–1967

As the University's building stock increased, so too did demand for maintenance and the space to house workshop equipment and estates staff. Robert Rogerson & Philip Spence designed the 2-storey, buff brick, workshop and office accommodation behind the old gymnasium in 1965.[153]

THE GREGORY BUILDING (GEOLOGY), LILYBANK GARDENS 1968–1980

On the recommendation of Wilson & Womersley, the University Court began assembling the site for the Geology building in 1968, purchasing some eight terraced houses in Lilybank Gardens for the purpose.[154] By December 1970, Ivor Dorward of J.L. Gleave & Partners had produced sketch plans both for the Geology building and a proposed long, narrow 3-storey car park for 280 vehicles to the north.[155] The plans were drawn to fit with a proposed widening of Ashton Lane to 60 feet by Glasgow Corporation as part of their redevelopment of Byres Road. The car park design was amended in 1971 to form a square-plan 6-storey building for 550 cars across the Great George Street end of Lilybank Gardens, which would also incorporate squash courts and a games hall. There was also some consideration of a bridge across Ashton Lane to the upper floors of the new shopping precinct, which might also contain University science buildings. Although compulsory purchases of the houses on the site took place, the revised car park plan was abandoned in favour of the current level surface car park in 1978.[156] The abandonment of the standard concrete aggregate panelling in favour of a buff-coloured brick is explained in a note of a meeting of the joint Corporation-University working group on the Hillhead developments in June 1972: 'Referring to the Planning Department's expressed preference for a continuation of concrete finishes for the buildings in this area, Mr Marshall [University Assistant Planning Officer] stated that the University would like to consider the use of other finishes with a view both to introducing variety and to blending the new buildings in a more sympathetic manner with existing non-University buildings on the perimeter of the zone. In addition concrete cladding was not much favoured by the University Grants Committee on grounds of cost'.[157] The building forms an L-plan at the curving southern end of Lilybank Gardens. A large 4-storey and basement block connects to a smaller 3-storey block via the entrance link. All the corners of the building are modishly chamfered (cut off) so that there are no external right-angled corners, and continuous strips of brown metal windows also help to give emphasis to horizontal elements, reducing the perception of height and bulk [FIG.199].

The most notable feature of the interior is the fine 7.6m mosaic in the entrance hall, designed by George Garson [FIG.202].[158] It depicts various geological structures and is comprised of fragments of common and rare specimen minerals, including M1217 crocidolite from South Africa and M2370 almondine from Bhilwara in Rajasthan, India, donated to the Hunterian Museum by two 19th-century benefactors, Theophilus Paton Esq. and His Highness the Maharana of Cacheypore, after whom the work is titled. Other original internal features include an angular staircase running the full height of the building and concrete coffered ceilings [FIG.201].

In 1998 the Geology building was renamed in honour of John Walker Gregory (1864–1932), the University's first Professor of Geology, from 1904 to 1929.[159]

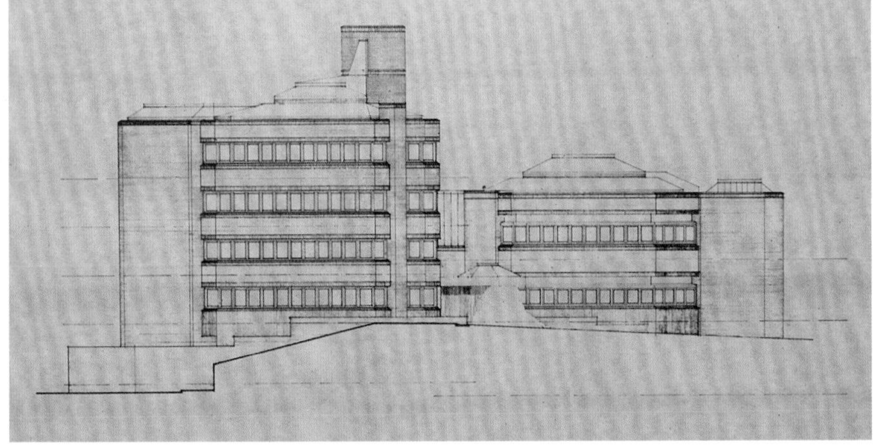

199 Gregory building elevation by Dorward, Matheson & Gleave
GUAS [ACCN 1626/4/25]

200 Design for the Hetherington building by Ivor Dorward, Matheson & Gleave 1971
GUAS [BE 141/8]

201 The main staircase, Gregory building, Lilybank Gardens

202 The mosaic mural entitled *Theophilus Paton Esq. and His Highness the Maharana of Cacheypore* by George Garson in the entrance hall of the Gregory building, Lilybank Gardens

GUPU [13–036–39]
By kind permission of the Estate of George Garson

THE HETHERINGTON BUILDING (MODERN LANGUAGES), BUTE GARDENS 1971–1984

The Hetherington building was first conceived in 1971 as accommodation for 'Arts-based' studies, including Modern Languages and English.[160] The Law Faculty was to occupy the old Modern Languages premises in University Gardens. The building was to be built in three phases to form a triangle occupying an enormous site bounded by Bute Gardens, Great George Street, Hillhead Street and Phase II of the Library. By 1978 it was clear that the scheme was over-ambitious, and it was scaled back to the rectangular plot fronting Bute Gardens.[161] Even then, consideration was given to retaining the existing townhouses, but their 1,500m² of floor space fell far short of the 2250m² of purpose-built space that could be achieved in a new building.[162] The tenements in Hillhead Street and Great George Street were to be converted to student residences.

Dorward, Matheson & Gleave began a feasibility study and sketch plans for the building as a Modern Languages centre in 1979.[163] Ivor Dorward was the supervising architect, with Sam Russell as project architect. The University Grants Committee gave their approval to progress the scheme in February 1981 and listed building consent was granted for demolition of the townhouses at 14 to 22 Bute Gardens in October of that year.[164] As a result of the scaled-back site and the growing need to take into account the surrounding residential character of the conservation area, the building is relatively low and aligned with the existing street pattern, rather than with the Gilbert Scott building.

As well as rejecting the alignment of the 1960s Modernist buildings, the Hetherington building was the first to adopt a Postmodern approach to design, incorporating a variety of historicist details, including a tiled Mansard (steeply sloping) roof, visible half-round gutters, individual windows and buff 'Mitford Silver Grey Rustic' brick walls. The brick was intended to match the colour of the adjacent stone tenements.

Originally conceived as an L-plan arrangement of academic offices off a spinal corridor, with larger teaching rooms and a language laboratory infilling the 'L' at the ground floor, the internal treatment was utilitarian. The entrance is at the south-west corner of the building, adjacent to the stairtower. Hypostyle Architects designed a new single storey resource centre addition fronting Great George Street and refurbished the main building in 2009. The Royal Fine Art Commission for Scotland found the final design interesting, 'with a height and size in keeping with its surroundings'. The Hetherington building is named after Hector Hetherington, Principal of the University from 1936 to 1961.

BUILDINGS BEYOND THE GILMOREHILL/HILLHEAD CAMPUS

Architects are noted in brackets.

1960	Wellcome Surgical Laboratory and extension, Garscube (W.N.W. Ramsay)
1960	Staff Recreation Centre, Garscube (W.J. Fairweather)
1963	Naval Architecture Experimental Tank, Garscube (Keppie, Henderson & Partners)
1962	Large Animal Units, Garcube (W.N.W. Ramsay)
1964	Zoology Field Station, Rowardennan (Thomas McCrea & Sanders)
1964	Equine Research Unit and Foal House, Garscube (Building Design Partnership)
1964	Parasitology Research Unit, Garscube (Building Design Partnership)
1964	Queen Margaret Hall I, Bellshaugh Road, Kirklee (W.N.W. Ramsay)
1964	Wolfson Hall I, Garscube (on site of Garscube House) (Building Design Partnership)
1965–7	Queen Margaret Hall II, Bellshaugh Road, Kirklee (W.N.W. Ramsay)
1965–8	Wolfson Hall II, Garscube (Building Design Partnership)
1965	Large Animal block, Cochno
1965	Dalrymple Hall, Belhaven Terrace West (W.N.W. Ramsay)
1966	Botany Research Laboratory, Garscube (Wylie, Shanks & Partners)
1966	Squash Courts, Garscube (D.C. Bailey)
1967	Staff Recreation extension, Garscube (W.N.W. Ramsay)
1967	Maclay Hall I, Park Terrace (W.N.W. Ramsay)
1967–9	Observatory, Garscube (Keppie, Henderson & Partners)
1967	Veterinary Field Station Stage I, Cochno (Lothian Barclay, Jarvis & Boys)
1968	Large Animal Unit, Garscube (Building Design Partnership)
1968–70	Alexander Stone Microbiology Building, Garscube (Boswell, Mitchell & Johnston)[165]
1969	Maclay Hall II, Park Terrace (W.N.W. Ramsay)
1969	Veterinary School, Garscube, Stage I (Building Design Partnership)
1969	Veterinary Surgery and Reproduction Units, Garscube (Building Design Partnership)
1969	Wellcome Surgical extension, Garscube (Building Design Partnership)
1968–70	Veterinary School, Stage II (Building Design Partnership)[166]
1969	Garscube Refectory (Building Design Partnership)
1969	Dental Hospital and School, Renfrew Street (Wylie Shanks & Partners)
1970	Wind Tunnel Building, Spencer Street
	Veterinary Field Station Stage II, Cochno

Chapter Ten

The Knowledge Economy 1980–present

203 The spire of the Gilbert Scott building reflected in Page\Park's remodelling of the Refectory (Fraser building), 2007–09

The University of Glasgow now competes in a global market for outstanding teachers, researchers and students. The quality of the working environment is recognised as an important factor in attracting the best talent to the University. The University also competes internationally to attract research contracts. Where quantity was the primary requirement of the 1960s building programme, the emphasis has shifted to quality. Another major shift affecting the design of buildings is from subject 'silos' towards a multi-disciplinary and outward-looking approach to teaching and research, with new flexible and collaborative networks and facilities, such as touch-down work spaces.[1] Under Principal Anton Muscatelli, there is now a prospect of relieving the longstanding chronic shortage of development land on the Gilmorehill/Hillhead campus through the University's re-acquisition of a large part of the Western Infirmary site on 31 March 2011. Redevelopment of the site will be a long and expensive process, but it opens the opportunity for a carefully planned and integrated expansion of the campus by about 25%. A Campus Development Framework by Page\Park Architects will provide strategic guidance to achieving coherent development across the Gilmorehill/Hillhead/Western Infirmary sites. Unlike the 1960s developments in Hillhead, the University is fully committed to community engagement and taking a wider view of the social, economic and environmental aspects of development.[2]

CONTEXTUAL AND ENVIRONMENTAL DESIGN

The period from 1980 to the present day has seen a revolution in the practice of architecture and design. Legislation and regulation at national and international levels have played their part in the changes, but so too have economic factors, computer-aided design (CAD), new construction materials and technology, globalisation, higher awareness of environmental and social impacts, more demanding requirements from clients and users, greater collaboration with other professional fields, and rising standards of planning, procurement, project and construction management.

For much of the 1980s and early 1990s the architectural revolution by-passed the university sector, which struggled just to maintain and upgrade its legacy of 1960s boomtime buildings in the face of increasing student numbers and cuts in capital funding. Many elements of the 1960s buildings, such as flat roofs, heating boilers and electrical services were coming to the end of their serviceable life after twenty years, and there were new requirements to meet under the Health and Safety at Work Act 1974 and the Fire Precautions Act 1971. During this time the University invested the small sums available in the conversion for departmental use of residential properties that had been purchased previously and were now too expensive to demolish and redevelop. Further modest purchases and conversions were made, such as Florentine House, Hillhead Street, in 1981.

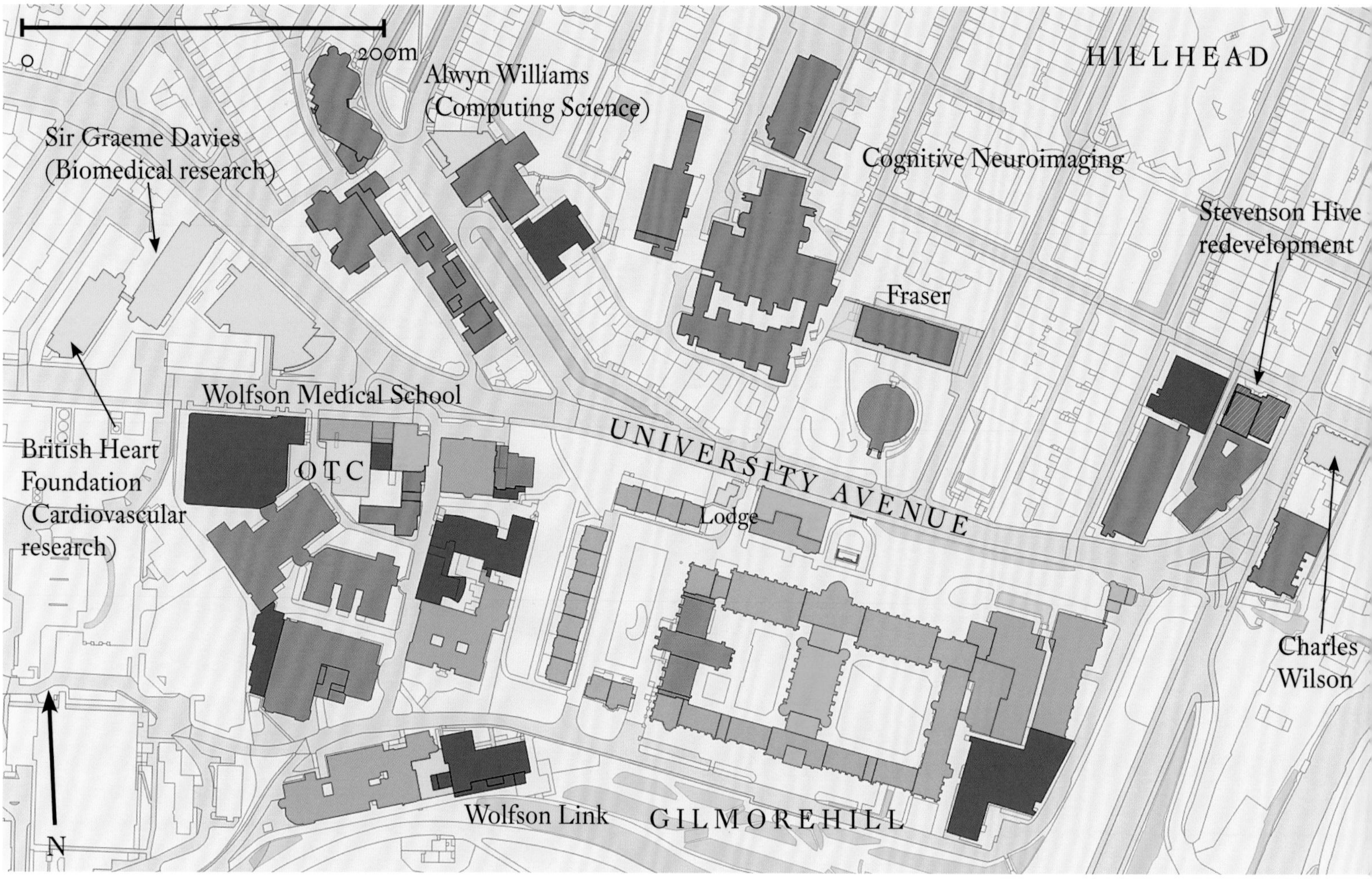

Perhaps one of the benefits of the long wait to recommence a coherent building programme was that when funds started to become available again in the mid-1990s, the resulting buildings were generally well-considered and of high quality contemporary design and materials. The glitzy excesses of Postmodern, 'Mockintosh', High-Tech and Iconic commercial architecture, which flourished in other parts of the city during the 1980s and 1990s, were largely avoided on the University's estate. Two strands of architectural Modernism that characterise the University's buildings of the late 1990s and the new millennium are their attention to the context of the surrounding townscape, and their concern with minimising environmental impact.

Much Modern Movement architecture in the years immediately after the Second World War had an idealistic, Utopian social programme with an emphasis on function and large-scale, standardized design. 'Contextual Modernism' perhaps best describes an approach to architectural design that has developed from the 1980s, rather than a distinctive style or coherent movement. While not looking to historic precedents, Contextual Modernist buildings are individually designed (rather than off-the-peg), minimalist in their detailing and take account of the scale, height, massing, density, materials and 'grain', or sense of place, of their surroundings. Typically, the design concerns extend into the spaces around the building and its integration into the pedestrian and road network. Often the design process for such buildings is people-centred, engaging with users, the community and other stakeholders.

As part of the University's more people-focused approach to the commissioning of buildings, the Disability Equality Action Plan 2006–2009, and subsequent updates, requires access issues to be considered and the Campus Infrastructure Disability Liaison Group (CIDLG) to be involved from the outset of all new-build projects. The University also has a programme to ensure existing buildings and facilities are accessible and 'so far as is reasonably practical' comply with physical access legislation.[3] The Environmental Association for Universities and Colleges was launched in 1996 with the aim of raising the profile of environmental management and facilitating improvement of

204 Development of Gilmorehill and Hillhead between 1980 and 2013

KEY

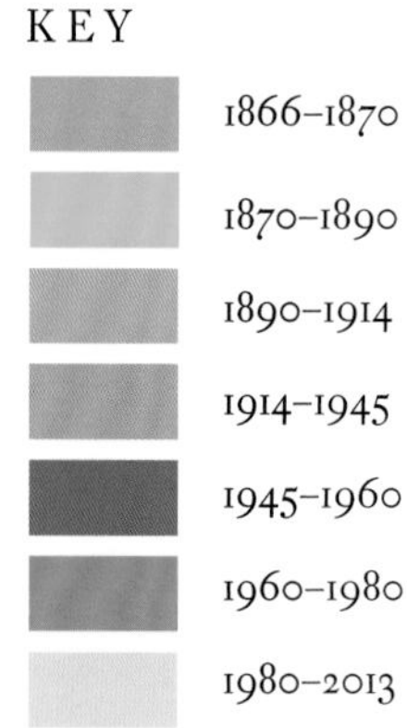

environmental performance in member institutions. The University was an early member, and began its commitment to sustainable design at this time. Glasgow was the first Scottish university to gain energy efficiency accreditation in 1998. From 2003, the University's new energy conservation brief required new buildings to be assessed for environmental performance under the Building Research Establishment Environmental Assessment Method (BREEAM). The method examines the environmental impact of new buildings in a number of areas. These include: management; operational energy; transport; health and well-being; water; materials; land use; site ecological value; and pollution. The University was an early adopter of BRE's *Green Guide to Specification* of 1996, which first set out a ranking of environmental impacts from A+ (best performance/least impact) to E (worst performance/highest impact).

In 2009, the year of the Climate Change (Scotland) Act, the University signed the Universities and Colleges Climate Commitment for Scotland and agreed to an ambitious carbon management plan with the Carbon Trust to reduce carbon emissions by 20% within the five-year life of the plan. As part of the plan, all new buildings should be high performance and energy efficient. The University will continue to upgrade inefficient buildings and replace inefficient appliances, and power will be bought or generated from renewable sources.

POLITICAL AND FINANCIAL BACKGROUND

By 1978 the University had entered a period of severe financial difficulties, which was predicted to last until at least 1990. This prediction was unfortunately accurate, coinciding largely with the period of power of Margaret Thatcher's Conservative government in Westminster. The government's cuts in public spending forced the University Grants Committee to implement savage 17% cuts in their grants for capital programmes from 1981. With the exception of the Hetherington building and the completion of the Hunterian Art Gallery and Mackintosh House, attention turned to adaptation of existing buildings on the main campus. As remarked in a statement from the University's Assistant Planning Officer to the city's Director of Planning on 20 July 1978,'Because of the virtual elimination of the Building Programme more minor works in altering or adapting older buildings to meet changing needs and requirements has been necessary'.[4] The Thatcher government instigated several major changes in higher education, notably under Kenneth Baker, the Secretary for Education from 1985. The Committee of Vice-Chancellors and Principals responded to the government's wish for an efficiency study of universities by setting up a steering committee under the chairmanship of Alex Jarratt, the former chief executive of Reed International. This committee recommended the introduction of performance indicators and wide-ranging changes in the management of universities to make them more businesslike. The McCallum Report, *The Future Strategy for Higher Education in Scotland* of 1985 similarly recommended more involvement of the business, commercial and professional communities in directing the content and method of courses.

Lord Croham headed a review of the University Grants Committee, which in February 1987 proposed its replacement with a University Funding Council. In taking forward the Croham recommendations through the White Paper, *Higher Education: Meeting the Challenge*, of April 1987 and ultimately the Education Reform Act of 1988, the government moved to create an internal market. Instead of obtaining grants to cover their costs, universities were required to enter contracts with the Universities Funding Council to provide specific academic outputs in return for resources. The process of academic auditing had already begun under the University Grants Committee, which instituted Research Assessment Exercises in 1986. The government now also required wider access to universities, more responsiveness to the needs of industry and commerce, less dependence on public funding and more cost-consciousness in the management of resources.[5] The University's constant and painful battle with the government's often capricious financial settlements, and politicisation of the funding mechanism throughout the 1980s, are charted elsewhere.[6] Such were the financial difficulties that parts of the Hunterian collections were threatened with sale. As has been noted above (page 173) eleven Whistler paintings were put up for sale in order to complete the construction of the Hunterian Art Gallery, and, as in previous times of crisis, the legality of selling the Hunterian coin collection was investigated. The position was similar across the United Kingdom. In 1984–85 the University Grants Committee's total investment in all major university building projects costing more than £1m was restricted to just £9m.[7] The following year Glasgow managed to attract major project funding for re-configuration of Chemistry and Life Sciences.[8] Under John Major's governments of 1990–97 the University's financial position became less acute, and Principal Sir William Kerr Fraser was able to reinvigorate the investment and development programmes for the estate. Capital grants from the short-lived Universities Funding Council to the University of Glasgow increased from £4,390,830 in 1990–91 to £8,407,070 in 1991–92.[9] Following the Further and Higher Education Act of 1992, funding of Scottish universities passed to the Scottish Higher Education Funding Council (Scottish Funding Council from 2005) and a new Higher Education Quality

Council (Quality Assurance Agency from 1997) was extablished. Five new universities were created from existing degree-awarding institutions in Scotland: Abertay; Glasgow Caledonian; Napier; Paisley (now merged with Bell College as the University of the West of Scotland) and Robert Gordon.

Tony Blair's Labour administration, famously committed to 'education, education, education', established a National Committee of Inquiry into Higher Education under Sir Ronald Dearing in 1997. The resulting Dearing Report was the most extensive review of the sector since Robbins in 1963, making ninety-three recommendations for reform. Evidence to the Committee by the National Academies Policy Advisory Group concluded that the dual support system of funding councils and research councils had shown 'remarkable adaptability and durability under great strain, but that strain has been carried mainly by the rundown of institutional infrastructure (eg libraries, experimental equipment, and building maintenance)'.[10] One immediate response to the Dearing Report was the establishment of the Joint Infrastructure Fund, which ran from 1998 to 2001, with over £700 million provided by the United Kingdom government and the Wellcome Trust to enhance and modernise the research infrastructure of the university sector. In 2002 a replacement funding scheme was put in place, the Science Research Investment Fund (SRIF), which operated on a 2-yearly cycle with a £1 billion budget for each cycle until 2008. From 1998 Principals Sir Graeme Davies and Sir Muir Russell bid successfully for funds towards the Biomedical Research Centre, the Wolfson Medical School, the James Watt Nanofabrication Centre, extension of the Computing Science building, the Centre for Cognitive Neuroimaging, as well as buildings at Garscube and Rowardennan. A new permanent capital investment fund was established within the science budget of the Department for Business Innovation and Skills to replace the SRIF scheme in October 2007. From 2005, the Scottish Funding Council's Learning and Teaching Infrastructure Fund (LTIF) has made significant grants towards the upgrading of laboratories and lecture theatres.

Following the establishment of a devolved Scottish Parliament in Edinburgh in 1999, the first independent committee of inquiry, led by Andrew Cubie, was appointed to investigate student finance. The Cubie Report recommended that tuition fees in Scotland should be scrapped, but graduates should contribute to a graduate endowment. This endowment in turn was scrapped in 2007. Three major consultation documents on aspects of the future of higher education in Scotland were undertaken *New Horizons: Responding to the Challenges of the 21st Century* and in 2007 *The Review of Higher Education Governance* and *Building a Smarter Future: Towards a Sustainable Scottish Solution for the Future of Higher Education* in 2012.

In 2001 the Scottish Parliament awarded the University of the Highlands and Islands, a federation of thirteen colleges and research institutions, higher education institute status. Full university status was awarded by the Privy Council in 2011. Queen Margaret University was awarded full university status in 2007.

The seven United Kingdom government-funded research councils were brought together in a strategic partnership known as Research Councils UK in 2002. The Higher Education Act 2004 related mainly to the introduction of student fees in England and Wales, but some aspects of the Act relate to Scotland, for example in the establishment of the Arts and Humanities Research Council. Another important funding measure recommended by the Dearing Report, but not implemented until April 2006, was authorisation to the seven United Kingdom research councils to pay 80% of the 'full economic cost' of research, which includes buildings and facilities, not just direct costs such as staff.

UNIVERSITY ORGANISATION AND ESTATE

At the start of the 1980–81 academic year matriculated student numbers at the University of Glasgow (excluding the Department of Adult and Continuing Education) stood at 11,041, of which 6,411 were men and 4,528 were women.[11] By 1990–91 these figures had risen to 13,812 total (7,530 men, 6,282 women), and in 2009–10 they stood at 22,110 (9,595 men, 12,515 women).[12] From 1995–96 there have been more female than male students.

In 1999 the University entered a partnership with other institutions to establish a liberal arts college at the former Crichton Hospital site in Dumfries. The same year saw a long-discussed merger with St Andrew's College of Education in Bearsden. Using the proceeds of the sale of the Bearsden site, the University constructed the St Andrew's Building in Eldon Street in 2003.

The three Faculties of Biomedical and Life Sciences, Computing Science, Mathematics and Statistics and Physical Sciences replaced the Science Faculty on 1 October 2000. From 1 August 2010 the University implemented a new organisational structure. The nine existing faculties were replaced by four colleges: Medical, Veterinary and Life Sciences; Arts; Science and Engineering; and Social Sciences. Each College comprises various schools and institutes.

PLANNING

During the early 1980s, when there was little prospect of resuming a building programme other than relatively small-scale conversions and upgrading of existing buildings, little was done in the way of new estate planning. However, from the late 1990s, estates management action plans were required to accompany funding applications. The latest planning and policy documents affecting the planning of the estates and design issues for individual buildings are:

- Landscape Management Plan 2008
- New Build and Demolition Policy 2010
- Maintenance and refurbishment Policy 2010
- Space Management Policy 2010
- Carbon and Energy Management Policy 2010
- University Strategic Plan 2010–15
- University Strategic Plan Glasgow 2020
- Estates Conservation Strategy 2012
- Campus Development Framework (in preparation)

THE BUILDINGS 1980–2013

ROBERTSON INSTITUTE OF BIOTECHNOLOGY, DUMBARTON ROAD 1992

The building is a 6-storey, square-plan tower tucked away behind the old Anderson College and Virology buildings on the corner of Church Street and Dumbarton Road. It is constructed of buff brick over the red brick ground and first floors and has a glazed corner. Designed by G.R.M. Kennedy & Partners, it is mildly Postmodern in character, with traditionally proportioned windows and a banded red brick plinth, after the manner of classical rustication.

It is named after the Robertson Trust, which provided funds for a new Chair of Biotechnology and construction of the Institute.

WOLFSON LINK 1995–1996

In 1995–96 Holmes Partnership designed the £2.4m Wolfson Link between the Davidson building and the neighbouring West Medical building, providing new laboratories and offices along with improved circulation and accessibility. At the heart of the link is a full-height covered courtyard. The link won the Glasgow Institute of Architects' Award in 1996.

KELVIN BRIDGE (UNBUILT) 1999

John McAslan & Partners were the winners of an international competition in 1999 to create a pedestrian link between the Gilmorehill campus and Kelvingrove Museum and Art Gallery. The main feature of the design was a sleek curving footbridge over the River Kelvin. Funding for the project was not secured, and the bridge remains unbuilt.

THE WOLFSON MEDICAL SCHOOL, UNIVERSITY AVENUE/UNIVERSITY PLACE 1999–2003

In 1997 the University began the phased purchase of the Western Court site, which formed part of a triangle between University Avenue, University Place and the back of the tenements on the east side of Byres Road, with a view to establishing a hub for medical/biomedical teaching and research.[13] At the time of purchase, the plot was not only an important new expansion site in its own right, but could potentially form a gateway between the Hillhead campus and the University's redevelopment of the Western Infirmary site, if the West Glasgow University National Health Service Trust should decide to relocate the Infirmary.

The first phase of purchase, the gushet site on the corner of University Avenue and University Place, was constrained on the south-west by the existing ugly brick pharmacy building (independent of the Western Infirmary and serving a number of Glasgow hospitals), which did not form part of the sale. The University had long contemplated bringing together various parts of the Medical School, and decided to allocate the site for this purpose. Reiach & Hall were appointed to design the Medical School building following a limited competition in 1999, which also included masterplanning for the site now occupied by the Sir Graeme Davies and British Heart Foundation Buildings. Landscape architects, Gross Max, designed the associated *Hortus Medicus* garden and Medics' Corner plaza.

The first major addition to the Gilmorehill/Hillhead campus in more than fifteen years, and the first to incorporate best energy efficiency practices from the outset, the building raised the bar of architectural quality by a significant degree. The design responded imaginatively not only to the University's specifications for teaching and research accommodation, but also to the broader context of the site, which had been degraded by the Council's demolitions of 1971 to alter the University Avenue alignment and the subsequent construction of poor-quality residential and occupational therapy blocks. Taking an overtly contemporary approach, but respecting the scale and grain of the surrounding townscape, a virtuoso arc of glass defines the prominent gushet between University Place and University Avenue, and a block clad with Northumberland Copp Cragg sandstone repaired the previously ragged street frontage along University Avenue [FIG.205].

The building comprises four distinct, but integrated elements, which together resolve the complicated functional requirements and geometries of the site. These four elements are the prominent curvilinear glazed block, which houses the Study Landscape (study resources and spaces) and administrative offices; a large

L-plan block of teaching spaces; a smaller L-plan block of service accommodation; and, finally, a triangular atrium serving as circulation space at the core of the complex.

The layout reflects a new approach to medical education at Glasgow, with a shift in emphasis from traditional instruction to problem-based learning. Using small groups of students facilitated by a tutor, this approach is intended to encourage self-motivation and skills in collaborative working, communication, effective problem-solving and self-directed learning. The tutorial rooms are small and numerous, while the communal Study Landscape, common room/café, seminar and practice ward spaces are generous and inviting to promote participation and interaction. The Study Landscape can operate independently from the rest of the building in order to allow 24-hour opening.

Lighting is an important component of the design: natural daylight wherever possible during the day; and clever use of a variety of artificial light sources to animate the building by night. The great sweep of glazing on the south-east elevation floods the Study Landscape with light, but the double skin reduces potential problems of glare, reflection and noise. Thermal gain is controlled by automated western red cedar louvres and convection currents between the double skin. The core of the building is also lit naturally by a pioneering glazed roof over the atrium, constructed using 16m-long structural laminated glass beams. These beams, designed in detail by Arup Façade Engineering, are believed to be the first use of glass engineering on this scale. The flush internal finishes are neutral and unfussy, with American Cherry timberwork and occasional splashes of bright colour on the lockers and furniture.

The Princess Royal opened the building formally on 3 April 2003. It was named the Wolfson Medical School to mark the major gift from the Wolfson Foundation towards the £17.5m cost of the project. The building was a Royal Institute of British Architects' Award winner in 2003.

THE SIR GRAEME DAVIES BUILDING (BIOMEDICAL RESEARCH) AND BRITISH HEART FOUNDATION GLASGOW CARDIOVASCULAR RESEARCH CENTRE, UNIVERSITY AVENUE/UNIVERSITY PLACE 2000–2006

Initially outline planning permission was granted for a new Institute of Virology on the western part of the University Avenue/University Place/Byres Road triangle, but funding was not secured. During 2000, Boswell, Mitchell & Johnston, who had previously investigated construction of a Biomedical research centre on the Boyd Orr car park, were invited to develop proposals for locating new Virology, Biomedical and Cardiovascular research centres on the Western Court site. Concerns about the density of development and the lack of funding for Virology resulted in a re-design to include only the Biomedical and Cardiovascular centres in the scheme of 2001.

The revised scheme envisaged two separate, but linked, parallel offset blocks running between University Avenue and University Place and containing 'wet' laboratories, specialist laboratories, offices and other ancillary accommodation. The Biomedical block, furthest from the tenements, is longer and taller, with five storeys plus basement and rooftop plant, while the western Cardiovascular block is four storeys to match the eaves height of the adjacent tenements. A public pedestrian route between the buildings links University Avenue to University Place, and has the potential to link with the Western Infirmary site in the future. To enable shared services, a bridge joins the glazed service stair/lift towers of the two buildings over the pedestrian route. The gable ends of the buildings facing University Avenue and University Place are clad in stone and angled to correspond with the geometry of the streets. The long elevations are clad in terracotta tiles and the south-facing windows have canopies to reduce solar glare. Inside, the rooms are of generic types to allow for future changes. Offices are arranged to face north-west and laboratories to face south-east, with a spine of ancillary service rooms.

205 The Wolfson Medical building, designed by Reiach & Hall in 1999

The Princess Royal opened the two buildings on 25 April 2006. The £17m Biomedical building is named in honour of Sir Graeme Davies, Principal from 1995 to 2003. The naming of the Cardiovascular Centre recognises the £5m contribution of the British Heart Foundation towards the £12m cost.

THE SIR ALWYN WILLIAMS BUILDING (COMPUTING SCIENCE), UNIVERSITY GARDENS 2002–2007

A new building for Computing Science had been mooted for the car park site to the south of the Mathematics building as far back as 1974, but the financial constraints of the 1970s, 1980s and early 1990s restricted the department to occupying remodelled townhouses at the southern end of Lilybank Terrace. The advent of the Joint Infrastructure Fund in 1999, and its successor, the Science Research Investment Fund, finally provided the prospect of extending into the triangular gap site between 17 Lilybank Gardens and Queen Margaret Union to create a new entrance and 2330m^2 of purpose-built research, seminar, office and ancillary accommodation. The landscaping of the streetscape linking Lilybank Terrace and University Gardens also formed part of the contract.

Sir Alwyn

06 The Sir Alwyn Williams uilding (Computer Science) esigned by Reiach & Hall in 002

The site was very constricted, an awkward shape, on a steep slope and set between a later 19th-century terrace of townhouses and a Brutalist building of 1968. Reiach & Hall's design cleverly resolved these difficulties and created a 5-storey building that works both as an eye-catching individual piece and as a link between its wildly contrasting neighbours [FIG. 206].

Externally, the key features, a *brise soleil* canopy over a fourth floor terrace and timber sunscreen louvres covering a south-facing glazed curtain wall, are borrowed from sunnier climes. Reiach & Hall's submission to the University acknowledges a number of sources for these features: Foster & Partners' Carré d'Art at Nîmes, (1984–93); Carlos Ferrater & Joan Guibernau's Casa Alonso-Planas in Barcelona (1995–98); Kengo Kuma's Fukushima River Filter Building in Japan (1996); David Morley Architects' Talacre Community Sports Centre, Kentish Town, London (2003); and Reiach & Hall's own 1998 Beacon development in St Vincent Street in Glasgow. The flanking walls are clad in glazed terracotta tiles.

Like the Wolfson Medical School, Reiach & Hall's design placed the offices, computer laboratories and seminar and research project rooms around a central triangular core containing circulation space with the addition of break-out areas and meeting rooms. The lift and stair service hub is set against the mutual wall with Lilybank Terrace to enable access to the existing departmental rooms in the Victorian terrace.

A bespoke pre-construction BREEAM assessment was carried out on the project. The Sir Alwyn Williams building was awarded a 'Very Good' BREEAM rating – a significant award given the site constraints. Materials were specified, where possible, in accordance with the Green Guide and to the BRE 'A' rating. Mixed-mode ventilation, that is, natural ventilation with supplementary displacement ventilation and local cooling, was adopted throughout. Externally a new streetscape links Lilybank Gardens and University Gardens, generating a much used public realm for the city centre campus.

Professor Anne Glover, Chief Scientific Advisor for Scotland, and Lady Joan Williams, the widow of Principal Sir Alwyn Williams, opened the £4.1m building on 22 June 2007.

CHARLES WILSON BUILDING, UNIVERSITY AVENUE 2004

The former Hillhead Congregational Church, designed by David Barclay of H. & D. Barclay in 1889, was purchased by the University in 2004 for use as an educational and conference facility. The conversion was designed by the University's Estates and Buildings office, and named after Principal Charles Wilson.

CENTRE FOR COGNITIVE NEUROIMAGING, BUTE LANE 2005–2008

This building was conceived as an interdisciplinary centre, bringing together researchers with an interest in cognitive neuroscience, functional neuroimaging, neuropsychology and computational modelling. Designed by Boswell, Mitchell & Johnston Architects, it occupies a constrained and discreet site along Bute Lane, behind the tenements of Great George Street and Hillhead Street. The new single storey, flat-roofed, building incorporates the lower floors of the old stone outshots of the 1890s tenements, with the large fMRI (functional Magnetic Resonance Imaging) and MEG (Magnetoencephalography) suites occupying the former garden grounds between the outshots. Externally, it has a red sandstone cladded block facing the Library and a lower rendered range facing Bute Lane.

The £4.32m cost of the project was divided almost evenly between the construction costs and the costs of the state-of-the-art scanning, imaging and other equipment. The building was opened on 28 November 2008.

STEVENSON HIVE BUILDING, UNIVERSITY AVENUE AND GIBSON STREET 2013–14

The new Stevenson Hive Building, designed by ECD Architects with Page\Park, replaces the old Glasgow University Union extension (see page 177). The new building, with a sandstone and white glass skin, also links to the Stevenson building to provide enhanced sport and leisure facilities.

THE FUTURE

It is perhaps most appropriate to finish this architectural history of the University of Glasgow with a view of the architectural future from David Page of Page\Park Architects, who has been commissioned to draw up an integrated Development Framework for Gilmorehill/Hillhead and the Western Infirmary site:

The realisation of acquiring additional land adjacent to the main campus offers a unique opportunity for the University of Glasgow to reshape the Gilmorehill campus in the West End of Glasgow. By taking time to carefully co-ordinate a Development Framework that is underpinned by an extensive consultation strategy, the University hopes to bring forward development aspirations in a cohesive and well-considered way. It is acknowledged that the scale of opportunity available to the University will take a number of years to deliver but the ultimate goal is to leave a positive lasting legacy for future generations.

Looking to the future of the estate and associated with the consolidation of the campus following the addition of the Western Infirmary, the University is undertaking an open dialogue within and with its wider constituency of support in the neighbouring community and beyond with a view to establishing the estate and campus vision for the next generation. Building on its 'Academic Strategy, A Global Vision 2020' focused on student experience, excellence in research and global reach, the ambition is to create a sustainable estate infrastructure and buildings fit for purpose for today and the future. Key to that vision are a number of important questions raised by the Principal and University leadership asking how the future will use the spaces within their buildings and the connections between them and the wider neighbourhood:

- *what physical spaces will support multidisciplinary and interdisciplinary activities?*
- *what is the nature of incubator and flexible knowledge exchange space to support research growth?*
- *how can the various challenges be overcome to deliver these unique settings?*

The University estates department in responding to these, is exploring how what seem micro relationships between people, influence the nature of the physical environment at the local, school then college level and ultimately inform the nature of the future campus as an experience for all. The exercise being undertaken is one of the first to ask whether the campus can evolve in response to this desire within the University to promote wider participation and by implication create a more open university at all levels, with its staff and students, funders, partners and neighbours. Initial investigation is that the wider campus opportunity offered by the Western Infirmary addition gives the University a unique flexibility to create these settings anew whilst adjusting but still respecting the traditions of the existing campus.

BUILDINGS BEYOND THE GILMOREHILL/HILLHEAD CAMPUS

Architects are noted in brackets.

1992 Murano Student Village, Ruchill (Assist Architects)

1995 Garscube Sports Complex

1995 The Weipers Centre for Equine Welfare, Garscube (Robert Potter & Partners)

1995 James Herriot Library, Garscube

1997 James Armour Stable Unit, Garscube (Robert Potter & Partners)

2001 Crichton Campus (Robert Potter & Partners) (RIBA Award 2001)

2003 St Andrew's Building, 11 Eldon Street (RMJM)

2005 Henry Wellcome Building for Comparative Medical Sciences, Garscube

2007 Scottish Centre for Ecology and the Natural Environment (SCENE) Field Station, Rowardennan (Page\Park)

2008 Beatson Institute for Cancer Research, Garscube (Reiach & Hall)

2009 Second Stable Block at the Weipers Centre for Equine Welfare

2009 New Small Animal Hospital, Garscube (Archial Architects) (RIBA Award; Glasgow Institute of Architects Award; RIAS Andrew Doolan Prize)

2010 Scottish Centre for Production Animal Health and Food Safety

2012 Wolfson Wohl Research Centre, Garscube (RMJM)

2014* Garscube Learning and Social Space (RMJM)

2014* Centre for Virus Research, Garscube (Sheppard Robson)

* Anticipated completion date

Appendix

PRINCIPALS OF THE UNIVERSITY OF GLASGOW

1460 Duncan Bunch
1475 Walter Bunch
1478 John Doby
1478 John Goldsmith
1480 John Brown
1483 Walter Leslie
1485 George Crichton
1488 John Goldsmith
1489 John Doby
1498 Patrick Coventry
1510 Thomas Coutts
1514 David Melville
1517 David Abercromby
1518 John Mair
1523 James Lindsay
1527 Alexander Logan
1540 Alexander Hamilton
1547 John Hamilton
1555 John Houston
1556 John Davidson
1574 Andrew Melville
1580 Thomas Smeaton
1585 Patrick Sharp
1615 Robert Boyd
1622 John Cameron
1626 John Strang
1651 Robert Ramsay
1653 Patrick Gillespie
1660 Robert Baillie
1662 Edward Wright
1684 James Fall
1690 William Dunlop
1701 John Stirling
1728 Neil Campbell
1761 William Leechman
1785 Archibald Davidson
1803 William Taylor
1823 Duncan MacFarlan
1858 Thomas Barclay
1873 John Caird
1898 Robert Story
1907 Sir Donald MacAlister
1929 Sir Robert Sangster Rait
1936 Sir Hector Hetherington
1961 Sir Charles Wilson
1976 Sir Alwyn Williams
1988 Sir William Kerr Fraser
1995 Sir Graeme Davies
2003 Sir Muir Russell
2009 Anton Muscatelli

CHANCELLORS OF THE UNIVERSITY OF GLASGOW

1451 William Turnbull, Bishop of Glasgow
1455 Andrew de Durisdere, Bishop of Glasgow
1474 John Laing, Bishop of Glasgow
1483 Robert Blackadder, Archbishop of Glasgow
1508 James Beaton, Archbishop of Glasgow
1523 Gavin Dunbar, Archbishop of Glasgow
1550 James Beaton II, Archbishop of Glasgow
1571 John Porterfield, titular Archbishop of Glasgow
1572 James Boyd of Trochrig, titular Archbishop of Glasgow
1581 Robert Montgomery, titular Archbishop of Glasgow
1585 William Erskine, titular Archbishop of Glasgow
1587 Walter Stewart, 1st Lord Blantyre, titular Archbishop of Glasgow
1598 James Beaton II, Archbishop of Glasgow
1603 John Spottiswoode, Archbishop of Glasgow
1615 James Law, Archbishop of Glasgow
1633 Patrick Lindsay, Archbishop of Glasgow
1642 James Hamilton, 3rd Marquess of Hamilton
1658 John Thurloe, Secretary to the Council of State
1660 William Cunningham, 9th Earl of Glencairn
1661 Andrew Fairfoul, Archbishop of Glasgow
1664 Alexander Burnet, Archbishop of Glasgow
1671 Robert Leighton, Archbishop of Glasgow
1674 Alexander Burnet, Archbishop of Glasgow
1679 Arthur Ross, Archbishop of Glasgow
1684 Alexander Cairncross, Archbishop of Glasgow
1687 John Paterson, Archbishop of Glasgow
1692 John Carmichael, 1st Earl of Hyndford
1714 James Graham, 1st Duke of Montrose
1743 William Graham, 2nd Duke of Montrose
1781 James Graham, 3rd Duke of Montrose
1837 James Graham, 4th Duke of Montrose
1876 Sir William Stirling-Maxwell of Pollock
1879 Walter Montagu-Douglas-Scott, 5th Duke of Buccleuch
1885 John Hamilton Dalrymple, 10th Earl of Stair
1904 William Thomson, 1st Baron Kelvin
1908 Archibald Primrose, 5th Earl of Rosebery
1930 Sir Donald MacAlister, 1st Baronet
1934 Sir Daniel Macaulay Stevenson
1947 Sir John Boyd Orr, 1st Baron Boyd-Orr
1972 Sir Alexander Kirkland Cairncross
1996 Sir William Kerr Fraser
2006 Professor Sir Kenneth Calman

Bibliography

ABERCROMBIE AND MATTHEW 1949
Patrick Abercrombie and Robert H. Matthew, *Clyde Valley Regional Plan*, Edinburgh, 1949

ADAM 1812
William Adam, *Vitruvius Scoticus: Plans, Elevations, and Sections of Public Buildings, Noblemen's and Gentlemen's Houses in Scotland*, Edinburgh, 1812, re-published 1980 and 2011 (James Simpson ed.)

ANNAN 1876
T. and R. Annan, *Memorials of the Old College of Glasgow*, Glasgow, 1876

ANNAN 1891
T. and R. Annan, *University of Glasgow Old and New*, Glasgow, 1891

ANONYMOUS 1903
Anonymous, *Unveiling of a stained glass window designed by Henry Holiday, in the Bute Hall, University of Glasgow on 17 October 1903. In memory of John Pringle Nichol, his son John Nichol, and his daughter Agnes Jane Nichol or Jack*, Glasgow, 1903

ANONYMOUS 1951
Anonymous, *The University of Glasgow Through Five Centuries*, Glasgow, 1951

ASHWELL AND NESBIT 1906
Ashwell and Nesbit, *The Latest Method of Heating*, Leicester, 1906

BLAIR AND JONES 1991
Céline Blair and David Jones, 'Furnishing the Hunterian Museum, Glasgow Style, 1809' in *Regional Furniture*, Burnley, 1991, pp.86–92

BONEY 1988
A.D. Boney, *The Lost Gardens of Glasgow University*, Glasgow, 1988

BRERETON 1844
William Brereton, *Travels in Holland, the United Provinces, England, Scotland, and Ireland 1634–35* (Edward Hawkins ed.), Manchester, 1844, p.117

BROWN AND MOSS 2001
A.L. Brown and Michael Moss, *The University of Glasgow: 1451–2001*, Edinburgh, 1996, updated 2001

BRUCE 1945
Robert Bruce, *First Planning Report to the Highways and Planning Committee of the Corporation of the City of Glasgow*, Glasgow, 1945

CHAPMAN 1820
Robert Chapman, *The Topographical Picture of Glasgow*, Glasgow, 1820

CITY PLAN 1951
Corporation of the City of Glasgow, *Development Plan*, Glasgow, 1951 (adopted 1954)

CLELAND 1816
John Cleland, *Annals of Glasgow*, 2 vols, Glasgow, 1816

COLVIN 1978
Howard Colvin, *A Biographical Dictionary of British Architects 1600–1840*, London, 1978

CORMACK 1902
J.D. Cormack (ed.), *Report of the Proceedings of the International Engineering Congress 1901*, Glasgow, 1902

COUTTS 1901
James Coutts, *Record of the Ninth Jubilee of the University of Glasgow*, Glasgow, 1901

COUTTS 1909
James Coutts, *A History of the University of Glasgow from its Foundation in 1451 to 1909*, Glasgow, 1909

CURRAN 2004
Samuel C. Curran, 'Dee, Philip Ivor (1904–1983)', *Oxford Dictionary of National Biography*, Oxford, 2004 [http://www.oxforddnb.com/view/article/31021]

DEARING 1997
National Committee of Inquiry into Higher Education, Dearing Report, London, 1997

DEVINE AND JACKSON 1995
Thomas Martin Devine and Gordon Jackson (eds), *Glasgow: Beginnings to 1830*, vol.1, Manchester, 1995

DICKSON 1888
William P. Dickson, *The Glasgow University Library: Notes on its History, Arrangements, and Aims*, Glasgow, 1888

DICTIONARY OF SCOTTISH ARCHITECTS
Dictionary of Scottish Architects 1840–1980, online resource, updated frequently: www.scottisharchitects.org.uk

DONNISON AND MIDDLETON 1987
David Vernon Donnison and Alan Middleton, *Regenerating the Inner City: Glasgow's Experience*, London, 1987

DUNCAN 1966
C.J. Duncan (ed.), *Modern Lecture Theatres*, Newcastle-upon-Tyne, 1966

DURKAN AND KIRK 1977
John Durkan and James Kirk, *The University of Glasgow: 1451–1577*, Glasgow, 1977

EMERSON 2008
Roger Emerson, *Academic Patronage in the Scottish Enlightenment: Glasgow, Edinburgh and St Andrews Universities*, Edinburgh, 2008

EVETTS 1988
Robin Evetts, *Architectural Expansion and Redevelopment in St Andrews, 1810–c.1894*, unpublished Ph.D. Thesis, University of St Andrews, 1988

FARR 2004
Dennis Farr, 'Young, Andrew McLaren (1913–1975)', *Oxford Dictionary of National Biography*, Oxford, 2004 [http://www.oxforddnb.com/view/article/56383, accessed 20 May 2012]

FENTON 2012
Clive Fenton, 'Northern Lights: university buildings in Scotland and northeast England' in *Sir Basil Spence: Buildings and Projects* (Louise Campbell ed.), London, 2012

FINLAYSON AND HAYWARD 2011
Gordon Finlayson and Danny Hayward, *Education towards Heteronomy: A Critical Analysis of the Reform of UK Universities since 1978*, University of Sussex, 2011

FORGAN 1986
Sophie Forgan, 'Context, Image and Function: A Preliminary Enquiry into the Architecture of Scientific Societies' in *The British Journal for the History of Science*, vol.19, no.1, Cambridge, 1986, pp.89–113

FOX AND GUAGNINI 1999
Robert Fox and Anna Guagnini, 'Laboratories, Workshops, and Sites: Concepts and Practices of Research in Industrial Europe, 1800–1914 (Concluded)' in *Historical Studies in the Physical and Biological Sciences*, vol.29, no.2, Californnia, 1999, pp.191–289, pp.291–94

GIBSON 1895
John C. Gibson (ed.), *Diary of Sir Michael Connal*, Glasgow, 1895

GLASGOW UNIVERSITY ARCHIVES 2007–
The University Story
http://www.universitystory.gla.ac.uk/2007 onwards

GLENDINNING 1997
Miles Glendinning (ed.), *Rebuilding Scotland: The Postwar Vision 1945–1975*, East Linton, 1997

GLENDINNING AND MUTHESIUS 1993
Miles Glendinning and Stefan Muthesius, *Tower Block: Modern Public Housing in England, Scotland, Wales and Northern Ireland*, New Haven and London, 1993

GOMME AND WALKER 1987
Andor Gomme and David Walker, *Architecture of Glasgow*, 2nd revised edition, London, 1987, pp.46–47, pp.169–70, p.177, p.249

GORDON 1872
A.E. Gordon, *The History of Glasgow from the Earliest to the Present Time*, Glasgow, 1872

GRANT 2005
David Grant, 'Removal of the University of Glasgow to Woodlands Hill 1845–9 and Gilmorehill 1853–83' in *Proceedings of the Society of Antiquaries of Scotland*, vol.135, Edinburgh, 2005, pp.213–58

HEALTH 1960
Department of Health for Scotland, *Report of the Department of Health for Scotland 1959*, Edinburgh, May 1960

HOWARD 1995
Deborah Howard, *Scottish Architecture from the Reformation to the Restoration, 1560–1660*, Edinburgh, 1995

HUTCHINS 2008
Roger Hutchins, *British University Observatories, 1772–1939*, Aldershot, 2008

INNES 1854
Cosmo Innes, *Munimenta Alme Universitatis Glasguensis: Records of the University of Glasgow, from its foundation till 1727*, 3 vols, Glasgow, 1854

JACKSON 1995
Stephen Jackson, 'The Blackstone Chair' in *Regional Furniture*, Burnley, 1995, pp.96–106

KEPPIE 2007
Lawrence Keppie, *William Hunter and the Hunterian Museum in Glasgow, 1807–2007*, Edinburgh, 2007

LAING 1841
David Laing, (ed.), *Letters and Journals of Robert Baillie A.M., Principal of the University of Glasgow, 1637–1662*, 3 vols, Edinburgh, 1841

LAW 1818
Robert Law, *Law's Memorials; or The Memorable Things that fell out within this Island of Britain from 1638 to 1684*, Edinburgh, 1818

LOWE 2012
Roy Lowe, *Education in the Post-War Years: A Social History*, Abingdon, 2012

MACAULAY 2009
James Macaulay, 'Sir George Gilbert Scott and the University of Glasgow' in *Essays in Scots and English Architectural History* (D. Jones and S. McKinstry eds), Donington, 2009, pp.71–81

MACGIBBON AND ROSS 1887
David MacGibbon and Thomas Ross, *The Castellated and Domestic Architecture of Scotland, from the Twelfth to the Eighteenth Century*, vol.IV, Edinburgh, 1887, pp.155–64

MACKECHNIE 1988
Aonghus MacKechnie, '*Evidence of a post-1603 court architecture in Scotland*' in *Architectural History*, vol.31, Edinburgh, 1988

MACKECHNIE 1993
Aonghus MacKechnie (ed.), *David Hamilton, Architect, 1768–1843: Father of the Profession*, Glasgow, 1993

MACKENNA 1981
Robert O. MacKenna, *Glasgow University Athletics Club: the Story of the First Hundred Years*, Glasgow, 1981

MACPHERSON 1992
Bill Macpherson, 'Restoring our Heritage: the Turnbull and Melville Rooms' in *Avenue* no.12, Glasgow, June 1992, pp.3–5

MARKUS 1985
Thomas A. Markus, 'Domes of Enlightenment: Two Scottish University Museums' in *Art History*, vol.8, no.2, London, June 1985, pp.158–77

MARWICK 1876
J.D. Marwick (ed.), *Extracts from the Records of the Burgh of Glasgow 1537–1642*, Glasgow, 1876

MARWICK 1881
J.D. Marwick (ed.), *Extracts from the Records of the Burgh of Glasgow, 1630–1662*, Glasgow, 1881

MARWICK 1908
J.D. Marwick (ed.), *Extracts from the Records of the Burgh of Glasgow, 1691–1717*, Glasgow, 1908

MARWICK AND RENWICK 1894
J.D. Marwick and Robert Renwick (eds), *Charters and Other Documents Relating to the City of Glasgow: AD 1175–1649*, VOL.II, Glasgow, 1894

MCFADZEAN 1979
Ronald McFadzean, *The Life and Work of Alexander Thomson*, London, 1979

MCKEAN, WALKER AND WALKER 1989
Charles McKean, David Walker and Frank Walker, *Central Glasgow: an Illustrated Architectural Guide*, Edinburgh, 1989, pp.179–85

MCKINSTRY 1991
Sam McKinstry, *Rowand Anderson: The Premier Architect of Scotland*, Edinburgh, 1991

METCALF 1965
Keyes DeWitt Metcalf, *Planning Academic and Research Library Buildings*, Harvard, *1965*

MKW 2010
MKW Design Partnership, *University of Glasgow, Senate Room, South Font: A Short Account of the History of the Alterations made to the Senate Room and Carnegie Room*, March 2010

MOFFAT AND BAXTER 1989
Alistair Moffat and Colin Baxter, *Remembering Charles Rennie Mackintosh: An Illustrated Biography*, Lanark, 1989

MORER 1702
Thomas Morer, *A Short Account of Scotland*, London, 1702

MOSS, MUNRO AND TRAINOR 2000
Michael Moss, J. Forbes Munro, Richard H. Trainor, *University, City and State: the University of Glasgow since 1870*, Edinburgh, 2000

MOSS, RANKIN AND RICHMOND 2001
Michael Moss, Moira Rankin, Lesley Richmond, *Who, Where and When: The History and Constitution of the University of Glasgow*, Glasgow, 2001

MURRAY 1927
David Murray, *Memories of the Old College of Glasgow: Some Chapters in the History of the University*, Glasgow, 1927

MUTHESIUS 2001
Stefan Muthesius, *The Post-War University: Utopianist Campus and College*, New Haven and London, 2001

NICHOLSON 1824
Peter Nicholson, *The Builder and Workman's New Director*, London, 1824

OAKLEY, 1973
C.A. Oakley, *A History of a Faculty: Engineering at Glasgow University*, Glasgow, 1973

PAC 1967
Public Accounts Committee, *Special Report – Parliament and Control of University Expenditure, with Proceedings, Evidence and Appendices (Committee of Public Accounts: 1966–7)*, London, January 1967

RCAHMS 1996
RCAHMS, *Tolbooths and Town-Houses: Civic Architecture in Scotland to 1833*, Edinburgh, 1996

RENWICK 1906
Robert Renwick, 'Buchanan's Connection with the University and Grammar School of Glasgow' in *George Buchanan – Glasgow Quater-Centenary Studies*, Glasgow, 1906, pp.33–41

RICHARDSON 1955
A. E. Richardson, *Robert Mylne, Architect and Engineer, 1733–1811*, London, 1955

ROBERTSON 1976
Paul L. Robertson, 'The Finances of the University of Glasgow before 1914' in *History of Education Quarterly*, vol.16, no.4 (Champaign, Illinois, winter 1976), pp.449–78 [accessed via JSTOR stable URL: http://www.jstor.org/stable/367725]

ROBERTSON 1990
Paul L. Robertson, 'The Development of an Urban University: Glasgow, 1860–1914' in *History of Education Quarterly*, vol.30, no.1 (Champaign, Illinois, spring 1990), pp.47–78 [accessed via JSTOR stable URL: http://www.jstor.org/stable/ 368755]

ROBERTSON 1998
Pamela Robertson, *The Mackintosh House*, Glasgow, 1998

ROBINS 1887
Edward Cookworthy Robins, *Technical School and College Building*, London, 1887

RODGER 1999
Johnny Rodger, *Contemporary Glasgow: The Architecture of the 1990s*, Edinburgh, 1999

ROSS AND HUME 1975
Anne Ross and John R. Hume, *A New and Splendid Edifice: the Architecture of the University of Glasgow*, Glasgow, 1975

SAINT 2007
Andrew Saint, *Architect and Engineer: A Study in Sibling Rivalry*, New Haven and London, 2007

SCALBERT 2001
Irénée Scalbert, *Architecture as a Way of Life: The New Brutalism 1953–1956*, paper from a report on the expert meeting, held at the Faculty of Architecture, TU Delft, on 5 November 2001: www.team100online.org/research/papers/delft1/scalbert.pdf [accessed 29 July 2012]

SCOTT 1857
George Gilbert Scott, *Remarks on Secular and Domestic Architecture, Present and Future*, London, 1857

SCOTT 1879
George Gilbert Scott and George Gilbert Scott Jr (ed.), *Personal and Professional Recollections by the late Sir George Gilbert Scott, R.A.*, London, 1879

SHANKS 1894
William Shanks, 'Glasgow Old College Inner Close' plate in *Edinburgh Architectural Association Sketchbook 1887–94*, new series VOL.II, Edinburgh, 1887–94, plate 39

SHARPLES 2004
Joseph Sharples, *Pevsner Architectural Guides: Liverpool*, New Haven and London, 2004

SIMPSON AND BROWN 2012
John Sanders, Tom Parnell, Nicholas Uglow and Cath Richards of Simpson and Brown Architects, *University of Glasgow Estates Conservation Strategy*, Leith, 2012

SMITH AND MITCHELL 1878
John Guthrie Smith, John Oswald Mitchell, *The Old Country Houses of the Old Glasgow Gentry*, Glasgow, 1878

SMITH 2009
Ken Smith, *The History of Particle Physics in Glasgow*, Glasgow, 2009 [published online: http://www.gla.ac.uk/schools/physics/research/groups/particlephysicsexperiment/ourheritage/]

STAMP 1999
Gavin Stamp, *The Light of Truth and Beauty: the lectures of Alexander 'Greek' Thomson, Architect, 1817–1875*, Glasgow, 1999

STAMP 2004
Gavin Stamp, 'Scott, Sir George Gilbert (1811–1878)' in *Oxford Dictionary of National Biography*, 2004 [http://www.oxforddnb.com/view/article/24869, accessed 27 January 2012]

STAMP AND MCKINSTRY 1994
Gavin Stamp and Sam McKinstry (eds), *'Greek' Thomson*, Edinburgh, 1994

STEVENSON 1880
John James Stevenson, *House Architecture*, London, 1880

SVIEDRYS 1976
Romualdas Sviedrys, 'The Rise of Physical Laboratories in Britain' in *Historical Studies in the Physical Sciences*, vol.7, California, 1976, pp.405–36

THOMPSON 1910
Silvanus Phillips Thompson, *The Life of Lord Kelvin*, 2 vols, London, 1910

THOMSON 1877
Allen Thomson, *Report by the Chairman of the University Removal Committee with prefatory notice of the earlier university buildings* (written May 1875), Glasgow, 1877

UFC ACCOUNTS [RELEVANT ACADEMIC YEAR]
University Funding Council, *Accounts 1988–92*, Bristol

UGC SURVEY [RELEVANT ACADEMIC YEAR]
University Grants Committee, *University Grants Committee Annual Survey* (London, published annually as a House of Commons Command Paper in the year after the end of the relevant academic year, e.g., survey for 1979–80 published in September 1981)

UGC RETURNS [RELEVANT ACADEMIC YEAR]
University Grants Committee, *Returns from Universities and University Colleges in Receipt of Treasury Grant* (London, published annually as a House of Commons Command Paper in the year after the end of the relevant academic year, e.g., report for 1959–60 published in September 1961)

UGC DEVELOPMENT [RELEVANT QUINQUENNIAL PERIOD]
University Grants Committee, *Quinquennial Report on University Development* (London, various years, published as a House of Commons Command Paper in the year after the end of quinquennial period, e.g., report for 1957–61 published in April 1962)

UNIVERSITY 1870
University of Glasgow, *Introductory addresses delivered at the opening of the University of Glasgow, session 1870–71 with a prefatory notice of the new building by Professor Allen Thomson*, Edinburgh, 1870

UNIVERSITY 1970
University of Glasgow, *Gilmorehill Centenary 1870–1970*, Glasgow, 1970

UNIVERSITY EQUALITY 2009
University of Glasgow, *Disability Equality Scheme 2009–2012*, Glasgow, 2009

UNIVERSITY REPORT [DATE]
University of Glasgow, Report of the University Court, 5 vols, Glasgow, 1964–71

WALKER 1975
David Walker, 'Scotland at the Turn of the Century' in *Edwardian Architecture and its Origins* (Alistair Service ed.), London, 1975, p.211

WALKER 1994
David M Walker, 'Listing in Scotland: Origins, Survey and Resurvey' in *Transactions of the Ancient Monuments Society*, vol.38, pp.31–96, London, 1994

WEIR, VEITCH AND COWAN 1871
D.H. Weir, J. Veitch and J.B. Cowan, *Memorials of the Old College of Glasgow*, Glasgow, 1871

WHYTE (LEEDS) 2008
William Whyte, '*The Modernist Moment at the University of Leeds, 1957–1977*' in *The Historical Journal*, vol.51, issue 01, Cambridge, March 2008, pp.169–93

WHYTE (LEICESTER) 2008
William Whyte, '"A Hell of a Job": Building the University of Leicester', Leicester, 2008 [lecture text, accessed 10 August 2012: www2.le.ac.uk/ebulletin/features/2000–2009/2008/02/nparticle.2008–02–28.0705916535]

WILLIAMSON, RICHES AND HIGGS 1990
Elizabeth Williamson, Anne Riches and Malcolm Higgs, *The Buildings of Scotland: Glasgow*, London, 1990, pp.338–40

WILSON 1961–62, 1962–63 AND 1963–64
Charles Haynes Wilson, *University of Glasgow Survey*, 3 vols, Glasgow, 1961–64

WRIGHT 1991
Elizabeth F. Wright, 'Thomas Hadden: architectural metalworker' in *Proceedings of the Society of Antiquaries of Scotland*, vol.121, Edinburgh, 1991, pp.427–35

YANNI 1999
Carla Yanni, *Nature's Museums: Victorian Science and the Architecture of Display*, Baltimore, 1999

Notes and References

ABBREVIATIONS

GLAHA Glasgow Hunterian Art Gallery Collections

GLAHM Glasgow Hunterian Museum Collections

GUAS Glasgow University Archive Services

GUL Glasgow University Library

RCAHMS Royal Commission on the Ancient and Historical Monuments of Scotland

RIAS Royal Incorporation of Architects in Scotland

RIBA Royal Institute of British Architects

SCRAN Scottish Cultural Resources Access Network

CHAPTER ONE · PAGES 13–25

1. Innes 1854, p.v.
2. J.H. McBrien, J.B. Kerr, et al., SUAT, *Recent work in Glasgow carried out by the Scottish Urban Archaeological Trust* (article for GAS). Also Glasdig 1 and 2 (newletter for urban archaeology support unit) and pamphlets/reports on Rottenrow and Bishops Castle excavations (1985).
3. Annan 1891, p.xiii.
4. Summary from the original Latin in Innes 1854, vol.I, p.iv.
5. Innes 1854, vol.I, p.67.
6. Innes 1854, vol.I, pp.67–68.
7. Innes 1854, vol.III, p.564.
8. Brereton 1844, p.117.
9. Durkan and Kirk 1977, p.32 .
10. Brereton 1844, p.117.
11. Innes 1854, vol.III, p.507.
12. Devine and Jackson 1995, p.45.
13. Innes 1854, vol.III, p.465.
14. Innes 1854, vol.III, p.467.
15. MacGibbon and Ross 1887, p.155.
16. Innes 1854, vol.III, pp.481, 484, 487, 488.
17. MacKechnie 1988, p.112.
18. MacKechnie 1988, p.112 and Innes 1854, p.481 (Caldwell, Rankin, Robert Boyd); p.487 (Patrick Colquhoun); p.498 (Johnstone).
19. Cleland 1816, vol.I, pp.446–47.
20. Innes 1854, vol.III, pp.481–82.
21. The accounts in this paragraph are all transcribed in Innes 1854, vol.III, pp.481–86.
22. Shanks 1894, vol.II, plate 39.
23. Innes 1854, vol.III, p.485.
24. Shanks 1894, plate 39.
25. Brereton 1844, p.117.
26. Innes 1854, vol.III, p.488.
27. For example, payment for a lock for 'the dor betwix the Brewhous and Kitching' in Innes 1854, vol.III, p.486.
28. Accounts of November 1655 refer to a spout of lead 'betwix the Librarie and the New Building'. By this time the 'new building' was the south range, see Innes 1854, vol.III, p.496.
29. The history of the gardens is recorded in Boney 1988.
30. For Clark's Deaconships see Cleland 1816, p.447. For the lease of the town quarry see Marwick 1881, p.445.
31. Laing 1841, p.313.
32. Innes 1854, vol.I, p.319.
33. Innes 1854, vol.III, p.492.
34. Innes 1854, vol.II, p.504.
35. Innes 1854, vol.III, pp.493–4.
36. Hunterian Museum and Art Gallery, ref. GLAHA 44157.
37. Innes 1854, vol.III, p.590.
38. Murray 1927, p.55.
39. RCAHMS 1996, p.74.
40. GUAS, ref. GB 248/30388B, 18 January 1741; receipt from James Adams, carver, for 'Carving the College arms above the Arch of the Steeple'.
41. Laing 1841, vol.III, p.384.
42. Laing 1841, vol.III, p.432.
43. Innes 1854, vol.III, p.507.
44. Howard 1995, p.130.
45. Murray 1927, p.33, quoting a letter from Principal Baillie to the Chancellor of Scotland, the Earl of Lauderdale in 1661.
46. Marwick 1881, p.454.
47. Innes 1854, vol.III, p.591.
48. Innes 1854, vol.III, p.581.
49. Innes 1854, vol.III, p.582.
50. GUAS, ref. 35083; account of 'Wainscutt furnished by the said Robert Donaldson to the finishing of the Wright-work in the Large Fore Hall of the College in Glasgow'.
51. GUAS, ref. 34921, 21 August 1745; account and receipt to the College of Glasgow by James Adams, carver, from April 1740 to May 1745 for work done in the New Library, Fore Hall and Fore-Gateway.
52. Brereton 1844, p.117.
53. Coutts 1909, p.158.
54. Coutts 1909, p.163.
55. Coutts 1909, p.173.

CHAPTER TWO · PAGES 27–41

1. Murray 1927, p.97.
2. Marwick and Renwick 1894, pp.356–58.
3. Law 1818, p.33.
4. Innes 1854, vol.III, p.597–98.
5. Marwick 1908, p.335, pp.338–41.
6. Innes 1854, vol.III, p.590.
7. GUAS, ref. FA 26634, 17 December 1722; Faculty Minutes vol.22, p.85.
8. GUAS, ref. FA 26634, 28 August 1723; Faculty Minutes vol.22, p.111.
9. The architect John Thomson drew up an early Greek style scheme in 1832 that was not executed, see GUAS, refs BUL 6/56/44 and 45.
10. Murray 1927, p.365 puts the rebuilding date at after 1761; GUAS, ref. 26640, March 1757; Faculty Minutes 1749–59, pp.212–13, Principal's House – 'plan given in by Mr Dreghorn'.
11. GUAS, ref. FA 26647, 13 November 1730; Faculty Minutes vol.35, p.25.
12. GUAS, ref. 34921, 21 August 1745; account and receipt to the College of Glasgow by James Adams, carver, from April 1740 to May 1745 for work done in the New Library, Fore Hall and Fore-Gateway.
13. GUAS, ref. 9447, 13 January 1832; account from L. Hill for 'Six pounds allowed for the Faculty for introducing gas light apparatus into his [Dr MacGill's] house'.
14. Murray 1927, p.393.
15. Innes 1854, vol.III, p.582.
16. Morer 1702, p.110.
17. National Records of Scotland, ref. GD 220/5/856/4–5; copy letter from the Duke of Montrose to Mungo Graham of Gorthie concerning the Duke of Chandos' grant of £500, 1721.
18. National Records of Scotland, ref. GD 220/5/1135/2; letter from Charles Morthland, Professor of Oriental Languages, to Mungo Graham of Gorthie, procurator to the Duke of Montrose, 1730.
19. National Records of Scotland, ref. GD 220/5/1214/3; letter from Charles Morthland to Mungo Graham, 14 March 1732.
20. GUAS, ref. 35022, 18 and 25 January, 1 and 16 February and 6 April 1732; minutes of the

Committee appointed by the Faculty of the College of Glasgow to take care of the building of the New Library. It is not known if James Adam, the 'mason in Stirling', was related to the Adam family of architects, but he seems to have been favoured by the College.

21. National Records of Scotland, ref. GD 220/5/1214/3; letter from Charles Morthland to Mungo Graham, 14 March 1732.

22. National Records of Scotland, ref. GD 220/5/1232; letter from William Adam to Mungo Graham of Gorthie, procurator to the Duke of Montrose, 6 May 1732. See also GUAS, ref. GB 248/35022.

23. GUAS, ref. 30387, 20 April 1832 and ref. 34923, 6 May 1732.

24. Adam 1812, pp.6–11.

25. National Records of Scotland, ref. GD 220/5/1271, letter from Charles Morthland to Mungo Graham, 26 June 1733.

26. GUAS, refs 34961–35084, 1732–45; various contractors' accounts.

27. GUAS, ref. GB 34921.

28. Colvin 1978, pp.238–39.

29. The galleries are described in Chapman 1820, p.144.

30. GUAS, ref. FA 26640, 8 April 1757; University Minutes vol.28, pp.219–20.

31. GUAS, ref. FA 26640, 6 May 1757; University Minutes vol.28, p.224.

32. Hutchins 2008, pp.37–40.

33. Quoted in Murray 1927, p.261.

34. GUAS, ref. FA 26640, 17 May 1758; University Minutes vol.28, p.262.

35. GUAS, ref. 58437/47, 17 March 1813; invoice from John Brash for £367.

36. GUAS, ref. FA 26694, 31 May 1792; Faculty Minutes vol.79, p.242.

37. GUAS, ref. FA 26694, 11 June 1792; Faculty Minutes vol.79, p.250.

38. GUAS, ref. FA 26694, 10 January 1793; Faculty Minutes vol.79, p.273.

39. GUAS, ref. FA 26694, 11 March 1793; Faculty Minutes vol.79, p.283, approved; p.297, 13 May 1793; payment of £125 to James Adam.

40. GUAS, ref. FA 26694, 22 April 1793; Faculty Minutes vol.79, p.288.

41. Coutts 1909, p.300.

42. GUAS, ref. FA 26696, 15 May 1806; Faculty Minutes vol.81, p.395.

43. See Markus 1985, pp.158–77 for an account of the establishment of both the Hunterian and Andersonian Museums.

44. Richardson 1955, p.120. Mylne was also connected to William Hunter though his marriage to Mary Home, the sister of Hunter's sister-in-law.

45. GUAS, ref. HUNT, 8 September 1797; letter from Robert Mylne to George Fordyce, one of the trustees of Hunter's will, quoting an earlier letter of 27 May 1797 from James Jardine, Professor of Logic and Rhetoric, to another trustee, Matthew Baillie.

46. GUAS, ref. HUNT 3/19, 8 September 1797; letter from Robert Mylne to George Fordyce, one of the trustees of Hunter's will.

47. GUAS, ref. HUNT 2/2/18, 17 May 1799; receipted account and precept to Robert Nimmo, writer, for the estate of the deceased John Clarkson, architect, for £5 for drawing designs and GUAS, ref. 5255, 18 December 1799; receipted account by David Hamilton for designs and drawings for the Hunterian Museum and 19 February 1801, precept in favour of David Hamilton for £28 10s for designs and drawings for the Hunterian Museum and GUAS, ref. 5269, 18 December 1799; David Hamilton account for 'Sundrie designs for a Museum'.

48. GUAS, ref. HUNT 3/22, 30 December 1800; letter from J. Millar to Matthew Baillie regarding the delay in responding to the Mylne proposals and the various considerations regarding the new museum.

49. Hunterian Art Gallery, refs GLAHA 42558–42573, no dates; various plans and elevations for 'Hunter's Museum'. Although he did not secure the Hunterian Museum commission, Hamilton seems to have developed good connections with at least two professors: James Jeffray, for whom he designed an extension to a house in Professors' Square, Hunterian Art Gallery, ref. GLAHA 42888–9, no date; and Professor Sandford, for whom he made alterations, GUAS, ref. 4950, 13 June 1831.

50. Registers of Scotland, Old Parish Register for Glasgow, 12 October 1798.

51. GUAS, ref. GB 248 HUNT 3/20, 26 September 1799; letter from Matthew Baillie to Principal Davidson.

52. GUAS, ref. HUNT 3/21, 15 October 1800; letter from Matthew Baillie to Principal Davidson complaining about the delay in considering Mylne's sketches.

53. GUAS, ref. FA 26635, 10 December 1730; Faculty Minutes vol.23, pp.144–45, GUAS, ref. HUNT 2/2/32; precept, 12 December 1803, and receipt 9 January 1804 from Peter Nicholson for 'Drawings of Plans, Elevations and a section for a second design for the Museum'. An unidentified drawing survives in the University Archives, which may be the west elevation of Nicholson's scheme (BUL 6/56/21), but a loose sheet of notes associated with the drawing suggests that it relates to the College Street scheme.

54. GUAS, ref. HUNT 3/28, 9 April 1803; draft letter from the Principal to Dr Baillie requesting that he decide between two sets of plans submitted for Dr Hunter's Museum by Mr Stark and Mr Hamilton.

55. GUAS, ref. BUL 6/56/65–69, 1803; plans and section of the museum for the College of Glasgow.

56. Colvin 1978, p.776.

57. GUAS, ref. FA 26696, 2 August 1804; Faculty Minutes vol.81, pp.307–08.

58. Murray 1927, p.207.

59. GUAS, ref. FA 26696, 22 December 1804; Faculty Minutes vol.81, p.342.

60. GUAS, ref. FA 26696, 4 August 1804; Faculty Minutes vol.81, p.324.

61. *Caledonian Mercury*, 12 September 1807, p.3; Keppie 2007, p.75.

62. GUAS, ref. HUNT 2/2/104, 19 April 1809; receipted account by William Stark, Architect, for 200 guineas for working drawings, specifications and designs supplied from 1804–09.

63. GUAS, ref. HUNT 2/2/85, 11 May 1809; receipt and accounts for Cleland & Jack for furniture bought for the Museum, also HUNT 2/2/114, 6 March 1810; receipted account by Cleland & Jack for work done on the furnishings of the Hunterian Museum. See Blair and Jones 1991, pp.86–92.

64. McLean Museum and Art Gallery, Greenock, Watt Collection, refs 1997.17, 20–25, 31 July 1807–5 September 1808; drawings and booklet for design of the Hunterian Museum heating system. Birmingham Central Library, ref. JWP 3/52, 1808; papers and plans concerning Mr [William] Strutt's stove, proposed for heating the Hunterian Museum, Glasgow, with draft letter from Watt to James Mylne and reply, and a letter from Strutt to Watt, also ref. JWP C4/D29, 1808; plans and drawings concerning Watt's proposals for revising the heating system of the Hunterian Museum, and ref. JWP C6/7, 1809–12; letters from Professor George Jardine about a prize essay and Hunterian stove and Professor Mickleham about the Hunterian heating.

65. GUAS, ref. 5252, 30 July 1809; letter from William Stark saying that Mr Brash will superintend the work on the Hunterian Museum and that Messrs Park, Galloway & Napier should start work at once, also HUNT 2/2/141, 20 September 1810; receipted account by John Brash for £6 6s for work done on the heating of the Hunterian Museum.

66. Keppie 2007, pp.46–50.

67. Murray 1927, pp.347–361.

68. Keppie 2007, p.64.

69. GUAS, ref. BUL 6/56/72 – 73, 17 January 1823; unexecuted elevation and plan by John Brash.

70. GUAS, ref. FA 26696, 11 March 1806; Faculty Minutes vol.81, p.389.

71. GUAS, ref. FA 26696, 13 March 1806; Faculty Minutes vol.81, p.390.

72. GUAS, ref. FA 26696, 7 April 1806; Faculty Minutes vol.81, p.393.

73. GUAS, ref. FA 26697, 29 October 1806; Faculty Minutes vol.82, p.14, and GUAS, ref. BUL 6/56/22–34.

74. Murray 1927, p.194.

CHAPTER THREE · PAGES 43–51

1. GUAS, ref. FA 26700, 19 December 1845; Faculty Minutes vol.85, p.219, copy letter of 13 November 1845.

2. GUAS, ref. FA 26700, 29 August 1845; Faculty Minutes vol.85, p.199.

3. Grant 2005, pp.213–58.

4. Smith and Mitchell 1878, LXI (Kelvingrove House), note 2.

5. GUAS, ref. FA 26701, 5 December 1849; Faculty Minutes vol.86, p.118.

6. GUAS, ref. FA 26700, 30 April 1846; Faculty Minutes vol.85, p.266.

7. GUSC, ref. MS Gen 1717/3/1/142, 12 January 1846; letter from Principal Macfarlan to James Mitchell, lawyer, asking him to write to GAMJRC stating it is necessary for John Baird and Macfarlan to proceed to Edinburgh to lay plans of projected buildings before Playfair 'in case evidence of professional man be required'. Also GUAS, ref. FA 26700, 17 January 1846; Faculty Minutes vol.85, pp.228–29, record of Playfair's refusal.

8. GUAS, ref. FA 26700, 26 January 1846; Faculty Minutes vol.85, p.232.

9. GUAS, ref. BUL 6/57/4–12. A bound volume of plans now only contains one plan, but other sheets relating to this scheme survive with stitch marks, suggesting that they have been removed from the same volume.

10. GUAS, ref. 26700, 30 October 1846; Faculty Minutes vol.85, p.290, revised ground plans laid before the Faculty.

11. GUAS, ref. 26700, 30 December 1846; Faculty Minutes vol.85, p.316, Faculty approval for transmission of the revised plans to the Commissioners for the College Removal.

12. GUAS, ref. 26700, 30 April 1847; Faculty Minutes vol.85, p.339, 'still more recently Mr Baird went to London to have direct communication with Mr Barry on the subject' and 4 August 1847, p.349, 'it had been farther arranged that when Mr Baird should have prepared revised plans embodying these changes, Mr Barry would revise the elevations'.

13. GUAS, ref. 26700, 25 September 1848; Faculty Minutes vol.85, p.441, copy of letter from the GAMJRC indicating their refusal to continue with the relocation proposals.

14. *Edinburgh Gazette*, 27 March 1849, p.305.

15. GUAS, refs 3400–09, 3411, 3413–14, 3416–22, 3425 and 3427–28, 24 January 1852; reports by the professors in answer to interrogatory concerning accommodation in Old College.

16. GUAS, ref. SEN 1/1/7, 7 February 1859; Senate Minutes vol.91, pp.1–4, new 'memorial' to Queen Victoria, repeating 1853 'memorial'.

17. Coutts 1901, p.425.

18. Universities (Scotland) Act 1858, section XXI, p.637.

19. GUAS, ref. 10470, 11 June 1860; report on the buildings of Glasgow University.

20. GUAS, ref. 3458, 12 March 1861; report of Improvements Committee concerning the state of the Library, the departments of Anatomy, Medicine and Natural History, with estimates for carrying out their proposals.

21. GUAS, ref. SEN 1/1/7, 14 March 1862; Senate Minutes vol.91, pp.176–77, copy letter from the Lords of the Treasury of 14 February 1862.

22. GUAS, ref. SEN 1/1/7, 15 December 1862; Senate Minutes vol.91, p.219.

23. A shelter was specified for this purpose at Gilmorehill when the University moved there: GUAS, ref. SEN 1/1/9, 29 July 1871; p.163, report of Buildings Committee.

24. GUAS, ref. SEN 1/1/7; Senate Minutes vol.91, pp.219–20, acceptance of estimate, 22 December 1862 and p.229, completion and rules for use of the shelter, 13 February 1863.

25. GUAS, ref. SEN 1/1/7, 4 April 1862; Senate Minutes vol.91, p.183. See Murray 1927, p.446.

26. University Review, 1884, p.5.

27. GUAS, refs. 10223–10226, 1 December 1863; notices served on the College by the City of Glasgow Union Railway Co. and Glasgow & North British Railway Co.

28. GUAS, ref SEN 1/1/7, 14 April 1864; Senate Minutes vol.91, pp.312–14, Removal Committee report to Senate.

CHAPTER FOUR · PAGES 53–77

1. GUAS, ref. 21215, 14 April 1864; Removal Committee Minute Book, advice of the Lord Advocate.

2. GUAS, ref. 10291, Schedule to the Glasgow (City) Union Railway Act, 1864.

3. GUAS, ref. 17146, 9 March 1865; Building Sub-Committee Minute Book no.1, p.32, letter to George Gilbert Scott from Allen Thomson regarding the layout and negotiations with Glasgow Corporation.

4. GUAS, ref. 78087, March 1853; feuing plan.

5. GUAS, ref. 10385, 1860; information as to proposed sites for the College of Glasgow.

6. Smith and Mitchell 1878, no.50.

7. Gordon 1872, p.1143.

8. RCAHMS, ref. DPM 1840/4/1; Dick Peddie design for gates, lodges, catacombs; RCAHMS ref. William Notman Collection, Roll 7, competition design under the name 'Alberti'.

9. *Glasgow Herald*, 6 October 1848, p.3. Anonymised plans for various housing schemes are held by GUAS, e.g. ref. 20844.

10. RCAHMS, ref. DPM 1840/6/1/5; perspective for proposed terraced housing at Gilmorehill. Signed: 'JDickPeddie /49'. Insc: cropped 'D'.

11. GUAS, ref. 17146, 9 March 1865; Building Sub-Committee Minute Book no.1, p.35.

12. GUAS, ref. SEN 1/1/8; Senate Minutes vol.92, pp.50–52, Clayslaps offer and p.53, 26 January 1865; Donaldshill purchase agreed. Also GUAS, ref. 4394, 17 February 1864; Finance Sub-Committee Minute Book, agreement to purchase Clayslaps.

13. GUAS, ref. 20818, June 1864; Burnet plan; GUAS, ref. 985, 27 November 1865; letter from John Burnet to Dr Allen Thomson concerning arrangements with Mr Smith, surveyor.

14. GUAS, ref. SEN 1/1/8, 7 November 1867; pp.198–99, purchase of Mrs Dalgleish's house and grounds at Hillhead.

15. GUAS, ref. SEN/1/1/10, 5 January 1875; p.149, offer for Hillhead House and portion of the grounds.

16. GUAS, ref. SEN 1/1/8; Senate Minutes vol.92, pp.46–47.

17. Stamp 2004.

18. Scott 1879, p.373.

19. Scott 1857, p.viii.

20. *Caledonian Mercury*, 3 June 1864, p.1.

21. GUAS, ref. 17146, 3 August 1864; Building Sub-Committee Minute Book no.1, pp.2–3.

22. GUAS, ref. SEN 1/1/8; Senate Minutes vol.92, pp.46–48.

23. GUAS, ref. 10546, 14 September 1864; part of copy letter to Loch & Maclaurin enquiring about Gilbert Scott, also Loch's response.

24. GUAS, ref. 17146, 30 September 1864; Building Sub-Committee Minute Book no.1, p.3, copy excerpt from the Senate Minutes approving an approach to George Gilbert Scott to serve as the College's architect.

25. GUAS, ref. 17146, 8 October 1864; Building Sub-Committee Minute Book no.1, pp.4–7.

26. GUAS, ref. 17146, 10 October 1864; Building Sub-Committee Minute Book no.1, p.8, copy of letter from George Gilbert Scott at 20 Spring Gardens, London, accepting the appointment as architect for the new buildings.

27. GUAS, ref. 17146, 10 October 1864; Building Sub-Committee Minute Book no.1, pp.8–14, memorandum of requirements to the architect.

28. GUAS, ref. 937, 20 October 1864; letter from George Gilbert Scott to Professor Allen Thomson intimating visit to Glasgow on 26 October.

29. GUAS, ref. 17146, 28 October 1864; Building Sub-Committee Minute Book no.1, pp.14–15, minutes of meeting.

30. GUL, Special Collections, photos B26, B27 and B48.

31. GUAS, ref. 943, 6 December 1864; letter from George Gilbert Scott to Professor Allen Thomson enclosing the papers he needs and stating his hope of being able to propose a general arrangement and that he took notes of Edinburgh's College buildings.

32. GUAS, ref. 940, 7 November 1864; letter from Arthur B. Thompson, Scott's Private Secretary, to

Professor Allen Thomson acknowledging George Gilbert Scott's receipt of plans dated 1846 and GUAS, ref. 17146, 12–17 December 1864; Removal Committee Minute, pp.16–24, various amendments to requirements.

33. GUAS, ref. 17146; Building Sub-Committee Minute Book no.1, p.24, undated copy of letter from George Gilbert Scott concerning the services engineering.

34. Hunterian Museum and Art Gallery, refs GLAHA 42452, 51567, 51568, 54347 and 54351. GUAS, Main Building, refs BUL 6/1/1–320; Bute Hall, refs BUL 6/4/1–30; and West Wing and Chapel, refs BUL 6/5/1–240. RIBA Library, Drawings Collection, George Gilbert Scott contract and working drawings, design for great hall, 1867–70, working drawings for Forehall to great hall, design for great hall, 1875–76, refs, PA1708/ScGGS[44]/1–24, DR10/3/1–2, DR72/1/1–7; Scott and Scott design and working drawing for Bute Hall, refs, PA1739/ScGGJ+ScJ[3]/1, DR72/3; John Oldrid Scott drawings for Randolph Memorial Hall and contract drawing for completing tower and spire, 1887, refs PA1738/ScJ[23]/1,2,4, and 5. RIBA Library, Scott Family Collection, John Oldrid Scott Account Books 1873–1916, refs ScJO/1–3. Mitchell Library, Dean of Guild Collection, spire drawings, ref. 1/399. Peterborough Museum, John Thompson Drawings Collection, vol.1 (57 drawings).

35. GUAS, ref. 17146, 24 October 1866; Building Sub-Committee Minute Book no.1, p.147, contract specifications: tracings.

36. Thomson 1877, p.39.

37. GUAS, ref. 17147, 3 May 1871; Building Sub-Committee Minute Book no.2, p.131, enquiry into completion of contracts.

38. For example, J.M. Bignell wrote to Allen Thomson on 4 February 1868 to say that he had sent on sketches of classrooms, the south block and central tower and plans of the professors' houses, GUAS, ref. 1087.

39. GUAS, ref. 944, 13 January 1865; letter from George Gilbert Scott to Professor Allen Thomson stating that he encloses a plan of proposed site and that he has arrived at a general arrangement which seems to meet the requirements, except the financial ones.

40. GUAS, ref. 946, 19 January 1865; letter from George Gilbert Scott to Professor Allen Thomson declaring his wish that criticism be delayed until he can bring his complete designs before the committee.

41. GUAS, ref. 17146, 21 February 1865; Building Sub-Committee Minute Book no.1, p.29, letter from George Gilbert Scott to Allen Thomson.

42. GUAS, ref. 17146, 29 December 1865; Building Sub-Committee Minute Book no.1, pp.53–54, copy of letter from Giles Gilbert Scott to William Hill, Honorary Secretary to the University.

43. Scott 1879, p.272.

44. GUAS, ref. 17146, 30 March 1866; Building Sub-Committee Minute Book no.1, p.97, removal of cloisters from the design.

45. GUAS, ref. 17146, 29 September 1865; Building Sub-Committee Minute Book no.1, p.38, glass roofs not suitable for the Library and Museum.

46. Saint 2007, pp.138–40.

47. GUAS, ref. 17146, 23 May 1867; Building Sub-Committee Minute Book no.1, p.260, minutes regarding appointment of hospital architect.

48. McFadzean 1979, pp.199–202.

49. GUAS, ref. 17146, 2 February 1866; Building Sub-Committee Minute Book no.1, p.61, copy letter from George Gilbert Scott to Allen Thomson, thanking him for his letter to Mr. Thompson. Gavin Stamp records Jacinta Feltis' discovery of this reference in Stamp 1999, p.87, n.1.

50. GUAS, ref. 17146,14 October 1865; Building Sub-Committee Minute Book no.1, p.47.

51. Stamp 1999, p.79.

52. Stevenson 1880, p.375. The author is grateful to Ranald MacInnes for drawing this quotation to his attention.

53. Dictionary of Scottish Architects, Rochead entry, accessed 20 April 2012.

54. GUAS, ref. 17146, 13 May 1865; Building Sub-Committee Minute Book no.1, pp.33–34, copy of letter from Allen Thomson to Giles Gilbert Scott detailing cost calculations.

55. GUAS, refs. 3051–3058, May-June 1865; reports and circular letters regarding fundraising.

56. GUAS, ref. 2210, 27 April 1865; Draft Minute Book of the Sub-Committee on Subscriptions, vol.1, press cutting.

57. Connal, p.128, entry for 28 March 1866.

58. GUAS, refs 957–961, 963, 965, 967–68, 970, 974, 981, 982, 984, 988, 1 June – 20 December 1865; various letters between Scott's office, Edgar, Burbridge and Allen Thomson, Convenor of the Building Sub-Committee, regarding the perspectives. GUAS, ref. 17146, 29 December 1865; Building Sub-Committee Minute Book no.1, p.51, copy letter from Allen Thomson to Gilbert Scott regarding the arrival of the perspective and its display in the Royal Exchange.

59. GUAS, ref. 1185, 3 October 1868; memorandum from C.L. Cockburn, manager, Artistic Engraving Association, to 'The Headmaster, University Glasgow' asking for a photograph of the drawing of the new buildings to submit to the editor of *The Builder*.

60. *Glasgow Herald*, 6 May 1867, p.5.

61. GUAS, ref. 17146, 19 January 1866; Building Sub-Committee Minute Book no.1, pp.57–58, Senate grant of powers to the Building Sub-Committee and authority to co-operate with the Subscriptions Sub-Committee.

62. GUAS, ref. 17146, 16 January 1866; Building Sub-Committee Minute Book no.1, p.55, copy letter from George Gilbert Scott to Dr Allen Thomson regarding old Gilmorehill quarries, appointment of a Clerk of Works and other matters.

63. GUAS, ref. 17147, 25 November 1869; Building Sub-Committee Minute Book no.2, p.94, John Thompson's progress report to the Building Sub-Committee.

64. GUAS, ref. 17146, 24 October 1866; Building Sub-Committee Minute Book no.1, p.137, copy letter from George Gilbert Scott to Dr Allen Thomson.

65. GUAS, ref. 17146, 2 October 1866; Building Sub-Committee Minute Book no.1, p.121, tenders for painterwork.

66. The author is grateful to Sam McKinstry for information on Robert Rowand Anderson and his work for Scott in Leith and Glasgow. The discussions regarding Anderson and the Clerk of Works post are as follows: GUAS, ref. 17146, Building Sub-Committee Minute Book no.1, pp.53–54, pp.58–59, p.61, pp.62–64, p.66, p.68, p.69, pp.70–73, p.74, pp.81–82, p.83, p.90; and refs 997–999, 6 February 1866 – 15 February 1866; letters regarding selection of Anderson as Clerk of Works.

67. GUAS, ref. 17146, 23 January 1867; Building Sub-Committee Minute Book no.1, p.244, report on award of contracts.

68. Thomson 1877, p.18.

69. See the website for the Heritage Group of the Chartered Institution of Building Services Engineers [http://www.hevac-heritage.org/homepage.htm, accessed 30 January 2012].

70. Dickson 1888, p.46, page note (no number).

71. Thomson 1877, p.18.

72. GUAS, ref. 17147, 10 February 1869; Building Sub-Committee Minute Book no.2, p.69, report of building works.

73. GUAS, ref. 17146, 5 February 1868; Building Sub-Committee Minute Book no.1, p.298, report on building progress.

74. GUAS, ref. 17147, 10 February 1869; Building Sub-Committee Minute Book no.2, p.82, report of foundation laying ceremony. See Thomson 1877, p.19.

75. GUAS, ref. 17147, 10 February 1869; Building Sub-Committee Minute Book no.2, pp.66–68, minutes of contract approvals.

76. GUAS, ref. 17147, 10 February 1869; Building Sub-Committee Minute Book no.2, pp.76–79, John Thompson's progress report to the Building Sub-Committee.

77. GUAS, ref. 17147, 25 November 1869; Building Sub-Committee Minute Book no.2, pp.92–94, John Thompson's progress report to the Building Sub-Committee.

78. GUAS, ref. 17147, 25 November 1869; Building Sub-Committee Minute Book no.2, p.97, financial report.

79. GUAS, ref. 17147, 25 November 1869; Building Sub-Committee Minute Book no.2, p.100, minutes regarding lightning conductors and keys.

80. Thomson 1877, p.36.

81. GUAS, ref. 17147, 25 November 1869; Building Sub-Committee Minute Book no.2, p.101, minutes regarding fatalities on site.

82. GUAS, ref. 17147, 3 May 1871; Building Sub-Committee Minute Book no.2, p.130, consideration of the future progress of the works.

83. GUAS, ref. 17147, April 1872; Building Sub-Committee Minute Book no.2, p.182, statement of extras prepared by George Gilbert Scott.

84. Thomson 1877, p.31.

85. GUAS, ref. 17147; Building Sub-Committee Minute Book no.2, p.134, 10 May 1871, sums required for completion of contracts and p.146, 11 November 1871, Museum fittings.

86. Thomson 1877, p.33.

87. GUAS, ref. 17147; Building Sub-Committee Minute Book no.2, p.192, 1 May 1877, accounts submitted for authority to pay – A. Wells for painting cases in the Museum; Glasgow Post Office Directory 1871–72, p.388.

88. GUAS, ref. 17147, 1 May 1877; Building Sub-Committee Minute Book no.2, pp.191–92, accounts submitted for authority to pay – A. MacKenzie for curtains and upholstering work in the Museum.

89. GUAS, ref. 17147, 1 May 1877; Building Sub-Committee Minute Book no.2, pp.190–91, accounts submitted for authority to pay – John Young.

90. GUAS, ref. 17147, 1 May 1877; Building Sub-Committee Minute Book no.2, p.191, accounts submitted for authority to pay – D. & G. Graham for hanging bells and erecting speaking tubes in the Museum.

91. GUAS, ref. SEN 1/1/10, 21 September 1875; p.247, work in the Museum.

92. GUAS, ref. SEN 1/1/10, 1 May 1873; p.5, summer works.

93. GUL, Special Collections, ref. MacLehose 770, 1 December 1896; report of the proceedings at the unveiling of the Sandford and Veitch memorials in the University of Glasgow.

94. Thomson 1877, pp.22–23, p.29; GUAS, ref. BUL 6/1/86, 1872; plan and elevation of Court Room fireplace, postmarked 1872.

95. GUAS, ref. BUL 6/1/88–89. Macpherson 1992, p.3, suggests that Oldrid Scott's furniture designs were never constructed.

96. GUAS, ref. BUL 6/1/91–93. The replacement panels are not fielded to match the originals.

97. GUAS, ref. CI/1/77, 6 October 1969; p.9.

98. Thomson 1877, p.28.

99. GUAS, ref. 34921, account and receipt to the College of Glasgow by James Adams, carver, from April 1740 to May 1745.

100. Thomson 1877, p.30.

101. GUAS, ref. SEN 1/1/9, 7 December 1871; p.196, committee on small class-room furnishings.

102. MKW 2010, p.2.

103. The cupola was a late addition to the plans after the contract drawings of November 1868, on which it did not appear.

104. Some fragments of copper cable from the classroom are preserved in the Hunterian Museum: e.g., ref. GLAHM 113590. Pieces of equipment, scientific instruments and other objects and documents relating to Lord Kelvin form part of the Hunterian Museum collections.

105. GUAS, ref. BUL 6/1/252–283.

106. GUAS, ref. CI/1/60; p.104, 15 December 1952, report of Committee on Stair Memorial and p.225, 28 April 1953, Stair Memorial.

107. GUAS, ref. CI/1/77, 6 October 1969; p.9, Senate Room/Carnegie Room.

108. GUAS, BE/146/6, 7 June 1971; supplementary agenda for the Works Committee.

109. GUAS, ref. 17146, 25 October 1864; Building Sub-Committee Minute Book no.1, p.13, memorandum as to accommodation required in the New Buildings to be submitted to Mr Scott.

110. GUAS, ref. 17146, 23 March 1866; Building Sub-Committee Minute Book no.1, p.92, professors' houses.

111. GUAS, ref. 17146, 23 May 1867; Building Sub-Committee Minute Book no.1, p.257, plans of Principal's and professors' houses.

112. GUAS, ref. 17147, 28 November 1868; Building Sub-Committee Minute Book no.2, copy contract between the Senate and John Thompson and specification by Scott for the professors' houses and ref. BUL 6/2/1–9, 28 November 1868; contract drawings.

113. GUAS, ref. 17147, 10 February 1869; Building Sub-Committee Minute Book no.2, p.68, plans of professors' houses approved of and to be proceeded with.

114. GUAS, ref. 17147, 25 November 1869; Building Sub-Committee Minute Book no.2, p.94, statement of progress.

115. Thompson 1910, vol II, p.780.

116. GUAS, ref. CI/1/69, 9 January 1962; p.134, Principal's lodging.

117. Thomson 1877, p.21.

118. GUAS, ref. SEN 1/1/9, 24 March 1870; p.21, arrangements for removal of Library.

119. Murray 1927, p.597.

120. Thomson 1877, p.28.

121. Thomson 1877, p.43.

122. GUAS, ref. SEN 1/1/11, 29 April 1875; p.214, Sir G. Gilbert Scott acct as architect of the College Buildings.

CHAPTER FIVE · PAGES 79–95

1. Moss, Munro and Trainor 2000, p.63.

2. Mackenna 1981, p.9.

3. GUAS, ref. 4621, 3 November 1870; notes and suggestions on the duties of College servants, janitor, bedellus, chamberlain, bell ringer and gardener.

4. GUAS, ref. SEN 1/1/9, 25 April 1872; p.260, report of summer works.

5. GUAS, ref. SEN 1/1/9, 23 May 1871; pp.156–60, buildings to be proceeded with.

6. GUAS, ref. SEN 1/1/9, 17 September 1872, p.289, stone wall on west side of quadrangle.

7. Thomson 1877, p.24.

8. GUAS, ref. 11942, 23 August 1870; letter from McGrigor, Stevenson & Fleming, Writers, to Mitchell, Macnie & Mitchell and GUAS, ref. 11938, 18 November 1870; letter from McGrigor, Stevenson & Fleming, Writers, to Alexander Macnie, WS.

9. GUAS, ref. 17147, 11 November 1871; Building Sub-Committee Minute Book no.2, p.146, Anent carved and inscribed stones at the Old College.

10. GUAS, ref. SEN 1/1/11, 12 December 1878, p.317, Committee on College Church graveyard and p.351, 27 February 1879, report of Committee on College Church Burying Ground.

11. Stevenson 1880, p.373.

12. Anonymous 1951, p.25.

13. Gibson 1895, p.141; Keppie 2007, p.85.

14. J.B. Kerr, 'Glasgow, High Street, College Goods Yard, foundations, pits, drain, sherd' in *Discovery and Excavation Scotland*, Edinburgh, 1984, p.25.

15. GUAS, ref. 1184, 3 October 1868; letter from James Allen Campbell to Allen Thomson.

16. GUAS, SEN 1/1/11, 22 November 1877; p.186, the Marquess of Bute's offer to build the Common Hall.

17. RIBA, ref. Scott 23–25.

18. RIBA, ref. Scott 27–32. GUAS, ref. SEN 1/1/11, 13 December 1877; p.198, report of Committee.

19. GUAS, ref. BUL 6/4/6–9.

20. Scott 1879, p.381.

21. Scott 1879, p.379.

22. GUAS, ref. 5513, 7 March 1885; letter from J. Oldrid Scott to Professor Berry concerning the confusion of his accounts and the Finance Committee's decision to pay him the balance after a certain length of time.

23. *Glasgow Herald*, 1 February 1884, p.8 (describes Mr Wood as Clerk of Works). GUAS, ref. BUL 6/4/6–9, 6 May 1878; contract drawings signed by Wood.

24. GUAS, ref. SEN 1/1/11, 14 August 1878; p.198, Minute of Agreement.

25. GUAS, ref. SEN 1/1/11, 18 November 1878; pp.295–300, letter from Robertson & Ross enclosing text of Charles Randolph's will.

26. GUAS, ref. SEN 1/1/11, 30 July 1878, 6 August 1878 and 14 August 1878; pp.201–11, copy of contract between the Principal and Professors of the University of Glasgow and John Thomson [sic] for Erection of Bute Hall and Substructure.

27. GUAS, ref. 21136, 1878; pp.6–9, specification of works in the erection of the Bute Hall for the University of Glasgow from designs of the late Sir George Gilbert Scott and under the direction of his sons, George Gilbert Scott and John Oldrid Scott.

28. *Glasgow Herald*, 2 February 1884, p.2.

29. *Glasgow Herald*, 1 February 1884, p.8. GUAS, ref. SEN 1/1/14, 13 January 1887; p.297, placing of portraits.

30. GUAS, ref. BUL 6/4/10, 14 December 1881; contract drawing for the Randolph Hall.

31. GUAS, ref. 2209, 10 February 1897; Works Committee Minute Book no.1, pp.136–37, Electric Lighting. GUAS, ref. BUL 6/4/34–36, 1950; drawing for proposed standard lamps by John Keppie, Henderson & J.L. Gleave. Information from David Gleave indicates that Joe Gleave was responsible for much of the design work in respect of the Bute Hall and Randolph Hall redecoration project of 1948–50.

32. GUAS, ref. 17146, 25 October 1864; Building Sub-Committee Minute Book no.1, pp.11–12, memorandum as to accommodation required in the new buildings to be submitted to Mr Scott.

33. *Glasgow Herald*, 20 June 1929, p.10.

34. GUAS, ref. BUL 6/4/28; design for Principal's chair.

35. GUAS, ref. C1/1/11, 11 February 1904; p.145, new organ for Bute Hall (records offer of April 1903 by Mr Carnegie to fund the organ) and ref. C1/1/12, 2 November 1905; p.24, report of Organ Committee on completion of the new organ.

36. GUAS, ref. BUL 6/4/25, n.d.; design for a gasolier to hang over the platform. GUAS, ref. 2209, 10 February 1987; Works Committee Minute Book no.1, pp.136–37, electric lighting.

37. GUAS, ref. 2210, 10 April 1899; Works Committee Minute Book no.2, pp.35–36, Caird Memorial Window.

38. Nichol 1903.

39. GUAS, C1/1/56, 24 February 1949; p.110, proposed re-decoration of the Bute Hall and p.176, 14 June 1949, proposed re-decoration of the Bute and Randolph Halls and their approaches, and C1/1/57, 8 November 1949; p.33, the Bute and Randolph Halls.

40. *Glasgow Evening Times*, 20 June 1951, p.2.

41. *Glasgow Herald*, 24 November 1984, p.3.

42. GUAS, ref. SEN 1/1/14, 5 November 1885; pp.182–83, screens in Cloisters.

43. GUAS, C1/1/56, 13 October 1948; p.5, McGill Memorial.

44. *Glasgow Herald*, 1 February 1884, p.8.

45. GUAS, ref. SEN 1/1/9, 10 February 1870; Senate Minutes 1869–73, p.15, minute of petition regarding erection of a gymnasium.

46. GUAS, ref. SEN 1/1/9, 28 July 1870; Senate Minutes 1869–73, p.67, report on gymnasium.

47. Peter C. McIntosh, 'MacLaren, Archibald (1819?–1884)', *Oxford Dictionary of National Biography*, 2004 (online edition, October 2009) [http://www.oxforddnb.com/view/article/50298, accessed 5 February 2012].

48. GUAS, ref. 2198, 9 February 1871; subscription prospectus.

49. GUAS, ref. 2174, 12 April 1872; letter from P.S. Young with enclosed order by Mr Burnet in favour of Hunter & Marshall for £294 5s 3d. *Building News*, 23 February 1872.

50. *Glasgow Herald*, 1 October 1852, p.2.

51. Mackenna 1981, pp.19–20.

52. GUAS, ref. SEN 1/1/10, 23 April 1874; p.86, athletic sports.

53. GUAS, ref. SEN 1/1/11, 6 March 1879; p.356, pavilion and p.363, 29 March 1879, pavilion.

54. Mackenna 1981, p.15.

55. GUAS, ref. 2210, 10 July 1899; Works Committee Book no.2, p.55, bicycle stable.

56. GUAS, ref. 2209, 5 May 1892; Works Committee Book no.1, p.32, new pavilion for Athletic Club. Mitchell Library, Dean of Guild Collection, ref. 1/1736, 25 February 1892; pavilion for Athletic Club.

57. Mitchell Library, Dean of Guild Collection, ref. 2/663, 3 September 1905, football pavilion.

58. Mackenna 1981, pp.31–32.

59. GUAS, refs. 15981–2, 17 June 1881; correspondence from John Burnet regarding the University's share of the costs of the lodge on Dumbarton Road.

60. GUAS, SEN 1/1/11, 4 November 1886; Senate Minutes, p.266, record of Andrew Cunninghame legacy and drawing by A.G. Thomson for completion of the spire. J.O. Scott to be consulted on stability of the tower and new spire.

61. GUAS, SEN 1/1/11, 25 November 1886; Senate Minutes, pp.281–82, copy of John Oldrid Scott's report on the tower.

62. Ibid.

63. Ibid.

64. GUAS, SEN 1/1/12, 7 October 1887; Senate Minutes, p.20, plans to be sent to Sir William Fettes Douglas.

65. GUAS, SEN 1/1/12, 7 October 1887; Senate Minutes, p.20, Sir William Thomson to provide specification of the lightning conductor.

66. GUAS, SEN 1/1/12, 28 July 1887; Senate Minutes, p.19, Scott provides plan and estimate for the clock and bells.

67. John Taylor & Co. Bell Catalogue, 1894, p.26; GUAS, SEN 1/1/12, 10 August 1888; Senate Minutes, p.177, mechanism working well and Mr Joyce's account of £207 to be paid, withholding £10 for 12 months.

68. GUAS, SEN 1/1/12, 26 July 1888; Senate Minutes, p.173, Old College bell sold to John Taylor & Co. for £29.

69. GUAS, refs 2411–15 and 56450, 1915–22; correspondence mainly with John Burnet & Son, concerning the installation in the tower of a clock donated by Major John Garroway.

70. GUAS, SEN 1/1/15, 24 August 1888; p.180, copy of Queen Victoria's address to the University.

71. GUAS, SEN 1/1/14, 29 January 1885; p.103, proposed Glasgow University Union.

72. GUAS, SEN 1/1/14, 12 November 1885; p.188, Students' Union – plans of proposed building.

73. *Glasgow Herald*, 13 December 1930, p.3.

74. GUAS, SEN 1/1/14, 29 April 1886; p.249, Students' Union building.

75. GUAS, SEN 1/1/14, 26 July 1886; p.252, Union building.

76. GUAS, SEN 1/1/15, 28 February 1888; p.113, Union building.

77. GUAS, SEN 1/1/15, 15 December 1887; p.56, gates at Union building.

78. GUAS, C1/1/4, 8 March 1893; pp.51–52, Union extension.

79. GUAS, ref. BUL 6/8/19–22, 10 June 1931; plans by T. Harold Hughes.

80. GUAS, SEN 1/1/14, 16 June 1885; p.170, removal of front of Old College.

81. GUAS, ref. 15728, August 1885; copy report from A.G. Thomson to Principal Caird on Pearce Lodge tenders.

82. GUAS, ref. 15727, 30 November and 6 December 1886; p.3, contract between Principal and Professors of the University of Glasgow and Morrison & Mason for removal and re-erection of the gateway building.

83. GUAS, ref. 21833, April 1892; design for railing extension by A.G. Thomson and ref. C1/1/6, 9 March 1899; p.190, resolve to replace wooden fence with iron railings from the old gateway at the West End Park to a point at the end of the professors' houses and ref. 2210, 6 March 1899; Works Committee Book no.2, p.34, railings in University Avenue.

84. GUAS, SEN 1/1/15, 12 January 1888; p.71, final building accounts and water account for Pearce Lodge and p.113, 23 February 1888, final payment to Thomson.

85. GUAS, SEN 1/1/14, 11 November 1886; p.272, old Forehall doorway to be installed at the head of the lion and unicorn stair with a new oak door.

CHAPTER SIX · PAGES 97–111

1. Moss, Munro and Trainor 2000, pp.106–07.

2. Coutts 1909, pp.457–63.

3. Coutts 1909, pp.465–66.

4. Thompson 1910, vol.2, note on p.1193 (Kelvin's house lighting).

5. GUAS, SEN 1/1/14, 23 April 1885; p.143, wire to Western Fire Office and SEN 1/1/15, 24 November 1887; p.42, proposed cloakroom.

6. GUAS, ref. C1/1/6, 8 March 1900; p.418, new Botanical laboratory, electric and gas lighting and ref. C1/1/8, 5 June 1901; p.69, electric lighting of University buildings.

7. Robins 1887, p.152 and plate 51.

8. GUAS, ref. C1/1/9, 5 March 1902; p.47, payment of account no.7 for lantern screen fixings.

9. GUAS, SEN 1/1/15, 30 May 1988; Senate Minutes, pp.168–70, statement by Frederick Bower on the state of the Botany Department.

10. GUAS, ref 6431, 1901; printed statement and appeal.

11. *Glasgow Herald*, 19 March 1900, p.4.

12. GUAS, ref. C1/1/6; unnumbered printed report at the back of this volume of Court Minutes relates to the Court meeting of 14 April 1899. The long and involved history of site selection for Botany and Engineering is retold here.

13. GUAS, ref. C1/1/5; Court Minute Book May 1895–February 1897, pp.285–86, 4 December 1896, minute recording alternative site plans prepared by Mr Burnet. For the first time there is a suggestion that the north boundary of the site at University Avenue might be used for a low building.

14. Dictionary of Scottish Architects, John James Burnet entry, accessed 21 February 2012.

15. See David M. Walker, 'Burnet, Sir John James (1857–1938)', *Oxford Dictionary of National Biography*, Oxford, 2004 (online edition, October 2008 [http://www.oxforddnb.com/view/article/32187, accessed 22 February 2012].

16. Mitchell Library, Dean of Guild Collection, plans registered 1 June 1891 by J.J. Burnet, ref. H/237.

17. GUAS, ref. C1/1/4, 17 April 1894; p.262, architect for Engineering laboratory and Botany Class buildings.

18. GUAS, ref. C1/1/4, 17 April 1894; p.263, Anatomy buildings at QMC.

19. Mackintosh had worked closely with Burnet on the construction of the Pathological Block at the Western Infirmary in 1894. His success here, and later in establishing the new out-patient department, led to a number of advisory positions on new hospital projects including the Glasgow Royal Infirmary, Glasgow Royal Hospital for Sick Children, Glasgow Maternity Hospital, Perth Infirmary, and further afield in South Africa. The laboratory study was presumably undertaken in anticipation of work for the University.

20. GUAS, ref. C1/1/5; Court Minute Book May 1895 – February 1897, pp.51–53, 22 July 1895, copy letter from Professor Barr to the Court requesting support for a trip to North America to view engineering laboratories and minute recording the Court's approval of £100.

21. Dictionary of Scottish Architects, John James Burnet entry, accessed 7 March 2012.

22. Information courtesy of Professor David M. Walker.

23. GUAS, ref. C1/1/20, 12 June 1913; p.109, the late Mr Oldrid Scott.

24. GUAS, ref. BUL 6/16/1–7, March 1914; block plans of various arrangements for new buildings.

25. The author is grateful to the 'Mackintosh Architecture: Context, Making and Meaning' Project Team for access to as yet unpublished material on the Queen Margaret College Anatomy building (www.mackintosh-architecture.gla.ac.uk).

26. GUAS, ref. C1/1/4; Court Minute Book, pp.262–63, 17 April 1894, architect for Engineering laboratory and Botany class buildings/ Anatomy buildings at QMC and ref. 2209; Works Committee Book no.1, p.76, 19 April 1894, architect for Engineering laboratory, Botany Class buildings and Anatomy buildings at QMC.

27. Dictionary of Scottish Architects, John Honeyman entry, accessed 7 March 2012.

28. Dictionary of Scottish Architects, John Honeyman entry, accessed 7 March 2012.

29. Hunterian Museum and Art Gallery, ref. GLAHA 52311–18, June 1894; sketch plans and elevations of Queen Margaret College Anatomy building and GLAHA 52311 signed 'John Honeyman & Keppie Architects. 140 Bath Street, Glasgow. June 1894', the rest 'John Honeyman & Keppies' Architects.

30. GUAS, ref. C1/1/4, 8 November 1894; Court Minute Book, pp.389–90, report of Commitee of Whole Court on QMC Anatomy Deptartment plans. Mitchell Library, Dean of Guild Court Collection, Register of New Buildings I, B4/11/1, 13 September 1894.

31. GUAS, ref. 2209, 19 April 1894; Works Committee Book no.1, p.83, QMC Anatomy buildings.

32. *Evening Times*, 7 March 1895.

33. Moffat and Baxter 1989, p.30.

34. *Glasgow Herald*, 11 April 1895, p.4 (report of the Glasgow Fine Art Institute). *British Architect*, 10 January 1896, p.22 and pp.26–27. *Academy Architecture* vol.8, May 1896, p.70, perspective and p.148, plans. The original pen and ink drawing was sold at Christie's, King Street, London, on 6 November 2002.

35. Hunterian Art Gallery, ref. GLAHA 52307–10 and 52354–5, June 1904; plans for a union hall and hall of residence.

36. GUAS, ref. DC233/2/13/1/2; Queen Margaret College Hall Co. Ltd share application, 1894. The author is grateful to Dr Nicky Imrie of the 'Mackintosh Architecture: Context, Making and Meaning' project for this reference and other information on this building (www.mackintosh-architecture.gla.ac.uk).

37. Coutts 1909, p.468.

38. *The Builder*, 28 April 1900, p.422.

39. Coutts 1901, pp.82–96.

40. J.W. French, 'Barr, Archibald (1855–1931)', Revd Iain F. Russell, *Oxford Dictionary of National Biography*, Oxford, 2004 (online edition, October 2005) [http://www.oxforddnb.com/view/article/30615, accessed 28 February 2012]

41. GUAS, ref. 55422; 19 November 1891; Memorial to the University Court regarding a site for the proposed Engineering laboratories from the Professor of Engineering.

42. GUAS, ref. C1/1/4, 11 January 1894; p.464, letter from Professor Barr.

43. GUAS, C1/1/9, 6 January 1902; p.30, payment to William Shireffs '*on account of Modelling and Stone Carving Work at Engineering Laboratory*'. Shireffs was a fellow member of the Glasgow Art Club with Burnet.

44. Mitchell Library, Dean of Guild Collection, drawings registered 28 September 1899, ref.1/7416.

45. GUAS, BUL 6/6/1–88; plans 1895–1901.

46. GUAS, C1/1/9, 4 February 1902; p.36, payment of £250 to the Otis Elevator Co. Ltd.

47. Cormack 1902, p.20.

48. GUAS, ref. C1/1/6, 3 May 1900; p.464, donation of volumes to the Engineering library. Lindsay, Burnet & Co. supplied the new building's air heater and valves.

49. GUAS, ref. C1/1/27, 21 January and 4 May 1920; p.47 and p.93, extension of Engineering Department.

50. *Glasgow Herald*, 5 November 1959, p.8.

51. GUAS, ref. C1/1/6, 12 October 1899; p.310, J.B. Thompson bequest and ref. C1/1/6, 9 April 1900; p.440, increase in Thompson grant for Anatomy.

52. GUAS, ref. BUL 6/7/1–5; plans by John Burnet & Son, January 1884.

53. GUAS, ref. C1/1/55, 25 September 1947; p.14, Anatomy Department – cloakroom accommodation.

54. GUAS, ref. C1/1/7, 23 July 1900; pp.55–56, Surgical laboratory plans.

55. GUAS, ref. C1/1/8, 4 March 1901; p.37, Surgical laboratory.

56. GUAS, ref. C1/1/28, 27 June 1922; p.103, Surgery Department water sprinklers.

57. GUAS, ref. 72710, n.d.; instructions to architects submitting Designs for 1. A New Building for the Department of Natural Philosophy; and 2. A New Building for the Departments of Physiology, Materia Medica, and Forensic Medicine and Public Health.

58. GUAS, ref. C1/1/9, Appendix, 6 December 1901; reports on the needs of the University at the present time in regard to equipment.

59. GUAS, ref. C1/2/1, 8 January 1903; pp.52–55, Joint Committee on laboratory requirements.

60. GUAS, ref. C1/2/1, 1 October 1903; pp.110–11, new buildings for Natural Philosophy, Physiology, etc.

61. Dictionary of Scottish Architects, Glasgow University, Materia Medica and Physiology buildings, accessed 24 March 2012.

62. GUAS, BUL 6/9/12–14, 10 December 1902; various block plans by James Miller for the Natural Philosophy and Medical departments.

63. GUAS, ref. 73394, December 1902; memoranda on proposed new buildings by James Miller, Honeyman, Keppie & Mackintosh, H.E. Clifford and MacWhannell & Rogerson and GUAS, ref. BUL 6/12/1–3, circa December 1902; McWhannell & Rogerson plans and elevations for the West Medical building.

64. The author is grateful to Dr Nicky Imrie of the Hunterian Museum and Art Gallery's 'Mackintosh Architecture: Context, Making and Meaning' project for drawing his attention to this unpublished letter. Quoted by kind permission of the Werkbundarchiv, Museum der Dinge, Berlin [Muthesius Collection, letter from Mackintosh to Muthesius, 19 November 1902].

65. Ashwell and Nesbit, 1906, p.13.

66. GUAS, ref. C1/2/2, 1 November 1906; p.162, Animal Houses.

67. *Glasgow Herald*, 24 April 1907, pp.4–5.

68. GUAS, ref. C1/1/76, 7 October 1968; p.17, Department of Pharmacology, West Medical building.

69. GUAS, ref. C1/2/2, 14 December 1905; p.40, electric light in Natural Philosophy department.

70. GUAS, ref. C1/2/3, 6 June 1907; p.11, tests in physical laboratory.

71. GUAS, ref. C1/1/29, 4 January 1922; p.37, Natural Philosophy laboratory – Mr James Miller's fee.

72. GUAS, ref. BUL 6/15/1, 1 May 1911; plans issued from 245 St Vincent Street, the office of the architects H. & D. Barclay, according to the Glasgow Post Office Directory of 1912–13 and Simpson and Brown 2012, building 123.

73. Simpson and Brown 2012, p.116.

CHAPTER SEVEN · PAGES 113–29

1. GUAS, ref. C1/2/4, 3 July 1913; p.271–73, Carnegie Trust Grant.

2. GUAS, ref. 73394, 11 March 1914; report by John James Burnet LLD on University buildings extension and 28 April 1914, report of the Buildings Committee. GUAS, ref. C1/2/4, 14 May 1914; p.338, report of New Buildings Committee and C1/1/21, 11 December 1913, p.26, new buildings, payment of fee for preliminary report and plans.

3. GUAS, ref. C1/2/4, 1 October 1914; p.376–78, new buildings for Arts and Zoology – agreement with architect.

4. GUAS, ref. C1/2/7, 6 July 1922; p.268, purchase of no.1 University Gardens for Women's Union.

5. *Nature* no.147, 5 April 1941, p.411, University of Glasgow: air raid damage.

6. GUAS, ref. C1/1/56, 2 December 1946; p.39, main building – south front.

7. Moss, Munro and Trainor 2000, pp.190–91.

8. GUAS, ref. BUL 6/16/2–7, March 1914; plans and elevations for proposed Zoology building.

9. GUAS, ref. C1/2/5, 13 December 1917, p.322, letter from Professor Graham Kerr.

10. GUAS, ref. 56588, 12 July 1920; approximate cost of new Natural History building – trade estimates provided by Dansken & Purdie, Surveyors; GUAS, ref. BUL6/16/8–95, May 1921 – December 1922; plans, elevations, sections and details for proposed Zoology building.

11. GUAS, ref. C1/2/7, 9 March 1921; p.40, new Zoology building tenders; C1/2/7, 10 November 1921; p.157, contracts for new Zoology building; ref. 56448; 1921, legal papers and correspondence relating to new Zoology/Natural History building, including contracts between University and various contractors. The Clerk of Works was John Martin (also for Natural Philosophy and West Medical) and the main contractors were: Alexander Muir & Sons (mason, brick and excavation); Stuarts Granolithic Co. (patent concrete floors and roofs); Ashwell & Nesbit (heating, ventilation); Dansken & Purdie (measurers); Redpath Brown & Co. (structural steel); and Bennets (furnishings).

12. Dictionary of Scottish Architects, Norman Aitken Dick entry, accessed 25 March 2012.

13. GUAS, ref. 56461, 1920–5, Zoology building correspondence. A number of the letters from Professsor Graham Kerr refer to Norman Dick.

14. GUAS, ref. 30 October 1923; letter from John Martin, Clerk of Works, to Alan Ernest Clapperton, Court Secretary, regarding worm holes in the new teak benches of the Zoology building.

15. *The Builder*, 30 October 1925, p.634.

16. GUAS, ref. 56461, February 1924; various correspondence about the cinematograph projector purchased by Professor Graham Kerr without checking the electrical connections.

17. GUAS, ref. C1/1/72, 13 January 1964; p.12, Department of Zoology – alterations; ref. C1/1/76, 2 December 1968; p.113, minor works programme for 1967–68.

18. GUAS, ref. BUL 6/16/3, March 1914; block plan showing proposed additions.

19. GUAS, ref. C1/1/67, 12 January 1960; p.527, W.92, Zoology Department.

20. GUAS, ref. 72653, 28 March 1927; letter from John Burnet, Son & Dick to the University Court.

21. GUAS, ref. BUL 6/5/106–199, November 1923; survey and proposal drawings for the lion and unicorn stair.

22. GUAS, ref. C1/2/7, 11 January1923, pp.338–39; report of committee on new Arts building.

23. Drawings of the stonework were marked 'rough for carver', e.g., BUL 6/5/159.

24. GUAS, ref. 72653, 26 April 1927; letter from John Burnet, Son & Dick to Alan Clapperton.

25. GUAS, ref. 72653, 1922–28; Memorial Chapel papers, including correspondence about the organ. Embarrassingly Burnet consulted with organ makers Hill, Norman & Beard for twelve years on the advice of the eminent Glasgow chemist, Sir George Beilby, but when the Court came to commission the work, they opted for the rival firm of Willis & Son.

26. GUAS ref. 72653, 7–18 August 1928; various correspondence regarding the carved work in the Chapel. *Glasgow Herald*, 18 April 1938, p.13; obituary of Dawson describes him as being responsible for 'the internal wood carvings and stone mouldings of Glasgow University Memorial Chapel'.

27. *Glasgow Herald*, 4 October 1929, p.5 and p.12; and 5 October 1929, p.5 and p.9. see also GUAS, ref. 57404, 9 April 1929, invoice from Galbraith & Winton.

28. GUAS, ref. 8/669, 8 December 1930; p.3, Dr Strachan's report on stained glass windows of Chapel.

29. GUAS, ref. 72653, 1951–57; various correspondence between Hector Hetherington, Joe Gleave, Sadie McLellan and Gordon Webster.

30. GUAS, ref. 8/671, 29 October 1958; letter from Principal Hetherington to Sir Basil Spence regarding selection of an artist for the east window of the Chapel.

31. GUAS, ref. 8/671, 3 November 1958; letter from Sir Basil Spence to Principal Hetherington regarding selection of an artist for the east window of the Chapel.

32. *Glasgow Herald*, 14 May 1962, p.6.

33. GUAS, ref. 56389, 1979; Court correspondence concerning the competition for stained glass windows on the occasion of the fiftieth anniversary of Glasgow University Chapel, including details of competition, list of competitors and the final result.

34. GUAS, ref. C1/1/57, 28 April 1953; p.224, University Chapel.

35. GUAS, ref. 72653, 14 January 1959 and 15 January 1959; letters between Hector Hetherington and Ian G. Lindsay regarding lighting in the Chapel. RCAHMS, ref. IGL W627/1–3, August 1967; perspectives, plans and elevations for new seating and lighting at the west end of Glasgow University Memorial Chapel. GUAS ref. BUL 6/5/224–5, no date; copies of some of the RCAHMS material.

36. GUAS, ref. BUL 6/17/1–3, July 1915; designs for the Hunter Memorial.

37. *Glasgow Herald*, 4 December 1930, p.7.

38. *Glasgow Herald*, 12 December 1930, p.5 and 13 December 1930, p.3.

39. GUAS, ref. C1/1/55, p.116, 19 February 1948; new Refectory.

40. *Glasgow Herald*, 27 January 1963, p.1; Wilson 1962–63, p.10.

41. GUAS, ref. C1/2/11, 8 February 1934; pp.220–23, needs of the University: Chemistry Institute etc.

42. GUAS, ref. C1/212, 27 June 1935; p.95, new Chemistry building.

43. GUAS, ref. C1/2/12, 21 April 1936; pp.240–41, new Chemistry building.

44. Dictionary of Scottish Architects, Thomas Harold Hughes entry, accessed 27 March 2012.

45. GUAS, ref. C1/2/11, 6 June 1934; p.317, University Athletic Ground – pavilion at Garscadden.

46. GUAS, ref. C1/2/12, 7 October 1936; p.311, appeal for funds for new Chemistry building and other purposes.

47. GUAS, ref. C1/2/13, 9 July 1937; p.50; new Chemistry building.

48. GUAS, ref. C1/2/13, 9 July 1937; pp.44–53, new Chemistry building.

49. *RIAS Quarterly* no.50, August 1935; p.11.

50. GUAS, C1/2/13, 31 October 1939; p.391, Chemistry building and Reading Room.

51. GUAS, ref. DC 008/608, 1939–40; correspondence between Principal Hetherington and the Admiralty.

52. GUAS, ref. C1/2/12, 4 June 1940; p.475, camouflage for new buildings.

53. GUAS, ref. C1/1/56, p.40, 2 December 1946; p.40, Department of Chemistry – Inorganic Chemistry block.

54. GUAS, ref. BUL 6/19/14–32, August 1947 to September 1949; drawings by Hughes & Waugh for the Inorganic Chemistry department and ref. C1/1/55, 13 May 1948, p.180; Chemistry building.

55. GUAS, ref. C1/1/57, 3 February 1953; p.146, W159 Chemistry Department.

56. GUAS, ref. C1/1/66, 4 November 1958; p.75, Chemistry building: metal windows.

57. GUAS, ref. BUL 6/19/36–45, March 1958 to September 1961; plans by Alexander Wright & Kay, UGC 1960–61, p.5.

58. GUAS, ref. C1/2/13, 2 June 1937; p.513, communication fom University Grants Committee.

59. GUAS, ref. C1/2/13, 3 May 1939; p.32 new Reading Room donation by Bellahouston Trustees.

60. GUAS, ref. DC 8/806, 1 June 1937; letter from Hector Hetherington to John Beresford, University Grants Committee.

61. *The Builder*, 17 October 1941, pp.348–50.

62. GUAS, ref. C1/2/12, 2 June 1937; pp.505–07, sale of Observatory.

63. GUAS, ref. C1/2/12, 2 June 1937; p.507, offer for ground in University Gardens.

64. Dictionary of Scottish Architects, Stewart & Paterson entry, accessed 7 April 2012.

65. GUAS, ref. BUL 6/23/2–12, October 1937 to August 1938; drawings for the Observatory, University Gardens, by Stewart & Paterson.

66. Roy 1993, p.395.

CHAPTER EIGHT · PAGES 131–47

1. GUAS, ref. BE/57/3, 10 January 1945; minute of meeting of the Works Committee of the University Court.

2. GUAS, ref. C1/1/56, 2 December 1946; p.39, main building – south front.

3. GUAS, ref. C1/1/67, 12 January 1960; pp.169–70, war damage repairs.

4. GUAS, ref. C1/1/54, 20 June 1946; p.163, War Memorial.

5. Moss, Munro and Trainor 2000, p.217.

6. UGC Development 1962–67, p.148, paragraph 476.

7. Muthesius 2001, p.106.

8. GUAS, C1/1/54, 15 May 1947; p.147, extra-mural medical schools, Anderson College, St Mungo's College.

9. Moss, Munro and Trainor 2000, p.223 and p.230.

10. GUAS, C1/1/56, 14 June 1949; p.176, alterations to University offices.

11. GUAS, ref. C1/1/54, 17 April 1947; p.129, ground at Garscube and 15 May 1947; pp.148–49, Garscube ground and C1/1/55, 19 February 1948; p.114, Garscube House. *Glasgow Herald*, 30 October 1947, p.4.

12. GUAS, ref. C1/1/57, 27 October 1949; pp.29–30, Fifth Centenery (plans for celebrations).

13. GUAS, ref. 69991, 19 March 1954; programme for inauguration of new buildings by the Rt Hon. James Stuart, Secretary of State for Scotland.

14. Moss, Munro and Trainor 2000, pp.251–53.

15. GUAS, ref. BE/57/3, 10 January 1945; minute of the Works Committee of the University Court.

16. Dictionary of Scottish Architects, Frank Charles Mears entry, accessed 23 April 2012.

17. GUAS, ref. C1/1/55, 19 February 1948; p.117, development programme, site plan.

18. GUAS, ref. C1/1/56, 14 June 1949; p.174, underpinning at old mineral workings.

19. GUAS, C1/1/57, 6 July 1950; Ministry of Town and Country Planning: communication to the Secretary of University Grants Committee.

20. Local authorities were first required to produce local development plans under the provisions of the Town and Country Planning (Scotland) Act 1947.

21. GUAS, ref. C1/1/58, 19 April 1951; p.205, development plan – report by Sir Frank Mears.

22. City Plan 1951, p.13, p.54, p.58 and accompanying loose 'main proposals' and 'proposed arterial road system' maps.

23. GUAS, ref. C1/1/56, 28 October 1948; p.28, area of development.

24. GUAS, ref. BE/57/3, January 1951; University of Glasgow proposed redevelopment plan, p.14.

25. GUAS, ref. C1/1/56, 6 October 1948; p.2, alternating current electrical supply and rewiring.

26. GUAS, ref. C1/1/56, 6 October 1948; p.2, transfer of departments.

27. GUAS, ref. C1/1/54, 4 June 1947; p.155, Natural Philosophy calculator, duplicator.

28. GUAS, ref. C1/1/55, 8 October 1947; p.21, applications for apparatus.

29. Curran 2004.

30. GUAS, ref. C1/1/54, 23 January 1947; p.66, Natural Philosophy Department: Department of Scientific & Industrial Research: Synchrotron and grant towards purchase of high-voltage generator.

31. Fenton 2012, p.118.

32. GUAS, ref. C1/1/55, 13 May 1948; p.180, Natural Philosophy building – plans.

33. GUAS, C1/1/56, 24 November 1948; p.40, extension to Natural Philosophy Department.

34. GUAS, ref. C1/1/55, 5 February 1947; p.107, Natural Philosophy extension.

35. GUAS, ref. C1/1/56, 5 February 1947; p.75, Natural Philosophy extension.

36. GUAS, ref. C1/1/55, 5 February 1947; p.107, building programme and Natural Philosophy extension and p.138, 18 March 1948, building programme.

37. GUAS, ref. C1/1/55, 13 May 1948; p.180, motion by Professor MacRobert.

38. GUAS, 1/1/55, 8 July 1948; p.224, Natural Philosophy extension.

39. GUAS, ref. 8/939, 1959; circular from Professor Philip Dee to Professor Thomas Wilson, reassuring him on the possible dangers in the University houses and gardens from radiation hazards caused by the Synchrotron.

40. GUAS, C1/1/56, 14 June 1949; p.175, Natural Philosophy extension.

41. Smith 2009.

42. RCAHMS, Sir Basil Spence Archive, ref. SGF 1940/1/1–55.

43. Duncan 1966, p.A40 (advertisement for 'Race' seating).

44. GUAS, ref. C1/1/55, 15 April 1948; p.157, Engineering building – architect.

45. GUAS, ref. IC1/1/55, 13 May 1948; p.180, Physiology Department lecture room.

46. *Glasgow Herald*, 5 November 1959, p.9.

47. GUAS, ref. C1/1/69, 6 February 1962; p.169, Engineering south building.

48. Sharples 2004, p.225.

49. GUAS, ref. C1/1/66, 3 March 1959; p.224, Engineering south building and GUL Special Collections, ref. MS Gen 537/54–74, 2 July 1958 – April 1960; miscellaneous letters from

Eric Kennington to Eric Stanford regarding the 'Progress of Science' sculpture.

50. *Glasgow Herald*, 5 November 1959, p.8.

51. Wright 1991, p.432 and p.434.

52. Information courtesy of David Sutherland Gleave.

53. GUAS, ref. C1/1/57, 17 September 1953; p.310, letter from Glasgow Institute of Architects – building programme.

54. GUAS, ref. C1/1/57, 15 December 1952; p.105, new Arts building – architectural competition (selection of architect) and p.128, 7 January1953, new Arts building – architectural competition (payment of competitor and assessor fees). Also, *The Builder* 30 January 1953, pp.188–89, p.200.

55. GUAS, ref. C1/1/57, 6 January 1953; p.126, new Arts building (exhibition of entries).

56. GUAS, ref. C1/1/66, 30 September 1958; pp.4–5, Arts building.

57. GUAS, ref. 56389, 9 October 1979; letter from Secretary of the University Court to W.N.W. Ramsay.

58. Dictionary of Scottish Architects, Anderson's College Medical School entry, accessed 18 January 2012.

59. Fenton 2012, p.120.

60. RCAHMS, Basil Spence Collection, ref. SPE SCT/34/2/1/1 (Virology only perspective sketch); SPE SCT/34/2/2/1 (layout and sketch designs for Virology and Genetics).

61. GUAS, ref. C1/1/68, 8 November 1960; p.72, Anderson College Development.

62. GUAS, ref. C1/1/66, 2 December 1958; p.105, tenders for Virology.

63. GUAS, ref. C1/1/69, 10 January 1961; p.168, Institute of Genetics.

64. GUAS, ref. C1/1/45, 9 December 1937; p.120, report of committee on building policy.

65. GUAS, ref. C1/1/45, 13 January 1938; p.131, University Avenue – Gibson Street site.

66. GUAS, ref. C1/1/53, 12 August 1946; p.177, architects for building schemes.

67. GUAS, ref. C1/1/66, 30 September 1958; pp.6–7, Physical Education building.

68. GUAS, ref. C1/1/65, 3 March 1958; p.225, Physical Education building.

69. *Glasgow Herald*, 9 January 1961, p.8 and p.12.

70. GUAS, C1/1/56, 24 November 1948; pp.36–37, report of sub-committee on heating system.

71. GUAS, C1/1/57, 8 November 1949; p.31, contract for construction of new boilerhouse.

72. GUAS, ref. C1/1/69, 6 March 1962; p.206, boilerhouse.

73. GUAS, ref. C1/1/68, 23 March 1961; p.275, new buildings – Garscube, records concerns about inadequacies in Coia's organisation during construction of the Veterinary Hospital and p.418, 13 July 1961, enquiries about Coia's organisation are inconclusive and the Court Secretary is unable to reassure the Court that future commissions will be 'less troublesome than the last'.

74. GUAS, ref. C1/1/68, 9 May 1961; p.326, Biochemistry building and p.365, 6 June 1961, Biochemistry building (heating and ventilation).

75. GUAS, ref. C1/1/59, 22 March 1962; p.220, Biochemistry building.

76. GUAS, ref. C1/1/54, 5 March 1947; p.97, new Surgery building.

77. GUAS, ref. C1/1/55, 8 July 1948; p.224, new buildings.

78. GUAS, ref. C1/1/56, 14 June 1949; p.174, Garscube Estate – proposed site for Animal Hospital.

79. GUAS, ref. C1/1/56, 8 August 1949; p.174, Garscube House – use of present building.

CHAPTER NINE · PAGES 149–83

1. For an example of the critical articles, see *Architects' Journal* 9 January 1958, p.37.

2. Muthesius 2000, pp.11–58.

3. UGC Development 1957–61, p.19, p.28.

4. PAC 1967, p.160.

5. University of Warwick Library, Modern Records Centre, ref. MSS.399/3/BDG/2, June 1965-June 1970; Committee of Vice-Chancellors and Principals of the Universities of the UK, building sub-committee minute books.

6. Health 1960, p.101.

7. Donnison and Middleton 1987, p.74.

8. Glendinning and Muthesius 1993, p.224.

9. Glendinning 1997, p.78.

10. GUAS, ref. BE 56383, 1967; part development plan for Partick Comprehensive Development Area.

11. Glendinning 1997, p.78.

12. GUAS, ref. BE/55/02, 3 November 1966; letter from Glasgow Corporation to the Secretary to the University Court.

13. Walker 1994, p.81.

14. GUAS, ref. BE/94/8, July 1978; University development plan – explanatory statement.

15. *Architectural Review*, vol.136, July, 1964, p.9, 'University in the City' editorial.

16. GUAS, ref. C1/1/67, 28 January 1960; pp.192–93, building programme 1964–68, quoting letter of 8 January 1964 from the University Grants Committee to the Principal.

17. GUAS, ref. C1/1/68, 23 February 1961; p.221, Carnegie Trust, Eleventh Quinquennial Distribution, 1962–67.

18. University Report 1964–66, p.3.

19. National Archives, ref. CAB 129/114, 30 September 1963; p.1, memorandum by the Chief Secretary to the Treasury and Paymaster General, John Boyd-Carpenter, in response to the Robbins Report.

20. National Archives, ref. CAB 129/114, 30 September 1963; p.2, memorandum by the Chief Secretary to the Treasury and Paymaster General, John Boyd-Carpenter, in response to the Robbins Report.

21. *Glasgow Herald*, 27 April 1961, p.9.

22. Hansard, House of Commons Debate (Balance of Payments, Government Measures), 27 June 1965, vol. 717, cc228–41.

23. UGC Development 1962–67, p.152.

24. *Glasgow Herald*, 17 January 1968, p.1.

25. GUAS, ref. BE 56383, 10 September 1970; minutes of Corporation/University working party on University development.

26. UGC Survey 1979–80, p.13.

27. Whyte (Leicester) 2008, pp.12–13.

28. University Report 1964–66, p.3.

29. *Glasgow Herald*, 11 December 1971, p.13.

30. UGC Returns 1960–61, p.36.

31. University Report 1970–71, p.64.

32. Moss, Munro and Trainor 2000, p.283.

33. GUAS, ref. C1/1/67, 28 January 1960; pp.332–34, memorandum to the UGC on numbers and buildings.

34. *Glasgow Herald*, 19 June 1954, p.7.

35. Dictionary of Scottish Architects, Joseph Lea Gleave entry, accessed 24 July 2012.

36. *Edinburgh Gazette*, 21 January 1958, p.36.

37. *Edinburgh Gazette*, 23 September 1960, p.1.

38. GUAS, ref. 56383, 11 April 1959; copy letter from Town Clerk Depute to the Secretary of the University Court.

39. GUAS, ref. BE/139/8, 1 August 1960; copy letter of appointment from the Secretary of the University Court to J.L. Gleave.

40. GUAS, ref. BE/139/8, 3 August 1960, letter from Sir Hector Hetherington to Joseph Gleave.

41. Whyte (Leeds) 2008, pp.181–83.

42. GUAS, ref. BE/139/8, 15 March 1960; minute of meeting of representatives of Court and Senate. This refers to Gleave being 'already in a position to present a report'.

43. GUAS, ref. BE/139/8, 20 June 1960; Hillhead Development Committee minutes.

44. GUAS, ref. BE/139/9, 16 March 1962; minute of meeting of architects engaged on projects in the Hillhead Development Area.

45. GUAS, ref. BE 139/8, 30 May 1960; letter from J. L. Gleave to Robert Hutcheson, p.2.

46. *Glasgow Herald*, 20 October 1960, p.16.

47. GUAS, ref. BE 139/8, 15 March 1962; minute of a meeting of architects engaged on projects in the Hillhead Development Area, p.3.

48. *Glasgow Herald*, 21 August 1963, p.14.

49. GUAS, ref. BE/139/8, 30 July 1962; letter from D. Mansley to J.L. Gleave.

50. GUAS, ref. BE/13/10, November 1965; Hillhead Precinct: Report Number One, by Hugh Wilson and Lewis Womersley.

51. GUAS, ref. 54/26, 13 May 1966; University of Glasgow – Hillhead Development: landscape principles.

52. GUAS, ref. BE/146/6, 1970–71; various correspondence between Robert Hutcheson and Sir Hugh Wilson regarding the appointment of an architect/planner.

53. GUAS, ref. 56383, 29 April 1971; minute of Corporation/University Working Party on University development.

54. GUAS, ref. BE/146/7, 1971; University development plan – preliminary report.

55. GUAS, ref. BE/146/7, 7 November 1974; University of Glasgow expansion report by the Planning Department of Glasgow Corporation, p.3.

56. GUAS, ref. BE/146/7, March 1978; '*Report on the Future Planning of the University of Glasgow*' by J.H. Rae, Director of Planning at the City of Glasgow District Council.

57. GUAS, ref. BE/146/7, 20 July 1978; explanatory statement attached to a letter from the University's Assistant Planning Officer to the Director of Planning at the City of Glasgow District Council.

58. GUAS, ref. BE/94/8, 5 December 1980; letter from the Secretary of the University Court to the Director of Planning.

59. GUAS, ref. BUL 6/58/45, November 1978; environmental and landscape strategy plan.

60. GUAS, ref. 53929, June 1967; development report on Veterinary Site, Garscube, Building Design Partnership.

61. University Report 1964–66, pp.17–18.

62. University Report 1964–66, p.13.

63. UGC Development 1957–61, p.19.

64. *Glasgow Herald*, 10 February 1958, p.6.

65. GUAS, ref. BE/139/8, 30 September 1960; copy letter from Secretary of University Court to Frank Fielden.

66. *Glasgow Herald*, 31 May 1966, p.12 (Construction Review).

67. GUAS, ref. CI/1/69, 6 March 1962; p.210, Refectory.

68. *Glasgow Herald*, 21 August 1963, p.14.

69. GUAS, ref. BE/139/8, 21 October 1960; Hillhead Development informal meeting, p.1.

70. GUAS, ref. CI/1/68, 23 March 1961; p.277, reports of the Refectory Committee and p.315, 27 April 1961; report of the Refectory Committee.

71. *Glasgow Herald*, 31 May 1966, p.12 (Construction Review).

72. GUAS, ref. CI/1/76, 3 February 1969; p.197, Hillhead Refectory (costs).

73. *Glasgow Herald*, 1 July 1981, p.3 and 15 May 1982, p.3.

74. GUAS, ref. CI/177, 6 October 1969; p.15, Hillhead Refectory landscaping.

75. Julie Gardham, text describing the University's copy of Fuchs' great herbal, *De Historia Stirpium*, at: http://special.lib.gla.ac.uk/exhibns/month/oct2002.html [accessed 3 June 2012].

76. GUAS, ref. BE/139/8, 26 October 1960; Hillhead Development Committee minutes, p.2.

77. GUAS, ref. BE/139/8, March 1960; proposed new Social Studies building – provisional list of subjects to be accommodated.

78. Moss, Munro and Trainor 2000, p.284.

79. University Report 1966–67, p.15.

80. GUL, Special Collections, ref. MS Gen 1751/2/1/4/3, 31 October 1959, memorandum on planning of a new Library.

81. GUAS, ref. BE/139/8, 26 October 1960; Hillhead Development Committee minutes, p.1.

82. GUAS, ref. CI/1/68, 24 November 1760, p.83, Hillhead Development and p.148, 19 December 1960; Hillhead Development ref. BE/139/8, 21 and 23 November 1960; letters from Leslie Martin and Frederick Gibberd declining work on the Hillhead Development.

83. GUAS, ref. CI/1/68, 7 February 1961, p.207, Hillhead Development, Library and Art Gallery.

84. GUL, Special Collections, MS Gen 1751/2/1–2, 1962–68; papers of Robert MacKenna relating to the construction of the new Library, including notes of visits, equipment, furnishings, furniture and correspondence and meetings with William Whitfield.

85. GUL, Special Collections, [uncatalogued], 4-page typescript 'Glasgow University Library' with building outline and specifications; 5-page typescript brief 'University of Glasgow: outline programme for new library building (revised: July 1962)'; reports of the Library Committee, sessions 1961–62 to 1971–72.

86. GUAS, ref. CI/1/68, 13 July 1961, p.405; Library and Art Gallery.

87. GUL, Special Collections, ref. MS Gen 1751/2/2/1, 1964; various dates, copy letters from R.O. MacKenna to overseas librarians arranging visits with William Whitfield.

88. GUL, Special Collections, ref. MS Gen 1751/2/1/4/1, 1954–62; new library building: early steps in planning.

89. GUAS, ref. CI/1/68, 13 July 1961; p.405, Library and Art Gallery.

90. Glendinning 1997, pp.140–41 and Saint 2007, p.405.

91. Glendinning 1997, p.142.

92. GUAS, ref. CI/1/69, 17 April 1962; p.245, University Library.

93. GUAS, ref. CI/1/65, 5 February 1968; p.179, Library stage I.

94. *Design*, vol.206, London, February 1966, p.62.

95. GUAS, ref. CI/176, 3 February 1969; p.197, Library.

96. GUAS, ref. CI/1/76, 2 June 1969; p.362, Library stage I.

97. A number of heating, ventilation and other mechanical faults are identified in Robert MacKenna's papers: GUL, Special Collections, ref. MS Gen 1751/2/, 1962–68; papers of Robert MacKenna relating to the construction of the new Library.

98. GUAS, ref. BE/146/7, 20 July 1978; explanatory statement attached to a letter from the University's Assistant Planning Officer to the Director of Planning at the City of Glasgow District Council.

99. GUL, Special Collections, ref. MS Gen 1751/2/10/3–4, 15 March 1972 – 21 April 1972; plans relating to the construction of the new entrance to the Library.

100. GUAS, ref. BE/94/8, 16 February 1979; letter from the University Buildings Officer to J.H. Rae, Director of Planning regarding the Hetherington Building and Library extension. See also unexecuted plans by Whitfield Partners for phase 2 of the Library and GUL, Special Collections, ref. MS Gen 1751/2/11, 3 June 1972; two alternative schemes for extending the Library to the north by Whitfield Partners.

101. Rodger 1999, pp.89–90

102. Farr 2004.

103. Keppie 2007, pp.106–07.

104. GUAS, ref. 56384, April 1962; memorandum on the Fine Art building.

105. GUAS, ref. CI/1/73, 20 December 1965; p.128, Art Gallery.

106. GUAS, ref. 56384, 24 April 1970; minute of the Museum Extension Progressing Committee.

107. GUAS, ref. 56384, August 1972; memorandum from the Honorary Keeper, Andrew McLaren Young.

108. GUAS, ref. 56384, March 1971; 'The New Building by the University of Glasgow for the University Art Collections and for Temporary Exhibitions' by Andrew McLaren Young.

109. GUAS, ref. 56384, 7 June 1971; supplementary minutes of the Works Committee.

110. There are numerous Court Minute Book references to the problems at the Art Gallery during the late 1970s. A sample can be found at GUAS, ref. CI/1/85/1; appendices to the minute of the Works Committee of 3 October 1977, p.6.

111. GUAS, ref. CI/1/86/1; appendices to the minute of the Works Committee of 2 October 1978, p.8 (Hunterian Art Gallery).

112. Moss, Munro and Trainor 2000, p.300.

113. GUAS, ref. 62967, 15 January 1976 to 15 February 1977; various minutes and correspondence between the University and the Scottish Arts Council regarding the Paolozzi doors.

114. Scalbert 2000. GUAS, ref. BE/139/9, 15 June 1976; minute by J. McCargow, Secretary to the University Court, recording Paolozzi's praise of Whitfield's design.

115. The history of the house and its contents is described comprehensively in Robertson 1998.

116. GUAS, ref. CI/1/56, 15 March 1949; p.118, 78 Southpark Avenue.

117. GUAS, ref. CI/1/57, 2 December 1952; p.84, 78 Southpark Avenue.

118. See Walker 1994 for a history of listing.

119. GUAS, ref. CI/1/68, 19 November 1960; p.147, transcript of letter of 30 January 1960 from the department of Health for Scotland regarding reports in the *Glasgow Herald* of demolition proposals for 78 Southpark Avenue.

120. GUAS, ref. BE/139/8, 30 May 1961; letter from William Whitfield to R.T. Hutcheson, Secretary of the University Court.

121. GUAS, ref. BE/139/8, 30 May 1961; letter from William Whitfield to R.T. Hutcheson, Secretary of the University Court.

122. GUAS, ref. CI/1/69, 22 March 1962; p.232, Hillhead Development.

123. Information courtesy of the 'Mackintosh Architecture: Context, Making and Meaning' project: (www.mackintosh-architecture.gla.ac.uk).

124. Unpublished transcript of Simpson & Brown Architects' interview with Sir William Whitfield and Andrew Lockwood, 26 August 2010, p.54.

125. GUAS, CI/1/68, 8 November 1960; p.74, Union extension.

126. GUAS, CI/1/68, 9 May 1961; p.326, Union extension.

127. GUAS, CI/1/77, 3 November 1969; p.73, Students' Union beer bar extension.

128. GUAS, ref. CI/1/68, 27 October 1960; p.49, Gilmorehill Church.

129. GUAS, ref. CI/1/68, 7 February 1961; p.206, Gilmorehill Church and p.24, 7 March 1961, Gilmorehill Church.

130. Rodger 1999, p.90.

131. GUAS, ref. CI/1/68, 7 February 1961; p.211, new building.

132. GUAS, ref. CI/1/69, 22 March 1962; p.232, Queen Margaret Union.

133. GUAS, ref. BE/139/8, 9 May 1961; minute of the Hillhead Committee, and 27 May 1961, letter from the Secretary of the University Court to Robert Gray, JP.

134. Dictionary of Scottish Architects, Queen Margaret Union entry, accessed 24 June 2012.

135. GUAS, ref. BE/139/8, 29 March 1960; letter from the Secretary of the University Court to J.L. Gleave.

136. *Glasgow Herald*, 15/03/1968, p.8.

137. GUAS, ref. BE/13/10, November 1965; '*Proposed Circulation Pattern Plan*' annexed to Wilson & Womersley's *Hillhead Precinct Report Number One*.

138. GUAS, ref. BE/55/02, 6 December 1966; letter to the Secretary of the University Court from Wilson & Womersley.

139. GUAS, ref. CI/1/76, 7 October 1968; p.11, Mathematics and p.108, 2 December 1968, Mathematics (to be accepted on 9 December 1968).

140. GUAS, ref. CI/1/77, 6 October 1969; p.16, Mathematics building.

141. University Report 1968–69, p.11.

142. Wilson 1963–64, p.4.

143. Information courtesy of David Sutherland Gleave.

144. GUAS, ref. 56381, 9 September 1968; letter from Charles Wilson to Sir John Wolfenden, Chairman of the University Grants Committee and ref. CI/1/76, 7 October 1968; p.13, Basic Science building and p.68, 4 November 1968, Basic Science building (to start on site 18 November 1968).

145. Wilson 1963–64, p.4.

146. *Building Design*, 3 November 1972, p.4.

147. GUAS, ref. BUL/6/29/1–15, various dates, August-September 1964; contract drawings by Keppie Henderson & Partners, signed for Gilbert Ash Scotland Ltd, general contractors.

148. GUAS, BE/13/10; 16 November 1965; letter from the Glasgow Corporation Depute Master of Works to Keppie, Henderson & Partners, marked as received by 'RD' on 17 November 1965.

149. The author is grateful to Clive Fenton for the identification of 'Sievo' mosaic tiles and drawing his attention to the double beam construction of the Kagawa Prefectural Government Hall.

150. GUAS, ref. BE13/10, 26 January 1965; letter from J.M. Dick of Keppie, Henderson & Partners to J.C. Wingate, Assistant Secretary to the University Court.

151. GUAS, ref. BE/13/10 54/29, 9 November 1965; letter from Keppie, Henderson & Partners to J.C. Wingate, Assistant Secretary to the University Court.

152. *Glasgow Herald*, 22 September 1970, p.5.

153. GUAS, ref. BUL 6/15/8; University 1970, p.47.

154. GUAS, ref. CI/1/76, 7 October 1968; p.13, Geology building.

155. GUAS, ref. BE/146/6, 15 December 1970; letter to Sir Hugh Wilson from Robert Hutcheson, Secretary of the University Court and response of 6 January 1971.

156. GUAS, ref. BE/146/7 94/8, 20 July 1978; explanatory statement attached to a letter from the University's Assistant Planning Officer to the Director of Planning at the City of Glasgow District Council.

157. GUAS, ref. 56383, 16 June 1972; minute of meeting of a Corporation/University Working Party on University development.

158. GUAS, ref. CI/1/86/2, 7 May 1979; p.278, Geology building and p.289, 23 May 1979, Department of Geology: entrance hall mural.

159. GUAS, ref. CI/1/108, 7 May 1997; p.104, request to rename building.

160. GUAS, ref. 56383, 29 April 1971; minutes of the Corporation/University Working Party on University development, p.2; and 12 January 1972, circular to all members of staff from the Principal, Charles Wilson.

161. GUAS, ref. BE/94/8, 20 July 1978; explanatory statement attached to a letter from the University's Assistant Planning Officer to the Director of Planning at the City of Glasgow District Council.

162. GUAS, ref. HG/30/3, 17 February 1981; minute to the Principal from J.S. Kay, Assistant Buildings Officer.

163. GUAS, ref. BE/94/8, 16 February 1979; letter from the University Buildings Officer to the Director of Planning.

164. GUAS, ref. HG/30/3, 1 October 1979; listed building consent notice.

165. GUAS, ref. CI/1/76, 7 October 1968; p.15, Microbiology building, Garscube.

166. GUAS, ref. CI/1/76, 7 October 1968; p.17, Veterinary School stage 2, phase 1, Garscube.

CHAPTER TEN · PAGES 185–94

1. GUAS, ref. CI/1/110, 27 April 1998; p.121, minutes of the Estates Planning and Strategy Committee, EP148.

2. GUAS, University of Glasgow Campus Development Framework Brief 2012, p.7.

3. University Equality 2009, pp.19–20.

4. GUAS, ref. BE/94/8, 20 July 1978; explanatory statement attached to a letter from the University's Assistant Planning Officer to the Director of Planning at the City of Glasgow District Council, p.5.

5. Finlayson and Hayward 2011.

6. See Moss, Munro and Trainor 2000, pp.300–29.

7. UGC 1984–85, p.14.

8. UGC 1988-89, p.1.

9. UFC 1991-92, p.18.

10. Dearing 1997, section 11.15.

11. Brown and Moss 2001, p.118.

12. Brown and Moss 2001, p.118 and University of Glasgow Business and Planning Unit statistics (headcounts 2005–6 to 2009–10).

13. GUAS, ref. CI/1/107, 29 January 1997; p.79, purchase of Western Court.

Copyright and Photographic Credits

The publisher wishes to thank all the individuals and institutions who have kindly supplied photographs and given permission to reproduce them in this book.

The University of Glasgow:

Archive Services, University of Glasgow (GUAS)

Maps, Official Publications and Statistics, University of Glasgow Library (GULMOPS)

Photographic Unit, University of Glasgow (GUPU)

Special Collections, University of Glasgow Library (GULSC)

The Hunterian, University of Glasgow (GUHMAG)

Alan Blackburn and family

Estate of David Donaldson

Faculty of Procurators, Glasgow

Estate of George Garson

Glasgow Art Club

Glasgow City Council

Glasgow City Libraries

Glasgow University Chaplaincy Centre

David S. Gleave

Estate of Eric Kennington

Dhruva Mistry

Mitchell Library, Glasgow

National Library of Scotland, Edinburgh

Newsquest (Herald & Times)

Trustees of the Paolozzi Foundation

Estate of Walter Pritchard

Royal Commission on the Ancient and Historical Monuments of Scotland (RCAHMS)

Royal Institute of British Architects, London (RIBA)

Scottish Cultural Resources Access Network (SCRAN)

Scottish National Portrait Gallery, Edinburgh

Sir John Soane Museum, London

Eric Stanford

Vivacity Peterborough Culture and Leisure

D.G.H. Waugh

The publisher would also like to acknowledge the photographers who have contributed to this book.

Nick Haynes: p.8 and illustrations 14, 63, 89, 90, 91, 92, 99, 100, 101, 102, 133, 134, 135, 136, 138, 143, 156, 157, 160, 162, 164, 180, 185, 186, 187, 188, 189, 194, 201 and 203
©Nick Haynes
www.conservationscotland.com

Keith Hunter: cover and jacket illustrations and illustration 205
©Keith Hunter
www.keithhunterphotography.com

Andrew Lee: illustration 179
©Andrew Lee
www.andrewleephotographer.com

Karl Williams: illustrations 76 and 132
©Karl Williams
www.karlwilliamsphotography.co.uk

Paul Zanre: illustration 206
©Paul Zanre
www.pzphotography.com

Index

NB: page numbers in *italics* denote illustrations